*Punc*   error in punctuation

*No Punc*   punctuation should be omitted

**Punctuation Symbols**

⊙   period   10.1

!   exclamation mark   10.3

?   question mark   10.2

⌃   comma   11.1
     with co-ordinate clauses   11.1
     after introductory
     element   11.2
     with non-restrictive
     modifiers   11.3
     with interrupting
     elements   11.4
     in a list or series   11.5
     for clarity   11.6
     conventional uses   11.7

*No* ⌃   omit comma   11.8

⌃   semicolon   12.1

⌃   colon   12.2

/--/   dash   13.1

(/)   parentheses   13.2

"   quotation marks   14.1

⌐/⌐   brackets   13.3

/.../   ellipses   14.2

/=/   hyphen   15.2

⌄   apostrophe   15.3, 6.2

*Ref*   reference of pronoun unclear   7.1

*Rep*   careless repetition   25.5

*Rest*   error in punctuation of restrictive
or non-restrictive modifier   11.3

*Shift*   shift (inconsistency)
     in pronoun form   7.6
     in verb tense   8.1

*SL*   sentence length ineffective   25.2

*Sp*   spelling error   17

*Sub*   faulty subordination   3.4, 3.5, 26.2

*T*   error in use of tense   8.1

*Trans*   needs better transition   21.3

*Trite*   trite expression   24.3

*Var*   ineffective or insufficient
sentence variety   26.1

*Vb*   error in verb form   8

*Wdy*   wordy   25.3

*WW*   wrong word   17.2, 23.3

//   elements should be parallel in form

⌒   close up space

\#   separate with a space

∧   omission

X   careless error

✓   good

**Other Symbols**

ISBN 0-7715-1758-0

Printed and bound in Canada

3 4 5 6 7 8 9 0  BP  86 85 84 83 82 81 80

**Acknowledgments**

The sources of quotations used for illustrative purposes are indicated in the text.

*Reprinted by permission of:* American Medical Association, excerpt from "Coronary Thrombosis" by William A.R. Thompson, M.D. in *Today's Health* (September 1952), published by the American Medical Association. J.A. Corry, excerpts from "Free Trade in Ideas" by J.A. Corry © 1954. Joan Daves, excerpt from *I Have a Dream,* © 1963 by Martin Luther King, Jr. Farrar, Straus & Giroux, Inc., a selection from "The Lottery" by Shirley Jackson. Copyright 1948, 1949 by Shirley Jackson. Copyright renewed © 1976 by Laurence Hyman, Barry Hyman, Mrs. Sarah Webster and Mrs. Joanne Schnurer. "The Lottery" appeared originally in *The New Yorker.* Gage Publishing Limited, excerpts from *S: Portrait of a Spy* by Ian Adams. Harper and Row, Publishers, Inc., excerpt from *One Man's Meat* by E.B. White. Copyright 1940, 1941 by E.B. White; excerpt from *The Second Tree From the Corner* by E.B. White. Copyright 1954 by E.B. White. *Maclean's* and Allan Fotheringham, excerpt from "Guy Lafleur? Barth Gimble? What ministry do they work in?" (June 12, 1978) © 1978 by Allan Fotheringham. The Macmillan Company of Canada Limited, excerpts from *The Loved and the Lost* by Morley Callaghan © 1951 by Morley Callaghan; excerpts from "The New Barbarians" by Geoffrey Durant, "A Word to the Wise" by Joseph Gold, "Is English Destroying Your Image?" by Michael Hornyansky, "Mrs. An Obsolete Industry?" by F.E.L. Priestly, and "Picking Up the Thread" by George Whalley, all from *In the Name of Language,* Joseph Gold ed. © 1975; excerpt from *Return of the Sphynx* by Hugh MacLennan © 1970; excerpt from "Cranes Fly South" by Edward McCourt from *Stories From Western Canada,* Rudy Wiebe ed. © 1972. Macmillan Publishing Co., Inc., excerpt from *The Aims of Education* by Alfred North Whitehead. Copyright 1929 by Macmillan Publishing Co., Inc., renewed 1957 by Evelyn Whitehead. Martin, Secker and Warburg and Mrs. Sonia Brownell Orwell, excerpt from "Marrakech" from *Such, Such Were the Joys* by George Orwell. Harold Matson Co., Inc., excerpts from *Desert Solitaire* by Edward Abbey, © 1968 by Edward Abbey; excerpt from *Two Fishermen* by Morley Callaghan © 1961 by Morley Callaghan. The Canadian Publishers, McClelland and Stewart Limited, Toronto, excerpt from *Frontenac: The Courtier Governor* by W.J. Eccles; excerpt from *Arcadian Adventures with the Idle Rich* by Stephen Leacock; excerpts from *Son of a Smaller Hero* by Mordecai Richler; excerpt from "The Painted Door" in *Lamp at Noon and Other Stories* by Sinclair Ross. Grace McInnis, excerpt from "Thy Kingdom Come" by J.S. Woodsworth, in *Sermons for the Unsatisfied,* Grain Growers' Guide, June 1915. Methuen Publications, Toronto, excerpt from "Newfoundland Dialect" by G.M. Story; excerpt from "Red River Dialect" by S.O. Scott, both in *Canadian English* © 1970. *Saturday Night,* excerpt from "Our Strange mistaken battle against French Canada" by Ramsay Cook (December 1977). *Saturday Review,* excerpt from "The Charlie Christian Story" by Ralph Ellison (May 17, 1958) © 1958 by Saturday Review. Lister Sinclair, excerpt from "The Canadian Idiom" in *Here and Now* No. 4, June, 1949. Mrs. James Thurber, excerpt from *Alarms and Diversions.* Copyright © 1957 by James Thurber. From "The Psychosemanticist Will See You Now, Mr. Thurber" in *Alarms and Diversions,* published by Harper and Row. Originally printed in *The New Yorker.* University of Michigan Press, excerpts from "A Way of Writing" by William Stafford from *Writing the Australian Crawl,* © 1978 The University of Michigan. University of New Mexico Press, excerpt from *The Way to Rainy Mountain* by N. Scott Momaday. Copyright © 1969 by The University of New Mexico Press. R.E. Watters, excerpts from "Stephen Leacock's Canadian Humor" from *Canadian Anthology,* Carl F. Klinck and R.E. Watters eds.

# Handbook of Current English

**Canadian Edition**

**Jim W. Corder**
Texas Christian University

**Grammar and Usage**

**Punctuation and Other Conventions**

**Canadian Edition prepared by**
**Walter S. Avis**
Royal Military College of Canada

**Composition**

**Diction**

**Sentences and Paragraphs**

 **gage** PUBLISHING LIMITED
TORONTO ONTARIO CANADA

**Practical Writing Tasks**

# To the Instructor

The Canadian edition of the *Handbook of Current English* endorses certain convictions that have characterized the book from its beginning: that selective and thoughtful use of language is important in everyday life as well as in school; that some forms of expression are more effective and more appropriate in given situations than other forms are; and that "good" language is that language best suited to the speaker or writer, to the subject at hand, and to the audience it is intended for. This edition, however, has been prepared with the needs of Canadian students in mind: although it contains virtually all the subject matter of the 5th American edition, in some instances what was therein has been compressed to make room for new material relating to the Canadian situation. Moreover, certain changes have been made so that the text will conform to Canadian modes of expression and, in some minor matters, to the personal preferences of the Canadian adapter.

New material appears in several areas, including the section on language and those on abbreviations and numbers, variant spellings, dictionaries, and reference books. There are also some modifications in the Glossary of Usage.

Of special significance in this Canadian edition is the shift to the metric system in conformity with the Canadian adoption of Le Systeme International d'Unités (SI), moreover, the Celsius scale replaces the Fahrenheit. Again, where instructions are offered for addresses relating to correspondence, the designations established by Canada Post for abbreviating the names of provinces and territories are used—as is the proper form and position of the Canadian Postal Code. Finally, in the treatment of figures and dates, the designated metric formula is also followed—as is the 24-hour system for specifying the time of day.

**Introduction: The Kinds of Language We Use.** The introduction is a discussion of the English language; it includes an account of distinctions between speaking and writing and of some varieties of English and the ways they can be used. The introduction suggests some ways of moving among varieties of English according to the principle of appropriateness. Some recommendations made throughout the text may be clearer if students read this material at the start of the course.

# Part One: Resources for Composition

**Sections 1 through 9: Grammar and Usage.** These sections review the grammar of English sentences and the functions of various kinds of words and word groups.

**Sections 11 through 17: Punctuation and Other Conventions.** These sections discuss and illustrate the principles governing the use of punctuation, mechanics, and other conventions, as well as various customs for using capital letters, apostrophes, abbreviations, and numbers. The final section, Spelling, suggests ways to overcome various spelling problems.

The sections in this first half of the *Handbook* treat single, definite topics. Grammatical definitions are included where they are relevant and necessary to the discussion. Many particular matters of usage are discussed at the point where they relate to general principles, but many more are included in the Glossary of Usage.

# Part Two: Practices in Composition

The second half of the *Handbook* serves as a brief rhetoric and as a practical guide to college and university writing.

**Sections 18 through 21: Composition.** These beginning sections focus on the processes of discovering what can or should be written and on the first steps in giving shape and character to the writing. Section 19 uses the experience of other writers to suggest some of the approaches and methods possible for student writers. These four sections constitute a discussion of what might be called prewriting.

**Sections 22 through 24: Diction.** These sections discuss the dictionary and deal with appropriate and effective uses of words.

**Sections 25 through 27: Sentences and Paragraphs.** These sections discuss means by which sentences and paragraphs can be managed and controlled to shape meaning; they show ways of using various sentence patterns and various patterns of paragraph construction to develop ideas.

**Sections 28 through 30: Practical Writing Tasks.** Problems of revising and practical matters in whole compositions are taken up here. Section 28, on revising, suggests ways of altering emphasis, mood, tone, and direction to suit the needs of the writing at hand. A sample of a student paper is included on pages 384-387, showing the first version, with the instructor's comments, and the revision.

Section 29 discusses and illustrates some particular kinds of writing, including answers to essay examinations, literary analyses, and business letters and résumés.

The final section is devoted to the special problems of research writing. A sample research paper is included.

**Glossary of Usage.** The Glossary gives succinct advice about many of the words and constructions that cause confusion in writing.

**Exercises.** Most of the exercises in this edition of the *Handbook* require the students to do some writing themselves, rather than to respond to another person's writing, although there are also exercises that call for sentence correction and for thought and discussion. The exercises may appear as is customary at the end of the sections; often, however, they are placed within the sections, immediately following the pertinent material. Thus, for example, when section 22.2 discusses "Learning to use your dictionary," appropriate exercises occur within the section, asking the students to apply what has just been discussed. Colored triangles mark exercises wherever they occur within the sections.

**Marginal tabs and correction charts.** The colored marginal tabs correspond to each of the six main divisions discussed above. In the margin of each right-hand page is also the pertinent correction symbol or abbreviation to indicate the material on those pages.

Themes can be marked by using either the correction symbols or the section numbers; the two are co-ordinated in the correction chart on the inside front cover as well as on the marginal tabs. In the text itself, the handwritten correction symbols appear with specific suggestions for revision, printed in color. Students should study the text that follows each suggestion whenever they are not sure why revision is necessary.

Appearing on the back end-cover of the book is a checklist for revision; it should be helpful for students to review their work with these questions in mind before handing in their themes.

Jim W. Corder
Walter S. Avis

# Contents

## Part Two:   Practices in Composition
Composition

## Diction

## Sentences and Paragraphs

## Practical Writing Tasks

# To the Student

*Handbook of Current English* is designed to be used both as a classroom text and as a reference book about particular points of grammar, usage, and rhetoric. If you take a little time to familiarize yourself with the organization and features of the book, you should be able to use the book easily and effectively.

**Introduction: The Varieties of Language We Use.** The introduction is a discussion of the English language. It includes a summary of the distinctions between spoken and written language and the varieties of English such as formal, general, informal, and nonstandard. It also suggests some ways of deciding what level or variety is most appropriate to the situation. Some of the recommendations made throughout the text may be clearer if you read this material at the start of the course.

## Part One: Resources for Composition

**Sections 1 through 9: Grammar and Usage.** These sections review the grammar of English sentences and the functions of the parts of speech.

**Sections 11 through 17: Punctuation and Other Conventions.** These sections discuss and illustrate the principles governing the use of punctuation marks, mechanics, capital letters, apostrophes, abbreviations, and numbers. Section 17, Spelling, suggests ways to overcome various spelling problems.

## Part Two: Practices in Composition

The second half of the *Handbook* serves as a brief rhetoric and as a practical guide to college and university writing.

**Sections 18 through 21: Composition.** These beginning sections focus on what might be called prewriting: Section 18 offers advice on finding and shaping a subject; section 19 discusses the modes of rhetoric and the situations each is most appropriate to; section 20 discusses organization; and section 21 discusses the first draft of the paper.

**Sections 22 through 27: Diction.** These sections discuss the dictionary and deal with the appropriate and effective use of words.

**Sections 25 through 27: Sentences and Paragraphs.** These sections discuss means by which sentences and paragraphs can be managed and controlled to shape meaning; they show ways of using various sentence patterns and various patterns of paragraph construction to develop ideas.

These sections and the ones on diction constitute discussions on what is usually called *style*.

**Sections 28 through 30: Practical Writing Tasks.** Problems of revising and certain practical matters relating to whole compositions are taken up here. Section 28 is concerned with revising a paper; section 29 discusses and illustrates some particular kinds of writing, including answers to essay examinations, essays about literature, and business letters and résumés; section 30 is devoted to the special problems of writing a research paper.

**Glossary of Usage.** The glossary is a quick reference guide to the correct use of some of the most troublesome or confusing words and constructions.

**Marginal tabs.** The colored marginal tabs correspond to each of the six main divisions listed above. In the margin by the tab is also the pertinent correction symbol or abbreviation indicating the material covered on those pages. The tabs and symbols should help you quickly find the subject you are looking for.

**Correction charts.** Appearing on the inside covers are two guides to correction and revision. The correction symbols on the inside front cover correspond to rules for revision of specific and general points of discussion. These rules are printed in red within the text, and offer a quick preview of the discussion to follow. Your instructor will probably use either these symbols or the section numbers to mark your papers, and expect you to follow the advice of the *Handbook* in correcting your papers.

The chart on the inside back cover, A Checklist for Revision, is a list of questions to ask about your papers before you hand them in; they are intended to ensure you have paid attention to both the specific details and more general aspects of composition.

**Index.** A full index provides a quick means of locating both general and particular points of discussion in the text. Used in conjunction with the marginal tabs in the *Handbook,* the Index can be a valuable tool.

# Canadian English

Language in Canada, as in most countries, is taken for granted. Unfortunately, however, a great deal of nonsense is taken for granted by many Canadians. Some people, especially recent arrivals from the United Kingdom, refuse to accept the fact that the English spoken in Canada has any claim to recognition. Others, who themselves speak Canadian English, are satisfied with the view that British English is the only acceptable standard. To these people, the argument that educated Canadians set their own standard of speech is either treasonable or ridiculous.

One Canadian I know had his eyes opened in a rather curious way. While shopping in a large Chicago department store, he asked where he might find chesterfields. Following directions to the letter, he was somewhat dismayed when he ended up at the tobacco counter. He soon made other discoveries as well. Blinds were "shades" to his American neighbors; taps were "faucets," braces "suspenders," and serviettes "napkins."

Before long his American friends were pointing out differences between his speech and theirs. He said *been* to rhyme with "bean," whereas for them it rhymed with "bin"; and he said *shone* to rhyme with "gone," whereas for them it rhymed with "bone." In fact, their Canadian friend had quite a few curious ways of saying things: *ration* rhymed with "fashion" rather than with "nation"; *lever* with "beaver" rather than "sever"; *z* with "bed" rather than "bee." Moreover, he said certain vowels in a peculiar way, for *lout* seemed to have a different vowel sound from *loud,* and *rice* a different vowel from *rise.*

The Englishman is also quick to observe that Canadians talk differently from himself. For example, he doesn't say *dance, half, clerk, tomato, garage* or *war* as Canadians do; and he always distinguishes *cot* from *caught,* a distinction that few Canadians make. He also finds that many of the words he used in England are not understood by people in Canada. Suppose he gets into a conversation about cars. Says he, "I think a car should have a roomy boot." No headway will be made till somebody rescues him by explaining that in Canada the boot is called a "trunk." Before the session is finished, he will probably learn that a bonnet is called a "hood" and the hood of a coupé is "the top of a convertible." Similarly, he must substitute *muffler* for *silencer, windshield* for *windscreen, truck* for *lorry,* and *gas* for *petrol.*

The examples I have mentioned suggest, quite correctly, that Canadian English, while different from both British and American English, is in large measure a blend of both varieties; and to this blend must be added many features which are typically Canadian.

The explanation for this mixed character lies primarily in the settlement history of the country, for both Britain and the United States have exerted continuous influence on Canada during the past two hundred years.

As the several areas of Canada were opened to settlement, before, during, and after the Revolutionary War in the 1770's, Americans were prominent among the settlers in many, if not in most, communities. American influence has been great ever since: Canadians often learn from American textbooks, read American novels and periodicals, listen to American radio programs, and watch American T.V. and movies. Moreover, Canadians in large numbers are constantly moving back and forth across the border, as emigrants, as tourists, as students (especially on athletic scholarships), and as bargain hunters. Finally, Canada shares with the United States a large vocabulary denoting all manner of things indigenous to North America. One need only leaf through the unabridged (or the concise) *Dictionary of Canadianisms* or the *Dictionary of Americanisms* to appreciate this fact.

On the other hand, Britain has also made an enormous contribution to the settlement of English-speaking Canada. For more than a century and a half, Britishers in an almost continuous stream and speaking various dialects have immigrated to Canada. In most communities, especially those along the Canadian-American border (where most of Canada's population is still concentrated), these newcomers came into contact with already established Canadians; and, as might be expected, their children adopted the speech habits of the communities they moved into. Only in certain settlement areas where relatively homogeneous Old Country groups established themselves did markedly British dialectal features survive through several generations. Such communities may be found in Newfoundland, the Ottawa Valley, the Red River Settlement in Manitoba, and on Vancouver Island. For the most part, however, the children of British immigrants, like those whose parents come from other European countries, adopt the kind of English spoken in Canada. Yet in the very process of being absorbed, linguistically speaking, they have made contributions to every department of the language.

That part of Canadian English which is neither British nor American is best illustrated by the vocabulary, for there are hundreds of words which are native to Canada or which have meanings peculiar to Canada. As might be expected, many of these words refer to topographical features, plants, trees, fish, animals, and birds; and many others to social, economic, and political institutions and activities. Few of these words, which may be called Canadianisms, find their way into British or American dictionaries, a fact which should occasion no surprise, for British and American dictionaries are based on British and American usage, being primarily intended for Britons and Americans, not for Canadians.

Prominent among Canadianisms are proper nouns, including names of regions: *Barren Grounds, French Shore, Lakehead*; names given to the natives of certain regions: *Bluenoses, Newfies, Herringchokers*; names associated with political parties: *New Democratic Party, Parti Québécois, Union Nationale.* In addition, there are a host of terms identified with places or persons: *Digby chicken, McIntosh apple, Quebec heater, Winnipeg couch.*

Languages other than English have contributed many Canadianisms to the lexicon: (from Canadian French) *brulé, caribou* (a drink), *joual, lacrosse, Métis, portage*; (from Amerindian) *babiche, Dene, kokanee, pemmican, shaganappi*; (from Eskimo) *atigi, Inuit, komatik, kuletuk, ulu, oomiak.* Sometimes the origin of such loanwords is obscured in the process of adoption; thus *carry-all, mush, siwash, snye,* and *shanty* derive from Canadian French *cariole, marche, sauvage, chenail,* and *chantier.*

Other Canadianisms are more or less limited to certain regions—to Newfoundland: *jinker, nunny bag, screech, tickle, tilt*; to the Maritimes: *aboideau, gaspereau, longliner, sloven*; to Ontario: *concession road, decker, dew-worm, fire-reels*; to the Prairie Provinces: *bluff* (clump of trees), *grid road, local improvement district*; to British Columbia: *rancherie, saltchuck, skookum, steelhead*; to the Northland: *bush pilot, cat-swing, cheechako, utilidor.*

Hundreds of Canadian words fall into the category of animal and plant names: *caribou, fool hen, inconnu, kinnikinnick, malemute, oolichan, saskatoon, sockeye, whisky-jack* or *Canada jay.* Many more fall into the class of topographical terms: *butte, coulee, dalles, sault.* Yet another extensive class includes hundreds of terms of historical significance: *Family Compact, Klondiker, North canoe, Red River cart, wintering partner, York boat.*

For many terms there are special Canadian significations: *Confederation, francization, Grit, height of land, reeve, riding, warden.* From the sports field come a number of contributions, especially from hockey and a game we used to call *rugby,* a term now almost displaced by the American term *football: boarding, blueline, convert, cushion, dasher, puck, rouge, snap.* And in the same area there are a number of slang terms that merit mention: *chippy, homebrew, import, rink rat.* Other slang or informal terms include: *fuddleduddle, horseman* ( = mountie), *moose pasture, peasouper, redeye.*

In pronunciation, as in vocabulary, Canadians are neither American nor British, though they have much in common with both. Although most Canadians pronounce *docile* and *textile* to rhyme with *mile*, as the British do, it is probable that most pronounce *fertile* and *missile* to rhyme with *hurtle* and *missal*, as the Americans do. And no doubt Canadians pronounce some words in a way that is typically Canadian. Most of us, for example, would describe the color of a soldier's uniform as *khaki*, pronounced (kär′kē). Yet no non-Canadian dictionary recognizes this Canadianism. Americans say (kak′ē), while the British say (kä′kē). In Canada, many people put flowers in a vase, pronounced (vāz); Americans use a (vās) and the British a (väz). To be sure, a number of Canadians say something like (väz), especially if the vase is Ming.

If we take imported dictionaries as our authority, such pronunciations as (kär′kē) and (vāz) are unacceptable. But surely the proper test of correctness for Canadians should be the usage of educated natives of Canada. Here are some other examples of pronunciations widely heard among educated Canadians; many of them are not recorded in our imported dictionaries: *absolve* (ab zolv′), *arctic* (är′tik), *armada* (är mad′ə), *chassis* (chas′ē), *culinary* (kul′ə ner′ē), *evil* (ē′v əl), *finale* (fə nal′ē), *fungi* (fung′gi), *jackal* (jak′ə l), *longitude* (long′gə tūd), *official* (ō fish′ əl), *opinion* (ō pin′yən), *placate* (plak′ āt), *plenary* (plen′ə rē), *prestige* (pres tēj′), *resources* (rizôr′səz), *senile* (sen′īl), *species* (spē′sēz), *Trafalgar* (trəfol′gə r).

Of course, not everyone uses all of these forms; yet all are used regularly by educated Canadians in large numbers. Who can deny that (ri zôr′səz) and (spē′sēz) are more often heard at all levels of Canadian society than (ri sôrs′ə z) and (spē′shēz), the pronunciations recommended in nearly all available dictionaries? Surely, when the evidence of usage justifies it, forms such as these should be entered as variants in any dictionary intended to reflect Canadian speech.

Another of the functions of a dictionary is to record the spellings used by the educated people of the community. In spelling, as in vocabulary and pronunciation, Canadian usage is influenced by the practice of both the Americans and the British. In areas where American and British practices differ, Canadian usage is far from uniform. Until recent years, British forms have predominated in most instances, for example, in *axe, catalogue, centre, colour, cheque, mediaeval, plough, skilful,* and *woollen* (and words of similar pattern), in spite of the obvious practical advantages of the

American forms: *ax, catalog, center, check, color, medieval, plow, skillful,* and *woolen.* In some cases, however, American spellings have asserted themselves to the virtual exclusion of the corresponding British forms, as in *connection, curb, jail, net, recognize, tire,* and *wagon* for *connexion, kerb, gaol, nett, recognise, tyre,* and *waggon.*

In recent years there have been indications that American spellings are becoming more commonly used in Canada. Many have, for example, been long ago adopted by Canadian newspapers, especially those in the larger centres, and by magazine and book publishers. Young people seem to use such spellings as *color, center, defense, medieval, program, skillful,* and *traveler* much more frequently than was formerly the case, the implication being that at least some American forms are accepted as proper in many Canadian schools. The fact is that usage is very much divided, varying from province to province and often from person to person. For the most part, however, Canadians respond to these variants with equal ease. Under such circumstances, a Canadian dictionary should include both forms, for here, as elsewhere, the lexicographer's obligation is to record usage, not to legislate it.

It has been argued in these pages that there is such a thing as a distinctive variety of English that is Canadian; yet it should be observed that this distinctive variety is referred to as "Canadian English" and not as "the Canadian language." The fact is that Canadians share one language with Britons, Americans, Australians, and a host of other people, both inside the Commonwealth and beyond it. To claim that there is a Canadian language, or, as many Americans do, an American language, is to distort the meaning of the word *language* for nationalistic purposes. On the other hand, it is a form of blindness to insist, as many do, that "English is English" and that only fools "dignify the slang and dialect" of Canada by giving it serious attention.

W.S.A.

# Introduction

# The Languages We Use

*What is written without effort is in general read without pleasure. — Samuel Johnson*

*There is no substitute for learning to write. Speech will not do as a substitute because it lets us off the hook too easily—both speaker and listener—through the persuasive shorthand of gesture, facial expression, and intonation. . . . Hence the great importance traditionally (and correctly) placed in humane education upon writing. There is really no other way of coming to terms seriously with language than by trying to write it well. To accept the proposition that writing is outmoded, that society is no longer "verbal" enough for skilful conduct of writing to be "relevant," is to arrest the development of those who . . . are unaware how easily—by "reading badly"—they can be made mute victims of cynical manipulation (social, commercial, and political) and could become emotional cripples and intellectual dwarfs. — George Whalley, "Picking up the Thread"*

Everyone who will use this textbook speaks English. Those who are native speakers of English know the language long before it is studied in school. We can usually understand sentences that other people utter, even though we may have never heard words in precisely those combinations before. By the time older people will admit that we have learned to talk, we can say sentences that we have never heard or said before. In fact, we can say sentences long before we know that there are such things as sentences. But even if we know English before we study it, there is ample reason to study it in school and throughout our lives. It is a medium through which we can conduct our affairs, whether trivial or important. We need to know what we can about the language and work toward using it wisely and well.

Paradoxically, English is both easy and difficult to study: easy, because we already do know the language; difficult, because English isn't one thing, but many things. It is varied; it changes. When we speak, we don't all sound alike, and when we write, we don't all write in the same way. Each of us knows English in various versions, and each of us uses one version when talking to a close friend, say, and another when speaking to a forty-year-old English teacher. In the talk that we hear every day, we understand many different ways of speaking; and we can read and understand still other ways of speaking in print.

Yet using a language well depends on more than an awareness of our abilities to speak and understand different varieties. It is also more than writing "complete" sentences, using correct verb forms, making verbs agree with their subjects and pronouns with their antecedents. Beyond these forms and conventions, using a language well is a matter of choosing from the broad range of that language the words and constructions that will best convey our ideas to a particular audience in a particular situation, that will best enable us to present ourselves fully and honestly to another. But no one can make choices unless choices are available; no one can choose among beans, corn, and broccoli unless beans, corn, and broccoli are on the table for the choosing. To make good choices in language, we must recognize the different versions of English and know the various ways English is used in contemporary writing and speaking.

## THE ELEMENTS OF LANGUAGE

Basically a language consists of a system of sounds, a collection of words, some changes in word forms, and some patterns into which the words fit to convey meaning. It may or may not have a system of writing and printing.

### Sounds

English has between thirty and thirty-five distinctive speech-sounds (about eighteen vowels, the rest consonants) and variations in pause, pitch, and stress. Each sound is used with slight modifications in actual speech; for example, some people have a full *r* and others a very slight indication of the sound. The pronunciation of words varies considerably among the different regions in which English is used, so that we can easily identify some people as being from Newfoundland, say, or Cape Breton.

### Words

Counting everything from slang and local words to rarely used words and limited scientific terms, English has a vocabulary of well over two million words. Many of these are used in several different senses—one dictionary giving forty different meanings for the word *check*. An unabridged dictionary has about 500 000 entries; a college dictionary has about 150 000 entries; a college student probably uses or recognizes over 50 000 basic words, not including derivatives made by adding syllables like *-ed* and *-ly*. English forms many new words by adding prefixes (*in-, anti-, re-, super-*) and suffixes (*-er, -ish, -ship, -teria*), and it makes compounds freely by putting two or more words together (*bookcase, streamlined*).

## Word Forms

Some languages are *inflected;* that is, their words change form to express grammatical relations in case, number, gender, person, tense, and the like. Latin and German, for example, are highly inflected. English uses very few changes in word forms: only a few endings, like the *-s* or *-es* of nouns (*boys, churches*), the *-s, -ed, -ing* of verbs (*asks, asked, asking*), *-er* and *-est* for comparing adverbs and adjectives (*hotter, hottest; nearer, nearest*), and a few internal changes, like the changes in vowels in *man-men, sing-sang*. These changes in form are one basis for grouping words into parts of speech.

## Constructions

English has two basic ways of combining words into groups; by phrases centred on nouns or their equivalents (*in the morning; crossing the street*) and by clauses centred on verbs (*he runs the forty-yard dash; when she saw the results*). We interpret the meaning of these familiar patterns very largely from the order in which the words stand, an order that we pick up naturally as children and follow almost instinctively. Out of these simple word groups, we build sentences of varying length and complexity. The study of the relationships between words and word groups in sentences is *syntax,* the principal division of *grammar.*

## Writing Practices

English, which, like other languages, first existed as speech, is represented in writing and printing by the twenty-six letters of the alphabet, a dozen or so punctuation marks, and such devices as capitals and italics. Our accepted practices of spelling, punctuation, capitalization, and so on were developed mostly by printers and serve chiefly to represent the spoken language.

These are the *materials* of language. What we do with them is another matter. This book is about *current* English, which appears in many forms. The book by and large uses—and usually recommends—standard English, that is, a kind of English to be expected from a person who has spoken, heard, written, read, and examined English enough to know some of its traditional characteristics and some of the ways it is habitually used in books, magazines, classrooms, and public meetings. Another way to describe standard English is to say that those who use it will generally have accepted the judgments on usage made by many people in many places over a long period of time.

There is good reason to do so. When you talk to other people, you are with them; they can watch your face and your hands; they see whether you lean toward them or turn coolly away; and they know instantly whether you are speaking uncertainly or boldly. But when someone else reads what you have written, you can't count on being there. More often than not, you are *not* there. That may mean that you will want or need to address your readers in a language whose characteristics you can expect them to understand. You and your readers may not ever be together unless you hold a language in community property. Qualities that a language accumulates in many places over a period of some time are likely to be clearer to readers, more accessible to them, than qualities that belong only to you or to you and a close circle of friends.

## VARIETIES OF ENGLISH USAGE

Living languages undergo continual growth and change. Ordinarily the changes are slow and barely noticeable — slightly different pronunciations, new shadings in the meaning of words, and gradual shifts in grammatical constructions — but their cumulative effect can be dramatic. The works of Shakespeare, written four centuries ago, present difficulties to the modern reader: many of the words are unfamiliar and the grammar occasionally seems strange. The writings of Chaucer, who lived a few centuries earlier, are hard to read without a large glossary and a grammar guide. Still earlier works, like *Beowulf,* can be understood only by specialists who have studied Old English much as they would study a foreign language. Yet all these works are written in a language that can claim to be called English and have been admired by many generations of readers of English.

Obviously our language has passed through many changes in the course of its history, and it will go on changing from generation to generation. But the language doesn't just change as time passes; at any given moment in its history, it also shows many internal variations. The work and worry and play of everyday life include all kinds of activities and situations, and English, both spoken and written, must serve them all. There are differences in the words and constructions typically used in different kinds of publications, even within a range no wider than that from newspapers to textbooks, and we use different language in writing or speaking to different people and for different purposes.

If in your writing you needed to say something about an object presented as something that it is not, you might use any one of the following words: *simulated, spurious, fraudulent, counterfeit, imitation, false, sham, pseudo, phony, bogus,* perhaps *put-on.* Which you use depends on a number of things. When you use one of the words, you may not think of it as an act of choice, and it may not be. You may simply use the word that you are most accustomed to using, or to hearing. If you do make a deliberate choice, however, the choice depends on many things—who you are, where you live, the people you spend most time with, the audience that will receive what you say or write, how much of your own personal language you are willing to use, and other factors. But you do have some choice among the words in this series, and in most other instances, especially when you write.

*Intro*

Since choices in vocabulary and construction are often available, it seems foolish to trust what we already know about language and to take for granted that the way we use words is going to be sufficient. There is not always one "right" choice to make; no language should be forced into or kept in a neat mold. Until fairly recently, it was common for students of language to assume that "good" English was fixed, that departure from an inflexible set of rules governing its use was automatically "bad" English. This highly *prescriptive* approach to language study reflected the belief that there was some ideal form of English, orderly and uniform. Students had merely to learn the laws and apply them, just as they would in studying physics or chemistry. Although the prescriptive approach often produced good results, both practical experience and modern linguistic scholarship—called *descriptive* because it studies and describes the language as it *is*—have shown it to be less than satisfactory. No single system of conventions and rules can accurately describe a complex, changing language. Whether we like it or not, our language is changing and varied, and because it is, it offers choices.

But choices are not choices unless we know what they are. There is no perfect way of describing or listing all the possible forms of spoken English. *One* way to catch the variety of spoken English is to start with highly personal language, and then see what happens to personal language in groups, in special times, in special places.

## Idiolects

Everyone has a personal language. It may be remarkably different from the language of someone who lives two hundred miles away, or even next door; it may be scarcely distinguishable from another person's language. This personal language is called an *idiolect,* a modern word formed by the blending of two Greek forms *idio-* (originally meaning "personal" or "one's own") and *-lect,* taken from *dialect,* which originally meant "talk" or "speech" although today it refers to one of the several varieties of a language. An idiolect, then, is the total language stock—words, grammar, pronunciations, and so on—of one speaker at a given point in his life. In fact, no idiolect is identical with any other, for each grows in the context of the individual's life and as the circumstances of his life change, so his idiolect changes. Each of the speakers in the passage that follows begins to be recognizable, even in a few lines. The first speaker's language, in particular, tells something about his age, his location, the manner of life he has led.

> "Ain't no whoopin' cranes nowadays," the old man said disconsolately.
>
> Lee spoke very slowly now, trying hard to be patient. "At Becker's slough. Honest. I saw the black tips of his wings just as clear!"
>
> "And you feel like you want to go, too," Grandpa said. "Breaks your heart almost, you want to go that bad, when you hear the thunder right over your head—like a big, long freight train passin' in the nighttime."
>
> His voice rose in an unexpected harsh croak. "At Becker's slough, you say? A whoopin' crane—a real, honest-to-gosh whooper? Boy, I ain't seen a whooper for forty years!"—Edward McCourt, "Cranes Fly South"

The writer in the passage below, however, owns and uses a different language. It is a language that is both active (some fifteen verbs and a number of nouns or modifiers made from verbs—*spincasting, calling, shielded*) and easy, with familiar pronoun references and pleasantly varied sentences that range from six to fifty-seven words.

> Trotlines from shore to shore get you more fish and bigger ones, but they're also more labor. After I'd finished with the line I worked along the beach, spincasting bootlessly for bass. Four Canada geese came diagonally over the river, low, calling, and in a moment I heard a clamor at the head of the island, shielded from me by the island's duned fringe and by willows. I climbed up through them to look. At least 200 more honkers took off screaming from the sand bar at the upper end of the bare plain. The passenger ran barking after them. Calling him back, I squatted beside a drift pile, and in the rose half-light of dusk watched through the field glass as they came wheeling in again, timid but liking the place as I liked it, and settled by tens and

twenties at the bar and in the shallows above it where the two channels split. — John Graves, *Goodbye to a River*

One's idiolect is not necessarily restrictive. For although each of us speaks an idiolect—our own personal language—we can easily understand other idiolects we hear and read, and almost everyone at times shifts from one way of speaking to another. Nevertheless, it is possible for a personal language to be so uniquely personal as to be incomprehensible to a hearer or reader—as in forms of baby talk, or in some kinds of family lingo, or perhaps even in portions of a tough, private poem like Christopher Smart's *A Song to David:*

*Intro*

> Gamma supports the glorious arch
> On which angelic legions march,
>     And is with sapphires paved;
> Thence the fleet clouds are sent adrift,
> And thence the painted folds, that lift
>     The crimson veil, are waved.

## Dialects

When a community of speakers and writers uses idiolects that have much in common in pronunciation, grammar, and vocabulary, the combined idiolects are often referred to as a *dialect.* Usually we think of a dialect only as the language of a particular geographical region, but we can use the word to name any gathering of idiolects that share essential characteristics. A dialect is almost like a code: speakers and writers of a dialect can usually converse with and write to speakers of the general language, but they also know the special language of some group or region. When Paul Simon wrote and sang that he was "Lookin' for fun and feelin' groovy," his language linked him to some people who used the language in a similar way. When another speaker says, "He jumped aboard of that dory some quick, eh?" he or she is using a dialect common in the Maritimes. But dialects occur everywhere; people who live and work on farms sometimes use distinguishable dialects, to be sure, and so do people who teach the third grade, and so do people whose language is often supposed to be remarkably proper. In the passage that follows, for example, a language is used that belongs to a dialect influenced by religious, psychological, and sociological studies:

> How is the humanization of sex impeded? First it is thwarted by the parading of cultural-identity images for the sexually dispossessed, to make money. These images become the tyrant gods of secular society, undercutting its liberation from religion and transforming it into a kind of neotribal culture. Second, the authentic seculariza-tion of sex is checkmated by an anxious clinging to the sexual stan-

dards of the town, an era so recent and yet so different from ours that simply to transplant its sexual ethos into our situation is to invite hypocrisy of the worst degree. — Harvey Cox, *The Secular City*

As we will see a little later, this passage, shown here as a kind of dialect, is close to still another kind of language that might be called *professional language,* or *craft language,* or *shoptalk.*

**Regional dialects.** There are, of course, many *regional dialects;* some of them are readily recognizable. Migration habits, work habits, geographical features, plant and animal life, and other characteristics of a particular region sometimes help to create a language for the region that is easily distinguishable from other dialects. A regional dialect may be marked by special words; people in the Prairies, for example, have more occasion to talk about *sloughs* and *coulees* than people in Ontario do, because of western topography.

A regional dialect may be identified at times by special pronunciations of ordinary words. After the election of Georgian Jimmy Carter as President of the United States in 1976, newspapers often printed pieces on "how to speak Southern," with definitions—"bard" means *borrowed,* "gull" means *girl,* "stow" means *store,* "ahmoan" means *I am going to,* as in "Ahmoan go eat dinner."

A regional dialect may be marked, too, as in the following passage, by characteristic constructions (*folks begin to git their eyes open*), by pronunciations (*infarnal, leetle*), and by words not commonly used elsewhere:

Then mimicking his voice and manner, he repeated Allen's words with a strong nasal twang, " 'A'most time for you to give over the clock trade, I guess, for by all accounts they ain't worth havin', and most infarnal dear, too; folks begin to git their eyes open.' Better for you, if you'd 'a had your'n open I reckon; a joke is a joke, but I consate you'll find that no joke. The next time you tell stories about Yankee pedlars, put the wooden clock in with the wooden punkin-seeds, and hickory hams, will you? The Bluenoses, Squire, are all like Zeb Allen: they think they know everythin', but they get gulled from year's eend to year's eend. They expect too much from others, and do too leetle for themselves. . . ."—T.C. Haliburton, "Gulling a Bluenose"

**Temporal dialects.** Another kind of dialect might be called *temporal.* Language changes faster in some communities than in others; sometimes a person or a group preserves usages or words out of the past while another person or group hurries into acceptance of new words, new usages. Martin Luther King's speech in Washington, D.C., on August 28, 1963, as the passage below will testify, gained a part of its power to move and to exhilarate from its recollection of rhythms, words, and constructions from the King James Bible:

> I have a dream that one day every valley shall be exalted, every hill and mountain shall be made low, the rough places will be made plane and crooked places will be made straight, and the glory of the Lord shall be revealed, and all flesh shall see it together.
>
> This is our hope. This is the faith that I go back to the South with. With this faith we will be able to hew out of the mountain of despair a stone of hope. With this faith we will be able to transform the jangling discords of our nation into a beautiful symphony of brotherhood. With this faith we will be able to work together, to pray together, to struggle together, to go to jail together, to stand up for freedom together, knowing that we will be free one day.

*Intro*

**Occupational dialects.**    We have already mentioned professional languages, craft languages, and shoptalk, all of which might be called *occupational dialects.* A wide range of such dialects is before us a good part of the time. We frequently borrow words from occupations for use in conversation, less frequently for use in writing—for example, *feedback, input, bug, huddle, fade-in, fade-out, close-up,* or *program* (as used with computers). Occupational dialects, of course, would occur most frequently in speech or writing in the discussion of particular occupations and their work, but as the words listed above may suggest, parts of some occupational dialects have come into common use and after a while no longer call attention to themselves as forms of dialects. But occupational dialects occur in many ways. In professional journals and specialized books, for example, we may expect to find languages that are common to people within given occupations. The passage below, though it appeared in a fairly popular publication, depends heavily on language taken from studies in education and psychology:

> The child-centred syndrome sounded humane and friendly enough and took its force from a swing of opinion among educators against rigid curricula, bad instruction, and inflexible methodology. The new fashion was intended to contrast with, rather than rejuvenate, subject-centred and teacher-centred instruction. This new panacea was given added urgency by the cry for greater student freedom and the desire for increased course choices. Students knowing nothing of the ingredients were to write their own recipes. Government alarm at rapidly escalating classroom costs, inevitable if instructional excellence was to be maintained in small classes and in traditional curricula, further augmented these changes. A highly educated and literate population can be achieved only at enormous cost.—Joseph Gold, *In the Name of Language*

**Public dialects.** We hear and read some special languages that we might call *public dialects*. Most of us hear, see, speak, read, and sometimes write words, phrases, and constructions that come from television, magazines, motion pictures, politics, and other forms of public communication. How many people said "At this point in time" instead of "now" during the Watergate hearings in the summer of 1973? How many people take over words or phrases from the King of Kensington or Archie Bunker, or other popular television characters? The public language of television and magazine advertisements is a fantasy language, never quite specific, always full of promise—"This is an unretouched photograph of Bonnie wearing Cornsilk—the makeup that gives you the look of innocence," or "There's a skin cleanser that leaves your skin the way nature intended," or "You're going to be beautiful ... both of you, in Chatelaine Formals."

## General English

Most of the language you hear or read in a week, however, probably doesn't belong to any one of these dialects, though the *public dialects* are extraordinarily pervasive. If we take into account all of the language you hear or read in a week, from television, classrooms, friends, overheard conversations, radio disc-jockeys, newspapers, magazines, and elsewhere, a good part of it doesn't have the distinctive character of personal idiolect, regional dialect, occupational dialect, or even public dialect. Much of it is in that broad range of language so commonly used that it attracts no attention to itself, and of course there are varieties of language within that range. These varieties we might call *general dialects*. In writing, the vocabulary and sentence structure of the general dialects seem natural—and close to those of speech. Punctuation is usually relatively light, and sentences are likely to vary widely in length and complexity.

In the following passage, the author talks about our capital, Ottawa, but the language he uses is community property:

> Early September in Ottawa makes the residents forgive and forget too easily the brain-numbing harshness of the winter months. September evenings are long and somnolent. The air moves softly, caresses the bared skin. For those who live downtown, the Rideau canal is the focal point of these evenings. The paths and parkland that stretch beside the canal become crowded with strollers taking the evening air. Families crowd the park benches until long after their children's bedtimes, finally surrendering the benches to couples who will linger until the early morning hours. Here and there, runners, dressed in flimsy shorts and undershirts, lope

silently through the knots and clusters of people.—Ian Adams, *S, Portrait of a Spy*

The general dialects are not limited to transmitting matters of general interest; they will also carry specialized information:

> Yet if our agriculture-based life depends on the soil, it is equally true that soil depends on life, its very origins and the maintenance of its true nature being intimately related to living plants and animals. For soil is in part a creation of life, born of a marvelous interaction of life and nonlife long eons ago. The parent materials were gathered together as volcanoes poured them out in fiery streams, as waters running over the bare rocks of the continents wore away even the hardest granite, and as the chisels of frost and ice split and shattered the rocks. Then living things began to work their creative magic and little by little these inert materials became soil. Lichens, the rocks' first covering, aided the process of disintegration by their acid secretions and made a lodging place for other life. Mosses took hold in the little pockets of simple soil—soil formed by crumbling bits of lichens, by the husks of minute insect life, by the debris of a fauna beginning its emergence from the sea.— Rachel Carson, *Silent Spring*

While general English may sometimes seem flat or uninteresting, it may also be interesting and precise. In this passage from a short story the language is a compressed form of what we all might say (except perhaps "the world leaps into proportion"), but it has the quality of feeling that we associate with literature:

> The man who expected to be shot lay with his eyes open, staring at the upper left-hand corner of his cell. He was fairly well over his last beating, and they might come for him any time now. There was a yellow stain in the cell corner near the ceiling; he had liked it at first, then disliked it; now he was coming back to liking it again.
>
> He could see it more clearly with his glasses on, but he only put on his glasses for special occasions now—the first thing in the morning, and when they brought the food in, and for interviews with the General. The lenses of the glasses had been cracked in a beating some months before, and it strained his eyes to wear them too long. Fortunately, in his present life he had very few occasions demanding clear vision. But, nevertheless, the accident to his glasses worried him, as it worries all near-sighted people. You put your glasses on the first thing in the morning and the world leaps into proportion; if it does not do so, something is wrong with the world.— Stephen Vincent Benét, "The Blood of the Martyrs," *Thirteen O'Clock*

## Dialect Modifications

Most of the English that we hear, read, speak, and write falls within what we have called the *general dialects*. Some versions of language within this range are far more casual and informal than others. Many of us, even if our speech or writing shows no other distinguishing marks (such as the work we do, or the place we live), use language that is breezy and often uncomplicated. Sentences are often short, and words and phrases may be more characteristic of speaking than of writing: *cop, deadpan, biffy, chancy, phony, peeve, whodunit.* Such words as these and others we use may be labelled *informal* (or colloquial) in dictionaries, which means that they occur more often in speech than in writing.

When writing or speaking informally, we are likely to make some use of *slang:* newly made words (*peacenik, hippie, groupie, teenybopper*), or old words with new meanings (*cool, straight, trip, far-out*), or phrases conspicuously overused (*good deal, right on*). For many reasons, a continuing flow of such words and phrases enters the language. Sometimes we adopt one or another of them because we want to be different or because we feel that new experiences need new names; sometimes we want to set ourselves apart from some other group (parents, say) by adopting expressions they don't use. Most slang is short-lived, but some proves useful enough to be absorbed into the general vocabulary.

If being informal, we are apt to use quite a few *localisms,* words or phrases characteristic of a certain region and often associated with a *regional dialect.* People often use regional names for common things (*coal oil* or *kerosene; gaspereau* or *alewife; shadberry, saskatoon berry,* or *juneberry*), special names for certain occupations (*longlinerman, draegerman, boom man*), or special names for features of the landscape peculiar to a region (*tickle, bogan, thrum-cap, butte, bench, muskeg, bluff* "clump of trees."). Some of these words are old forms put to new uses; others are borrowings from Canadian French or from Amerindian languages.

## Non-standard English

Some of the varieties of language mentioned above are *non-standard* forms of English. A *standard* may be defined as an accepted measure of quality. If a measure of quality is accepted, that means it has wide use. Idiolects, dialects, and the various dialect modifications are associated with particular people, particular groups, particular places, particular times. In this special sense then, they are *non-standard,* not languages for wide use.

Any language may appear in non-standard form. If grammatical errors occur, if spelling is inconsistent, if punctuation is inadequate, if usage is that not widely accepted, such language may be called *non-standard.* Errors in form mean that the language is not meeting an accepted measure of quality. Indeed, you should already know that the most common way of judging a language is by its propriety and consistency in grammar, spelling, punctuation, pronunciation, and usage.

You should also remember that language can be used to deceive, to betray, to oppress. Moreover, each of the varieties of language—those primarily spoken forms already mentioned and the primarily written forms discussed in the following sections— can become unacceptable and therefore non-standard because it contains contradictions, ambiguities, and other violations of clear thinking. In short, we can consider as non-standard any language that is inconsistent within itself and fails to communicate as effectively as possible.

Some styles of language are *non-human* and thus unacceptable. If a speaker says "From the beginning of our session together, I want to get you programmed to give me instant feedback," then no matter what his or her intention is, the speaker is thinking of us as objects, electronic machines. An educator who says "We must get the new students conditioned to the self-paced learning programs" is, whether he or she intends to or not, visualizing students as Pavlovian dogs. Some styles may be *mean-spirited.* They focus on the speaker and his own interests and associates excluding all others from the magic circle of human communication. Some styles are simply agencies for *falsehood* ("termination with extreme prejudice" substitutes for "execution"). And all of our idiolects sometimes fall short of their *possibilities* in failing to say all that they might say.

## EDITED ENGLISH

No perfect system exists for classifying and naming all versions of the English language. The idiolects, dialects, and versions of language mentioned above are examples only. All of them are forms of spoken English. Some of them can also be written effectively.

But for use in writing, almost any language has to be edited for it is ordinarily being presented publicly. Such public presentation— as opposed to private conversation—requires careful preparation and revision; in short, it needs editing. *Edited English* is a version of the language that you may associate with schools, good newspapers, good books, or good public speakers. It is an idiolect or dialect that has been modified to produce a measure of uniformity consistent with the grammatical standards traditionally taught in English, Canadian, and American schools, using a vocabulary shared by people in different places and different times. Edited English has been produced by a kind of filtering process. Motivations for promoting the use of edited English as *the* standard English are no doubt mixed, but there are good reasons. In the filtering process, what separates people from each other linguistically is supposed to be trapped and discarded, while what binds people together linguistically is left free for use. Few people speak edited English; many write it. What we should keep in mind, is that though edited English is just another available variety of language, it is one of the most important.

We do not, of course, mean that all forms of edited English are alike. The forms of spoken English mentioned above, when edited for public presentation, can become appropriate edited English. The casual language of our private conversations, of our idiolects and dialects, can provide a kind of *informal* edited English. The general spoken English that was described earlier is the foundation for *general* edited English. The *formal variety* of usage, found chiefly in writing, is principally a development from general spoken English but still more fully edited and more complex than general edited English. It is more influenced by reading and follows more closely the conventions built up by writers and editors in the past. It usually occurs in discussions of specialized topics and in writing addressed to somewhat limited audiences.

The vocabulary of formal English includes most of the general words but very few from regional dialects. Necessarily, formal English uses the specialized vocabulary of the subject matter being discussed; it also may use a good many abstract words. The grammatical constructions tend to be fuller than in general English, and very often the sentences are somewhat longer and more complex. Formal writing tends to follow older practices in punctuation and to use *close* punctuation—more frequent marks than are typical in general English, and *heavier* ones, such as a semicolon where a comma might serve.

The formal English used in academic, scientific, technical, and scholarly writing is usually impersonal. Good formal writing, however, is not stilted or dull. This account of the mapping of Switzerland shows the single-minded attention to the subject, the compact and orderly statement of ideas, and the moderate use of technical terms that characterize impersonal formal English:

The heroic task of making a topographic survey and map of Switzerland fell to the lot of General Guillaume Henri Dufour (1787–1875). Under his personal supervision the work was begun in 1830 and the first sheet was published in 1842. Thirty-four years later the entire survey, on a scale of 1:100,000, was finished and the last of the 25 sheets came from the press. Soon after, the map appeared in atlas form, published at Berne. Far from being a pioneering effort that would require immediate revision, the Dufour atlas proved to be a model of accuracy and artistic delineation, not only for future map makers of Switzerland, but for cartographers at large. The sheets of the atlas were used as a basis for later surveys on different scales, and on the sheets of Switzerland's new survey references were made to the corresponding sections and subsections of the original Dufour map. The art work and conventional signs on the new map were almost identical with those on the Dufour originals. The lettering and bench marks (figures denoting heights), prominent buildings, roads, boundaries and forests were printed in black. Small slopes and passes, ravines and narrow defiles that could not be shown by equally spaced contour lines were printed in brown hachures. Black hachures were used to indicate rocky prominences and precipices, the general effect being a pictorial representation by oblique lighting. Horizontal surveys were shown in bronze and water was indicated by shades of blue. — Lloyd A. Brown, *The Story of Maps*

A more personal type of formal English is shown in the following passage. Some of the words and phrases are formal— *inert knowledge, radical error,* and *delicate, receptive, responsive to stimulus.* The constructions are full: note the sentence beginning *Whoever was the originator* and the following sentence, beginning *But whatever its weight of authority.* But some constructions (*I appeal to you, as practical teachers. So far, so good.*) carry an unmistakable personal emphasis and keep us aware that the writer is expressing himself as an individual:

I appeal to you, as practical teachers. With good discipline, it is always possible to pump into the minds of a class a certain quantity of inert knowledge. You take a text-book and make them learn it. So far, so good. The child then knows how to solve a quadratic equation. But what is the point of teaching a child to solve a quadratic equation? There is a traditional answer to this question. It runs thus: The mind is an instrument, you first sharpen it, and then use it; the acquisition of the power of solving a quadratic equation is part of the process of sharpening the mind. Now there is just enough truth in this answer to have made it live through the ages. But for all its half-truth, it embodies a radical error which bids fair to stifle the genius of the modern world. I do not know who was first responsible for this analogy of the mind to a dead instrument. For aught I know, it may have been one of the seven wise men of Greece, or a committee of the whole lot of them. Whoever was the originator, there can be no doubt of the authority which it has acquired by the continuous approval bestowed upon it by eminent persons. But whatever its weight of authority, whatever the high approval it can quote, I have no hesitation in denouncing it as one of the most fatal, erroneous, and dangerous concepts ever introduced into the theory of education. The mind is never passive; it is a perpetual activity, delicate, receptive, responsive to stimulus. You cannot postpone its life until you have sharpened it. Whatever interest attaches to your subject-matter must be evoked here and now; whatever powers you are strengthening in the pupil, must be exercised here and now; whatever possibilities of mental life your teaching should impart, must be exhibited here and now. That is the golden rule of education, and a very difficult rule to follow. — Alfred North Whitehead, *The Aims of Education*

These are some versions of our language—countless idiolects, many dialects, regional, occupational, general, public, edited English, formal language. Each version can be used to move or to inform; each can be warm, generous, and powerful; each can be used with point and precision; and each must be used with due regard for meaning since effective communication cannot be achieved without a firm grasp of this important aspect of language. Indeed, meaning is a house of many mansions, all of which are always open for inspection. To ignore this invitation is to be blind to the dangers of misunderstanding that lie in the abuse and misuse of language and to forego the deep satisfaction that comes from using good language in a clear, concise, and pleasing way.

In what follows, we will examine the question "What is 'good' language—especially with reference to written English?"

## SOME QUALITIES OF GOOD LANGUAGE

A "good" language is not just a gathering of specific practices in vocabulary, grammar, and usage that you must invariably follow. Many languages are available, all equally reputable and, in certain circumstances, all equally "good." The objective in writing is not first to conform to some previously established system of usages, but to use the resources of the language to communicate fully, precisely, and honestly. Good writing is not born of a system of rules and usages; systems of rules and usages are born of good writing.

## Some Versions of English — A Summary

### Spoken language

IDIOLECT: an individual's personal language, influenced by environmental factors (geographical area, occupation) and internal factors (age, sex, personality).

DIALECT: the combined idiolects of a *community of speakers.* Dialects can overlap, but can be classified by such terms as regional, temporal, occupational, social.

DIALECT MODIFICATIONS: slang, localisms, fad words.

GENERAL ENGLISH includes the languages above and might be called the dialect of the great majority of speakers of Canadian English without the strong modifications of other dialectal factors.

NON-STANDARD ENGLISH does not meet the accepted measure of quality in usage, grammar, pronunciation, and so on.

### Written language: Edited English

INFORMAL ENGLISH is characterized by short sentences and "breezy" style; it includes personal and journalistic writing.

GENERAL ENGLISH is characterized by the constructions and vocabulary of general English, more attention being paid to grammatical form; it is found in most books, newspapers, and magazines.

FORMAL ENGLISH is characterized by full constructions and specialized vocabulary; it is generally impersonal, found mostly in, academic, scientific, technical, and other scholarly writing.

*Intro*

A language can enable us to remember our experiences and get them straight in our minds. A language can enable us to put our experiences in order and establish connections between them. A language can enable us to speculate on our experiences and draw conclusions from them. A language can enable us to praise or to blame. As the previous section suggests, many varieties of language are available to serve these purposes, each suitable in particular circumstances. Each of these varieties may have its own distinct structure, and each can be written.

It is here that writers meet a special problem, already noted. When we speak to someone, we are there. We can "finish out" what we intend by our words. The tone of voice, a shift of shoulders, a gesture with the hands, a movement of the eyes—all these complement the words. And when we speak to people, often we can tell if they are comprehending or accepting what we say by their expressions; if we sense that they are not, then we have the immediate opportunity to start over, speaking in a different way and using different words to get over the difficulty.

When it comes to writing, we are rarely present when someone reads what we have written. Our meaning and intention rest in the words on the page, and these are sometimes inadequate. No language we use permits us to communicate two things at once under normal circumstances; when we say one thing, we're *not* saying another; if we acquire the capacity to use a formal language, we often risk losing the rich words that name particular local features in a regional dialect. When we write, there is a further problem, for written words have to stand on their own. We are not there to explain, to modify, to fill in, to shift emphasis. We should, then, give our greatest care to writing, to insure as best we can the precision and the fullness of our meaning. Readers are likely to be people much like ourselves. They have their own varied interests and preoccupations. They think their own thoughts. They can't be expected to fill in gaps we leave out. They can't be expected to attend closely just because we've written something.

Writing is a kind of contract between writer and reader. The writer asks the reader to spend time in reading; in return the writer is obliged to give care to the writing. The reader requires of the writer some worth in what is written and owes the writer at least a little curiosity, a little patience, a little willingness to listen. Any language that clearly demonstrates precision and fullness of meaning and also promotes rapport between reader and writer is likely to be "good" language.

## APPROPRIATE LANGUAGE

This *Handbook,* however, customarily recommends what we earlier called edited English, for several sound reasons. In the first place, as we have already mentioned, no single handbook can fully describe all the versions of English; it is doubtful that a single handbook could describe *two* versions fully; it is doubtful, indeed, that a single handbook can describe a *single* version of the language fully. Since the book can't describe all, or even some, it sets out to describe and recommend the kind of language that appears most commonly in print, that is, the primary medium of communication in most books, newspapers, and magazines in Canada. Edited English is valuable because it is widely used, and it is widely used because it is flexible and will serve many purposes. It is a language suitable to sociological research and to cookbooks, to personal letters and to political commentary. We recommend it, finally, because it is a language we can speak, hear, and read in common. Its widespread use in publications and in schools makes it accessible to many people. The language does not belong to any single person, or to any single group or region. Widely used and commonly accessible, edited English is a shared language in which we can take mutual delight. We have not tried to list here all the characteristics of edited English: the rest of this *Handbook* tries to show what edited usage is like. When we say, "Many writers prefer to ..." or "It's usually best to say ..." or "Try to avoid ... ," we are recommending general Canadian English edited for written use.

Any language, in principle, can be a "good" language if used appropriately. Consequently, edited English can be governed by a standard of appropriateness. When you write a language, the choice of vocabulary, usage, and construction is, in a way, not yours alone. The subject you are talking about makes certain demands. The audience you reach may have certain expectations and these merit your respect. When we make our choices from the range language offers, we must use words in trust and place ourselves in community with others. We cannot use language solely as if it were our private toy. Nor can we use language solely to please others. If we are to use a language well, we must use it so that it is appropriate to us as speakers or writers, appropriate to its audience, and appropriate to the particular situation we find ourselves in.

*Intro*

## Appropriateness to Speaker or Writer

As a writer, you dominate the writer-reader relationship; your judgment and sense of fitness control the language you use. Whatever your purpose in writing, express your ideas in language that seems natural. Your writing, in fact, should be an honest expression of your own character. Your language alone is what presents you to a reader; you cannot be everywhere your writing is, and only your language can bring a distant reader and you into any accord. The most fitting language for you, then, is that which gives you and your ideas fullest expression.

This does not mean that the idiolect or dialect that you already speak is a language you can rest content with. Nor does it mean that your idiolect is necessarily "bad" language. It does mean that you should strive to master other versions of general English because they are appropriate in situations you may expect to face in future. One place to start the process of choosing an appropriate language is in your own present language. How well do you understand the way you already speak and write? What is your present language like? Does it have special traits that you can't reasonably expect other people to understand? Are you sure of yourself in spelling, punctuation, sentence structure? When you write a paper for a college course, do you choose the best part of your natural language, or do you adopt an entirely different variety of English? If you return to a paper that you wrote some time ago and read it aloud, does it sound at all like something you would or could say? If it doesn't, can you tell what happened to your language in the paper? Or what has happened to it since?

The suggestions and the pressures of teachers or critics may have some brief effect on the way you use language, but in the long run you set your own standard. The language you use is your responsibility. Good English is not primarily a matter of rules, but of judgment. You are not struggling under a series of *don'ts* but trying to discover among the wide resources of modern English the language that best suits your purpose, your audience, and yourself.

## Appropriateness to Reader or Listener

If you are trying to reach particular types of readers, you may have to adjust your subject matter and your manner of expression more or less to their expectations. You have to be more than merely understandable; you may have to meet your readers, who are real people, largely on their own ground. If your language—though right for you—is not language your readers can use and respond to, then they will not get your meaning. You can enjoy in cold comfort the knowledge that you are right in what you say, but you can hardly expect applause from those who understand little of what you say. Meeting readers on common ground, or even on their ground, is not as hard as may appear at first. After all, some adjustments in language are made almost automatically in letters, for one writes in different ways to different people. The big problem lies in having to write without knowing who will be reading the words. Yet you must learn to overcome such difficulties through practice under critical direction. In writing a class paper, try to direct it to some particular audience, say, the group in your course of study. This technique will help you judge what words and what kinds of sentences are appropriate. In this way, you will learn to use language that is clear, correct, interesting, and proper.

*Intro*

**Clarity.**   Since the aim in writing is to communicate, you must use clear and exact words that your readers will understand. If the subject demands unfamiliar words, try to use them so that the meaning is clear; if necessary, include a concise explanation. Occasionally, you may have to provide a formal definition. Clarity also calls for sentences that are not excessively long and that have a natural, direct movement—though you also must remember the demands of the subject and situation. Experienced readers can grasp more elaborate sentences than those who read little or read hurriedly. Nevertheless, everyone finds pleasure in reading direct, straightforward sentences.

Careful attention to punctuation is also necessary if you are to make your statements clear to your readers. The various marks—commas, dashes, semicolons, and periods among them—indicate the groups of words that are to be understood as units and often show the relationship between these units. Omitted or misused marks may force a reader to go over a passage two or three times to get its intended meaning; superfluous marks may prevent him from recognizing words belonging together or may slow his reading-speed to the point of exasperation.

**Correctness.**   Part of a writer's duty to his readers is to meet their expectations in language by taking care to avoid thoughtless, elementary errors. Such will certainly convince some readers that you are not giving them the consideration they deserve; they may very well refuse to take you seriously. When you finish writing a paper, take time to check it carefully for errors in grammar, spelling, punctuation, and other matters of usage.

**Interest.**   All readers appreciate some liveliness in what they read, both in the writer's expression and in the choice of material. Too many students seem to feel that serious writing requires flat pompous language. On the contrary, in striving for liveliness, there is no need to seek novelty through words that are out of the ordinary. Instead, use just those words you might use in an intelligent, reasonably animated conversation. Avoid monotonous sentences that drag; vary their length and pattern so as to please active, alert minds. Attract your readers' interest by making reference, when appropriate, to things people have said and done, and use details to illustrate your ideas.

One warning is needed: in gearing your writing to your readers' background and expectations, don't underestimate their intelligence, thus compromising yourself and insulting them. Visualize them at their best and write for them at that level.

## Appropriateness to Purpose and Situation

The teacher in your composition class may be interested in seeing essays and other forms of writing in which you use a wide variety of language types and styles, exercises in your own idiolect that use dialect forms, and so on. But many of your other teachers, perhaps all of them, will not be so receptive to such experiment in the papers they assign. In all probability, they will expect—and appreciate—well-written edited English, as described earlier.

The standards of written usage in a composition course are about the same as what would be expected in published material of similar nature. This means that papers about personal experiences, college activities, or your own private reflections might be suitably set forth in general English. It also means that papers required in other courses, will usually be more formal revealing less of your own personality and attitudes; such papers focus with greater concentration on an impersonal subject and require the writer to meet other expectations and objectives.

This standard for college writing is not the result of an arbitrary decision that a given variety of language is nicer or more correct than others. When you are able to use a more formal variety of language, you have, by acquiring that ability, mastered a larger vocabulary, a wider variety of sentence structures, and a greater degree of control. Such mastery of mature language is necessary if you wish to say anything of merit about academic subjects. Consider this single instance. Suppose you are in a philosophy course where one of your assignments is to write a critique of a book on philosophy, including an examination of the author's premises, the mode of his argument, and the style of his presentation. To complete the assignment requires, among other things, that you know what a *critique* is, and also that you must command a language that will let you talk about *premises, modes of argument,* and *styles of presentation.*

*Intro*

The rather formal language that will enable you to discuss these things may not, however, be useful in a meditative essay about sitting on the prairie at midnight under hosts of twinkling stars. If you pay attention to purpose and situation, you should be able to treat most subjects in appropriate language. Inexperienced writers frequently use language that is too heavy to be appropriate to them or to their subjects. For example, a student who wanted to say that he had rebelled against his parents despite having come from a happy home wrote:

> Although my domestic environment was permissive and munificent and my sibling relationships were good, I found it necessary to express my generation's mores in reaction to paternal supervision.

The student may seriously have believed that this kind of writing was better than a simple statement. He would almost certainly object to being told that his sentence was bad English, worse perhaps than if it contained some inaccurate or illogical expressions. But inaccuracies can be quite easily corrected, whereas inflated and inappropriate language must be completely rewritten to be effective. The artificial "formality" of such language is not found in good formal writing, and it should be avoided in student papers.

Once you find the tone that is right for your situation, you should stay with it unless there is some special reason for changing. Although the lines between the varieties of usage cannot be drawn precisely, conspicuous shifts from one to another should ordinarily be avoided, as in the second of these two sentences:

> In the distant pines the rising wind whined as it played among the needles. And when the storm broke, the rain came down in buckets.

Superficial consistency is not so important as fundamental appropriateness, but ordinarily one variety of English should be used throughout a piece of writing.

Reading the work of practised writers is one good way to increase your sensitivity to language and its various uses. Before attempting to write for an unfamiliar situation, read and study some good examples of writing done for a similar purpose. After all, it makes little sense to try to write an article for a magazine you have never read or to try to write a technical report or reference paper without ever having seen one. First you must learn what is typically done in a given situation. When you have learned, follow the accepted practices unless there is good reason to do otherwise.

▶ **EXERCISE**

A good part of the time most of us take for granted the languages we use regularly and the languages we hear regularly. We may not pay much attention to language differences unless we hear words or phrases that are new to us or startling in their context. One way to work toward using your language thoughtfully and well is to pay close attention to what you say and hear, thus becoming more conscious of the way language is used.

1. What are the identifying marks of the variety of language used by those people you were closest to in your early years? List words, expressions, special ways of saying things that you have heard from family and friends, but do not commonly hear elsewhere.
2. If you are in school, list new expressions and ways of saying things that you have heard since starting school. Which of them have you started using yourself?
3. Which words and expressions that you use or hear appear to have been popularized by their use on some television program?
4. Which words and expressions are used to express approval by your family? Your friends and associates now? Which words and expressions are used to express disapproval by your family? By your current friends and associates?
5. Which words and expressions seem to recur most frequently around you?
6. Which words and expressions that you use or hear seem to be associated with some particular region in Canada?

# PART ONE

# Resources for Composition

## GRAMMAR AND USAGE

## PUNCTUATION AND OTHER CONVENTIONS

# Grammar of Sentences

*. . . the right to utter a sentence is one of the very greatest liberties; and*
*we are entitled to little wonder that freedom of utterance should be,*
*in every society, one of the most contentious and ill-defined rights.*
*The liberty to impose this formal unity is a liberty to handle the*
*world, to remake it, if only a little, and to hand it to others in a shape*
*which may influence their actions. — Richard Weaver,* THE ETHICS OF
RHETORIC

The *sentence* is the primary constructed unit in edited English as it
is in all other varieties of English. Indeed, a sentence form of some
kind exists in most, if not all, languages.

What appears to happen in the English sentence form is that two
or more kinds of experience are combined to make a new and
more complete statement of experience. You may know what
*pants* are and what *tearing* is, but when you read the sentence
"My pants are torn," you can understand it without stopping to
think about the separate things, *pants* and *tearing.* The sentence is
something new and different from the kinds of experience that it
includes. In the common sentence form the two (sometimes
more) kinds of experience are stated, usually one as a subject, the
other as a verb. Sometimes, however, one or the other or both of
the experiences are not stated, but supplied by the context:

> He went to town yesterday. [In this sentence, the different kinds of
> experience or reality included are the person referred to as *He* and
> the act of *going.*]

> Why weren't you there? [In this sentence, the two are the person re-
> ferred to as *you* and the idea of *being in some place.*]

> Please try to be on time. [In this sentence, one is omitted, but since
> we can understand that the speaker is talking directly to someone,
> we know that what is left out is *you.*]

> Why not? [Here all of the experiences are omitted from the sentence,
> and we would have to depend on the circumstances in which the
> words appear to know what the experiences are. They might, for
> example, be a shortened form of "Why can't I go to town?"]

> Good! [Here again we would have to depend on the circumstances
> in which the word appears to know what the statement is.]

All these constructions are sentences, though they look very
different from each other. A written sentence is a message of one
or more words punctuated as an independent unit. A sentence,
then, is made complete by its grammatical form and meaning or, in

special circumstances, by the context in which it appears.

A writer has to twist and turn sentences this way and that so as to get the message across most effectively. You must therefore understand how different kinds of sentences are made and what each kind can do. If you know the inner structure of sentences and the way the parts fit together, your control of the several kinds of sentence will improve and so will the quality of your writing. This section reviews the basic grammatical terms needed in analysing and describing sentences and in discussing the relations between the several parts.

**1.1**

*Gr s*

## 1.1 MAIN SENTENCE ELEMENTS

Most English sentences are made with a subject and a verb. You may see this pattern referred to as the "major" or "favorite" sentence type in English.

### The Subject

The subject (s) of a sentence is a noun or noun equivalent (pronoun, noun clause, gerund, infinitive) that is the starting point of the sentence. The *simple subject* is a single word, like *students* in the first sentence below. The *complete subject* consists of the simple subject together with its modifiers — *Hurried students:*

       s
Hurried **students** often make careless mistakes. [noun]
  s
**She** runs faster than her brother does. [pronoun]
       s
**What he doesn't know** is that he talks too much. [noun clause]
  s
**Talking** is his only exercise. [gerund]
   s
**To listen** is to suffer. [infinitive]

### The Verb

A verb (v) is a word which has forms like *ask, asks, asked* or *sing, sang, sung, singing* and which in a sentence agrees with the subject. In the typical sentence, the verb follows the subject and, like the subject, is often a nucleus for modifying words. The verb may consist of one or more words:

      s         v

Hurried students often **make** careless mistakes.

    v    s    v

**Does** he **listen** to what she says?

      s         v

Leslie Jones **has driven** for twenty years without getting a ticket.

            s            v

Perhaps the defendant **should be given** the benefit of the doubt.

    The *predicate* is the verb and whatever words are related to it, such as objects, complements, and modifiers. In the following sentences, the complete predicate is in boldface type, the verb itself being marked with a v:

      s         v

Hurried students **often make careless mistakes.**

      s    v

The doorbell **rang.** [The verb is the complete predicate.]

                     s     v

After finishing his second year, George **spent two long sessions talking with his advisor about his major.**

## The Object

The *direct object* (o) of a verb is a noun or noun equivalent that completes the statement. It answers the question asked by adding "what" or "whom" after the verb. (Hurried students often make what? Careless mistakes.):

      s         v             o

Hurried students often make careless **mistakes.** [noun]

      s       v         o

The Sherwoods have decided **to buy a home.** [infinitive phrase]

  s     v        o

He wondered **what he should do.** [noun clause]

The *indirect object* (io) is used with verbs of telling, asking, giving, receiving, and so on. It names the receiver of the message, gift, or whatever, answering the question "to whom or what" or "for whom or what." It comes *before* the direct object:

  s   v      io           o

He gave the **church** a memorial window.

The same meaning can usually be expressed in a prepositional phrase placed *after* the direct object:

  s   v          o

He gave a memorial window **to the church.**

## The Complement

A complement (c) is a noun or an adjective in the predicate which follows a linking verb (LV). In contrast to an object, a complement is related to the subject rather than to the verb, because a linking verb (sometimes called a *copula*) expresses a condition rather than direct action. A noun used as a complement is called a *predicate noun;* an adjective used as a complement is called a *predicate adjective:*

**1.1**

*Gr s*

S      LV        C<br>
Mary Enderby is a skilled **architect.** [predicate noun]<br>
S      LV       C<br>
The tenor sounded a little **flat.** [predicate adjective]

The most common linking verb is *be* in its various forms: *is, are, was, were, has been, might be.* Other linking verbs include *seem* and *appear* and, in some contexts, *feel, grow, act, look, smell, taste,* and *sound.*

See also 9.2, Predicate Adjectives.

▶ **EXERCISE**

List both the main sentence elements (subject, verb, direct object, indirect object, complement) and the complete predicate of each sentence in the paragraph below.

The [Iroquoian] bride was usually chosen by the young man's mother, who arranged matters with the girl's mother, frequently without consulting either of the two fathers or the bridegroom himself. If everything seemed satisfactory, the two families exchanged presents and the marriage was accomplished. The young man went to live with his bride's parents, but there was no set period of service expected of him. There was a feast, of course, and one interesting custom was that of giving the bride bundles of firewood as wedding presents. The older women knew that going out into the forest to get firewood was one of the most tedious tasks facing the newly married girl.—Douglas Leechman, *Native Tribes of Canada*

## Word Order

In English, we identify the main sentence elements chiefly by their position in the sentence—that is, by word order. Although the form of the words is the same, it makes a lot of difference whether their order is "the ball hit the boy" or "the boy hit the ball."

**Typical word order.** The typical order of the main elements is subject–verb–object (or subject–linking verb–complement). This is the order in which we make most statements and the means by which we understand them.

In "The class congratulated Rachel," we know through experience that *class* is the subject of *congratulated* because it comes before the verb, and that *Rachel* is the object because it follows the verb. When the verb is in the *passive voice* (a past participle following some form of the verb *be*), the order of sentence elements remains subject—verb: "Rachel was congratulated by the class."

So familiar is this order that we recognize it even though the statement itself may be gibberish, or "jabberwocky," as in these lines by Lewis Carroll:

> . . . the slithy toves
> Did gyre and gimble in the wabe. . . .

Whatever the meaning, most people would agree that because of the order of the words, the subject is *toves* and the verbs are *did gyre* and *gimble*.

**Inverted order.** The typical order of sentence elements is reversed in questions, exclamations, and emphatic statements:

>               V     S      O
> QUESTION: Have you a minute to spare?
>                         C                S     LV
> EXCLAMATION: How wasteful these meetings are!
>                            O  S       V
> EMPHATIC OBJECT: A better job I never had.

In sentences with *there* or *it* as an *anticipating subject* (AS), or *expletive,* the real subject comes after the verb:

> AS LV      C       S
> It is a difficult choice.
>   AS     LV     C       S
> There are several reasons for the difficulty.

When the usual order of elements is reversed, the subject of the sentence can be found by locating the verb and identifying what word answers the question formed by putting "who" or "what" before it. Thus in the expression "A lot he knows about it," *knows* is the verb, and since the answer to "*Who* knows?" is obviously *he, he* (rather than *lot*) is the subject.

## Main Sentence Elements

SUBJECT: A noun or noun equivalent that performs an action or is in a particular state of being; it usually appears before the verb and determines the number (singular or plural) of the verb.

**1.1**

VERB: A word that is inflected to show tense, person, and number. It signifies the action or state of being of the subject.

PREDICATE: The verb and all words related to it.

DIRECT OBJECT: A noun or noun equivalent that answers the question asked by adding *what?* or *whom?* to the verb.

INDIRECT OBJECT: A noun that names the receiver of some action, answering the question *to whom or what?* or *for whom or what?* added to the verb. It comes before the direct object.

COMPLEMENT: A noun or adjective in the predicate, following a *linking verb;* it refers to the subject rather than the verb, because a linking verb expresses a condition rather than direct action.


**Examples:**

```
             S      V         DO
```
Careless drivers may injure pedestrians.
```
     S      V      IO          DO
```
Charity may give the needy financial aid.
```
         S    LV         C
```
Some drivers are often careless.
```
     S    LV              C
```
Charity is often the last resort of the needy.
```
   AS   LV    C      S
```
There are many hotels in Vancouver.

## 1.2 SECONDARY SENTENCE ELEMENTS

In addition to the main sentence elements (subject–verb–object or subject–linking verb–complement), most sentences also contain secondary elements. Secondary elements are typically used as modifiers (M)—they describe, limit, or make more exact the meaning of main elements. The table on page 34 shows the various ways in which modifiers—single words, phrases, and clauses—might be used to qualify or expand a simple statement.

### Adjectives and Adverbs as Modifiers

Single words used as modifiers are ordinarily related to the element they modify by means of word order. *Adjectives* relate to nouns and usually stand before the words they modify, but sometimes they come immediately after; in both examples, *climb* is the word modified:

>     M      M
> It was a **slow, dangerous** climb.
>
>              M          M
> The steepness of the slope made the climb **slow** and **dangerous.**

*Adverbs* are more varied in position because often they relate to the sentence as a whole. However, when they modify a particular word (verb, adjective, or adverb) they usually stand close to it:

>     M
> They **particularly** wanted to go. [modifies *wanted*]
>
>                                M
> He came home from the movies **quite** late. [modifies *late*]

See 9, Adjectives and Adverbs.

### Other Words and Word Groups as Modifiers

In English a noun often modifies another noun: *glass* jar, *ski* pants, *dance* hall. Nouns used in this way are usually called *modifiers* (not adjectives) or, more exactly, *nouns used attributively.* (See 6.4, Noun Modifiers.)

Prepositional phrases function as modifiers in the majority of English sentences:

>                        M
> An apartment dweller **in a large city** [modifies *apartment dweller*]
>
>         M                              M
> can live **in the same place** [modifies *can live*] **for a year** [modifies *in*

M
*the same place*] and never speak **to his next-door neighbor.** [modifies
*speak*]

Verbal phrases and subordinate clauses also can function as
modifiers:

**1.2**

M
**Finding no one at home,** he scribbled a note and left it under the front
door. [participle phrase modifying *he*]
M
He needed a way **to make money.** [infinitive phrase modifying *way*]
M
People **who live in glass houses** shouldn't throw stones. [subordinate
clause modifying *People*]

See 3, Subordinate Clauses, and 4, Verbals.

## Appositives

An appositive (A) is a noun or noun equivalent placed beside
another noun to supplement or complement its meaning. It has the
same grammatical function as the noun to which it relates. In
speech, it is marked by a pause and a change in pitch:

A
Your lawyer, **Mr. Jenkins,** is on the telephone.
A
The story takes place in Thebes, **a city in ancient Greece.**

See 11.3, Appositives.

## Modifiers of Modifiers

Words, phrases, and clauses that modify the main sentence elements may themselves be modified. These expressions are called
*modifiers of modifiers:*

MM        M            S        V        M        M        O
The **local** high-school orchestra played several difficult selections
MM    M
**very** well.

▶ **EXERCISE**

Notice how the sentence *The girl sang* can be expanded to make this
sentence: *The delicately beautiful girl, made even more attractive by
her nervousness, sang so sweetly that every person in the audience
hoped she would win the contest.*

## Modifiers

### Modifiers of the subject:

           M      S
A WORD: The **local** orchestra played a selection.

             S                    M
A PHRASE: The orchestra, **consisting largely of amateurs,** played a selection.

             S                  M
A CLAUSE: The orchestra, **which had practised hard for several weeks,** played a selection.

### Modifiers of the verb:

                   V                M
A WORD: The orchestra played the selection **badly.**

                   V                M
A PHRASE: The orchestra played the selection **with more enthusiasm than technique.**

                 V                M
A CLAUSE: The orchestra played the selection **as if they had never rehearsed together before.**

### Modifiers of the object:

                       M     O
A WORD: The orchestra played a **difficult** selection.

                     O        M
A PHRASE: The orchestra played a selection **of old folk-tunes.**

                         O      M
A CLAUSE: The orchestra played a selection **which no one in the audience had ever heard before.**

### Modifiers of the main clause:

           M
A WORD: **Nevertheless,** the orchestra played the selection.

           M
A PHRASE: **Considering their lack of experience,** the orchestra played the selection fairly well.

           M
A CLAUSE: **Since there were no other requests,** the orchestra played the selection.

Expand the following sentences in a similar way, using modifiers, to at least twelve words each:

1. Dogs bark.
2. This typewriter works well.
3. The car runs.

**1.3**

## 1.3 PHRASES AND CLAUSES

English sentences are constructed of single words, phrases, and clauses. Main (or independent) clauses form the principal grammatical units of sentences; they express completed statements and can stand alone. Phrases and subordinate clauses, on the other hand, are dependent on other sentence elements and are used very much like single words.

### Phrases

Phrases are groups of related words connected to a sentence or to one of the elements in it by means of a preposition or a verbal. A phrase has no subject or predicate and cannot stand alone.

**Prepositional phrases.** A prepositional phrase consists of a preposition (*at, from, by, in, of, under,* etc.) followed by a noun or noun equivalent and whatever modifiers that it may have. It functions like an adjective or adverb, depending on what element it modifies:

> He came **from a small town** [modifies the verb *came*] **in northeastern New Brunswick** [modifies the noun *town*].

**Verbal phrases.** A verbal phrase consists of a participle, gerund, or infinitive (none of which has full verb function) plus its object or complement and modifiers. A participle phrase functions as an adjective; a gerund phrase as a noun; and an infinitive phrase as either a noun, an adjective, or an adverb. (See 4, Verbals.)

> Sentences **containing several unrelated ideas** [participle phrase modifying *Sentences*] are seldom effective.

> **Containing the enemy** [gerund phrase used as subject] was their first objective.

> The easiest way **to understand grammatical construction** [infinitive phrase modifying *way*] is **to analyse your own sentences** [infinitive phrase used as complement].

## Clauses

A *main* (or independent) clause contains a subject and predicate and is the grammatical core of a sentence. In the three sentences below, the main clauses are in boldface. Each is a complete expression and could stand alone as a sentence:

   S     V
**I laughed** because I couldn't help myself.
   S    V    O      S   V           O
**She hated English,** but **she needed one more course to graduate.**
           S    V         O
If I were you, **I would find a new job.**

A *subordinate* (or dependent) clause also has a subject and a predicate, but it functions as *part* of a sentence. It is related to the main clause by a connecting word that shows its subordinate relationship, either a relative pronoun (*who, which, that*) or a subordinating conjunction (*because, although, since, after, if, when,* etc.):

I laughed **because I couldn't help myself.**

Subordinate clauses are used like nouns (as subjects, objects, or complements), like adjectives (modifying nouns or pronouns), or like adverbs (expressing relationships of time, cause, result, degree, contrast, and so forth). The subordinate clauses are emphasized in the following examples:

He confessed **that he loved me.** [noun clause, object of *confessed*]

Many of the criminals **whose cases crowded the docket each year** were third- or fourth-time offenders. [adjective clause modifying *criminals*]

**After you plant the seeds,** you should water the garden right away. [adverb clause of time]

The peas in his garden were stunted **because he did not water them soon enough.** [adverb clause of cause]

See 3, Subordinate Clauses and Connectives.

▶ EXERCISE

Start with this sentence: *She walked.*

1. Add a *phrase* that tells where she walked.
2. Add a *phrase* that tells how she walked.
3. Add a *phrase* that tells when she walked.

4. Add a *phrase* that tells where she walked and a *clause* that tells why she walked there.
5. Add a *clause* that tells when she walked, a *phrase* that tells where she walked, and a *clause* that tells to what place she walked.

## 1.4 SENTENCES CLASSIFIED BY CLAUSE STRUCTURE

**1.4**

*Gr s*

Sentences may be classified according to the kind and number of clauses they contain as *simple, compound, complex,* or *compound-complex.*

### Simple Sentences

A simple sentence contains one independent clause and no subordinate (dependent) clauses:

> The man went across the street.

Although simple sentences contain only one clause, they need not be limited to a minor idea. They may, moreover, contain a number of modifiers, and either the subject or the predicate (or both) may be compound:

> Words go up and down the social scale: *knight* and *knave* once meant the same, "a young fellow," but now one has gone up and the other down the scale. [compound subject]—M.H. Scargill, "The Changing Language"

> He got off the northbound train at the first stop after Manawaka, cashed in his ticket, and thumbed a lift with a truck to Winnipeg. [compound predicate]—Margaret Laurence, "Horses of the Night"

> Adam and Padre Doorn climbed out of their jeep and went inside. [compound subject and compound predicate]—Colin McDougall, *Execution*

### Compound Sentences

Compound sentences contain two or more main clauses and no subordinate clauses:

> We of the steerage were careless in our dress [first main clause], but he was always clad in immaculate white linen, with pointed, yellow shoes to match his complexion.—John Buchan, *Prester John*

Each clause in a compound sentence is independent and is *co-ordinate* (of equal rank) with the other clauses. The clauses may be joined (or separated) in one of three ways:

**With co-ordinating conjunctions.**   Independent clauses are most frequently linked by the co-ordinating conjunctions *and, but, or, nor, for, yet* or the correlatives *either . . . or, neither . . . nor, both . . . and, not only . . . but (also):*

> It rained all morning, **but** it cleared up for the picnic.
> **Either** you play to win **or** you don't play at all.

**Without connectives.**   Independent clauses not joined by co-ordinating conjunctions are conventionally separated by semicolons:

> They are generous-minded; they hate shams and enjoy being indignant about them; they are valuable social reformers; they have no notion of confining books to a library shelf. — E. M. Forster, *Aspects of the Novel*

**With conjunctive adverbs.**   The clauses in a compound sentence are sometimes linked by a conjunctive adverb such as *accordingly, also, consequently, however, nevertheless, therefore, then.* However, the function of these connectives is one of modification. When they come between one clause and another, they are preceded by a semicolon:

> The urban renewal program has many outspoken opponents; **nevertheless,** some land has already been cleared.

See 12.1, Semicolons.

## Complex Sentences

A complex sentence consists of one main clause and one or more subordinate clauses:

> As far as I could determine [subordinate clause], Paris hadn't changed at all [main clause] since I last visited it ten years before [second subordinate clause].

In published writing today, complex sentences are used far more frequently than the other three types are. Often, as many as half of the sentences in a particular piece of writing are complex. Complex sentences offer more variety than simple sentences do; it is often possible, for example, to shift subordinate clauses around in the sentence in order to get different emphases or different rhythms. Look at the example above again. It could be changed in various ways by keeping essentially the same words but changing the emphasis:

> Since I last visited Paris ten years ago [subordinate clause], it hadn't changed at all [main clause], as far as I could determine [subordinate clause].

> Or,

**1.4**

> Paris hadn't changed at all [main clause], as far as I could determine [subordinate clause], since I last visited it ten years ago [second subordinate clause].

The tone changes slightly in these examples: in the first example the idea emphasized is that Paris hadn't changed at all; the second sentence emphasizes the visit ten years before; and the third places more doubt on the idea of Paris not changing because *as far as I could determine* gets heavier emphasis. And complex sentences are often more precise than compound sentences are: a compound sentence gives two ideas equal weight; a complex sentence establishes a more exact relationship.

## Compound–Complex Sentences

A compound–complex sentence contains two or more main clauses and one or more subordinate clauses:

> When two men fight a duel [first subordinate clause], the matter is trivial [first main clause], but when 200 million people fight 200 million people [second subordinate clause], the matter is serious [second main clause]. — Bertrand Russell, *The Impact of Science on Society*

Compound—complex sentences occur least often in English because they are apt to be unwieldy.

▶ **EXERCISES**

1. Combine the short sentences in each group below into a single sentence by reducing some to phrases or subordinate clauses. Arrange the parts in any way necessary to create sentences:

   a. He left before sunrise. He reached his old country-home by noon. He had time to look around a while. He went on to his aunt's house.

   b. The ball took a bad bounce. It hit the second-base player in the eye. She picked it up anyway. She threw it to first base. The runner was out. The second-base player fell to her knees.

   c. The wind died. It was sunset. The night was clear. The wisp of moon was not out yet. There were stars. It was still. The crackling of the fire was the only sound.

2. Write one sentence on each model shown below. An example of each is given:

   a. compound: main clause + conjunction + main clause
      *He ate the squash, but he didn't like it.*

   b. complex: subordinate clause + main clause
      *When he had planted the beans, he marked the row with two stakes.*

   c. compound–complex: subordinate clause + main clause + conjunction + main clause
      *After he bought the car, he regretted his haste, but then it was too late.*

   d. complex: main clause + subordinate clause
      *He disliked the car because it used too much gas.*

   e. compound—complex: main clause + subordinate clause + conjunction + main clause + subordinate clause
      *He went to the country whenever he could, and he visited as many of his old friends as possible.*

## 1.5 SENTENCES CLASSIFIED BY PURPOSE

Sentences are conventionally classified by meaning or purpose as follows:

**Statements** (often called *declarative sentences*):

   Jim laughed.
   Most of the sentences we speak and write are declarative.

**Questions:**

   At what temperature does water boil?
   Why do you ask?

**Commands** (including requests and instructions):

   Write soon.
   When the water boils, turn off the burner.

**Exclamations** (feelings, facts, or opinions expressed in an emphatic way):

   How lucky you are!
   He should be thrown out!

## 1.6 UNORTHODOX SENTENCES

While the great majority of written sentences contain both subjects and verbs, some do not. In speech, we may express ourselves by a single word ("Yes." "Oh?"), a phrase ("In a minute."),
or a clause ("If you say so."). Similarly, we occasionally find
single words, phrases, and subordinate clauses as sentences in
published material:

> And so on to Bangkok. Spit and hiss of water, the gramophone quiet.
> The lights out along the deck, nobody about. — Graham Greene, *The
> Shipwrecked*

We do not have to supply any "missing" words to get the author's
meaning (such as "And so *the ship sailed* on to Bangkok."). Such
statements are meaningful and complete as they stand. But they
are minor types, exceptions to the typical English sentence pattern
with subject and predicate. When they appear in print, they are
used deliberately and for a special purpose — to imitate dialogue,
for example, or to create emphasis, or to avoid colorless,
repetitious verbs.

### Subjectless Sentences

Commands and requests generally do not have subjects:

> Don't let me hear you say that again.
> Please try.

The subject is sometimes omitted in informal writing (seldom
in serious writing) when it is easily carried over from the preceding sentence by the context:

> They took no interest in civilized ways. Hadn't heard of them,
> probably. — Clarence Day, *Life with Father*

### Verbless Sentences

Several types of sentences without a main verb are used in all
levels of speaking and writing. The verbs are not left out; they
are not thought, spoken, or written. The statements are complete
and independent without them.

**Exclamations.** *Ouch!, Oh!,* and similar words make complete exclamations, as do such phrases as *What luck!* and *How terrible!*

**Answers to questions.** Short answers without a main verb (*Yes. No. Not if I can help it.*) are considered complete sentences. Occasionally a writer may use a verbless construction to answer a question he has raised himself:

> What is a hero? **The exceptional individual.** How is he recognized, whether in life or in books? **By the degree of interest he arouses in the spectator or the reader.** — W. H. Auden, *The Enchaféd Flood*

**Descriptive details.** Descriptive details are sometimes set off in sentences by themselves for emphasis or to avoid such neutral verbs as *is, are, has:*

> To understand what a fine place Montreal is when spring is coming you must know the winters that come first. **Chill grey mornings; sun bright in the cold noon sky but giving off no heat to speak of; skies darkening again early in the afternoon; long frosty nights with that window-banging wind whipping in burning hard from the north, pushing people before it like paper, making dunes and ridges that hurt the eye to look at on the mountain snows, burning children's cheeks red and cutting like a knife across flat frozen ponds. Old men blowing on their wrinkled hands, boys with blue lips and women with running noses all huddled up and knocking their feet together in the bitter cold waiting for liquor commissions to open and banks to shut, late dates, street cars.** . . . —Mordecai Richler, *Son of a Smaller Hero*

# 2

# Common Sentence Errors

Except for misspelled words, which sooner or later will attract someone's attention, probably the three most conspicuous errors in sentence construction are fragmentary sentences, comma faults, and fused sentences.

**2.1**

*Frag*

These three faults are very common, should they occur in your writing, they will be criticized because they suggest either that you are unable to recognize and distinguish independent grammatical constructions, or that you have not checked your writing carefully.

## 2.1 FRAGMENTARY SENTENCES

*Frag*    Revise the fragment marked by joining it to another sentence, by making it into a complete sentence, or by rewriting the passage.

A *fragmentary sentence* is an incomplete statement—a phrase or a subordinate clause—punctuated as a complete sentence. Fragmentary sentences occur frequently in our speech, and they often make good enough sense there, as responses to what someone else has said, for example, or as additions to what we have already said. A coach might say to his players at practice, "Let's take a ten-minute break to get these last two plays straight. And to give you a chance to catch your breath." His players would certainly have no difficulty in understanding him even though the latter statement is a fragment. But they were listening to him and watching him; they could tell that while he was talking about the plays he could see they were tired. As an afterthought, he adds the fragment. When you write something down, however, you can't superimpose gestures and tone; a reader has only the written words as a guide to your meaning. A fragmentary sentence is likely to be a fragmentary idea that needs to be completed or joined with another idea in a grammatically sound sentence.

A sentence fragment can be corrected in various ways:

1. by joining it to another sentence;
2. by supplying a subject and a predicate;
3. by rewriting the passage in which it occurs.

Each of these ways is illustrated below. (See 1.6 for a discussion of the occasional effective use of fragmentary sentences.)

## Joining a Fragment to Another Sentence

A fragmentary construction usually belongs to the preceding sentence. If you read the passage aloud, you will notice that you pause only slightly before the sentence fragment and do not drop your voice as noticeably as you do at the end of complete sentences. This means that the fragment should be joined to the preceding sentence, usually with a comma. Sometimes it should also be rephrased.

> SENTENCE FRAGMENT: The next afternoon we made our way through Caen. **That town in Normandy which became famous during World War II.**
>
> REVISED: The next afternoon we made our way through Caen, a town in Normandy which became famous during World War II.

**Phrases as fragments.**    Phrases are subordinate sentence elements and should not be punctuated as complete sentences:

> FRAGMENT: I cite these examples to show you how interesting accounting can be. **And to give you an idea of the kind of problems an accountant has to solve.** [The fragment has no main subject and verb. It is an infinitive phrase — *to give* belongs in the first sentence parallel with *to show*.]
>
> REVISED: I cite these examples to show you how interesting accounting can be and to give you an idea of the kind of problems an accountant has to solve.
>
> FRAGMENT: For the past five years I have been contributing annually to the Heart Foundation. **Without ever suspecting that one day a member of my own family might benefit from my contributions.** [prepositional phrase]
>
> REVISED: For the past five years I have been contributing a small amount annually to the Heart Foundation, without ever suspecting that one day a member of my own family might benefit from my contributions.
>
> FRAGMENT: Professor Brown suddenly glanced up from his notes. **His eyes twinkling with suppressed laughter.** [Twinkling is a participle, not a full verb.]
>
> REVISED: Professor Brown suddenly glanced up from his notes, his eyes twinkling with suppressed laughter.

*Explanatory phrases* beginning with *such as, for example, that is, namely,* and similar expressions belong in the same sentence as the statement they explain:

> FRAGMENT: Their mother had a hard time cooking for them because they disliked so many things. **For example, squash, sweet potatoes, beets, okra, cabbage, apricots, and peaches.**
> REVISED: Their mother had a hard time cooking for them because they disliked so many things, for example, squash, sweet potatoes, beets, okra, cabbage, apricots, and peaches.

**2.1**

*Frag*

**Subordinate clauses as fragments.**  *Subordinate clauses* are only parts of sentences and should not stand alone without a definite reason. A relative pronoun (*who, which, that*) or a subordinating conjunction (such as *although, because, if, when, while*) indicates that what follows is a subordinate clause and that it should be combined with a main clause:

> FRAGMENT: At the time, my old rowboat with its three-horsepower motor seemed a high-speed job to me. **Although it only attained a speed of about twelve miles an hour.** [adverb clause, beginning with *Although*]
> REVISED: At the time, my old rowboat with its three-horsepower motor seemed a high-speed job to me, although it only attained a speed of about twelve miles an hour.

> FRAGMENT: The whole area is honeycombed by caves. **Many of which are still unexplored.** [adjective clause, introduced by *which*]
> REVISED: The whole area is honeycombed by caves, many of which are still unexplored.

## Making a Fragment into a Sentence

If the fragment deserves special emphasis, it can be made into a sentence by inserting a subject and a predicate:

> FRAGMENT: He talked for fifty minutes without taking his eyes off his notes. **Apparently not noticing that half the class was asleep.** [*Noticing* is a participle, not a verb.]
> REVISED: He talked for fifty minutes without taking his eyes off his notes. Apparently he did not notice that half the class was asleep. [The subject is *he;* the predicate is the verb *did notice* plus the words related to it.]

> FRAGMENT: National elections and student elections may be compared as closely as an object and its photograph. **The only difference being in size.** [*Being* is a participle, not a verb.]
> REVISED: National elections and student elections may be compared as closely as an object and its photograph. The only difference is in size. [*Is* is the verb, and *difference* is the subject.]

## Rewriting a Fragment

Sometimes involved or hopelessly snarled sentence fragments have to be completely revised. The following long "sentence" has three phrases that seem to be subjects, but there is no *main* verb. A number of verbs appear, but each one is in a subordinate construction:

> FRAGMENT: **The people** who only said, "Oh, too bad," on seeing the lifeless puppy, **the small boy** who removed the dead puppy from the gutter, and the **middle-aged man** who kept saying that people were making a greater fuss about this incident than had been made over his own accident at this same corner a year ago, when he was almost run over by a taxi.

> REVISED: When the small boy removed the dead puppy from the gutter, some people only said, "Oh, too bad." But the middle-aged man kept saying that people were making a greater fuss about this incident than they had made over his own accident at this same corner a year ago, when he was almost run over by a taxi.

▶ **EXERCISES**

1. Sentence fragments often appear in advertisements. The name of a product by itself is sometimes followed by a period to create emphasis. Short phrases punctuated as if they were sentences may seem more direct and to the point. When words and phrases are punctuated as sentences, they can be more readily moved around for purposes of design and visual effect. Find three advertisements that depend on fragments (Advertisements by automakers are good places to look) and rewrite the text with complete sentences. Be prepared to discuss which you think is more effective.

2. Rewrite the following sentences so that they contain no fragments:
   a. Statistics are not yet available to show the actual decrease in accidents. Since this program is still in the process of being completed and traffic has doubled in the past few months.
   b. The area thrives on competition since the same kind of shops are all grouped together. An example of this being the three supermarkets, which are within a mile of each other.
   c. Public transportation will have to be subsidized by the government. Because it will be too expensive for people to ride otherwise.
   d. A popular person usually has three good personality traits. A good sense of humor, considerateness of others, and good grooming.
   e. The professor was obviously displeased with the performance of the class. His eyes looking as angry as lightning bolts.

## 2.2 COMMA FAULTS

*C Ƒ*

**Change the marked comma to a period or semicolon or revise the passage to make an acceptable sentence or sentences.**

A *comma fault* (or a *comma splice*) occurs whenever two or more independent clauses not joined by a co-ordinating conjunction are written with only a comma between them. The result is that one clause is simply backed up against the other.

**2.2**

*C Ƒ*

> The card catalogue is the key to the books in the library, many large libraries have separate catalogues for certain collections of books.

Each of the two clauses joined here is a main clause that could stand alone as a simple sentence. The clauses should be separated by a period or joined into a compound sentence by a semicolon or an appropriate connective:

> The card catalogue is the key to the books in the library; many large libraries have separate catalogues for certain collections of books.

> The card catalogue is the key to the books in the library, and many large libraries have separate catalogues for certain collections of books.

Those who understand clause structure and know how and when to use clauses will not have much trouble with comma faults. If you make this error often, review 1.4, Sentences Classified by Clause Structure. You may also find it helpful to read your papers aloud. If your voice drops or if you pause noticeably at a comma, check the sentence to see if it is actually two independent statements. For example, read this sentence aloud to see how much more marked the pause is at the comma following *past* (a comma fault) than at the comma following *five-thirty:*

> The long shopping-days along downtown streets are a thing of the past, the stores now open for business at 10:00 and close at 17:30, including Saturdays.

The marked pause indicates that there are two separate statements here; a new sentence should begin after *past*.

### Making Two Sentences

A comma fault may be removed by using a period instead of the comma, making two full sentences:

COMMA FAULT: He took a couple of steps, stopped, reached out, and turned a valve, as he did so he told us the valves had to be checked daily.

REPUNCTUATED: He took a couple of steps, stopped, reached out, and turned a valve. As he did so, he told us the valves had to be checked daily.

This is usually the best solution when the ideas are clearly distinct or when there are many commas in either or both statements. However, correcting a comma fault by putting a period between two very short, closely connected statements may result only in two weak sentences:

I opened the door noisily, he didn't move. [Here joining the clauses by **but** is preferable to making each a separate sentence.]

## Using a Semicolon

Comma faults may sometimes be corrected by substituting a semicolon for the comma. This is appropriate when the ideas expressed in the two clauses are closely related:

COMMA FAULT: Charley then crossed the room and threw a switch which started the motor, returning, he wiped the sweat from his forehead with the back of his hand.

REPUNCTUATED: Charley then crossed the room and threw a switch which started the motor; returning, he wiped the sweat from his forehead with the back of his hand.

A great many comma faults in student papers occur with "conjunctive" adverbs such as *however, accordingly, consequently, therefore.* When such adverbs appear at the junction of two independent clauses, the conventional punctuation is a semicolon. Although such words show the connection between ideas in the clauses, their connective function is weak.

COMMA FAULT: The person with a university degree has an education far beyond that to be obtained solely from books, **therefore** his or her chances for success may be greater than are those of a person without this education.

REPUNCTUATED: The person with a university degree has an education far beyond that to be obtained solely from books; therefore, his or her chances for success may be greater than are those of a person without this education.

Other uses of adverbs like *however* and *therefore* are discussed on page 160.

## Revising the Passage

Often the best way to remove a comma fault is to revise the sentence, using a connective that will show the relation between the statements. The connective may be a co-ordinating conjunction (such as *and* or *but*), a subordinating conjunction (*although, because, if, since, when*), or a relative pronoun (*who, which, that*) referring to a noun in the first statement. Sometimes one statement can be revised as a phrase, as in the third example:

**2.2**

*C F*

> COMMA FAULT: It is a personal matter, everyone has to cope with it sooner or later.
>
> REVISED: It is a personal matter **that** everyone has to cope with sooner or later.
>
> COMMA FAULT: I enjoy being in the midst of a party, particularly if I feel some responsibility for its success, conversation is a stimulant more powerful than drugs.
>
> REVISED: I enjoy being in the midst of a party, particularly if I feel some responsibility for its success, **because** conversation is a stimulant more powerful than drugs.
>
> COMMA FAULT: Many companies are looking for experts in pollution control, this is a rapidly expanding field.
>
> REVISED: Many companies are looking for experts in pollution control, a rapidly expanding field.

There are many ways of correcting comma faults. The revision chosen in most situations will depend on the writer's intention and understanding of the passage where the fault occurs. Consider this comma fault:

> The war provided the setting for many novels, three of them were especially outstanding.

Suppose this occurs in the opening paragraph of a paper in which you intend to review a number of war novels very briefly and then focus at some length on three that you think are outstanding. You might revise the sentence as shown below, subordinating the first statement to show that the review of several novels is less significant in the paper than the close study of three (see 3 and 26.2):

> While the war provided the setting for many novels, three of them were especially outstanding.

If you intend in your paper to give equal time and attention to the review of several novels and to the close study of three, you might revise the fault in this way:

> The war provided the setting for many novels. Three of them were
> especially outstanding.

If the review of a number of novels is what is most important
in your paper, and the three novels are simply being used as
examples, then you might revise in this way:

> The war provided the setting for many novels, including three that
> were especially outstanding.

► EXERCISE

Comma faults can often be corrected in several different ways, as the
example below suggests. Study the example, and then correct the
following sentences in the way that you feel is most effective. Be
prepared to discuss your revisions.

*Comma fault:* The Expos traded Rusty Staub, it was a big mistake.
*Revised as a compound sentence:* The Expos traded Rusty Staub; it was a
big mistake.
*Revised as two sentences:* The Expos traded Rusty Staub. It was a big
mistake.
*Revised by rewriting:* It was a big mistake for the Expos to trade Rusty
Staub.
When the Expos traded Rusty Staub, they made a big mistake.
Trading Rusty Staub was a big mistake for the Expos.

1. I'd like to own a bigger car, I don't think I could afford the gas.
2. Bricklayers were hired on a contingency basis, that is, they weren't
   paid until the building was finished.
3. Jim hit a single down the right-field line, David scored from second
   base.
4. Julie is an excellent guitarist, she taught herself.
5. The electricity went off during the storm, we could not read or
   watch television.

## 2.3 FUSED SENTENCES

 Use a period or semicolon between the two statements, or revise the passage to make an acceptable
sentence or sentences.

A *fused sentence* is the same kind of error as a comma fault, except
that no punctuation at all appears between the main clauses. It
should be corrected in the same way as a comma fault:

1. make two sentences of the fused sentence;
2. use a semicolon to separate the two main clauses;
3. rewrite the passage.

> FUSED SENTENCE: Two volumes of this work are now completed the first will be published next year.
>
> POSSIBLE REVISIONS: Two volumes of this work are now completed. The first will be published next year.
>
> Two volumes of this work are now completed, the first **of which** will be published next year.

**2.4**

*Mix*

▶ **EXERCISE**

Following the suggestions in the text, repair the fused sentences below:

1. The birds began to sing it was late in the afternoon.
2. The steak was very expensive prices have been going up lately.
3. "What is the purpose in this?" he asked he did not believe in fraternity initiations.

## 2.4 MIXED CONSTRUCTIONS

*Mix*  Revise the mixed construction to make an acceptable sentence or sentences.

When several sentence faults are combined or when a construction is not one of the standard sentence types, the result is sometimes called a *mixed construction.* Repunctuating cannot correct errors of this kind; the whole passage must be rewritten into acceptable sentence units:

> MIXED CONSTRUCTION: I had always admired his novels, and when I had a chance to meet him, a real delight. [independent and subordinate clauses improperly joined by *and*]
>
> POSSIBLE REVISION: I had always admired his novels and was delighted when I had a chance to meet him.
>
> MIXED CONSTRUCTION: Charles was a hard worker, but I wondered how was he going to get everything finished on time? [shift from statement to question]
>
> POSSIBLE REVISION: Although Charles was a hard worker, I wondered how he was going to finish everything on time.

MIXED CONSTRUCTION: Of course, the Haitian diet is quite different from ours, this is obvious consisting largely of beans and rice. [a comma fault and a misplaced modifying phrase]

POSSIBLE REVISION: Of course, the Haitian diet, consisting largely of beans and rice, is quite different from ours.

Since mixed constructions usually involve a combination of errors, their variety is almost infinite. The only sure way to avoid them is to learn the principles of sentence construction thoroughly and to practise writing well-constructed sentences in coherent paragraphs (See 27.3, Continuity).

# Subordinate Clauses and Connectives

A subordinate clause has a subject and a predicate, but it is shown to be an incomplete statement — a subordinate part of the sentence — by a special kind of connective that relates it to the main clause. In the following sentence, *when* and *that* are the connectives; *few people thought* is the main clause:

> **When Hatfield ran for re-election in 1978,** few people thought **that he could win.**

Subordinate (dependent) clauses are used in sentences as modifiers, subjects, objects, or complements. Depending on the grammatical function they serve, they are classified as adjective clauses (3.1), adverb clauses (3.2), or noun clauses (3.3).

About half the sentences in most kinds of writing contain one or more subordinate clauses, for subordination shows the relationship between ideas much more exactly than a series of simple or compound sentences. Effective use of subordinate clauses is discussed at the end of this section. For a further discussion of subordination and style, see 26.2, Subordination to Control and Clarify Meaning.

## 3.1 ADJECTIVE CLAUSES

A clause that modifies a noun or pronoun is an adjective clause. The relative pronouns *who, which,* and *that* (p. 92) are the words most frequently used to introduce adjective clauses; these pronouns also serve as subjects or objects within the clause:

> Some people **who buy modern paintings** are interested in them more as investments than as art. [*Who* is the subject of the clause, which modifies *people*.]

> The goals **for which he had fought all his life** no longer seemed important to him. [*Which* is the object of the preposition *for;* the clause modifies *goals*.]

> Many books **that are commercially successful** do not qualify as serious literature. [*That* is the subject of the clause, which modifies books.]

> He received a letter from an uncle **whom he had not seen for twenty years.** [*Whom* is the object of the verb *had seen;* the clause modifies *uncle*.]

Adjective clauses may also be introduced by the relative adverbs *when, where,* and *why:*

It was a day **when everything went wrong.** [The clause modifies *day.*]

She returned to the town **where she had lived as a girl.** [The clause modifies *town.*]

The reason **why these early settlements disappeared** has never been explained satisfactorily. [The clause modifies *reason.*]

## Clauses Without Relative Words

Sometimes an adjective clause is a restrictive modifier, a modifier that is essential to the sentence because it limits the meaning (see 11.3). In this case, the relative word is often omitted, especially when the following word is a pronoun or proper name:

The only books [that] Alice read in high school were those [that] her teacher assigned.

He is a person [whom] everyone admires.

These clauses without relatives (they are still subordinate clauses) have long been used in English and are acceptable in all varieties of writing.

## And Which

*And* is sometimes needlessly used between an adjective clause and the rest of a sentence. The relative pronoun *who, which,* or *that* is the only connective needed; the use of *and* or *but* is superfluous and obscures the subordination:

CARELESS: The sea anemone is a fascinating creature **and which** looks more like a plant than an animal.

REVISED: The sea anemone is a fascinating creature which looks more like a plant than an animal.

## 3.2 ADVERB CLAUSES

A subordinate clause that modifies a verb, adjective, adverb, or main clause is an adverb clause. It usually expresses a relationship of time, place, direction, cause, effect, condition, manner, or concession:

He lived abroad for seventeen years but returned to Canada **when war broke out.** [The clause modifies the verb *returned.*]

During her husband's absence she managed the business better **than he had.** [The clause modifies the adverb *better.*]

He becomes very stubborn **when he meets opposition.** [The clause modifies the predicate adjective *stubborn.*]

**Because she was a woman of principle,** even her opponents respected her. [The clause modifies the main statement, *even her opponents respected her.*]

**3.3**

*Sub*

English has many connectives for expressing these adverb relationships. The following are among the most common:

| | | | |
|---|---|---|---|
| after | because | since | unless |
| although | before | so | until |
| as | if | so that | when |
| as if | in order that | though | where |
| as long as | provided that | till | while |

See also 3.4, page 58, Using Exact Connectives.

## 3.3 NOUN CLAUSES

Because they function as nouns, subordinate clauses used as subjects, objects, complements, and appositives are called noun clauses. Most noun clauses are introduced by *that,* but *whatever, whoever, who, what, why, when, where,* and *whether* are also used.

### As Objects

Noun clauses are most frequently used as direct objects:

The Prime Minister said **that his meeting with the provincial Premiers had been fruitful.**

No one knows **why these early settlements disappeared.**

They wondered **what would happen next.**

Noun clauses also serve as objects of prepositions:

From **what you have told me,** I think he is making more money than he deserves.

There is a prize for **whoever gets there first.**

In the last sentence, *whoever* is the correct form rather than *whomever* because the pronoun is the subject of the clause.

### As Appositives

Noun clauses are quite often used as appositives:

> Most people still accept the myth **that progress is inevitable.**
> The fact **that he might lose** never occurred to him.

### As Subjects

Sentences beginning with a subject clause introduced by *that* or *whether* sometimes seem rather stilted, especially if the clause is relatively long. In most kinds of writing, constructions of this kind can more easily appear *after* the verb:

> STILTED: **That he could raise his grade by studying harder** had never occurred to him.
> REVISED: It had never occurred to him **that he could raise his grade by studying harder.**

> STILTED: **Whether or not we should revise our foreign policy** was the principal topic of discussion.
> REVISED: The principal topic of discussion was **whether or not we should revise our foreign policy.**

Subject clauses introduced by other words are common in all levels of writing:

> **Whatever is worth doing at all** is worth doing well.
> **Where he disappeared** is a matter of conjecture.

### As Complements

Noun clauses sometimes occur as complements, particularly in definitions and explanation. Such constructions are often awkward, however, and it is often better to substitute a different wording:

> AWKWARD: Usually the winner is **whoever has the most endurance.**
> BETTER: The person with the most endurance usually wins.
> OR: Whoever has the most endurance usually wins.

> AWKWARD: Our materialism is **why some Europeans criticize us.**
> BETTER: Some Europeans criticize us for our materialism.
> OR: Our materialism is criticized by some Europeans.

After "The reason *is* (or *was*) . . ." the preferred connective in formal and general writing is *that* rather than *because* (*because* means "the reason that"):

> The reason he lost the election was **that** [preferable to **because**] he lacked organized support.

▶ **EXERCISE**

Combine the following pairs of sentences by making one of the sentences into a subordinate clause:

1. The hamster is a handsome animal. It looks like a bundle of fur.
2. He was a strong man. He was feared and admired.
3. The rain has fallen for two days. It has washed the bridge away.
4. Those delegates are not here yet. They attended a big party last night.
5. He was fourteen years old. He began to shave.

**3.4** ◀

*Sub*

# 3.4 SUBORDINATION FOR EXACT STATEMENT

*Sub* Show the intended relationship between ideas by using appropriate subordination, or correct the faulty subordination.

Ideas that deserve equal emphasis should be grammatically co-ordinate (as in *My son is in high school and my daughter is in university*). But an important part of writing is discriminating among ideas that do *not* deserve equal emphasis. Statements that describe or explain another statement or tell how, when, where, or why something happened should be expressed in subordinate constructions whenever the relationship is not immediately clear from context. For example, there is no reason why three separate sentences should be made of these obviously related ideas:

> Mozart made his first trip to Italy in 1769. He was thirteen years old. His father went with him.

If the first statement is the one the writer wants to emphasize, it can stand as a main clause while the other two are reduced to a secondary level:

>   1. In 1769 Mozart made his first trip to Italy
>     2. when he was thirteen years old
>     2. accompanied by his father

Then the sentence would look like this:

> In 1769, **when he was thirteen years old** [subordinate clause], Mozart made his first trip to Italy [main clause], **accompanied by his father** [verbal phrase].

## Showing the Relative Importance of Ideas

A subordinate clause usually indicates that the matter subordinated is less important to the subject being discussed than the main statement. To judge the rightness of subordination it is necessary to know what the emphasis of the passage is. For instance, in joining the two statements "The lightning struck the barn" and "Mother was setting the table for supper," the first would be the main statement in a general account of the event:

> The lightning struck the barn [main clause] just as Mother was setting the table for supper [subordinate clause].

But if the point to be emphasized is what Mother was doing when the lightning struck, the sentence would probably be written like this:

> When the lightning struck the barn [subordinate clause], Mother was setting the table for supper [main clause].

The paragraph would then probably go on to tell what Mother did in the crisis.

In revising sentences, then, it is important to see that the parts are related according to their relative importance.

## Using Exact Connectives

Subordinate clauses are exact because their connectives show a precise and specific relationship to the main clause. Co-ordinating conjunctions, especially *and,* are much less definite in meaning than adverb connectives like *because, since, when, while* or the adjective connectives *who, which, that:*

> CO-ORDINATE STATEMENT: Sandra was waiting for the bus and she saw a purse on the sidewalk.
> ONE STATEMENT SUBORDINATED: **While she was waiting for the bus,** Sandra saw a purse on the sidewalk.
> CO-ORDINATE STATEMENT: "Anglosaxon Street" is one of Earle Birney's best-known poems, and it has been reprinted in many anthologies.
> ONE STATEMENT SUBORDINATED: "Anglosaxon Street" **which is one of Earle Birney's best-known poems,** has been reprinted in many anthologies.

In speaking we tend to rely on only a few of the conjunctions available for expressing adverb relationships (see 3.2), but in writing greater exactness is required. Particular care should be taken so that the common conjunctions *as* and *so* are not overused.

**Using** *as* **and** *so.* The conjunction *as* may introduce various kinds of adverb clauses:

**3.4**

*Sub*

> DEGREE OR MANNER: I went as fast **as I could go.**
> TIME: Our guests arrived **as the sun was setting.**
> CAUSE: **As it was getting dark,** we made for home.
> COMPARISON: Lettuce is not as fattening **as spaghetti is.**
> ATTENDANT CIRCUMSTANCE: **As the fire spread,** the sky grew darker.

The variety of its meanings makes *as* a word to be watched in writing. In some instances it is the proper and only connective to use—to express comparisons, for example (We went as far *as the others did*), or in clauses of manner (*As the twig is bent,* so grows the tree). But in many other constructions, *while, when, since,* or *because* would be more exact and emphatic:

> **While** [not *as*] we were walking, he told us stories.
> The war was almost over **when** [not *as*] he was captured.

*As* is especially weak in the sense of *because.* To introduce clauses of reason, purpose, or result, *since* or *because* is better in most writing:

> He refused to join in the square-dancing **because** [not *as*] he was afraid of making a fool of himself.

Like *as,* the word *so* (or *and* so) is an overworked and often inexact connective. In most writing it should be replaced by a more definite word:

> INEXACT: She couldn't find a job, **so** she decided to go to summer school.
> REVISED: **Since** she couldn't find a job, she decided to go to summer school.

> INEXACT: He was new to the district, **so** he had few friends.
> REVISED: **Because** he was new to the district, he had few friends.

The inexact sentences are not wrong; in both, *so* means *therefore* or *consequently.* But the revised sentences are better; *since* and *because* are signals alerting the reader at the outset that cause-effect relationships occur in the sentences.

In clauses of purpose, *so that* is preferable to *so:*

> He went to Toronto **so that** [not *so*] he could find a job in publishing.

► **EXERCISE**

Combine the following pairs of sentences, choosing one of the statements to be the subordinate idea. Use a connective that accurately shows the relationship.

1. They pawned his big pocket watch. They needed money for groceries at the end of the month.
2. They knew what to expect of the weather. They had lived on the prairies for forty years.
3. The angry farmers had assembled and now stood shouting in front of the Peace Tower. The Prime Minister came out to address them.
4. He got the garden planted by April 15. It cost him forty dollars for fertilizer, a new hoe, and a sore back.

## 3.5 FAULTY SUBORDINATION

Faulty subordination usually results from a careless stringing together of ideas as they happen to come into the writer's mind. Consider, for example, the haphazard use of dependent constructions in the following sentence:

> Because her mother died when Barbara was five years old, and since her father lived a solitary life, Barbara had a very unhappy childhood, having no family to confide in.

The elements in this cluttered statement might be rearranged to establish a better sense of order and proportion:

> Barbara had a very unhappy childhood. She was five years old when her mother died, and since her father led a solitary life, she had no family to confide in.

When you go over the first draft of your papers, revise any subordinate elements that weaken your sentences or obscure their meaning.

### Tandem Subordination

It is usually best to avoid statements in which a series of dependent clauses are strung together, one after another. Too many clauses beginning with similar connectives (*who, which, that; when, since, because*), each built upon the preceding one, are called tandem subordination, or "house-that-Jack-built" constructions:

> TANDEM SUBORDINATION: He had carefully selected teachers **who** taught classes **that** had a slant **that** was specifically directed toward students **who** intended to go into business.

REVISED: He had carefully selected teachers who specifically slanted their courses toward students intending to go into business.

TANDEM SUBORDINATION: The recordings **which** I bought last week were scarce items **that** are essential to people **who** are making collections of folk music **which** comes from Spain.

REVISED: Last week I bought some scarce recordings that are essential to collectors of Spanish folk music.

**3.5**

*Sub*

Sentences that begin and end with the same kind of subordinate clauses are awkward because of their seesaw effect:

**When** he came home from work, Dad would always complain **when** the children weren't there to meet him.

Such constructions can be improved by changing one of the connectives. Usually it is possible to choose a connective that is more exact:

When he came home from work, Dad would always complain **if** the children weren't there to meet him.

## Inverted Subordination

Putting the main idea of a sentence in a subordinate clause or phrase ("inverting" the proper relationship between statements) may result in an awkward or incongruous statement:

INVERTED: She was eighteen when her hands were severely burned, which meant that she had to give up her goal of becoming a concert pianist.

MORE ACCURATE: When she was eighteen, [main clause:] **her hands were severely burned.** As a result, [main clause:] **she had to give up her goal of becoming a concert pianist.**

Inverted or "upside-down" subordination frequently occurs in sentences that trail off into weak participle phrases:

The road was blocked, **causing us to make a twenty-mile detour.**

Such sentences can be improved by putting the less important statement in an adverb clause:

We had to make a twenty-mile detour **because the road was blocked.**

▶ **EXERCISE**

Practise further with subordination by rewriting the first three to five paragraphs of several newspaper articles. You should be able to combine some sentences by turning some short ones into subordinate clauses.

# 4

# Verbals

Because *verbals* are forms of *verbs,* the two are sometimes confused. *Verbs* (see 8) are often described as finite, or limited, because one form only can be used to show time. *Verbals,* which are discussed in this section, are described as non-finite, meaning that they do *not* change their form to indicate time or tense. It may help to get the distinction clear if we note differences between finite and non-finite forms.

If we say "Joe went to the movies this afternoon," or "Joe went to the movies yesterday," the verb *went* (a form of *go*) is finite. That means that we can tell from the form of the verb that the action took place at a particular time in the past. *Went* is finite because it can only be used to record past action. If we say "Joe will go to the movies tomorrow," the verb *will go* is finite; it can only be used to refer to future action. Other forms of verbs are finite in similar ways.

*Verbals,* however, are not so limited. We can say "Joe has always liked *to go* to the movies" (in past time), or "Joe likes *to go* to the movies" (present time), or "Joe will always like *to go* to the movies" (future time). In each instance, the infinitive *to go* keeps the same form because it is non-finite.

Verbals, then, are non-finite verb forms; they are used in sentences as nouns (subjects, objects, complements) or modifiers. They have many qualities of verbs: aided by auxiliary verbs, they can show tense, for example, and they can take objects, but they cannot serve as full, finite verbs to make sentences or clauses. In many sentences, however, verbal phrases function very much like subordinate clauses in showing the relationship between main and subordinate ideas:

> **When she graduated from Acadia,** she went to Halifax in search of a job. [subordinate clause]
> **Having graduated from Acadia,** she went to Halifax in search of a job. [verbal phrase, modifying *she*]

Verbals are classified by form and function as

1. **infinitives** (*to ask, to buy*), which can serve either as nouns or as modifiers;
2. **participles** (*asking, asked, buying, bought*), which modify nouns and pronouns; and
3. **gerunds** (*asking, buying*), which are verbal nouns.

Although the present participle and the gerund are identical in form, they can be distinguished by the way they are used in sentences:

> PARTICIPLE: a **dancing** figure [modifier]
> GERUND: **dancing** takes skill [noun]

The forms and principal uses of verbals are illustrated in the table on page 64. See also 8, Verbs.

**4.1**

*Vbl*

## 4.1 USING VERBAL PHRASES

Like full verbs, verbals can take objects, complements, and adverbial modifiers. In some constructions they also take a subject, if the meaning of that term is stretched a little:

> **Slowly weaving its way from twig to twig,** the spider built its nest. [*way* is the direct object of the participle *weaving,* which is modified by the adverb *slowly; way* is modified by the prepositional phrase *from twig to twig;* the entire participle phrase modifies *spider,* the subject of the sentence]

> He avoided the accident by **running his car onto the shoulder of the road.** [*car* is the direct object of the gerund *running,* which is modified by the phrase *onto the shoulder of the road;* the verbal phrase is the object of the preposition *by*]

> She wanted **to be an architect or industrial designer.** [*architect* and *designer* are complements of the infinitive *to be;* the verbal phrase serves as object of the verb *wanted*]

### Subjects with Infinitives

An infinitive phrase often has an expressed subject:

> He wanted **the whole department** [subject of the infinitive] **to be reorganized.**

If the subject of an infinitive is a pronoun, it is in the object form:

> They asked **him** [subject of the infinitive] **to be secretary.**
> Their mother told **them** [subject of the infinitive] **to behave.**

### Subjects with Gerunds

When a noun or pronoun precedes a gerund, serving as its "subject," some questions of usage arise: sometimes the possessive form is used, sometimes the common form. The writer must de-

## Forms and Uses of Verbals

### Infinitives

An infinitive is (1) the base form of a verb (with or without *to*) or (2) any verb phrase that can be used with *to* to function in a sentence as a noun, an adjective, or an adverb.

| Forms: | Active | Passive |
|---|---|---|
| PRESENT | (to) ask, (to) be asking | (to) be asked |
| PAST | (to) have asked, (to) have been asking | (to) have been asked |

**Principal uses:**
SUBJECT: *To be called* to the principal's office makes little boys nervous.
OBJECT: He does not like *to express his opinion.*
MODIFIER **(adjective):** I have plenty of work *to do.* (Modifies *work*)
MODIFIER **(adverbial):** The students came *to learn French.* (Modifies *came*)
ABSOLUTE PHRASE MODIFYING THE MAIN CLAUSE: *To tell the truth,* he is a bore.

### Participles

A participle is a verb form, typically ending in *-ing* or *-ed,* used as a modifier.

| Forms: | Active | Passive |
|---|---|---|
| PRESENT | asking | being asked |
| PAST | having asked | asked, having been asked |

**Principal uses:**
MODIFIER OF A NOUN: a *smiling* candidate; a *clogged* drain
PARTICIPIAL PHRASE MODIFYING A NOUN: The candidate *getting a majority of the votes* will be nominated.
ABSOLUTE PHRASE MODIFYING THE MAIN CLAUSE: *Everything considered,* a portable typewriter seems the most practical gift.

### Gerunds

A gerund is a verb form, typically ending in *-ing* or *-ed,* used as a noun.

| Forms: | Active | Passive |
|---|---|---|
| PRESENT | asking | being asked |
| PAST | having asked | having been asked |

**Principal uses:**
GERUND AS SUBJECT: *Having been asked* made him happy.
GERUND PHRASE AS SUBJECT: *Taking anthropology* opened a whole new field.
GERUND AS OBJECT: She taught *dancing.*
GERUND AS COMPLEMENT: Seeing is *believing.* (*Seeing* is also a gerund.)
GERUND AS A MODIFIER OF A NOUN: the *dining* room, a *fishing* boat
GERUND AS APPOSITIVE: He had only one hobby, *collecting stamps.*

pend partly on the sound in choosing the form that seems more natural, but the following principles should serve as guides:

1. When the subject of a gerund is a personal pronoun or a proper noun, the possessive form is generally used:

    The less said about **his** singing, the better.
    They insisted on **Bob's** playing the piano.

**4.1**

*Vbl*

2. When the subject is stressed, the common form is usually preferred with nouns and the object form with pronouns:

    Did you hear about the **mayor** being arrested for speeding?
    I can't imagine **him** winning an award.

3. When the subject is a plural noun, the common form is usually preferred:

    The manager disapproves of **people** smoking in meetings.
    The staff will not tolerate **visitors** coming and going at will.

4. If the subject is abstract, the common form is used:

    It was a case of **panic** getting the upper hand.
    There is a danger of the **temperature** dropping suddenly.

5. When the subject is modified by other words, the common form is used:

    There was something suspicious about the **daughter** of the sponsor winning the $10 000 prize.

    At the beginning of the election, no one in Ottawa foresaw the possibility of the **Finance Minister,** who had angered so many people with his tax bill, retaining his seat in the Commons.

6. With other noun forms, usage is divided. If you are writing a formal paper, it is usually best to use the possessive form, but the common form of the noun is widely used in general English:

    FORMAL: The neighbors complained about the **dog's** barking at night.
    GENERAL: The neighbors complained about the **dog** barking at night.

    FORMAL: Jones worried about his **secretary's** taking another job.
    GENERAL: Jones worried about his **secretary** taking another job.

► **EXERCISE**

Write sentences that include the terms shown below. Let the noun or pronoun be the subject of the gerund.

*Example:* Richard/strumming on his old guitar
*Sentence:* The dog howled at the sound of Richard's strumming on his old guitar.

1. the cousin of the senator/getting the contract for the bridge
2. orchestra/talking during rehearsal
3. pronoun referring to Richard/giving up
4. my mother/saying such things
5. fear/overcoming his sense of responsibility

## 4.2 IDIOMATIC USE OF INFINITIVES AND GERUNDS

Sometimes we say things in a particular way, not because it is grammatically proper, but simply because it is a way of speaking or writing that has for a long time been customary. When we say that we *put up with* something, the expression doesn't make much sense grammatically, but we know that it means *tolerate* because it is an *idiom* that we are familiar with.

Some expressions are regularly completed by infinitives (privileged *to attend*), others by gerunds (the privilege *of attending*). When one form is substituted for the other, the result is an unidiomatic construction: for example, "eager *to join*" is a standard idiom, but "eager *of joining*" is not. Here are typical expressions, some that call for a gerund, others for an infinitive. You will find others in your dictionary under the key (main) word of the construction:

| **Gerund** | **Infinitive** |
|---|---|
| cannot help going | compelled to do |
| capable of working | able to work |
| skilled in writing | the desire to write |
| the habit of giving | the tendency to give |
| successful in getting | manage to get |
| ignore saying | neglect to say |
| my object in paying | my obligation to pay |
| satisfaction of doing | satisfying to do |

With many words, especially common ones, either a gerund or an infinitive is idiomatic: a way *of doing* it, a way *to do* it.

### The *and* of in Gerund Phrases

Gerunds are more direct when they are not preceded by *the* and when they are completed by a direct object rather than an *of* phrase:

AWKWARD: In **the** revising **of** the first draft, writers should check their spelling.

DIRECT: In revising the first draft, writers should check their spelling.

## *To* **with Infinitives**

Most infinitive constructions are introduced by *to,* "the sign of the infinitive":

> She needed time **to think.** They hoped **to get** home before dark. His efforts **to be promoted** failed.

*To* is not used, however, after auxiliary verbs (*can, may, must, shall, will*):

> I can **see.** You must **try** it. We may **go** to Europe next fall.

With a few verbs (*do, dare, help, need,* etc.) usage varies:

> I did see him. It did me good **to see** him.
> I helped him [**to**] **learn** to drive.

## **Split Infinitives**

If an adverb comes between *to* and an infinitive (I don't want *to ever see* him again) the phrase is called a *split infinitive.* A writer should avoid split infinitives that are obviously awkward or that call undue attention to themselves:

> AWKWARD: I will not describe the circumstances of our meeting, or even attempt **to** physically **describe her.**
> BETTER: I will not describe the circumstances of our meeting, or even attempt **to describe** her physically.

But constructions of this sort are not always awkward. When the normal position of the adverb is after the word *to,* a split infinitive is standard usage (The receptionist asked them *to please sit* down). Putting the adverb modifier immediately before or after the infinitive would be clumsy or misleading in some statements:

> CLUMSY: Autumn is the time **really to see** Europe.
> BETTER: Autumn is the time **to really see** Europe.

## 4.3 MISRELATED MODIFIERS

Revise the sentence so that the expression marked is clearly related to the word or statement that it modifies.

Verbals, either as single words or in phrases, are most often used as modifiers of individual words:

I first noticed him **sitting alone in a corner.** [present participle, modifying *him*]

The city hall, **completely renovated four years ago,** always impresses visitors. [past participle, modifying *city hall*]

He still had three years **to serve in prison** before he would be eligible for parole. [infinitive, modifying *years*]

Like other modifiers, verbal modifiers should be clearly related to the words that they modify. When a verbal construction seems from its position to refer to a word that it cannot sensibly modify, it is said to be *misrelated,* or *misplaced.* Participle phrases usually give writers the most trouble:

MISRELATED: On the other side of the valley, **grazing peacefully like cattle,** we saw a herd of buffalo. [the participle phrase seems to refer to *we*]

REVISED: On the other side of the valley **we** saw a herd of buffalo, **grazing peacefully like cattle.** [the phrase clearly refers to *buffalo*]

Misrelated modifiers may be momentarily confusing to the reader (or unintentionally humorous) and should therefore be avoided. Sometimes the correction can be made by putting the modifier immediately before or after the word it is meant to modify, as in the example above, but often it is better to rewrite the sentence completely:

MISRELATED: One early-day western politician is said to have passed out campaign cards to the voters **pinned together with five-dollar bills.** [the participle phrase seems to refer to *voters*]

REVISED: One early-day western politician is said to have pinned five-dollar bills to the campaign cards he passed out to voters.

Occasionally modifiers are placed so that they seem to refer to either of two elements in the sentence. These constructions (sometimes called *squinting modifiers*) can be avoided by changing the position of the modifier or by otherwise revising the sentence:

SQUINTING: The woman who was standing in the doorway **to attract attention** dropped her purse.

REVISED: The woman who was standing in the doorway dropped her purse **to attract attention.**

OR: The woman, standing in the doorway **to attract attention,** dropped her purse.

Other types of misrelated modifiers are discussed in 9.5, Position of Adverbs.

## 4.4 DANGLING MODIFIERS

*ᗡ m*    **Revise the sentence to include the word to which the dangling modifier refers.**

*Dangling modifiers* refer to a word that is implied rather than actually stated in the sentence. Like misrelated modifiers, they can make a sentence confusing or ludicrous:

> **Having moved at fifteen,** his hometown no longer seemed familiar.

This error often occurs when passive rather than active verbs are used:

> DANGLING: **In painting four of these pictures,** his wife was used as his model.
>
> REVISED: **In painting four of these pictures,** he used his wife as his model.
>
> DANGLING: **To find the needed information,** the whole book had to be read.
>
> REVISED: **To find the needed information, I** had to read the whole book.

Usually the easiest way to correct a dangling modifier is to name the agent or "doer" of the action immediately after the phrase, as in the revisions shown above. It is often better, however, to revise the sentence entirely, making the relationships more accurate by using other constructions. Changing the verbal phrase to a subordinate clause often improves the sentence:

> DANGLING: **Having been delayed by a train accident,** the leading role was played by a local actress.
>
> REVISED: **Because the leading lady was delayed by a train accident,** her role was played by a local actress.

## 4.5 ABSOLUTE MODIFIERS

A writer should distinguish clearly between verbal modifiers that obviously dangle, such as those cited above, and *absolute modifiers*—participle or infinitive phrases that modify the statement as a whole and thus do not need a specific reference word in the main clause. As the word *absolute* suggests, these modifiers are complete and independent; their form does not depend on anything else in the sentence.

A number of absolute constructions are commonly used expressions:

> **Everything considered,** this plan seems best.
> **To make a long story short,** we bought the house.
> **Considering the cost of lumber,** the price is reasonable.

Absolute modifiers can usually be converted easily into subordinate clauses: *When everything is considered,* this plan seems best.

An absolute phrase with a subject is sometimes called a *nominative absolute.* This construction is often used effectively in descriptive and narrative prose for adding details or parenthetical material:

> Their bench was cut by a side coulee, and they tipped and rocked down, the rumps of the horses back against the dashboard, Ray's hand on the brake, **the shoes** [subject] **shrieking** [participle] mud from the tires,—Wallace Stegner, "Carrion Spring"

> Everyone was preparing to go home, **mothers** [subject] **buttoning** [participle] their children's coats, **children** [subject] **clutching** [participle] ... their balloons and whistles and paper baskets full of jelly beans.—Alice Munro, "The Shining Houses"

▶ EXERCISE

Some of the sentences below contain misrelated or dangling modifiers. Rewrite the sentences to make the relationships clear. The sentences with absolute modifiers need no revision. Notice that the sentences needing correction can be revised in more than one way. In the first revision below, the subject *their actions* is dominant; in the second revision, using *I* as the subject makes it dominant.

*Example:* Having grown tired of them, their actions no longer concerned me.

*Revision:* Because I had grown tired of them, their actions no longer concerned me.

*Revision:* Having grown tired of them, I felt that their actions no longer concerned me.

1. Being thoroughly persuaded of them myself, the beliefs I hold seem to me to be obviously true.
2. My spirits often sink in despair, however, trying to find ways to convince others of these truths.
3. After having convinced a friend against his will, both he and I find that our friendship is in doubt.

4. It does not really persuade anyone to accept my beliefs by citing authorities to prove my point.

5. To be honest about it, my friends have grown weary of my arguments and often try to avoid me.

6. After having satisfied my own mind in every detail of an argument, the decision I reach seems incontrovertible.

7. My position tends to harden very rapidly, my decision having been reached, and I am not likely to change my mind.

8. To be perfectly frank, it is unwise for you to pretend that you are convinced by what I say to be polite.

9. Above and beyond the call of mere friendship, being more important, truth is what matters.

10. To do justice to any friendship based on truth, it takes absolute candor on both sides.

**4.5**

*abs m*

**5**

# Agreement of Subject and Verb

*agr*  Make the marked verb agree grammatically with its subject.

In English, parts of speech that change form to show number, gender, or person should agree, or correspond, when they are related to each other. Pronouns agree with their antecedents (see 7.2) and verbs with their subjects. Agreement, or correspondence, means, in this case, that if a subject is plural, then its verb ought to be plural as well.

Agreement between subject and verb is not always a problem in general English because most verbs seldom change form. The verb *be* is an exception, for it has several forms; but other verbs have only two forms in the present tense and only one form in the past tense. Although we say *I swim* and *you swim,* we change the form for the third person singular to *he swims, she swims,* or *it swims.* In the past tense, we use *swam* for all situations. There are departures from this practice in certain English dialects. Some, for example, consistently use only one form in the present tense: *I do, you do, he do, she do, it do.* See 8, Verbs, for a discussion of English verb forms.

Questions about agreement of subject and verb are most likely to arise when verbs have compound subjects or collective nouns as subjects, or when the number of the subject (singular or plural) is obscured by other words occurring between the subject and verb. These problems are discussed in the following sections.

## 5.1 VERBS WITH COMPOUND SUBJECTS

A compound subject is made up of two or more words, phrases, or clauses joined by *and, or, nor.* The number of the verb depends on which conjunction is used and on the meaning of the subject.

### Subjects Joined by *and*

The conjunction *and* is used to join co-ordinate items, to link them. Accordingly, subjects joined by *and* usually take a plural verb:

**Bob, Ted,** and **Sandra swim** with the national team.

The first **draft** of your paper and the **version** finally turned in might **differ** in several ways.

*Exception:* When the words of a compound subject refer to the same person or are considered together as a unit, the verb is usually singular:

**5.1**

*agr*

His warmest **admirer** and severest **critic was** his wife.

**Law and order means** different things to people with different political opinions.

## Subjects Joined by *or, nor*

Compound subjects joined by *or, nor, either . . . or, neither . . . nor* sometimes take singular verbs and sometimes plural. Here are some ways to tell the difference:

1. When both subjects are singular, the verb ordinarily is singular:

    **One** or the **other is** certainly to blame.

    Neither **Premier Davis** nor **Premier Blakeney was able** to attend the federal-provincial conference.

*Exceptions:* In questions, where the verb precedes the subject, general usage tends to use a plural verb:

    **Are** [formal: *Is*] either **Clark** or **Broadbent** supporting the bill?

In general usage, a plural verb may also follow two singular subjects if they are not considered as separate:

    Neither **radio** nor **television provide** [formal: **provides**] adequate news coverage.

2. When both subjects are plural, the verb is plural:

    No artificial **colorings** or **preservatives are used.**

3. When one subject is singular and the other plural, usage varies. In formal writing, the verb usually agrees with the nearer subject:

    One major **accident** or several minor **ones seem** to occur at this corner every weekend.

    Neither the **revolutionists** nor their **leader was** to blame.

    In general usage, a plural verb is often used even if the nearer subject is singular:

    Neither the **revolutionists** nor their **leader were** to blame.

4. When the subjects are pronouns in different persons, formal usage requires that the verb agree in person and number with the nearer subject. In general usage (and even in formal usage if the alternative is awkward), the verb is usually plural:

FORMAL: Either **you** or **she is** likely to be elected.
GENERAL: Either **you** or **she are** likely to be elected.

FORMAL AND GENERAL: Neither **you** nor **I are** trained for that job. [*Am* would sound unnatural.]

Such problems of agreement can usually be avoided by substituting a different, more natural construction:

**One** of you **is** likely to be elected.
**Neither** of us **is** trained for that job.

## Subjects Followed by *as well as*

In formal usage, a singular subject followed by a phrase introduced by *as well as, together with, along with, in addition to* ordinarily takes a singular verb:

The **treasurer as well as the president was held** responsible for the mismanagement of the company.

But a plural verb is often used in these situations when the added phrase is clearly intended as a compound subject:

Both the **production** of small cars, **together with the supply** in the dealers' showrooms, **have been outstripped** by the demand.

A simple solution—and one that may make the statement more direct—is to use *and* wherever appropriate:

Both the **production** of small cars and the **supply** in the dealers' showrooms **have been outstripped** by the demand.

▶ EXERCISE

Write sentences using the subjects given below, making sure that the verb agrees with the subject.

*Example:* backaches, dizzy spells, and blinding headaches
*Sentence:* Backaches, dizzy spells, and blinding headaches *are* signals that you should see a doctor.

1. beer, wine, and champagne
2. neither codeine nor magnesia tablets
3. both alligators and crocodiles

4. neither drugs nor tobacco
5. the teacher together with the class

# 5.2 VERBS WITH COLLECTIVE NOUNS AS SUBJECTS

**5.2**

*agr*

Words that refer to a group of people or objects but are singular in form are called collective nouns or group nouns: *army, audience, choir, committee, crowd, faculty, gang, group, government, jury, mob, orchestra, public, team.* Verbs and pronouns used with collective nouns are either singular or plural, depending upon the meaning of the group word.

## Nouns Referring to the Group as a Unit

Singular verbs and singular pronouns are used with collective nouns that refer to the group as a unit:

> **Class is** dismissed.
> The **committee has** already held **its** first meeting of the year.
> The **audience is** requested to remain seated during intermission.

## Nouns Referring to Individuals in a Group

When a collective noun refers to the members of the group, especially if it represents them as acting individually, a plural verb and plural reference words are used:

> The graduating **class have** all agreed to have **their** pictures taken.
> The **committee are** arguing among **themselves.**
> The **audience have** taken **their** seats.

Sentences like these often sound rather unnatural, and in most cases it is better to substitute a clearly plural subject (the committee *members,* the *members* of the audience).

## Verbs with Measurements and Figures

Expressions signifying quantity or extent (*kilometres, litres, years, grams*) take singular verbs when the amount is considered as a unit:

> **Five dollars is** too much to pay for a book in that condition.
> **Four litres** of oil **is** all the crankcase holds.
> **Three months passes** in no time at all on a dude ranch.

When the amount is considered as a number of individual units, a plural verb is used:

> **Two more dollars are** missing from the till this morning.
> There are **two litres** of milk in the refrigerator.
> The last **three months have been** the driest in Saskatchewan's history.

In expressions of addition and multiplication, usage is evenly divided:

> Five and seven **is** [or **are**] twelve.
> Five times seven **is** [or **are**] thirty-five.

A singular verb is used in expressions of subtraction and division:

> Twenty-five from thirty-one **leaves** six.

## Verbs with *data, number, public*

*Data* is a plural form and is generally so considered in formal, particularly scientific, writing; but since the singular *datum* is rarely used, *data* is often used for both singular and plural in general writing; agreement often depends on context:

> SINGULAR IDEA: The **data** the president needs **has been analysed** by his assistant. [*data* refers to a body of facts]
> PLURAL IDEA: After the **data** [individual facts] **have been gathered** and **analysed,** you can decide which elements are most essential to your study.

*Number* as a collective noun may be either singular or plural: preceded by *the*, it refers to the total sum and takes a singular verb; preceded by *a*, it refers to the individual units and takes a plural verb:

> **A number** of pages **are** badly torn.
>
> **The number** of pages assigned for daily reading **was** gradually increased to twelve.
>
> Physicians were disturbed to find that **an** alarming **number** of bacteria **were** developing a tolerance to penicillin.

*Public* takes a singular verb if the writer wishes to signify the whole group (The *public is* invited to attend); it takes a plural verb if the writer is considering the individual members (The *public are* invited to express their opinions).

## Words Ending in *-ics*

*Physics, mathematics, economics, civics, linguistics,* and similar *-ics* words that refer to a science, art, or a body of knowledge are usually considered singular; other words ending in -*ics* that refer to physical activities or qualities (*athletics, acrobatics, tactics*) are generally treated as plurals.

> SINGULAR FORMS: **Physics was** my most difficult subject in high school.
>
> **Ballistics is** the study of the motion of projectiles.
>
> PLURAL FORMS: **Athletics have** been virtually abolished from some smaller schools.
>
> New **calisthenics are** designed for older people.

**5.3**

*agr*

Some words ending in -*ics* (*ethics, politics, acoustics*) may be used in either a singular or plural sense, according to the context:

> SINGULAR IDEA: In almost every group, **politics is** a controversial subject.
>
> PLURAL IDEA: Radical **politics were** offensive to the Family Compact.
>
> SINGULAR IDEA: **Acoustics is** a branch of science that is growing fast.
>
> PLURAL IDEA: The **acoustics** in this room **are** not all they might be.

When you are in doubt about the number of a word ending in -*ics*, consult a dictionary.

## 5.3 BLIND AGREEMENT

Sometimes writers make a verb agree with a nearby expression rather than with its actual subject. Since this often occurs when a writer accepts the nearest convenient word or phrase that looks like a subject, it is frequently referred to as "blind agreement." The error usually occurs in the following situations:

### Plural Nouns Between Subject and Verb

A singular subject followed by a phrase or clause containing plural nouns is still singular:

> Here and there a **man** [subject] such as Columbus, Galileo, and others **has** [not *have*] ventured into the unknown physical and intellectual worlds.
>
> The **lumberman** [subject] who previously sold only to carpenters and builders now **finds** [not *find*] hundreds of amateurs eager to build their own homes.
>
> I decided to see exactly how **one** of those new cars **is** [not *are*] put together.

## *one of those who*

In formal English, the verb in clauses that begin *one of those who* (or *that*) is plural:

> He is one of those men who never **care** how they look. [The verb is plural because its subject *who* refers to *men*, not to *one*.]

> "The Lottery" is one of those stories that **leave** you more puzzled when you finish than when you began. [*Stories* is the antecedent of *that*.]

Although a singular verb is common in spoken English ("one of those girls who *plays* in the band") and in a good deal of published material, the plural verb is customarily used in formal English.

*Exception:* When *the only* precedes *one of those who* the verb is singular, since the pronoun *who* then refers to one person or thing only:

> She is the only one of those women who **plays** bridge well.

## *there is, there are*

When a sentence begins with the introductory (or "dummy") word *there* (sometimes referred to as an "anticipating subject"), the number of the verb is determined by the subject which follows:

> There **are** conflicting **opinions** [subject] about smoking in the classrooms.

> There **is** great narrative and dramatic **power** [subject] in most of the novel.

> At our camp there **were** at least a dozen **men** [subject] who were familiar with the mountain trail.

In this construction a singular verb is frequently used before a compound subject, especially if a plural verb would be unidiomatic, as in the second example below:

> There **is food** and **drink** enough for everyone.
> There **was nothing** he could do and **little** he could say.

But notice that starting a statement with *there is* or *there are* is often wasteful and wordy:

> Great narrative and dramatic power are evident in most of the novel.

> At our camp, at least a dozen men were familiar with the mountain trail.

## Verb and Complement

A verb agrees with its subject and not with its complement or its object:

> Our chief **trouble** [subject] **was** [not *were*] the black flies that swarmed about us on the trip.

> The **black flies** [subject] that swarmed about us on our trip **were** [not *was*] our chief trouble.

> The **material** [subject] that was most interesting to me when I worked on my reference paper **was** [not *were*] the books that stated the facts forcefully.

**5.3**

*agr*

When subject and complement differ in number, the sentence usually sounds less awkward if the subject and verb are plural, as in the second example above.

## Inverted Word Order

When the word order is inverted, care must be taken to make the verb agree with its subject and not with some other word:

> Throughout the story **appear** thinly disguised **references** [subject] to the author's own boyhood.

> **Is** any **one** [subject] of these pictures for sale?

> Accompanying the actress **were** her **secretary** and two **members** of her legal staff. [The verb has a compound subject.]

Subjects like *series, portion, part, type* take singular verbs even when modified by a phrase with a plural noun:

> A **series** of panel discussions **is** scheduled for the convention.

> A substantial **portion** of the reports **is** missing.

> The most interesting **part** of the investigations **was** the discovery and identification of the forged letters.

▶ **EXERCISES**

1. Find the subject of the italicized verbs in the following paragraph. If the subject is a pronoun, indicate what word or idea it refers to.

   Epidemics *have taken* a great toll of lives in past generations. Death in infancy and early childhood *was* frequent and there *were* few families who didn't lose a member of the family at an early age.

Medicine has changed greatly in the last decades. . . . The use of chemotherapy, especially the antibiotics, *has contributed* to an ever decreasing number of fatalities in infectious diseases. Better child care and education *has effected* a low morbidity and mortality among children. The many diseases that have taken an impressive toll among the young and middle-aged *have been conquered.* The number of old people *is* on the rise, and with this fact come the number of people with malignancies and chronic diseases associated more with old age.—Elizabeth Kubler-Ross, from *On Death and Dying*

2. Determine the subject of each of the following sentences and select the verb form that agrees with it. If there is any problem of agreement, explain your choice of verb in terms of the points made in this section.

   a. The wages of sin (is, are) death.
   b. All (is, are) well.
   c. Comparison of things that are unlike and that, by their uniqueness (produces, produce) a sense of wonder in us, (show, shows) that the writer is just displaying his or her own cleverness.
   d. Too many metaphors (is, are) a sign of a young writer.
   e. "Patience and fortitude," though describing virtues, (is, are) a motto often used to counsel sloth.
   f. The United States (enjoys, enjoy) good relations with Canada.
   g. He is one of those people who (is, are) always making trouble.
   h. To have loved and lost (is, are) an experience most of humanity (has, have) suffered.
   i. Many of our tax dollars (go, goes) to defence commitments.
   j. Neither metaphor nor simile (is, are) useful if the image is confused.

3. Write sentences that include the following items:

   a. *Three semesters,* meant as a single unit, used as the subject
   b. The word *ethics* used as the subject in a plural sense
   c. A singular subject followed by a phrase that includes a plural noun
   d. *There are* at the beginning of the sentence
   e. The expression *one of those who*
   f. *A part of the audience* used as the subject

# 6

# Nouns

Nouns are words used in sentences chiefly as subjects of verbs, objects of verbs or prepositions, as complements following a linking verb, as appositives, or as modifiers of other words. They change their form to show number (by adding *-s, -es,* etc.) and possession ( *'s, s'* ). A noun may designate a person (*Henry Cartwright, child*), place (*Spain, home*), thing (*pencil, steak*), quality (*beauty, rage*), action (*hunting, logrolling*), or idea (*justice, reality*).

**6.1**

*Noun*

The table on page 82 shows the forms, functions, and customary ways of classifying nouns. The following sections focus on the common problems that writers may have with nouns: how to use plural and possessive forms conventionally, when to use *a* or *an* before nouns, and how to spot unidiomatic or clumsy noun modifiers.

## 6.1 PLURALS OF NOUNS

 **Change the marked noun to a standard plural form.**

Most English nouns form the plural simply by adding *-s* to the singular form (*cats, girls, books, things*). If the plural makes an extra syllable, *-es* is added to the singular form (*bushes, churches, kisses, Joneses*).

A few nouns preserve older methods of forming the plural, adding *-en* (*children, oxen*) or changing the vowel (*feet, teeth, geese, mice*). Some nouns have the same form for both singular and plural:

1. the names of some animals, such as *deer, fish, mink, sheep;*
2. all words ending in *-ics,* such as *athletics, civics, mathematics;*
3. a number of words rarely or never used in the singular, such as *barracks, headquarters, measles, pants, scissors.*

There are few hard-and-fast rules for troublesome plurals, however, and writers should learn to consult the dictionary whenever they are unsure of a plural form. If the plural of a noun is irregular, it will be shown under the entry for the singular form; if no plural is given, the plural is formed in the usual way, by adding *-s* or *-es.*

## Nouns: Forms, Functions, and Classes

### Forms

SINGULAR AND PLURAL FORMS
Singular: boy, mother, box, child, goose, hero, baby, phenomenon
Plural: boys, mothers, boxes, children, geese, heroes, babies, phenomena

COMPOUND NOUNS OR GROUP WORDS, two or more nouns (written as one word, as two words, or hyphenated) functioning as a single unit: bookcase, football; pine tree, high school; father-in-law, hangers-on

POSSESSIVE FORM: boy's, Harriet's, girls', cats'

GENDER. A few nouns in English have one form for the masculine, one for the feminine: actor, actress

### Functions

SUBJECT OF A VERB: The *tires* squealed as the *car* skidded around the corner.

OBJECT OF A VERB: The new company manufactured *toys*.

COMPLEMENT: A whale is a *mammal*. He became *president*.

OBJECT OF A PREPOSITION: The acrobats were performing inside the *tent*.

INDIRECT OBJECT: He gave the *church* a memorial window.

APPOSITIVE: Mr. McDermott, the insurance *agent*, is here.

MODIFIER OF A NOUN: He thought *cigarette* holders looked silly. *Mr. Tyler's* car was stolen.

MODIFIER OF A STATEMENT: *Each year* we make new resolutions.

### Classes

PROPER NOUNS, names of particular people, places, and things, written with an initial capital, or upper-case letter: Anne, George W. Loomis, London, Monday

COMMON NOUNS. In contrast with these proper nouns, all the other groups are common nouns and are written entirely in lower-case letters

CONCRETE NOUNS, names of objects that can be seen and touched: leaf, leaves, road, panda, manufacturer

ABSTRACT NOUNS, names of qualities, actions, ideas that are perceived mentally: kindness, hate, idealism, fantasy, concept

COLLECTIVE NOUNS, names of groupings of individuals: fleet, army, company, committee, bevy

MASS NOUNS, names of material aggregates or masses not defined as individual units: food, money, intelligence, justice

COUNT NOUNS, names of things perceived as individual units: car, shelf, pencil, cow, vase

Since writers ordinarily know when a plural form is needed, the chief problems with noun plurals are related to spelling. Section 17.3, Spelling, shows some groups of nouns whose plurals may cause such problems.

► EXERCISE

**6.2**

*Noun*

Write a sentence using the plural form of the following words. If you can use more than one of them in a single sentence, do so: *father-in-law, apparatus, commander-in-chief, sheaf, medium, phenomenon, berry, handful, thesis, tomato, auto, governor-general.*

## 6.2 POSSESSIVE (GENITIVE) CASE

Case refers to the form a noun or pronoun takes that shows its relationship to other words in the sentence. In English, nouns have only two case-forms, the common form (*dog, book, Ross*) with its plural (*dogs, books, Rosses*) and the possessive (*dog's, book's, Ross's*) with its plural (*dogs', books', Rosses'*). These forms are all pertinent to the written or printed language. The "possessive" relationship may also be conveyed by using a prepositional phrase governed by *of* (*of the dog, of the book, of Ross*), although one is not always interchangeable with the other in idiomatic usage.

### Uses of the Possessive

The possessive case is typically used to indicate ownership (the *student's* book) or close association or identification with (the *actor's* mannerisms). But it also shows other relationships:

**1. Description:** a *day's* work, a *suit's* style, *yesterday's* paper.
**2. Doer of an act:** the *wind's* force, the *dean's* permission.
**3. Recipient of an act:** the *bill's* defeat, the execution *of a spy.*
**4. Subject of a gerund** (see page 63): the *doctor's* warning.

### Forms of the Possessive

The possessive and plural forms are identical in sound so that in speech they can be distinguished only by the way they are used: the possessive is followed by another noun (The *boy's work* was finished), whereas the plural is not (The *boys worked* hard). It is impossible to distinguish between the singular and plural possessive except in the larger context of what is being said.

In writing, the apostrophe signals the possessive case, and the position of the apostrophe (*boy's, boys'*) ordinarily tells us whether a possessive is singular or plural.

 Insert an apostrophe where it belongs in the marked word or take out the unnecessary apostrophe.

## Position of the Apostrophe

Most singular nouns form the possessive by adding *'s*, as do the few plural nouns that do not end in *-s* (such as *men, women, children*):

> the **teacher's** remarks (the remarks *of the teacher*)
> a **day's** work (the work *of a day*)
> the **children's** playground (the playground *of the children*)

Plural nouns ending in *-s* form the possessive by adding an apostrophe alone:

> the **teachers'** meeting (the meeting *of teachers*)
> the **musicians'** union (the union *of musicians*)
> the **Joneses'** relatives (the relatives *of the Joneses*)

Singular nouns ending in *-s* either form the possessive by adding an apostrophe alone, just as plural nouns do, or by adding *'s* if an extra syllable occurs in the pronunciation. Either way is acceptable; consistency is, however, desirable.

> Mr. **Jones'** [or **Jones's**] business     the **hostess'** [or **hostess's**] gown
> **Delores'** [or **Delores's**] father     the **actress'** [or **actress's**] role

**Group words.** With group words or compound nouns the *'s* is added to the last term:

> The **Queen of England's** duties     the **attorney general's** job
> her **mother-in-law's** address     **someone else's** responsibility

**Nouns in series.** When two co-ordinate nouns (joined by *and, but,* or *nor*) are in the possessive, the apostrophe usually is added only to the last one if there is a joint relationship: *Ann and Tom's* mother. But if there is an individual relationship, the apostrophe is used with both nouns: *Ann's and Tom's* bicycles, *neither Ann's nor Tom's* teacher.

**Plural nouns as modifiers.**  The apostrophe is not used in some expressions in which the plural noun is considered a modifier: *teachers* college, Department of *Veterans* Affairs. Since plural noun-modifiers are being increasingly used, careful attention should be paid to letterheads, signs, official publications, and the like to determine the proper form in specific cases. In military circles, *officers'* mess is the preferred form.

**6.2**

*Noun*

## *of* Phrases and *'s* Forms

The *'s* form of the possessive is customarily used with reference to living things (my *uncle's* house, a *cat's* paw) and an *of* phrase with reference to non-living things (the door *of the room,* an angle *of inclination,* the beginning *of the end*). But in many instances, either form may be used, the choice depending largely upon the sound and intended emphasis of the expression (the *book's* cover, the cover *of the book*). Some idiomatic expressions are usually stated in one form only (a *week's* wages, a *moment's* hesitation, an embarrassment *of riches,* the wages *of sin*).

**Awkward use of *'s* forms.**  An *of* phrase is sometimes preferable to an *'s* form to avoid a clumsy or unidiomatic expression or a statement that may be ambiguous. When the modifying noun is separated from the word it refers to by a phrase or a clause, an *of* phrase should be used:

> The apartment **of the woman** who won the contest was ransacked last night. [not *The woman who won the contest's apartment* nor *The woman's apartment who won the contest*]

The *of* phrase is useful in distinguishing between the recipient and doer of an act, particularly if the meaning is unclear in context. *John's photographs* might mean either photographs *of* him or photographs taken *by* him; but *the photographs of John* would ordinarily mean that John was the subject of the pictures.

**The double possessive.**  In a few statements both the *of* and *'s* forms of the possessive are used, an idiom of long standing in English: that boy *of Henry's,* some friends *of my father's,* a remark *of the author's.*

▶ EXERCISE

Indicate which of the italicized nouns in these sentences are correctly written with *-s* endings and which should have *-'s* or *-s'*.

1. The *energies* of our system will decay, the *suns* glory will dim, and the earth will not tolerate the race that has disturbed *its* peace.
2. A wit of *Barries* said, "Facts were never pleasing.... He was never on *terms* with them until he stood them on their *heads*."
3. The din from the *childrens* playground tried the Joneses patience.
4. The king was "the *peoples* prayer ... and the old *mens* dream."

## 6.3 USE OF *A* AND *AN* WITH NOUNS

Whether *a* or *an* is used before nouns and noun phrases depends on the following *speech sound.* Use *a* before a consonant *sound: a* car, *a* yard, *a* Union, *a* European nation, *a* history book (also *a* historical novel, where *h* may be unpronounced). Use *an* before a vowel *sound: an* ape, *an* oar, *an* hour, *an* honest woman.

## 6.4 NOUNS AS MODIFIERS

Nouns are freely used in English to modify other nouns. Since they thus assume some of the functions of adjectives, such modifiers may be called *adjectivals* (or attributive nouns). In fact, many compound nouns are made up of just such sequences: *textbook, dog-train, maple sugar.* (See the table on p. 82.) Most compound nouns are today written in block, that is, as one word, though practice varies according to whether the block form is awkward in appearance, open to misreading, and so on: *book agent, motor inn, language laboratory, grab bag.*

In speech, such established compounds are tied together by a special pitch-stress pattern, the first noun bearing louder stress than the second, as *flypaper, fly swatter.* (See 15.2 for details about hyphenating compounds.) Once such sequences are commonly written as one word or with a hyphen, the adjectival loses its identity, having been absorbed into the compound-noun category.

Nevertheless, the free use of adjectivals remains typical of English syntax: *murder mystery, kitchen utensils, student council,* where the usual meaning is "of, related to, or having to do with." On occasion, however, adjectivals take on specialized meanings, as illustrated by *toy poodle,* the modifier *toy* designating a miniature breed of dog. Such specialized meanings are entered in dictionaries, as are many adjectival+noun sequences with special meanings, for example, *snow fence* and *water cooler.*

Most adjectivals are singular in form, just as adjectives always are: one *maple* leaf, two *maple* leaves; one *balloon* tire, two *balloon* tires. Note also that singular forms are used for compound (and therefore hyphenated) adjectivals expressing measurement: a *two-litre* jug, a *three-metre* jump, a *thirty-degree* temperature.

In certain situations, a writer may choose either an adjective or an adjectival: an *atomic* bomb or an *atom* bomb; but such freedom of choice is not always available or appropriate. In many situations, the adjective is preferable to a clumsy, imprecise, or unidiomatic adjectival: use *medical* (not *doctor*) school; *Canadian* (not *Canada*) money.

In proper names, as of government agencies, business firms, and so on, the adjectival *Canada* has long been in use alongside the adjective *Canadian:*
*Canada* Council, *Canada* Cycle and Motor Co., Ltd. (CCM), *Canadian* Broadcasting Corporation, *Canadian* Tire Corporation Ltd.

Moreover, Canadians should be aware of a peculiarly native innovation wherein the adjectival *Canada* occurs after the noun it modifies in such names. This development reflects French syntax and owes its origin to the federal government's policy of promoting bilingualism nationally: Air *Canada,* Parks *Canada,* Statistics *Canada,* and so on. Indeed, the practice has spread to other institutions of various kinds where national scope is implied: Loto *Canada,* Unity *Canada.* It has recently become fashionable even among business firms, domestic and multinationals: Career *Canada* Ltd., Bell *Canada.* Even magazines follow the vogue: *Nature Canada, Ski Canada.* Rapid growth of this syntactical Canadianism makes such a sentence as the following quite idiomatic: "Canadian hockey players get support from Sports Canada when playing for Team Canada in the Canada Cup series."

Just as nouns function as adjectives in some respects (adjectivals), so nouns function as adverbs, though much less often. A noun as adverb, called an *adverbial,* occurs in this sentence: *He walked home,* where the noun could be replaced by *there, quickly,* or some other adverb.

**6.4**
*Noun*

▶ **EXERCISES**

1. Ability to discriminate between one style and another in the use of nouns improves with experience in reading and exercise in writing. Count and classify the nouns occurring in any three paragraphs in each of the following sources according to these categories: plural, possessive, concrete, abstract, compound, adjectival.
   a. An article in a news magazine, as *Maclean's*
   b. An article in an opinion magazine, as *Canadian Forum*
   c. An article in a newspaper
   d. An editorial in a newspaper
2. Select the noun form you consider appropriate in each of the following sentences. Where the choice is not optional, create a

sentence in which the inappropriate form would be appropriate. If need be, consult your dictionary.

a. The (major-generals, majors-general) agreed on two possible (hypothesis, hypotheses).
b. Their (enemies, enemys) stormed into the (valleys, vallies).
c. All the (data, datum) were sent to the managers of the (auditoria, auditoriums).
d. "Television," she said, "is one of the (media, mediums) that contribute to a permissive attitude toward violence."

3. Proofread the following sentences carefully, correcting all errors in the use of noun forms:

a. The father-in-laws temper was aroused when wine was spilled on a bride's-maid dress.
b. Muskoxes are native to the Arctic's tundra.
c. The governor-general of Canadas office is held by a Canada-born person of recognized merit.
d. He used a two-horses wagon to carry his potatòs to market.

# 7

# Pronouns

The word *pronoun* means *for a noun*. A pronoun is a word similar to a noun in function, but it does not specifically name a person, place, thing, or idea. Usually it is used as a substitute for a previously stated noun, called its *antecedent*. A pronoun refers to its antecedent for its specific meaning, which is generally evident from the context:

**7.1**

*Ref*

> My uncle phoned last night. **He** is coming by plane.
>
> Men over forty are invited to join. **They** may apply by mail.
>
> Joe heard that credit cards cause many financial problems. **This** interested **him.**
>
> My friend and I are invited to a party with her cousins. **We** are going to **it** with **them.**

Pronouns eliminate the need to repeat nouns every time a person, place, thing, or idea already designated is referred to. They also, help bind statements together, for when a pronoun in a sentence refers to a noun in the preceding sentence, there is a natural connection between the two sentences. Notice how the pronouns in the following passage help give it continuity:

> The young man has formed an ideal of saving his money and he considers the bank the best place to accomplish his purpose. He understands the essentials of banking, if not the details; he understands how he appears to others (confused, incompetent, helpless, etc.) and also *why* he appears so; he understands what he does wrong while he does it; and above all he understands himself thoroughly, past and present, both his inner self and his outer appearance.—R.E. Watters, "Stephen Leacock's Canadian Humor"

Pronouns should be used more carefully in writing than they sometimes are in speaking. Remember that a reader cannot see the writer or hear his change in tone. Readers need to see pronouns in the form that indicates their function so that they will be able to follow a pronoun's reference to its antecedent without confusion. The following sections discuss the most common problems in using pronouns. The table on page 92 lists the various kinds of pronouns and their forms.

## 7.1 REFERENCE OF PRONOUNS

**Change the marked pronoun so that its reference will be exact and obvious; if necessary, substitute a noun for the pronoun or revise the sentence.**

## Pronouns Referring to a Definite Antecedent

The antecedent of a pronoun should be clearly stated, not merely implied, and the pronoun should refer specifically to this antecedent:

> INACCURATE: He had been vaccinated against typhoid, but **it** did not protect him. [No antecedent for *it*]
>
> ACCURATE: He had a typhoid **vaccination,** but **it** did not protect him. [*Vaccination* is the antecedent of *it*]

Instead of changing the antecedent, it is often better to substitute a noun for the inexact pronoun:

> INACCURATE: She couldn't understand how to make the cake until I wrote **it** out.
>
> ACCURATE: She couldn't understand how to make the cake until I wrote out **the recipe.**

A simple test for accurate reference is to see whether the antecedent could be substituted for the pronoun. If not, the sentence needs revision:

> INACCURATE: She talked a lot about the technique of horsemanship although, as a matter of fact, she had never ridden **one** [horsemanship?] in her life.
>
> ACCURATE: She talked a lot about the technique of horsemanship although, as a matter of fact, she had never ridden **a horse** in her life.

The antecedent of a pronoun should not be a noun used as a modifier or a noun in the possessive form:

> INACCURATE: To make an attractive tulip border, plant **them** close together. [*Tulip* is used as a modifier.]
>
> ACCURATE: To make an attractive border of **tulips,** plant **them** close together.
>
> INACCURATE: Bill provided a lot of excitement one afternoon when he was skipping rocks across the pond and cut open a young **girl's** head **who** was swimming under water. [A noun in the possessive functions as a modifier.]
>
> ACCURATE: Bill provided a lot of excitement one afternoon when he was skipping rocks across the pond and cut open the head of a young **girl who** was swimming under water.

## Ambiguous Reference

Sometimes the meaning of a pronoun is unclear because the pronoun could refer to two different antecedents. To eliminate such ambiguity, either substitute a noun for the pronoun or clarify the antecedent:

CONFUSING: When Stanton visited his father in February, **he** did not know that **he** would be dead within two months.

CLEAR: When Stanton visited his father in February, **he** did not know that **the old man** would be dead within two months.

Sometimes ambiguous reference may be avoided by making one of the antecedents singular and the other plural:

**7.1**

*Ref*

AMBIGUOUS: In the nineteenth century, many businessmen [plural] exploited the workers [plural] at every opportunity, not caring whether **they** were making a living wage, but only whether **they** were making a lot of profit.

CLEAR: In the nineteenth century many businessmen [plural] exploited the worker [singular] at every point, not caring whether **he or she** was making a living wage, but only whether **they** were making a lot of profit.

Using the same pronoun for different implied antecedents is particularly annoying to a reader and should be avoided:

CONFUSING: We pulled out our spare, which was in the trunk, and put **it** on. **It** dampened our spirits for a while, but we decided to go on with **it**. [The first *it* refers to the tire, the second to the mishap, the third to the trip.]

REVISED: We pulled out our spare, which was in the trunk, and put the tire on. Having to change a flat dampened our spirits for a while, but we decided to go on with the trip.

Identifying the antecedent by repeating it after the pronouns is a makeshift practice that should be avoided:

CLUMSY: Boswell first met Johnson when **he** (Johnson) was fifty-four.

REVISED: Johnson was fifty-four when Boswell first met **him.**

Ambiguity sometimes results from a careless use of possessive pronouns:

AMBIGUOUS: Mrs. Hurst was a very popular woman and **her accusation** scandalized everyone in town. [Was Mrs. Hurst the accuser or the accused?]

REVISED: Mrs. Hurst was a very popular woman and **the accusation she made** [or **the accusation made about her**] scandalized everyone in town.

## Pronouns Referring to Ideas and Statements

*This, that, which,* and *it* are often used to refer to ideas or situations expressed in preceding statements:

Always do right. **This** will gratify some people and astonish the rest. — Mark Twain

## Kinds of pronouns

### Personal pronouns

|  | Subject | Object | Possessive |
|---|---|---|---|
| First person |  |  |  |
| Singular | I | me | my, mine |
| Plural | we | us | our, ours |
| Second person |  |  |  |
| Singular and plural | you | you | your, yours |
| Third person |  |  |  |
| Singular |  |  |  |
| masculine | he | him | his |
| feminine | she | her | her, hers |
| neuter | it | it | its (of it) |
| Plural | they | them | their, theirs |

### Relative pronouns

| who | whom | whose |
|---|---|---|
| that | that |  |
| which | which | whose, of which |

### Interrogative pronouns

| who | whom | whose |
|---|---|---|
| which | which | whose, of which |
| what | what |  |

**Reflexive and intensive pronouns:** myself, yourself, himself, herself, itself, oneself, ourselves, yourselves, themselves

**Demonstrative pronouns:** this, these, that, those

### Indefinite pronouns

| | | | | |
|---|---|---|---|---|
| all | both | everything | nobody | several |
| another | each | few | none | some |
| any | each one | many | no one | somebody |
| anybody | either | most | nothing | someone |
| anyone | everybody | much | one | something |
| anything | everyone | neither | other | such |

**Reciprocal pronouns:** each other, one another

**Numeral pronouns:** one, two, three . . . first, second, third . . .

I just am a Canadian. **It** is not a thing which you can escape from. **It** is like having blue eyes.—Robertson Davies

They criticized me sometimes for being too much concerned with the average Canadian. I can't help **that**. I'm just one of them.—John Diefenbaker

In such constructions, the idea to which the pronoun refers must be obvious.

**7.1**

*Ref*

## Use of *who, which, that*

*Who* refers to persons, *which* generally refers to things, and *that* refers to either persons or things.

Students **who** [or *that*] plan to enter the university in the fall should forward transcripts of their records to the registrar.

In five minutes he solved a problem **that** [or *which*] I had struggled with for nearly five hours.

This is a matter about **which** more information is needed.

*That* always introduces restrictive clauses. *Who* and *which* are used both restrictively and non-restrictively. See 11.3, Commas with Non-restrictive Modifiers.

The use of *which* to refer to persons is not idiomatic English. *Which* is often used, however, to refer to impersonal organizations of people like groups, clubs, companies, and so on:

The provincial legislature, **which** [not *who*] passed the act despite the lieutenant-governor's protest, had its eye on getting more votes.

The Plowrite Company, **which** manufactured farm implements, has gone into bankruptcy.

## Use of *he or she*

The masculine pronoun (*he, him, his*) has customarily been used when referring to a noun or pronoun that includes persons of both sexes (*student, teacher, clerk, everyone, anyone, somebody*):

Each entering freshman is required to report promptly for **his** scheduled physical examination.

Everyone who is eligible to vote should make certain that **he** has registered before the deadline.

The masculine pronoun has been traditionally used in such situations simply because it is more convenient and less cumbersome to use a single pronoun than it is to use two pronouns to signify both sexes:

> Everyone who is eligible to vote should make certain that **he or she** has registered before the deadline.

It seems likely, however, that the use of both masculine and feminine pronouns will become more common, or that plural constructions will be used more frequently:

> **Every student** who wishes to can get **his or her** textbooks at the university bookstore immediately after registration.

> **All students** who wish to can get **their** textbooks at the university bookstore immediately after registration.

There is a third possibility, for *they* (*their, them*) as a common-gender singular is already widespread in spoken English, and may in time occur more frequently in writing, especially when the antecedent is an indefinite pronoun that includes both sexes: Everyone who wishes to can get *their* textbooks at the university bookstore.

▶ **EXERCISES**

1. Use pronouns to replace the repetitious nouns and make a single, smoother sentence.

   *Example:* John saw the sports car. John knew at once that he must own the sports car.

   *Revision:* John saw the sports car, and he knew at once that he must own it.

   a. Christopher lit George's cigar. The cigar glowed brightly.
   b. "My goodness, yes," Susan's husband said, "Susan's husband will tell you about Susan. Susan has left town."
   c. The second baseman told the first baseman that the second baseman wanted to take the first baseman to dinner after the game. The first baseman said no.
   d. When the teacher gave the students the students' assignment, the students groaned. Then the students did the work.

2. Revise each of the following sentences in which the reference of pronouns is inexact, misleading, or otherwise faulty.

   *Example:* A general-interest bookstore would probably do better in this town than an obscure one.

   *Revised:* A general-interest bookstore would probably do better in this town than a bookstore that specializes in obscure books.

   a. After he had studied *kung fu* for three months, he began to boast that he was an expert one.

b. An exercise room is available in the basement of the new physical-education building which can be used by both students and faculty.
c. Tolliver's wild-flower text is useful, but its description of the high-plains crocus is vague.
d. Football is a more complex game now than in the past, with its play books and game movies, but many are still brutally rough.
e. When the women were about to leave the exhibit of quarter-horses, they ran into their husbands.

**7.1**

*Ref*

## 7.2 AGREEMENT OF PRONOUN AND ANTECEDENT

*Agr*    **Make the marked pronoun agree in form with the word to which it is related.**

To be clear in meaning, a pronoun must agree in number with its antecedent – the particular noun to which it refers. When a pronoun serves as subject, the number of the verb is determined by the pronoun's antecedent. (See also 5, Agreement of Subject and Verb.)

### Personal Pronouns

Personal pronouns, like nouns, have both singular and plural forms, as listed in the table on page 92. A personal pronoun referring to a singular antecedent should be singular; one referring to a plural antecedent should be plural. Errors in agreement are most likely to occur when a pronoun is separated from its antecedent by some intervening element:

INACCURATE: Although the average **Canadian** believes theoretically in justice for all, **they** sometimes fail to practise it. [*Canadian* is singular; *they* is plural.]

ACCURATE: Although the average **Canadian** believes theoretically in justice for all, **he or she** sometimes fails to practise it. [*Canadian* and *he or she* are both singular, as are their verbs.]

INACCURATE: After reading his **arguments** in support of abolishing property, I found that I was not convinced by **it.** [*Arguments* is plural; *it* is singular.]

ACCURATE: After reading his **arguments** in support of abolishing property, I found that I was not convinced by **them.** [Both *arguments* and *them* are plural.]

When a pronoun's antecedent is a collective noun, the pronoun may be either singular or plural, depending on the meaning of the noun (see 5.2):

> The **class** planned **its** next field trip.
> The **class** had **their** pictures taken.

A pronoun referring to co-ordinate nouns joined by *and* is ordinarily plural:

> When **Linda and Gail** returned, **they** found the house empty.

Usually a singular pronoun is used to refer to nouns joined by *or* or *nor:*

> **Dick or Stan** will lend you **his** car.

In general, the principles governing agreement between a pronoun and co-ordinate nouns are the same as those governing agreement between a compound subject and verb; see 5.1.

## Relative Pronouns

When a relative pronoun is used as the subject of a dependent clause, the antecedent of the pronoun determines the number of the verb and of all reference words:

> George is one of those people who **have** trouble making up **their** minds. [The antecedent of *who* is the plural *people,* which requires the plural verb, *have; who* also requires the plural reference *their* for the same reason.]

> George is a person who **has** trouble making up **his mind.** [The antecedent of *who* is *person.*]

## Indefinite Pronouns

A number of words of greater or less indefiniteness often function as pronouns: *some, all, none, everybody, somebody, anybody, anyone.* Some of these words are considered singular; others may be singular or plural, depending on the meaning of the statement. In revising your papers, be sure that verbs and reference words agree in number with indefinite pronouns.

*Everyone, anybody, somebody. Everyone, everybody, anyone, anybody, someone, somebody, no one, nobody* are singular forms and are used with singular verbs (Everyone *has* left; Somebody *was* here; Nobody ever *calls*).

Spoken usage and written usage, however, often differ in the form of the pronouns used with these words. In writing, a singular reference word is standard (Everyone brought *his* book); in speaking, a plural reference word is often used.

> WRITTEN: Not **everyone** is as prompt in paying **his** bills as you are.
> SPOKEN: Not **everyone** is as prompt in paying **their** bills as you are.

**7.2**

*agr*

But more writers are using either *his or her* or accepting the plural reference that occurs often in speech. And in some statements a singular reference word would be puzzling or nonsensical with the indefinite pronoun:

> When I finally managed to get to my feet, everybody was laughing at me, and I couldn't blame **them** [*him* would be impossible] because I was a funny sight.

*All, some, none.*   *All, any, some, most, more* are either singular or plural, depending upon the meaning of the statement:

> All of the turkey **has** been eaten.
> All of these questions **were** answered.
> Some of the dialogue **is** witty.
> Some of the farmers **have** opposed marketing boards.

*None* may be either singular or plural, depending upon the context. In current usage, it is commonly used with a plural verb, but formal usage still prefers a singular verb unless the meaning is clearly plural:

> None of our national parks **is** more scenic than Banff.
> None of the charges **has** been proved.
> None of the new homes **are** as well constructed as the homes built twenty-five years ago. [The sentence clearly refers to all new homes.]

The emphatic *no one* is always singular:

> I looked at a dozen books on the subject, but no one **was** of any use to me.

*Each.*   *Each* is a singular pronoun and usually takes a singular verb and singular reference words:

> **Each** of the players on the football team **has his** own idea about physical training.

Although the use of the plural form to refer to *each* is considered informal (*Each* of the children ran as fast as *their* legs could carry *them*), this construction is sometimes found in writing when the plural idea is uppermost:

> Each of these peoples undoubtedly modified Latin in accordance with **their** own speech habits.—Albert C. Baugh, *History of the English Language*

However, unless you are prepared to justify your use of plural forms with *each,* you should use singular verbs and pronouns. See also 9.3, Demonstrative Adjectives, for agreement of *this* and *that* (*this kind, that sort*).

▶ **EXERCISE**

Rewrite the following sentences, changing the words indicated. Make all other changes that would naturally occur, including those in pronoun, noun, and verb forms.

*Example:*   Change *an athlete* to *athletes.* When an athlete gets out of shape, he is probably insuring the end of his career and the end of his team's winning record.

*Rewritten:*   When *athletes* get out of shape, *they* are probably insuring the end of *their* careers and the end of *their* team's (or *teams'*) winning record (or *records,* if *teams'*).

1. Change *a person* to *people.* When a person weaves in and out of traffic lanes, he is endangering the lives of other motorists as well as his own.
2. Change *Another* to *Other.* Another grocery store also reports that its meat sales have fallen off.
3. Change *anyone* to *everyone.* My sister wanted to be able to help anyone who looked insecure or troubled, and to make him feel at ease, no matter who it happened to be.
4. Change *one* to *some.* One actor may interpret the role of Hamlet one way, another another way: if one decides that the role is pathetic, another may decide that his view—the tragic one—is correct.
5. Change *each* to *all.* Until the law determining the age of legal majority was changed, each student was expected to provide her home address so that her grades could be sent to her parents.

## 7.3 CASE OF PRONOUNS

 *Case*     **Change the form of the marked pronoun to show how it functions in the sentence.**

### Subject and Object Pronouns

Most personal pronouns and the relative or interrogative pronoun *who* have one form when they are used as subjects (*I, she, he, we, they, who*) and another when they are used as objects (*me, her, him, us, them, whom*). A simple test may help you know which pronoun form to use. In a sentence like this, "He left the books for Sarah and (I, me)," omit *Sarah and.* Then it becomes clear that *me* is the form to use. Subject and object forms are listed in the table of pronoun forms on page 92.

**7.3**

*Case*

**After prepositions.**   The object form of a personal pronoun is used after a preposition (a letter for *him;* among *us* three). When a pronoun immediately follows a preposition, there is seldom any question about the proper form, but when there are two pronouns, or when a noun is used with the pronoun, writers are sometimes tempted to use a subject form:

INCORRECT: The work was divided between **she** and **I**.
REVISED: The work was divided between **her** and **me**.

INCORRECT: The same is no doubt true of what European and Asiatic nations have heard about **we** Canadians.
REVISED: The same is no doubt true of what European and Asiatic nations have heard about **us** Canadians.

**After *than* in comparisons.**   In written English, *than* is considered a conjunction, not a preposition, and is followed by the form of the pronoun that would be used in a complete clause, whether or not the verb appears in the construction:

I am older than **she** [is].
John dances better than **I** [do].
I like him better than **she** [does].
I like him better than [I like] **her**.

In speech, the object form is common with *than* when the pronoun stands alone (I am older than *her;* My room-mate was taking more courses than *me*). It is occasionally found in general writing, especially fiction, but in most college and university writing the subject form is preferable in these constructions.

*It is I, it's me.*   Formal English prefers the subject form after the linking verb be:

It is **I**.
That is **he**.

But educated as well as uneducated people frequently say *"It's me"* or *"That's him."* *Me* is more natural in this expression because the pronoun stands in the normal position of the object, right after a verb. All authoritative grammars and dictionaries now consider it's *me* acceptable general usage. However, this construction seldom occurs in writing, except in dialogue, where "It is *I*" would sound stilted.

The notion that *I* is somehow more "correct" or polite than *me* sometimes leads people to use the subject form even when the pronoun is the object of a verb: "Father took Jerry and *I* to the game." The object form should be used in such constructions: "Father took Jerry and *me* to the game."

*Who, whom.* The distinction between *who* and *whom* is rarely made in informal speech (the *Oxford English Dictionary* says *whom* is "no longer current in natural colloquial speech"), and it may eventually disappear in writing. For example, in the construction *Who* are you taking to the concert?, most would agree that *who* seems natural, since it is in the subject position, even though formal usage would require *whom,* as the direct object (You are taking *whom* to the concert?).

In most writing, it is probably best to make the distinction between *who* and *whom: whom* is the standard form when it is the object of a preposition and comes immediately after the preposition (To *whom* were you speaking? He was a man in *whom* we placed great trust). In other objective constructions *whom* is also used; use *who* when it is the subject of a verb, even in subordinate clauses which may themselves be in the objective case:

> Taxes will go up no matter **whom** we elect [*whom* is the direct object of the verb *elect*].
>
> Taxes will go up no matter **who** is elected [*who* is the subject of the verb *is elected*].

The easiest way to check your usage is to arrange the elements in the clause in a subject—verb—object order (we elect *whom; who* is elected); *whom* serves as object, *who* as subject. Sometimes intervening words cause problems, but the principle still holds:

> He made a list of all the writers **who** [subject of *were*] he thought were important in that century.

## Possessive Pronouns

In writing, the chief problem in the use of possessive forms of pronouns is the apostrophe. Remember that an apostrophe is not used with the possessives of personal pronouns (a relative of *ours;* the tree and *its* leaves), nor with the possessive of the relative pronoun *who* (a boy *whose* name was Tom).

Possessive of personal pronouns.    Personal pronouns have two forms for the possessive (see p. 92): one is used as a modifier before a noun (*my* roommate, *her* favorite hat); the other is used (by itself or in a phrase) after a noun (That pencil is *mine;* a friend of *hers*). While either form may be used in many statements (*our* government, this government of *ours*), there are some constructions in which one form is obviously better than the other:

**7.3**

*Case*

> CLUMSY: We decided to pool **their** and **our** resources.
> REVISED: We decided to pool their resources with **ours.**

*Its, it's.*    *Its,* without the apostrophe, is the possessive form of *it; it's,* with the apostrophe, is the contraction for *it is* or *it has:*

> Everything should be in **its** proper place.
> **It's** [it is] an ill wind that blows no good.
> **It's** [it has] been a long time.

One of the mistakes most frequently marked in student papers is the use of *it's* for *its.* If you tend to confuse these two forms you should check each instance of *its* (*it's*) when revising your papers: for example, if you've used *it's,* read the word as *it is* or *it has;* your meaning will reveal any errors.

**Possessive of indefinite pronouns.**    Several of the indefinite pronouns (*all, any, each, few, most, none, some*) are used only in *of* phrases for the possessive:

> They were both happy when things were going well, but adversity brought out the best side **of each.**

The apostrophe and *s* are used with the possessive forms of other indefinite pronouns, just as they are with nouns:

> **Anyone's** guess is as good as mine.
> One man's meat is **another's** poison.
> **Somebody's** books were left in the classroom.

When indefinite pronouns are used with *else,* the apostrophe and *s* are added to *else* and not to the preceding word:

> These notes are somebody **else's.**
> Anyone **else's** offer would have been accepted.

**Possessive of *who* and *which.***    *Whose* is the possessive form of the relative pronoun *who. Who's,* the informal contraction for *who is* or *who has,* is not used in most writing.

A well-known Canadian painter is A.Y. Jackson, **whose** paintings are familiar to thousands.

It is the white-collar worker **who is** [informal: *who's*] least likely to be affected by seasonal unemployment.

Although *whose* usually refers to persons and *of which* to things, *whose* is regularly used to refer to inanimate things when *of which* would be awkward:

. . . we would cross a room in which no one ever sat, **whose** fire was never lighted, **whose** walls were picked out with gilded mouldings. — Marcel Proust, *Remembrance of Things Past*

▶ **EXERCISE**

Read the following sentences and correct any pronouns used incorrectly.

*Example:* She answered the phone, trying to sound very dignified, and said, "Would you like to leave a message with I?"
*Revised:* *I* should be *me*.

1. She divided what was left of the cake equally between Margaret and I.
2. A book in which a man and a woman collaborate should deal accurately with human nature, for between him and her they represent the two sexes.
3. Most of the other actors have had more experience than me and make fun of my stage fright.
4. Whom do you think is going to be chosen as editor?
5. A letter came for Paul and I inviting us to a committee meeting.

## 7.4 REFLEXIVE AND INTENSIVE PRONOUNS

The reflexive form of a personal pronoun is used to refer back to the subject in an expression where the doer and recipient of an act are the same:

I had only **myself** to blame.
He hurt **himself** skiing.

The same pronoun form is sometimes used as an intensive to make another word more emphatic:

The award was presented by the Governor-General **himself**.
Life **itself** is at stake.

In certain constructions, *myself* is mistakenly considered by some people as more polite than *I* or *me* (My wife and *myself* accept with pleasure), but in standard English the reflexive form is not used as the subject or as a substitute for *me:*

> Another fellow and I [not *myself*] saw the whole thing.
> Sam invited John and me [not *myself*] to dinner.

*Hisself* and *theirselves* are not standard English forms.

**7.4**

*Pron*

## 7.5 CHOICE OF PERSONAL PRONOUN FORM

Personal pronouns indicate the person or persons speaking (first person: *I*, *we*), the person spoken to (second person: *you*), or the person or thing spoken of (third person: *he, she, it, one, they*). In writing, the choice of form may be a problem since the writer can refer to himself or herself as *I*, *one*, or *we*. Some questions that frequently arise in using these pronouns are considered here.

*I, we.*   There is no reason to avoid the pronoun *I* in any situation where it is needed. Some writers think that the use of *I* makes their writing too personal and subjective. Remember, however, that all writing is done by a person, that is, by an "I"; it is often better to present the fact plainly and honestly, rather than to try to get around the natural use of *I* by devices that only call attention to themselves:

> AWKWARD: After exploring the subject, **the writer** finds that mass hysteria is a rather common occurrence.
> REVISED: After exploring the subject, **I** find that mass hysteria is a rather common occurrence.

*We* is useful for general reference (*We* are living in an atomic age), but as a substitute for *I*, the "editorial *we*" is out of place in most writing:

> AWKWARD: The conclusions in **our** paper are based upon information **we** obtained from the local police.
> REVISED: The conclusions in **my** paper are based upon information **I** obtained from the local police.

*You.*   Overuse of the generalizing *you* (meaning people in general) should be avoided. Its implied reference to the reader may sometimes be irritating, misleading, or both:

AWKWARD: When **you** begin reading *The Waste Land,* **you** are totally confused.

REVISED: When **I** began reading *The Waste Land,* **I** was totally confused.

Even if not irritating, the use of *you* is often inappropriate and inaccurate. In the sentence above, *you* directs attention to some particular second person, but attention should go either to the writer (as in the revision) or to all readers. Use of the generalized *you* should be confined to informal situations which genuinely apply to everyone:

When **you** suddenly enter a dark room, it takes a while for **your** eyes to adjust.

*You* can be used successfully, as in a familiar essay, when the writer seeks to establish a close relationship with the reader.

*One.*    One is used, particularly in formal writing, to refer either to people in general or to the writer:

Watching the scene on television, **one** senses the drama of the situation.

But this use of *one* is impersonal, rather stiff, and often ungainly, especially when *one* is repeated several times. General English characteristically uses personal pronouns in such expressions:

Watching the scene on television, **I** [or *you*] can sense the drama of the situation.

In current Canadian usage, it is standard practice to refer to *one* (meaning the writer or anyone) by the third-person *he* and *his* or *she* and *her:*

**One** should be cautious if **he** wants to avoid offending **his** friends.

## 7.6 AVOIDING SHIFTS IN PRONOUN FORM

*Shift*    Make the marked words or constructions consistent in form. Pronouns should be consistent in person and number; verbs should be consistent in tense.

In using pronouns for general reference, be consistent and do not make unnecessary shifts from singular to plural forms or from *we* to *you* or *one:*

INCONSISTENT: After **one** has selected the boat **he** is going to learn in, it would be a good idea if **you** first learned the theory of sailing. Most of **us** have at least seen a sailing boat, but seeing one and sailing one are two different things. **One** might think that a boat can sail only with the breeze and not against it. Or **they** might think that a stiff breeze is necessary to sail a boat.

CONSISTENT: After **you** have selected the boat **you** are going to learn in, it would be a good idea if **you** first learned the theory of sailing. **You** have probably seen a sailing boat, but seeing one and sailing one are two different things. **You** may think that a boat can sail only with the breeze and not against it. Or **you** may think that a stiff breeze is necessary to sail a boat.

**7.6**

*Shift*

The pronoun *one* is more likely to lead to a shift in construction than are the other forms. Unless you intend to be impersonal and feel confident in your use of *one,* use *you, we, he, she,* or a noun substitute in these situations.

▶ EXERCISE

Revise the following sentences to correct the needless shifts in person or number.

*Example:* The modern car is very complex, and they are always
        breaking down.
*Revised:* The modern car is very complex, and *it is* always breaking
        down.
*Or:* Modern cars *are* very complex, and they are always breaking
        down.

1. Some writers think teachers use grammar as a means to block your creative abilities.
2. When a person has enjoyed a year of travelling, one is reluctant to return home to an ordinary job.
3. When a student has spent a lot of time on his compositions, they are apt to be disgruntled if all they get is grammatical criticisms.
4. Anybody would feel the same way if you had a teacher like mine.
5. Although a pocket dictionary can give some help, they cannot replace a standard desk dictionary.
6. Nobody in the class seemed very sure of their ability to analyse style.

# Verbs

 Change the marked verb form so that it conforms to standard usage.

The emphasized words in these sentences are verbs:

The hunter **shot** a deer.
Our next speaker **will be introduced** by the chairperson.
**Are** you ready?

Except in questions, verbs usually follow the subject. In meaning, they indicate action (*run, manufacture, write*), condition (*am, feel, sleep*), or process (*become, grow*). In form, they may be one word (*do*) or a phrase (*should have done*), and may add letters (prove*s*, prove*d*) or change internally (s*i*ng, s*a*ng, s*u*ng) to indicate person, number, tense, and voice. The table on page 117 lists the terms used to describe the principal characteristics of verbs.

The following sections discuss some of the most common problems in the use of verb forms. See also 4, Verbals, and 5, Agreement of Subject and Verb.

## 8.1 TENSE

*T* Make the tense of the marked verb conventional in form or consistent with others in the passage.

By means of the different tenses, writers set the time of the situation they are describing (as happening in the past, going on at present, or occurring in the future) and also show the continuity of the action or explanation. Consistent and conventional use of tense keeps the sequence of your writing in order and enables a reader to follow the sequence.

### Tense Forms

The appropriate form of a verb should be used to indicate each of its tenses. Problems seldom arise with regular verbs, because they have only two forms: the infinitive, or base form, used for the present tense (*walk, imagine, sleep*) and a form ending in -*ed*, -*d*, or -*t* for the past tense and past participle (*walked, imagined, slept*). See 8.2 for the forms of irregular verbs.

Except for the simple present and past tenses, English verbs show distinctions of time by various phrase combinations (*have walked, had walked, will walk,* etc.), often supported by adverbs (for example, "he is about to go" as a future). The table on page 108 lists the most frequently used active tenses and the verb phrases most commonly associated with time distinctions.

**8.1**

## Time and Tenses

The various tenses in English serve to indicate particular moments or periods in time:

PAST TIME:    *Past tense—***I cooked** meat pies yesterday. [indicates something that happened at a particular time in the past]

*Past progressive tense—***I was cooking** meat pies when they came in. [indicates something going on during a period of time in the past]

*Perfect tense—***I have cooked** meat pies many times. [indicates something that has happened at various times in the past]

*Past perfect tense—***I had cooked** meat pies long before I found the recipe I use now. [indicates something that happened before some time in the past]

PRESENT TIME:    *Present tense—***I cook** meat pies. [indicates something that happens, as customary practice, or that can happen in the immediate present]

*Present progressive—*I **am cooking** meat pies. [indicates something that is going on at the present time]

FUTURE TIME:    *Future tense—***I will cook** meat pies for dinner tomorrow. [indicates something that can happen at some time in the future]

*Future perfect tense—***I will have cooked** the meat pies before she gets home with the wine. [indicates something that will take place before some particular time in the future]

Notice how the tenses are used to indicate differences in time in these sentences:

He **has finished** supper [perfect] and **is looking** [present progressive] at television.

He **had finished** supper [past perfect] and **was looking** [past progressive] at television.

## Most Frequently Used Active Verb Tenses

|  | I | he, she, it | we, you, they |
|---|---|---|---|
| **Present tenses** | | | |
| PRESENT (immediate present) | ask | asks | ask |
| PRESENT PROGRESSIVE (continuing present) | **am** asking | **is** asking | **are** asking |
| **Past tenses** | | | |
| PAST | asked | asked | asked |
| PAST PROGRESSIVE (continuing period in past) | **was** asking | **was** asking | **were** asking |
| PERFECT (past time extending to the present; past participle with *have* or *has*) | **have** asked | **has** asked | **have** asked |
| PAST PERFECT (a time in the past before another past time; past participle with *had*) | had asked | had asked | had asked |
| **Future tenses** | | | |
| FUTURE (future time extending from the present) | will ask **am** going to ask | will ask **is** going to ask | will ask **are** going to ask |
| FUTURE PERFECT (past time in some future time; future tense of *have* with past participle) | will have asked | will have asked | will have asked |

He **had finished** supper [past perfect] when I **arrived** [past].
He **finished** supper [past] when I **arrived** [past].

When the verb of a main clause is in the past or past perfect tense, the verb in a subordinate clause is also past or past perfect:

They slowly **began** to appreciate what their teacher **had** [not *has*] **done** for them.

Up to that time I **had** never **seen** Slim when he **hadn't** [or *didn't have;* not *hasn't*] a wad of tobacco in his mouth.

*Exception:* A present infinitive is usual after a past verb:

**I would have liked** very much **to attend** [not *to have attended*] her wedding, but I was out of town.

## Consistent Use of Tenses

*Shift*   **Make the marked words or constructions consistent in form. Verbs should be consistent in tense; pronouns should be consistent in person and number.**

Unnecessary shifts in tense (as from the present to the past, or the past to the future) confuse the sequence of your writing:

UNNECESSARY SHIFTS: **I sit** down at my desk early with intentions of spending the next four hours studying. Before many minutes **passed, I heard** a great deal of noise down on the floor below me; a water-fight **is** in progress. **I forgot** about studying for half an hour, for it **is** quite impossible to concentrate on French in the midst of all this commotion. After things **quieted** down **I began** studying again, but **had** hardly **started** when a magazine salesman **comes** into my room. [mixture of present and past]

CONSISTENT: **I sat** down at my desk early with intentions of spending the next four hours studying. Before many minutes **had passed, I heard** a great deal of noise down on the floor below me; a water-fight **was** in progress. **I forgot** about studying for half an hour, for it **was** quite impossible to concentrate on French in the midst of all that commotion. After things had **quieted** down **I began** studying again, but **had** hardly **started** when a magazine salesman **came** into my room. [past tense throughout]

In single sentences inconsistencies in verb tenses often occur when a writer shifts the form of two or more verbs that should be parallel:

SHIFTED: For years I **have been attending** summer camp and **enjoyed** every minute of it.

CONSISTENT: For years I **have been attending** summer camp and **enjoying** every minute of it.

## 8.2 IRREGULAR VERBS AND AUXILIARIES

Some of the most commonly used verbs in English create problems in writing because of their irregular forms or optional uses.

### Irregular Verb Forms

A writer sometimes departs from the standards of edited English when he forms certain tenses of the irregular verbs. Such deviations are most likely to happen when he uses some dialect form or other non-standard form (He *seen* the show last week), or when he confuses forms with similar spellings (*choose, chose*). The following list shows the principal parts of irregular verbs that sometimes cause problems. The *past tense,* second column, is used in the simple past (She *wrote* a letter). The *past participle,* third column, is used with auxiliaries to form verb phrases (The bird *had flown* away; Soon this *will be forgotten;* The chimes *are being rung*). The past participle cannot be used alone as a full verb in the past tense.

When two forms are given, both are acceptable (He *lighted* a cigarette; He *lit* a cigarette). Verbs marked with an asterisk (*) are discussed in the sections following. For verbs not given here, consult a recent dictionary. Caution: If your dictionary labels the form in question *non-standard, obsolete, archaic, dialect,* or *rare,* that form is not suitable for most general writing.

| Infinitive | Past tense | Past participle |
|---|---|---|
| arise | arose | arisen |
| bear (carry)* | bore | borne |
| bear (give birth to)* | bore | borne, born |
| begin | began | begun |
| bite | bit | bitten, bit |
| blow | blew | blown |
| break | broke | broken |
| bring | brought | brought |
| burst | burst | burst |
| catch | caught | caught |
| choose | chose | chosen |
| come | came | come |
| dig | dug | dug |
| dive | dived, dove | dived |
| do* | did | done |

| Infinitive | Past tense | Past participle |
|---|---|---|
| drag | dragged | dragged |
| draw | drew | drawn |
| dream | dreamed, dreamt | dreamed, dreamt |
| drink | drank | drunk |
| drive | drove | driven |
| eat | ate | eaten |
| fall | fell | fallen |
| fly | flew | flown |
| forget | forgot | forgotten |
| freeze | froze | frozen |
| get* | got | got, gotten |
| give | gave | given |
| go | went | gone |
| grow | grew | grown |
| hang (a person) | hanged, hung | hanged, hung |
| hang (an object) | hung | hung |
| know | knew | known |
| lay (place)* | laid | laid |
| lead | led | led |
| lend | lent | lent |
| lie (recline)* | lay | lain |
| light | lighted, lit | lighted, lit |
| lose | lost | lost |
| pay | paid | paid |
| prove | proved | proved, proven |
| ride | rode | ridden |
| ring | rang, rung | rung |
| rise | rose | risen |
| run | ran | run |
| see | saw | seen |
| set* | set | set |
| shake | shook | shaken |
| shine | shone, shined | shone, shined |
| show | showed | showed, shown |
| shrink | shrank, shrunk | shrunk |
| sing | sang, sung | sung |
| sink | sank, sunk | sunk, sunken |
| sit* | sat | sat |
| slide | slid | slid, slidden |
| slink | slunk | slunk |
| speak | spoke | spoken |
| spring | sprang, sprung | sprung |
| steal | stole | stolen |
| swim | swam, swum | swum |
| take | took | taken |

**8.2**

*Vb*

| Infinitive | Past tense | Past participle |
|---|---|---|
| tear | tore | torn |
| throw | threw | thrown |
| wake | woke, waked | woke, waked |
| wear | wore | worn |
| wring | wrung | wrung |
| write | wrote | written |

## Forms of the Verb *be*

The verb *be* has eight forms, three more than any other verb in English. In addition to the infinitive, there are three forms in the present tense, two in the past tense, the present participle, and the past participle:

| | I | he, she, it | we, you, they |
|---|---|---|---|
| PRESENT TENSE: | am | is | are |
| PAST TENSE: | was | was | were |
| PRESENT PARTICIPLE: | being | | |
| PAST PARTICIPLE: | been | | |

The forms of *be* are not troublesome in ordinary situations, at least not for those reasonably well acquainted with edited English. Some speakers of dialect, in Newfoundland, for instance, do use *be* in a different way, as in *she be singing.* These forms are usually not found in general written English, however.

*Ain't.* *Ain't* is a dialectal and, in Canada, a non-standard contraction of *am not* (extended to the other forms of *be*); *aren't* and *isn't* are the standard forms. In questions with *I, am I not?* is formal; *aren't I?* is the form most often used. Since the forms are rarely needed in writing except in dialogue, the form most natural to the speaker would be used.

▶ EXERCISE

Rewrite this paragraph, filling in the proper forms of the verbs indicated in parentheses, including any necessary auxiliary verbs.

As the action begins, it is clear that the old man (perfect of *rise*) and (perfect of *bid*) the young soldier enter. The audience is aware that the young soldier (perfect of *know*) for a long time that it was the old man who (past perfect of *slay*) his father. When the soldier (past perfect of *return*) from the war, his mother (past perfect of *forsake*) her deathbed to tell him how the old man (past perfect of *steal*) into the house, (past perfect of *find*) the loaded gun on the night table, and, even as the mother (past of *shrink*) into the corner of the room, (past perfect of *shoot*) her husband. Laden with this heavy sorrow, her heart (past perfect of *burst*). Within the next few moments of action, the young soldier (future perfect of *bind*) the arms of the old man and (future perfect of *begin*) to lead him from the room.

## Choice of *can* or *may*

In all levels of usage *can* is used for ability (This car *can* do better than 150 kilometres an hour; He *can* walk with crutches), and *may* for possibility (That *may* be true; We *may* get there before dark).

**8.2**

To express permission, formal English and edited general English use *may* (*May* I go now? You *may* have any one you like). Although general spoken English increasingly uses *can* in such expressions (*Can* I go now? You *can* have any one you like); in writing, it is best to use *may.*

## *do–did–done*

Speakers of some dialects use *done* as a past-tense form (He *done* his best) where edited English requires *did,* the standard form. Particular care should be taken with the past tense and the past participle:

PRESENT TENSE:    I, we, you, they **do**; he, she, it **does**
PAST TENSE:       I, you, he, she, it, we, they **did**
PAST PARTICIPLE:  I, you, we, they have (had) **done**; he, she, it has (had) **done**

*don't, doesn't.* *Don't* is the contraction for *do not* (I *do not,* I *don't*), *doesn't* is the contraction for *does not* (he *does not,* he *doesn't*). The substitution of one form for the other (*Don't* she look pretty?) is not consistent with edited forms of the language.

**Idioms with** *do.* *Do* is used in many standard idioms (set expressions): *do* without, *do* away with, make *do.* In college and university writing, it is best to avoid informal expressions with *do,* like these:

When the Dean of Women arrived, she seemed **done in** [better: *exhausted*].
They **did** [better: *cheated*] the government out of $50,000.

Consult a dictionary whenever you are unsure about the appropriateness of a particular expression with *do* or *done.*

## *born–borne*

The past participle of *bear* in the sense of "carry" is spelled *borne:* a leaf *borne* by the wind, he had *borne* many hardships.

In the sense of "give birth to," the spelling is *born* in the passive voice, *borne* in the active: *born* in Truro, a *born* loser, a child *born* to her (but, she had *borne* a child).

### get–got–gotten

The principal parts of the verb *get* are *get, got,* and *gotten* or *got.* Both forms of the past participle are used in Canada:

> He could have **gotten** [or *got*] more for his money.
> Her efforts had **gotten** [or *got*] no results.

Used with *have* to show possession (see below), the form is always *got.* In other constructions, *gotten* is quite common.

*have got, have got to.* *Have got* in the sense of possession (I *haven't got* a black tie) or obligation (We *have got to* finish this experiment today) is widely used in speech and is acceptable in most kinds of writing. Some writers of formal English avoid the expression, regarding *got* as redundant and preferring *have* alone (I *haven't* a black tie; We *have to* finish this experiment today). Although *have* alone carries the meaning, it is so frequently used as a mere auxiliary of tense that it is not often considered as a verb of full meaning; in such cases either *have* or *have got* is considered acceptable.

**Idioms with** *get.* In many common idioms *get* is standard usage for all levels of speaking and writing:

| STANDARD: | get up | get along with (someone) |
|---|---|---|
| | get away from | get over (an illness) |
| | get ahead | get tired |

Other expressions with *get* are considered informal and would best be avoided in college or university writing:

> INFORMAL: Long-winded discussions **get** on my nerves.
> This modern music **gets** me.
> Some people seem to **get** away with murder.
> A stray bullet **got** him in the shoulder.

When you are in doubt about the standing of an idiom with *get,* consult a recent dictionary.

### lie–lay

*Lie* and *lie down* do not take an object. The principal parts are *lie, lay, lain:* You *lie* on the bed, or *lie down* on the job; Yesterday he *lay* in bed all morning; The log had *lain* across the road for a week. The present participle of *lie* is *lying:* The log was *lying* in the road; I found him *lying* in bed.

*Lay* and *lay down,* to put or place, take an object. The principal parts are *lay, laid, laid:* She *laid* her purse on the table; He should *lay down* his cards; The cornerstone was *laid;* The robin *laid* an egg. The present participle of *lay* is *laying:* He was *laying* the foundation.

**8.2**

*V.b*

### sit–set

The verb *sit* (as in a chair) does not take an object. Its principal parts are *sit, sat, sat:* I like to *sit* in a hotel lobby; He *sat* there an hour; I have *sat* in the same chair for three semesters.

The verb *set,* meaning to put something down, takes an object. Its principal parts are *set, set, set: Set* the soup on this pad; They *set* the trunk in the hall yesterday; She has *set* candles in the windows.

### shall–will

In current Canadian usage, *will* is generally used with all persons of the verb for the future tense (I *will* leave tomorrow. He *will* arrive at six. We *will* return later). To express determination or for emphasis, usage is divided about *will* and *shall* (I *will* not permit it. They *shall* pass). Some writers make the following formal distinctions between *shall* and *will:*

**Simple future**

| | | |
|---|---|---|
| FIRST PERSON: | I shall ask | we shall ask |
| SECOND PERSON: | you will ask | you will ask |
| THIRD PERSON: | he, she, it will ask | they will ask |

**Emphatic future**

| | | |
|---|---|---|
| FIRST PERSON: | I will ask | we will ask |
| SECOND PERSON: | you shall ask | you shall ask |
| THIRD PERSON: | he, she, it shall ask | they shall ask |

Such distinctions are seldom heard in conversation nowadays and rarely met at all except in very conservative formal writing. Observe that the distinctions are eliminated in conversation where the contractions are used: *I'll* ask; *we'll* ask; and so on.

*shall* **and** *will* **in questions.** In questions, *will* is used in all persons, but *shall* is often used, especially in formal English, if there is a notion of propriety or obligation:

Will I go? Where **will** we go next? What **will** you do now?
OBLIGATION: **Shall** I go? What **shall** she wear?

Some writers use *should* and avoid both *shall* and *will:*

Where **should** we go next? **Should** I go?

In the negative, *won't* is the regular form:

What **won't** they think of next?
Why **won't** you go?

**Overuse of** *shall. Shall* should not be used in statements where
*will* is the standard form:

Whether or not Parliament **will** [not *shall*] pass the bill is not for
me to guess.

Some people apparently think that *shall* is a more correct (or
elegant) form than *will.* It is not.

## should–would

*Should* and *would* are used in statements that carry a sense of
doubt or uncertainty:

It **should** be cooler by evening. [Contrast with the meaning of: It
*will* be cooler by evening.]

I wasn't ready as soon as I thought I **would** be.

*Should,* like *shall,* is often used to express the idea of propriety
or obligation:

You **should** wash your hands before meals.
I **should** answer her letter this week.

In polite or unemphatic requests, both *would* and *should* are
used for the first person and *would* for the second person:

I **would** be much obliged if you could help me.
I **should** be much obliged if you could help me.

**Would** you please give this your earliest attention?
I wish you **would** write more often.

In indirect discourse, *would* and *should* serve as the past tenses of
*will* and *shall:*

DIRECT DISCOURSE: Mary said, "I will go."
INDIRECT DISCOURSE: Mary said that she would go.

DIRECT DISCOURSE: "Shall we adjourn?" the president asked.
INDIRECT DISCOURSE: The president asked if they should adjourn.

## Terms Used in Describing Verbs

VERB FORMS (8.1). English verbs have three principal parts:

| INFINITIVE (the base form) | PAST TENSE | PAST PARTICIPLE |
| ask (to ask), go (to go) | asked, went | asked, gone |

REGULAR AND IRREGULAR VERBS (8.1 and 8.2). Regular verbs add -*ed* to form the past tense and past participle (ask, asked, asked). Irregular verbs change form in other ways (sing, sang, sung; go, went, gone).

**8.2**

*Vb*

TENSE (8.1). The "time" of a verb's action as expressed in the form of the verb:

PAST: I went        PRESENT: I go        FUTURE: I will go
**(For other tenses, see the table on p. 108.)**

TRANSITIVE AND INTRANSITIVE.
A verb is **transitive** when it has an object: The teacher *demanded*(v) *order*(o).
A verb is **intransitive** when it does not have an object: He *slept*(v) well.

ACTIVE AND PASSIVE VOICE (8.3). A **passive** verb is a form of *be* and a past participle: *is believed, was believed, had been believed, will be believed.* All other verbs are **active.**

MOOD (8.4). The manner in which a statement is expressed (an almost obsolete distinction now):
The **indicative mood** expresses a fact or a statement: I *am* thrifty.
The **subjunctive mood** is used in some conditions (as those contrary to fact: If I *were* king.) and in such constructions as: It is necessary that he *be* twenty-one.

AUXILIARY VERB (8.2). A verb used in a verb phrase to show tense, voice, etc.: *am* going; *had* gone; *will* go; *should have been* done.

LINKING VERB OR COPULA (1.1). A verb that "links" its subject to a predicate noun or an adjective: She *is* a teacher. The days *became* warmer.

FINITE AND NON-FINITE VERBS. A **finite verb** (from the Latin *finis,* meaning "end" or "limit") can be limited (5 and 8):
In **person** by a pronoun or subject (I *sing,* she *sings*)
In **time** by a tense form (she *sings,* she *sang*)
In **number,** by a singular or plural form (he *sings,* they *sing*)
Finite verbs are full verbs in sentences and clauses: I *had gone* before he *came.*

THE NON-FINITE VERB FORMS (participles, infinitives, gerunds) are not limited in person or number and are ordinarily used in phrases (4):
Before *leaving* I thanked our host. She needed a hat *to wear* to the party.

Writers sometimes use *would* with another verb to suggest continuous or habitual action: The man *would* always be waiting at the corner. He *would* give me a quarter for candy. I *would* refuse it. It's generally better to depend on the accurate verb tense of the primary verb: The man *was* always *waiting* at the corner. Every time he saw me he *offered* me a quarter for candy. I always *refused* it.

▶ **EXERCISES**

1. Supply the proper form of the verbs in parentheses in each of these sentences. Some of the constructions may call for an infinitive, participle, or gerund (see section 4).

   *Example:* Last night the wind (whip) the leaves so that they (spin) like the arms on a windmill.
   *Answer:* whipped, spun

   a. Once she had (do) the exercises, she (do) her reading with much greater pleasure.
   b. In the saloon, the dark-bearded cowboy pushed aside his beer and slowly (draw) his gun.
   c. He could have (get) a higher grade if he had worked a little longer on the project.
   d. Within minutes the care-(ride) policeman (ride) up to investigate.
   e. Before he called, she had (lie) down to rest a few minutes.
   f. A low moan was (wring) from his lips.
   g. He had (rid) the town of many criminals before.
   h. At the hitching post the horse (shake) his mane and nervously (paw) the ground.

2. Write sentences following the instructions below.

   a. a single sentence that uses both *can* and *may*
   b. a sentence that uses the past tense of *sit*
   c. a sentence that uses the past tense of *set*
   d. a sentence that uses *should* to express an obligation
   e. a sentence that uses *would* as the past tense of *will*
   f. a sentence that uses *should* as the past tense of *shall*

## 8.3 ACTIVE AND PASSIVE VOICE

When writers use *active* rather than *passive voice,* they do so because they wish the doer of the action denoted by the verb to be the subject of the sentence:

ACTIVE VERB: Jim's father **gave** him a car.
PASSIVE VERB: Jim **was given** a car by his father.

The passive consists of a form of *be* plus the past participle (*is given, are chosen, was taken, have been corrected*).

## Appropriate Passives

The great majority of English sentences use active verbs, but sometimes the passive is appropriate. Passive constructions are apt if the actor is unknown or unimportant to the statement, or when the writer chooses not to identify him:

**8.3**

*v/b*

> The game **was postponed** because of rain.
>
> The expressway **will be completed** by spring.
>
> One of the advantages of the new tank is that the engine **can be removed** and **replaced** in far less time than the same operation took for the old one.

A passive verb may also be appropriate if the writer wants to emphasize the object or the act rather than the doer:

> The fire **was discovered** by the watchman.
> The bill **is supported** by members of all parties.

## Inappropriate Passives

*Pass*    Change the passive verb or verbs to active.

Passive constructions are often weak or awkward and should be changed to the more direct active voice:

> WEAK PASSIVE: A distinction **is made** by sociologists between achieved and ascribed status.
>
> ACTIVE: Sociologists **make** a distinction between achieved and ascribed status.
>
> PASSIVE: All of the major Russian novelists **were studied** in my comparative literature course.
>
> ACTIVE: I **studied** all of the major Russian novelists in my comparative literature course.

It is sometimes awkward to combine an active and a passive verb in the same sentence:

> AWKWARD: The city **needs** more money to build new schools, and it **will** probably **be raised** through a bond issue.
>
> REVISED: The city **needs** more money to build new schools and **will** probably **raise** it through a bond issue.

▶ **EXERCISE**

Revise the sentences below so that they still mean the same thing, but are in the active voice.

*Example:* It has always been felt by me that the study of biology is boring.

*Revised:* I have always felt that studying biology is boring.

1. Biology is thought by students to be very time-consuming.
2. It is also felt that cutting up dead frogs is disgusting to some students.
3. Sometimes tests are given by biology professors which are thought to require too much memorizing.
4. Also, it is costly to some to pay the lab fees.
5. For these reasons, it is an opinion of mine that the abolishment of required biology should be considered by school authorities.

## 8.4 USE OF THE SUBJUNCTIVE MOOD

Certain instances of atypical verb forms are known as the subjunctive mood: He *ask* instead of *asks;* I, he, or she *were* instead of *was;* I, he, she *be asked* instead of *is* or *was asked.* The word *mood* is a variant of the word *mode* and indicates manner. A verb in the subjunctive mood, then, is a verb used in a particular manner, to express a future contingency or a condition contrary to fact. Use of the subjunctive forms in current English is quite limited and inconsistent, even in formal English. There is almost always an alternative construction, often with auxiliary verbs; therefore, writers seldom need to use the subjunctive.

### In Conditions

The subjunctive is sometimes used, especially in formal English, to express contrary-to-fact, impossible, or improbable conditions:

If I **were** in your position [I'm not], I wouldn't accept his offer.
He said that if he **were** in power [he isn't], he would remove them.

The subjunctive is sometimes found in simple conditions:

If the subject of a verb **be** impersonal, the verb itself may be called impersonal.

This use does not contribute to meaning and seems unnecessary.

### In *that* Clauses

The subjunctive is used in many set expressions (usually in a formal, often legal, context) for recommendations, demands, and so on:

> FORMAL: It is required that the applicant be over twenty-one.
> STANDARD: The applicant must be over twenty-one.

> FORMAL: I ask that the interested citizen watch closely the movements of these suspicious persons.
> STANDARD: I ask the interested citizens to watch closely the movements of these suspicious persons.

**8.4**
*V/b*

### In Formulas

The subjunctive is found in numerous formulas and set phrases, locutions surviving from a time when the subjunctive was used freely:

> If I were you    If only she were here    As it were
> Be that as it may    Come what may    God be with you

▶ **EXERCISE**

Complete the following sentences using subjunctive verb forms.

1. If I . . . .
2. She said if she . . . .
3. Were he to . . . .
4. It is necessary that each student . . . .
5. What would you do if she . . . .

## 8.5 IDIOMS WITH VERBS

 **Change the marked word or expression so that it will be idiomatic.**

An idiom is a usage that has become established through custom. Verbs and verb phrases should be both idiomatically correct and appropriate to the general level of a writer's style. The chart on page 122, lists some verb forms that should be avoided because they are clumsy or not in good edited form. Others are acceptable in informal or general usage but are sometimes frowned upon in formal English.

## Troublesome Idioms

ABLE TO: A clumsy and unidiomatic expression when used with a passive infinitive: "This shirt **can be** [not *is able to be*] washed without shrinkage."

AGGRAVATE, IRRITATE: In formal usage **aggravate** means to intensify or make worse; **irritate** means to vex or annoy: "The seriousness of his crime was **aggravated** by the prisoner's implication of innocent people." "Stop **irritating** me with those silly questions." Informally **aggravate** is used in the same sense as **irritate**: "I was never so **aggravated** in my life." The distinction between the two words should be observed in college writing.

BEING THAT: To introduce a dependent clause of reason or cause, **being that** is an unacceptable substitute for **because, since,** or **for**: "Randy decided to major in pharmacy **because** [not *being that*] his uncle was a successful pharmacist."

CONTACT: Many people dislike this verb as a substitute for "get in touch with someone," although it is widely used in business: "Will you **contact** our Mr. Hubble?" In general and formal writing "call" or "see" is ordinarily used.

ENTHUSE: Most dictionaries label **enthuse** informal, preferring **be enthusiastic about** or **show enthusiasm**. While **enthuse** is in fairly common use, it is generally better to use another form.

FIX: In general usage, **fix** commonly means repair or prepare (**fix** a broken clock, **fix** lunch for three). It also means to make fast or establish (**fix** the tent to its pegs, **fix** tariff prices). **Fix** is informal in the sense of to **get even with** (I'll **fix** you for that).

LEAVE, LET: **Leave** means to depart or to abandon; **let** means to permit: "They won't *let* us *leave.*" Using **leave** for **let** is inappropriate edited English.

PREDOMINATE, PREDOMINANT: **Predominate** is a verb: "The captain's will **predominated** throughout the voyage." **Predominant** is an adjective: "His **predominant** characteristic is laziness."

SUSPECT, SUSPICION: **Suspect** is the verb meaning to distrust or imagine: "The police **suspected** foul play." **Suspicion** is a noun, and when used for **suspect** is a localism, inappropriate in edited English except in dialogue.

TRY AND, TRY TO: Both are accepted idioms: **Try and** is the more common in general English, especially in informal speech (**Try and** get in on time); **try to** is the preferred form otherwise (**Try to** get in on time).

WANT, WANT TO, WANT THAT: In the sense of **ought** or **should, want** is informal: "You **should** [rather than *want to*] review your notes before the test." In statements of desire or intention, **want to** is the standard idiom: "I **want you to get** [not *for you to get* or *that you get*] all you can from this year's work." In such constructions, **want that** and **want for** are not standard.

▶ **EXERCISE**

Correct any faulty verb forms that you find in the following sentences.
Some of the constructions call for verbals (see section 4).

*Example:* He often had came to the same bar.
*Revised:* He often *had come* to the same bar.

**8.5**

1. The students were not use to seeing the Chancellor in Duffy's
   Tavern, ordinarily a student hangout.
2. It was raining hard, and he had almost drownded before he come
   upon a place to find shelter.
3. He was wet through and through, and he said that his feet were
   nearly froze.
4. Having rode across the prairie all day, Lonesome Jim was
   thoroughly wore out and could not get his legs unbended.
5. Early in the day, the TV stations broadcasted the news that the
   Prime Minister was going to make a speech that night.
6. Having born a pack, a shovel, a canteen, a map case, and a note-
   book for thirty miles, Jim laid down and went to sleep immediately.
7. There don't seem to be any way to keep him from sleeping when he
   is tired.
8. His grandfather believed that the family had originally came from
   northern Alberta.
9. He sat the overdue books on the counter and waited to pay the fine.
10. They got up before dawn, drunk coffee and ate rolls, checked the
    map, and taken back roads west for the next stage of their
    journey.

# Adjectives and Adverbs

*Adj /*
*Adv*  Use the appropriate form of the marked adjective or adverb.

Nouns and verbs can be used without adjectives and adverbs. However, adjectives and adverbs are not usually used alone, for adjectives are modifiers of nouns and pronouns, and adverbs are modifiers of verbs, adjectives, and other adverbs. They function as qualifiers, calling attention to a more specific quality of the thing or action referred to by the word they modify. Note the difference in meaning signalled by the adjectives in the following sentence:

> The can on the shelf contains tomatoes.
> The **red** can on the **lowest** shelf contains **fancy** tomatoes.

In the expanded sentence, the adjectives *restrict* the meaning of the nouns they modify, changing a general statement to one about a particular can on a particular shelf containing a specific grade of tomatoes.

The basic parts of a sentence—the simple subject, the verb, the object—do not always convey the full sense of what is intended. Adjectives and adverbs enable a writer to specify, to distinguish (not *shelf,* but *lowest shelf*). These modifiers may add descriptive details (a scene of *pleasant* memories; he laughed *loudly*), limit or make more specific the meaning of a key word (the *first* book; he left *immediately*), or qualify statements (*Perhaps* you've had enough).

In sentences an adjective or an adverb is identified by finding the word or word group to which it is related: remember that an adjective modifies a noun or pronoun, an adverb, or the whole sentence.

> ADJECTIVE: the **lucky** dog [modifies the noun *dog*]
> ADVERB: He **luckily** won the third round. [modifies the verb *won*]
> ADJECTIVE: The car is **fast.** [modifies the noun *car*]
> ADVERB: She drove **fast.** [modifies the verb *drove*]

Other examples are discussed in the sections that follow.

## 9.1 POSITION OF ADJECTIVES

Most writers have few problems with adjectives. The forms of adjectives are relatively simple, and they are usually easy to place in a sentence. The typical position of adjectives (and of participles and nouns used as adjectives) is immediately before the words they modify, though other positions are sometimes possible:

> An **unoccupied** farmhouse had been put at the bishop's disposal by a member of the congregation, on account of the **great** scandal the church was suffering. It was provided with ... **simple** furnishings, and the owner wanted no remuneration for it. Nearby, there lived an **old** woman who had agreed to look after the bishop.... —Wilfred Watson, "The Lice"

**9.1**

*adj /
adv*

> So on Saturday afternoons the **well-to-do** Jews walked up and down Decarie Boulevard which was their street. A street of **sumptuous** supermarkets and banks **built** of granite..., and delicatessens **rich** in **chromium** plating. —Mordecai Richler, *Son of a Smaller Hero*

Two or more adjectives are often placed after the word they modify to gain emphasis or to avoid a clumsy expression:

> He was hesitating awkwardly there at the door, **tall** and **dark,** in his fine expensive city clothes.... —Morley Callaghan, "Father and Son"

> ... the sailors thronged the streets in flapping blues and spotless whites— **brown, tough,** and **clean.**— Thomas Wolfe, *Look Homeward, Angel*

If an adjective is in a phrase, it often follows the noun:

> The old man, exceedingly **weary** from his trip, lay down to rest.

## 9.2 PREDICATE ADJECTIVES

Predicate adjectives—adjectives that follow linking verbs—refer back to the subject (see 1.1). The common linking verbs are *be* (*am, is, are, was, were, has been*), *seem, appear, become, grow, prove,* and verbs describing sensations like *taste, feel, smell, look, sound.*

Sometimes these verbs are followed and modified by adverbs (The weeds grew *rapidly*). To determine whether a predicate adjective or an adverb should be used, see whether the word modifies the subject or the verb. When it modifies or refers to the subject, use an adjective; when it modifies the verb, use an adverb:

> The children looked **unhappy.** [predicate adjective, describing *children*]

> As the rain continued to fall, the children looked **unhappily** out the window. [adverb, modifying *looked*]

Overnight the weather turned **cold.** [predicate adjective, modifying *weather*]

He turned **abruptly** when he heard his name called. [adverb, describing the way in which he *turned*]

## good–well

*Good* is an adjective (a *good* time; This cake tastes *good*). *Well* is either an adjective (He was a *well* boy; Are you feeling *well?* All is *well*), or an adverb (He writes *well*). Either *good* or *well* may be used as a predicate adjective with the verb *feel,* but with different connotations:

Don't you feel **well?** [referring to a state of health, not ill]

It made him feel **good** to pack his own bag and get into the front seat and drive his own car. [referring to a general attitude of bodily sensation—comfort, happiness, well-being]

Do not use the adjective *good* in place of the adverb *well:*

The team played **well** [not *good*] for five innings.

## bad–badly

As an adjective, *bad* is the usual form after linking verbs:

She feels **bad.** The milk tastes **bad.** The situation looks **bad** to me.

But *badly* is also used when the emphasis is on the verb: I feel *badly* [or *bad*] about your troubles. Many people object to such uses of *badly,* however, and it is just as well to avoid them in writing.

▶ **EXERCISES**

1. Write sentences following the directions given below.
    a. Write a sentence in which *good* is used as a predicate adjective.
    b. Write a sentence in which *bad* is used as a predicate adjective.
    c. Write a sentence in which *glad* is used as a predicate adjective.
    d. Write a sentence in which *good* is used as a predicate adjective and *well* is used as an adverb.

2. List ten magazine advertisements or television commercials that use sentences with predicate adjectives.

## 9.3 DEMONSTRATIVE ADJECTIVES

*This* and *that* (called *demonstrative* adjectives) are the only adjectives with plural forms: *this* idea, *these* ideas; *that* project, *those* projects. *This* and *these* usually refer to something nearby, or something the writer is more closely associated with or more interested in. *That* and *those* usually refer to something farther away, or something the writer is less immediately interested in:

**9.2**

*adj*

> **This** car is easy on gas.
> **That** car is a lemon.
> **These** books are required for this course.
> **Those** books are recommended for further reading.

*This* and *that* are often used with *kind* and *sort,* (see *kind,* p. 472), which as singular nouns should be preceded by singular modifiers:

> I like **this kind** of cake best.
> Jokes of **that sort** annoy me.

## 9.4 FORMS OF ADVERBS

Although a number of common adverbs have unmodified forms (*now, quite, there, too*), most are made by adding the suffix *-ly* to an adjective: *accidental-ly, real-ly, apt-ly, mere-ly.* A few others have the same form as the adjective, either ending in *-ly* (*early, friendly, likely*) or without an ending (*fast, hard, late, better*).

Some standard adverbs have been formed by adding *-wise* to a noun, as *otherwise, clockwise.* However, the practice of adding this suffix to a noun to mean "with regard to"—as in *budget-wise* or *company-wise*—is considered jargon and should be avoided.

### Long and Short Forms of Adverbs

Some adverbs have two forms: one with an *-ly* ending (long form), the other without (short form): *slow—slowly, loud—loudly, tight—tightly.* Adverbs used with or without the *-ly* ending include:

| | | | | | |
|---|---|---|---|---|---|
| bright | deep | fair | quick | sharp | straight |
| cheap | direct | loose | rough | slow | tight |
| close | even | loud | second | smooth | wrong |

The long and short forms are often interchangeable:

> Go **slow.** Go **slowly.**
> Don't talk so **loud.** Don't talk so **loudly.**
> The rope was drawn **tight.** The rope was drawn **tightly.**

But such is not always the case. For example, the *-ly* form is used between a subject and its verb (He *slowly* walked up the stairs.). On the other hand, the short form is used with short adjectives (participles especially), often as part of a compound modifier (*new*-found friends, but *newly* discovered mines). A few adverbs have only one form (They ran *fast.* They worked *hard.*) *Hardly* is an adverb, but it is used only in negative sentences, having developed a meaning different from *hard.* Whether to use one or another of adverbs having two forms is often a matter of personal choice, depending on the rhythm of the sentence and the tone of the writing.

## Bobtailed Adverbs

When an adverb has only the *-ly* form, take care not to drop the ending from such adverbs as *seriously* and *differently:*

> Twenty-five dollars is **considerably** more than I want to pay. [not *considerable*]
> People often told him that he should take things more **seriously.** [not *serious*]
> She worked **differently** from the others. [not *different*]

Dropping the *-ly* in such words is a dialectal characteristic and is a non-standard practice. If there is doubt, use a dictionary.

The bobtailed adverbs most often encountered are *bad, real, sure.* In general or edited English, these forms are adjectives only; the adverbs have *-ly:*

> He danced **badly.**
> It was a **really** outstanding performance.
> They were **surely** enjoying themselves.

Note that *some* for *somewhat* is dialectal or regional usage.

## almost — most

*Almost* is an adverb meaning "very nearly":

> I almost lost my mind. [adverb, modifying the verb *lost*]
> The train was almost always on time. [adverb, modifying the adverb *always*]

*Most* is an adjective meaning "the greatest number":

> **Most** fishermen are optimists. [adjective, modifying *fishermen*.]

You'll sometimes hear *most* used as an adverb in speech: This train is *most* always on time. When an adverb is needed in writing, use *almost*.

**9.4**

*Adv*

## 9.5 POSITION OF ADVERBS

### Adverbs Modifying a Single Word

Although adverbs are less limited than adjectives as to their position in a sentence, they should be placed in a position that clearly indicates the intended meaning and desired emphasis.

When an adverb modifies a single word, its typical position is immediately before that word:

> The party ended **quite** late [modifies *late*]
> They **never** finished the job. [modifies *finished*]

This principle often puts the adverb between an auxiliary and its participle:

> He had **quietly** withdrawn.

The adverb may follow the verb directly or follow the verb and its object:

> He withdrew **quietly.**
>       v       o
> They finished the job **hurriedly.**

See also 4.2, p. 67, Split Infinitives.

### Sentence Adverbs

A good many adverbial modifiers—single-word adverbs, phrases, or clauses—cannot sensibly be related to another single word in a sentence. It is conventional to say that these adverbs "modify the whole sentence" and to call them *sentence adverbs.* Their position is variable:

> **Unfortunately,** they had already left.
> They had already left, **unfortunately.**
> They had **unfortunately** already left.

This flexibility makes it possible to shift the position of many sentence adverbs for variety as well as for emphasis.

## Misplaced Adverbial Modifiers

*Mm*   **Revise the sentence so that the marked expression is clearly related to the word or statement it modifies**

Be careful not to misplace a modifier so that the meaning of a statement becomes ambiguous or even ludicrous:

> AMBIGUOUS: Using several pen names, the two editors have almost written every article in the magazine. [*almost* seems to modify *written*]
>
> CLEAR: Using several pen names, the two editors have written **almost** every article in the magazine.

Adverbs are sometimes placed so that they could modify an element that precedes or one that follows; these are sometimes called "squinting modifiers":

> Although it was often said that the old boat would sink **somehow** it seemed blessed with unsinkability. [*Somehow* might modify the preceding verb *sink* or the following clause. Adding a comma after *sink* would clear up the ambiguity.]

In some constructions, misplacing the modifier may alter the intended meaning:

> The way I can stand in front of a store window and persuade myself that I need useless articles **even** surprises me. [intended meaning: *surprises even me*]

See also 4.3, Misrelated Modifiers, and 4.4, Dangling Modifiers, for a discussion of the placement of verbal modifiers.

## Position of *only* and Similar Adverbs

In formal usage, limiting adverbs like *only, merely, hardly, just* are placed immediately before the element they modify:

> I need **only** six more to make a full hundred.
> The audience seemed **hardly** to breathe when the girl began speaking.

In informal spoken usage such adverbs usually stand immediately before the verb:

I **only** need six more to make a full hundred.

The audience **hardly** seemed to breathe when the girl began speaking.

This pattern, typical of speech, is acceptable in general writing, when no misunderstanding of the author's meaning will occur:

> When the brilliant lightweight boxer, Kid Lewis, stood for Parliament in his native borough, he **only** scored a hundred and twenty-five votes. — George Orwell, *The English People*

> He **only** remembers one verse of the song and he has been repeating it. — Eugene O'Neill, *A Moon for the Misbegotten*

**9.5**

*m m*

▶ EXERCISE

Study the following sentences carefully and state where you would place the indicated modifier within each sentence. If more than one position is possible, explain what change of emphasis would result from shifting the modifier.

*Example:* Add *almost:* The fire had burned down to nothing.
*With modifier:* The fire had *almost* burned down to nothing.

*Or:* The fire had burned down to *almost* nothing.

1. Add *certainly:* The fields were carpeted with snow that had fallen in the night, for there had been none yesterday.
2. Add *scarcely:* Some had landed, oddly enough, on the back patio, where the wind was now blowing.
3. Add *almost:* Farther out in the yard, the doghouse was covered to the roof so that it looked like a small mound of cotton.
4. Add *even:* The garden walks were so obliterated by drifts that my father, who had laid out the garden, did not know where they were.
5. Add *more or less:* You could tell where one path went by following the clothesline, which had a ridge of snow that made it visible from the house.
6. Add *only:* Yesterday I had seen the yard with a few flowers growing.
7. Add *definitely:* "It's beautiful to look at," my father said, "but you'll have to shovel the walks because your mother will want to hang out the wash she did last night."
8. Add *better:* Picking up the old battered shovel, I went out into the bitter wind, knowing I would be able to get the job done before the snow hardened.
9. Add *hardly:* Although I walked on the white snow-blanket softly, I had taken a few steps when I fell in a position from which I could extricate myself.
10. Add *merely:* Because it was a moderate snowfall, I laughed and went on with my work.

## 9.6 DOUBLE NEGATIVES

A statement in which a second negative needlessly repeats the meaning of the first negative is called a *double negative:* "The trip will *not* cost you *nothing.*" Such constructions do appear in other languages. In French, for example, two words (*ne* and *pas*) are needed to make a negative. In edited English, however, one negative is quite adequate: "The trip will cost you *nothing*" or "The trip will *not* cost you anything."

Obvious double negatives like *not* with *nothing* seldom cause problems. Watch for concealed double negatives, when *not* is combined with *but* or with adverbs of negative meaning such as *hardly, barely, scarcely.*

*Can't hardly, couldn't scarcely.*  Such common expressions as "I can't hardly hear you" and "There wasn't scarcely enough money left to pay the taxes" are double negatives because *hardly* and *scarcely* in this sense mean *almost not.* The standard idioms that should be used in writing are, "I *can* can hardly hear you" and "There *was* scarcely enough money left to pay the taxes."

*Can't help but.*  The construction *can't help but* (or *cannot help but*) is an established idiom. Many writers, however, avoid it, using instead one of the expressions in the following sentences:

> I **cannot but** feel sorry for him. [formal]
> I **can't help feeling** sorry for him. [general]

*Irregardless.*  *Regardless* is the standard usage. The suffix *-less* is a negative ending; the addition of the negative prefix *ir-* in *irregardless* creates a double negative, a non-standard usage.

## 9.7 COMPARISON OF ADJECTIVES AND ADVERBS

*Comp*   **Make the comparison of adjectives or adverbs more accurate or more appropriate.**

Most adjectives and adverbs have three different forms to indicate degrees of the characteristic they name. The positive degree (or simple form of the modifier) expresses no comparison (*red, slow, seriously*); the comparative form represents an increase or decrease in degree from the positive, or makes a specific comparison between two things (*redder, slower, more seriously,* or *less seriously*); the superlative indicates the greatest (or least) degree among three or more things (the *reddest* apple of all, the *slowest* runner on the team, the *most*—or *least*—*seriously* presented argument).

**9.7**

*Comp*

## Forms of Comparison

Most adjectives and adverbs are compared in one of two ways: by adding *-er, -est* to the positive form, or by prefixing *more, most* (or *less, least*).

|  | **Positive** | **Comparative** | **Superlative** |
|---|---|---|---|
| ADJECTIVES: | hot | hotter | hottest |
|  | brilliant | more brilliant | most brilliant |
|  | expensive | less expensive | least expensive |
| ADVERBS: | near | nearer | nearest |
|  | sincerely | more sincerely | most sincerely |
|  | often | oftener, more often, less often | oftenest, most often, least often |

In general, the *-er, -est* forms are used with words of one syllable (*longer, driest*), and *more, most* with words of more than two syllables (*more interesting, most rapidly*). With two-syllable words, a writer often has a choice of either form (*abler, more able; easiest, most easy*). In some cases, the rhythm of the sentence may dictate which form is chosen:

> After a night's sleep, his eyes were **steadier** and less **bloodshot;** his bearded face seemed **handsomer** and his voice **more resonant.**

A few common modifiers form the comparative and superlative degrees irregularly:

| | | |
|---|---|---|
| bad | worse | worst |
| good, well | better | best |
| far | farther, further | farthest, furthest |
| little | less, lesser, littler | least, littlest |
| many, some, much | more | most |

*worse–worst.* *Worst* is the appropriate form for the superlative: That was the *worst* [not *worse*] show I have ever seen.

*farther—further.* In formal English, a distinction is usually made between *farther,* referring to distance (It was six kilometres *farther* to town), and *further,* referring to abstract degree (We will study these suggestions *further*). In general English, *further* is commonly used for both distance and degree.

## Use of the Comparative Form

The comparative form of an adjective or adverb is ordinarily used when two things are compared:

> You're a **better** man than I am, Gunga Din!
> Blood is **thicker** than water.
> She works **more diligently** than her sister.

But in some expressions the comparative form is used when no actual comparison is mentioned (higher education, the lower depths, Better Business Bureau). In others, the reader is left to supply the comparison (Look younger, live longer . . . than what?). Writers of advertising copy are particularly fond of this use of the comparative because of the favorable inferences the reader may draw: Smoke a *milder* cigarette; More protection for *fewer* dollars; Sudso gets clothes *cleaner.* Such constructions are meaningless and should be avoided in edited English.

## Use of the Superlative Form

The superlative form ordinarily indicates the greatest degree among three or more persons or things:

> He was voted the member of his class **most likely** to succeed.
> Many critics consider *King Lear* the **greatest** of Shakespeare's trage-dies.

In spoken English, the superlative is sometimes used for comparing two things (Put your *best* foot forward). The same construction is occasionally seen in writing, but it is usually better to keep the superlative for comparisons among three or more.

Superlative forms also occur in expressions in which no direct comparison is implied (*best* wishes, *deepest* sympathy, *highest* praise, *most* sincerely yours). The form with *most* is frequently used as an intensive to signify a high degree:

> For example, Herbert Spencer (1820–1903), a **most** influential En-glish philosopher . . . .—Melvin Rader, *Ethics and Society*

The informal use of a heavily stressed superlative to indicate nothing more than general approval should be avoided in serious writing:

> Hasn't she the **sweetest** voice? (Better: Hasn't she a **sweet** voice?)

## Comparison of *unique* and Similar Words

Some people regard words such as *unique, perfect, dead, empty* as logically incapable of comparison or qualification because their positive forms express absolute states. Ordinarily, we wouldn't expect to say that something is *more unique, more perfect, deader,* or *emptier,* but in actual usage these terms are often qualified or modified by comparative forms, as in the following examples:

> We, the people of the United States, in order to form a **more perfect** union....—Preamble to the Constitution of the United States (1787)
>
> ... The **more unique** his nature, the more peculiarly his own will be the coloring of his language. —Otto Jespersen, *Mankind, Nation, and Individual from a Linguistic Point of View*

Whether words like *unique* should or should not be qualified is a matter that can be determined only by appropriateness. In college and university writing, such words should not be qualified; for, used with their full meaning, they are valuable words that say something precisely.

Qualifiers are acceptable in some instances. If you say that A is *more nearly unique* or *more nearly perfect* than B, you are not talking about absolute states that should not be qualified; you are saying that A is closer to being unique or perfect than B is.

## 9.8 MAKING COMPARISONS IDIOMATIC

**Change the marked expression so that it will be idiomatic.**

In writing, expressions of comparison should be more carefully and more fully stated than they often are in speaking. Expressions that might pass unnoticed in conversation (such as *all the higher the ladder will reach* or *the slowest of any runner on the team*) are too slipshod to be used in careful writing (where the same ideas would be expressed: *as high as the ladder will reach* and *the slowest runner on the team*).

## Comparing Comparable Things

When using comparisons in your writing, make certain that the things compared are logically comparable:

> TERMS NOT COMPARABLE: The rhinoceros has a hide almost as tough as an alligator. [*hide* and *alligator* are not comparable]
> COMPARABLE TERMS: The rhinoceros has a hide almost as tough as that of an alligator [*or* **as an alligator's**].
>
> TERMS NOT COMPARABLE: One reviewer compared these short stories to O. Henry.
> COMPARABLE TERMS: One reviewer compared these short stories to those written by O. Henry [*or* **to O. Henry's**].

## Completing Comparisons

Statements involving comparisons should be written out in full, particularly if any misunderstanding might arise through shortening one of the terms:

> AMBIGUOUS: I owe him less than you.
> CLEARER: I owe him less than I owe you. *Or:* I owe him less than you do.
>
> AMBIGUOUS: He admires Eliot less than other modern poets.
> CLEARER: He admires Eliot less than other modern poets do. *Or:* He admires Eliot less than he does other modern poets.

Double comparisons with *as . . . as, if . . . than* should be filled out in writing:

> He is **as** tall **as, if** not taller **than,** his brother. [*not:* He is as tall if not taller than his brother.]
>
> The styles vary **as** much **as, if** not more **than,** the materials.

Since the *if . . . than* construction tends to interrupt sentence movement, it is usually preferable to complete the first comparison and then add the second, dropping *than:*

> He is as tall as his brother, if not taller.
> The styles vary as much as the materials, if not more.

## Use of *other* in Comparisons

*Other* is used when the comparison involves things of the same class, but not when the things being compared belong to two different classes:

> She is a better dancer than the **other** girls.
> She dances better than any [not *any other*] boy in school.

*Blithe Spirit* was more successful than the **other** plays we produced.
I think movies are more entertaining than any [not *any other*] book.

*Other* is not used with superlative comparisons:

Pavlova was the best of all the [not *all the other*] Russian ballerinas.

The Egyptians had attained the highest skill in medicine that had up to that time been achieved by any [not *any other*] nation.

**9.8**

*fd*

## Use of *like* or *as* in Comparisons

To introduce a prepositional phrase of comparison, *like* is standard usage:

They are **like** two peas in a pod.
He looks **like** his father.
Bicycle riding, **like** golf, can be enjoyed at almost any age.

Avoid substituting *as* for *like* or *such as* in prepositional phrases like this:

Some writers **like** [not *as*] Buckler and Garner take their material from a particular region.

To introduce a clause of comparison with a definite subject and verb, formal and general English both prefer *as, as if, as though* to *like:*

He acted **as if** he didn't feel well.
He wanted to be a doctor **as** his father had been.
She took to skiing **as** a duck takes to water.

The use of *like* as a conjunction has increased in recent years; but the construction is still frowned upon by many who prefer *as, as if,* and *as though*—the standard forms.

He fights well, **like** a champion should.
Sue talks **like** she knows everything.
I'm going to tell it **like** it is.

▶ EXERCISES

1. Some of the adjective and adverb forms and expressions of comparisons in these sentences would be inappropriate in most college and university writing. Revise each sentence to make it acceptable.
   a. The ship lay in the cove like it was a natural fixture.
   b. It had been there so long that the weather had turned it more grey.
   c. Many things would be needed to refurbish it, as caulking, paint, new masts, and glass for portholes.

    d. All in all, it was the most 19th-century sight in the town.

    e. The ship looked as much if not more pathetic than an old hound lying forgottenlike nearby a deserted farmhouse.

    f. Still, the scene was real fine artwise, and camera enthusiasts were taking pictures most every clear day of the year.

    g. Picturesque as the sight was, everyone agreed it was the saddest.

    h. I thought wistfully of how trim and noble the ship must have been in her heyday, what with her tall masts and most every sail stretching out to catch the wind.

    i. The reason for its being there was most unique; the owner had died of a sudden before he could make it into a museum.

    j. A sailing ship is the most romantic, because it pits man against the elements more than any other motorized boat does.

    k. To sit on the wharf and watch the old ship rot, that's what made me feel badly.

    l. Much the most dreariest of sights is watching anything lose its former beauty.

    m. I only wished I could have seen her in her prime, when she was shipshape.

    n. Her prow was cut sharp back, so that she could cleave the waves like a knife through hot butter.

    o. She was clearly the best of all the other ships I have ever seen, bar none.

2. Fill in the modifiers called for in the paragraph below, choosing modifiers that will help create a consistent tone for the paragraph.

Sometimes, late in the evening, when I have worked (adverb) and (adverb) at my desk, I stop and lean back in my (adjective) chair and hear night sounds (adjective) and (adjective) in the distance. Sometimes I hear a (adjective) car passing, or someone calling far away, or (adjective) music from some car radio, or a bird song, (adjective) and (adjective). Then I remember that there is a world outside my window (adjective) (adverb), and I go to the door and stand a moment, looking out (adverb).

# End Punctuation

Every complete sentence requires a mark of punctuation at the end, either a period, a question mark, or an exclamation mark. The great majority of sentences are statements, requiring a period (.). Direct questions are followed by a question mark (?), and emphatic or exclamatory statements are ended with an exclamation point, or mark (!).

Periods and question marks also have several conventional uses in addition to their function as end stops.

## 10.1 PERIODS

 Insert a period at the place marked.

Periods are the most common end stops; they mark the end of all sentences that are not direct questions or exclamations.

### Periods After Statements

> Madagascar is an island off southeast Africa.
> "Where is he now?" she asked. "Tell me."
> "Oh." (Where no exclamatory force is intended.)

### Periods After Indirect Questions and Courtesy Questions

An indirect question is really a statement *about* a question, and is never followed by a question mark:

> He asked us where we got the money. (A direct question would be *Where did you get the money?*)

> They wanted to know what I had been doing since I graduated.

> Will you please return this copy as soon as possible. (This is a courtesy question, a polite request phrased as a direct question, but followed by a period.)

> May we hear from you at your earliest convenience.

### Periods After Abbreviations

A period is conventionally used after most abbreviations:

| | | |
|---|---|---|
| Mr. H.L. Matthews | Oct. | Ph.D. |
| Regina, Sask. | D.D.S. | etc. |

An abbreviation within a sentence may be followed by additional punctuation (After she gets her M.A., she might go on to get her Ph.D.), but at the end of a sentence, no additional mark is needed unless the sentence is a question or exclamation (Does he have a Ph.D.?)

Periods are sometimes omitted from abbreviations, especially if they are made from initial letters: UNESCO, NDP. Consult an up-to-date dictionary for the preferred form of particular abbreviations. If usage is divided (R.M.C. or RMC), follow a consistent style throughout any one piece of writing. (See 16.1, Abbreviations.)

## Periods with Figures

A period (decimal point) is used before fractions expressed as decimals and between whole numbers and decimals, and to separate dollars and cents:

|        |       |                  |            |
|--------|-------|------------------|------------|
| .05    | 4.6   | 3.141 59         | 95.6%      |
| $4.98  | $.98  | *but* 98 cents   | *or* 98¢   |

See 14.3 for periods used as ellipses to mark the omission of words.

## 10.2 QUESTION MARKS

?   Punctuate this sentence or sentence element with a
.   question mark.

## After Direct Questions

A question mark is used after a sentence expressing a direct question:

What can we do?
Did Napoleon dislike Elba?
Really?

When a sentence begins with a statement but ends with a question, the ending determines the punctuation:

Perhaps this explanation is poor, but is there a better one?

## After Questions Within a Sentence

A question mark stands immediately after a question that is included within a sentence:

Someone once remarked (wasn't it Mark Twain?) that old second-hand diamonds are better than no diamonds at all.

"Are you engaged?" he blurted.

When a question mark and quotation marks occur together, the question mark goes inside the quotation marks if the quotation is a question. The question mark goes outside the quotation marks if the whole sentence is a question:

He asked himself, "Is this the best of all possible worlds?"
Do you agree that this is "the best of all possible worlds"?

### To Indicate a Doubtful Statement

A question mark is used, with or without parentheses, to show **10.3** that a statement is approximate or questionable:

Geoffrey Chaucer, 1340?—1400
Geoffrey Chaucer, 1340(?)—1400

Sometimes writers place a question mark in parentheses to indicate humor or mild sarcasm:

She gave him an innocent (?) wink over her menu.

The question mark is better omitted. If humor or sarcasm requires a signal for the reader to recognize it, it would probably be better to revise the entire passage.

## 10.3 EXCLAMATION MARKS

Insert or remove exclamation mark at the place indicated.

An exclamation mark is used after an emphatic interjection (Oh! Ouch! Fire! Help! No, no, no!) and after statements that are genuinely exclamatory:

The building had disappeared overnight!
What torments they have endured!

There is seldom need for exclamation marks unless you are writing dialogue. Don't use an exclamation mark unless the statement is genuinely emphatic; it will not lend weight to a simple statement of fact, nor will the use of double and triple marks add anything.

► EXERCISE

Rewrite the following items, changing the end punctuation. Make any other changes you need in order to use different end signals.

1. My first job, as an elevator operator, was the most thrilling I've ever had! To me it was almost as if I were an actor, waiting my cue to speak and move!! My audience responded! How could they help it! They had to get off!!

2. What fear he must have felt while he swayed there!

3. He asked us where we got the money.

4. Win one of sixteen luxurious all-expense paid vacations in Québec!

5. How I hope we will win!

# Commas

 Insert a comma at the place indicated.

Commas mark a slight separation between grammatical units, similar to brief pauses in speech. They are highly important to the meaning of all kinds of sentences, and they are important in determining the pace and tempo of writing. About two-thirds of all punctuation marks used are commas.

To use commas well, you must know not only when to use them but also when to omit them. The principal uses of the comma are described in the following sections and summarized in the table on page 146. The table also lists some constructions in which commas should *not* be used, as discussed in 11.8, Misused Commas.

**11.1**

## 11.1  COMMAS BETWEEN CO-ORDINATE CLAUSES

A comma is customarily used before the conjunction linking the co-ordinate clauses in a compound sentence, especially when the clauses are long or when it is desirable to emphasize their distinctness. Notice that the comma always comes *before* the co-ordinating conjunction, not after it:

> This down does not actually exist, but it might easily have a thousand counterparts in America or elsewhere in the world.— Rachel Carson, *Silent Spring*

> They were lost as to what to do at first, so I provided a kind of verbal running commentary to accompany them.—Joseph Gold, ''A Word to the Wise''

### Short Clauses Joined by *and, or, nor*

The comma may be omitted before the conjunctions *and, or, nor* in compound sentences if the co-ordinate clauses are short and closely related in thought:

> Life is short [ ] and time is fleeting.
> He had to get home [ ] or his father would be furious.
> Nancy didn't like her [ ] nor did I.

General writing often omits the comma where formal writing would use one, as between the two independent clauses in this example:

> From time to time the room swayed around him and he was glad he wasn't the one who would have to drive home.—Mordecai Richler, *The Apprenticeship of Duddy Kravitz*

### Clauses Joined by *but, yet*

In both formal and general writing a comma is used between independent clauses joined by *but* or *yet* in order to emphasize the contrast:

> This was not the man they had known, but ten perilous and eventful years had passed since their last meeting.
>
> It is an imperfect system, yet it is better than none.

### Clauses Joined by *for*

A comma is necessary between clauses joined by *for* used as a conjunction, so that it won't be confused with the preposition *for:*

> He was an easy target, for anyone could pull the wool over his eyes. [*for* as a conjunction]
>
> He was an easy target for anyone who wanted to take advantage of him. [*for* as a preposition]

## 11.2 COMMAS AFTER LONG INTRODUCTORY ELEMENTS

Adverb clauses and long modifying phrases are usually set off by a comma when they precede the main clause. When these elements come at the end of a sentence, a comma may or may not be necessary.

### Adverb Clauses

Adverb clauses (see 3.2) are often placed at the beginning of a sentence for variety or emphasis. In this position they are usually separated from the main clause by a comma:

> **When he said that we would be expected to write a theme every day,** I nearly collapsed.

**Before penicillin and other antibiotics were developed,** pneumonia was often fatal.

The comma is often omitted after a short introductory clause closely related to the main clause, especially if both clauses have the same subject and provided no ambiguity or confusion results:

**When I lived in Toronto** [ ] I went to the theatre every month.
**After he seized control** [ ] the situation changed drastically.

When an adverb clause *follows* the main clause, no comma is used (as a general rule):

I nearly collapsed [ ] **when he said that we would be expected to write an essay every day.**

Pneumonia was often fatal [ ] **before penicillin and other antibiotics were developed.**

**11.2**

If, however, such an adverb clause is only loosely related to the main clause and would be preceded by a distinct pause in speech, it is separated from the main clause by a comma:

The new wing will be finished by spring, **unless, of course, unexpected delays occur.**

The college and the cadets were undoubtedly popular, **though it was a popularity not unmixed with envy.**—R.A. Preston, *Canada's R.M.C.*

## Long Modifying Phrases

Long modifying phrases are generally punctuated in the same way as adverb clauses. When they come before the main clause, they are followed by a comma:

**To fully understand the impact of Einstein's ideas,** one must be familiar with those of Newton. [infinitive phrase]

**Leaning far out over the balcony,** he stared at the waves below. [participle phrase]

**In such a situation,** the wisest thing to do is run. [prepositional phrase]

When the phrases are relatively short and create no ambiguity or confusion, the comma is often omitted:

**In this context** [ ] the meaning is entirely different.
**To evade the draft** [ ] he moved to Canada.

## Commas

**Commas are used:**

1. Between co-ordinate clauses (11.1)
   a. When they are joined by *and, or, nor* if the clauses are long or not closely related
   b. When they are joined by *but* or *yet*
   c. When they are joined by *for*
2. After long introductory elements (11.2)
   a. When an adverb clause precedes the main clause (usually optional if the introductory clause is short and closely related)
   b. When a long modifying phrase precedes the main clause (usually optional if the phrase is short and closely related)
3. With non-restrictive modifiers (11.3)
   a. To set off subordinate clauses and phrases that do not limit, define, or restrict the meaning of the term they modify
   b. To set off appositives
4. To set off interrupting and parenthetical elements (11.4)
5. To separate co-ordinate items in a series (11.5)
   a. In a series of words, phrases, or clauses not joined by conjunctions (optional before *and* joining the last item in a series)
   b. In a series of co-ordinate adjectives, all modifying the same noun
6. To separate constructions for clarity (11.6)
7. In certain conventional places (11.7)
   a. In numbers
   b. In dates
   c. In addresses
   d. With titles and degrees
   e. In correspondence
   f. With phrases identifying direct quotations

**Commas should not be used (11.8):**

1. Between main sentence elements
2. Between two words or phrases joined by *and*
3. Between main clauses without a connective
4. With restrictive modifiers
5. After the last item in a series

When the modifying phrase *follows* the clause, commas are unnecessary if the thought seems to flow smoothly from one to the other:

> One must be familiar with Newton's ideas [ ] **to fully understand the impact of Einstein's.**

> Special treatment may be necessary [ ] **in cases of severe malnutrition.**

> The local residents often saw Elgin [ ] **wandering among the ruins.**

But if the phrase is only loosely related to the clause or if it modifies some distant expression, a comma should be used to prevent confusion:

> Wilson nervously watched the man, **alarmed by his silence.** [The phrase modifies *Wilson,* not *man.*]

**11.2**

▶ **EXERCISES**

1. Complete the sentences started below, punctuating wherever necessary.

   a. When she hit . . . .
   b. If I can . . . .
   c. Although he . . . .
   d. At this particular time and place . . . .

2. Read the following sentences carefully. In which of the places marked with brackets would you insert a comma? In which do you consider a comma optional? Not appropriate? Give specific reasons for your choice of punctuation.

   a. When a man has done me an evil turn once [1] I don't like to give him the opportunity to do so twice.—Sir John A. Macdonald
   b. Let us all be happy and live within our means [1] even if we have to borrow money to do it.—Artemus Ward
   c. Whenever punctuation problems arise [1] it is a good idea to consult the text [2] and determine the proper usage.
   d. Walk right in [1] and sit right down.

## 11.3 COMMAS WITH NON-RESTRICTIVE MODIFIERS

*Rest*   **If the modifier marked is non-restrictive, set it off with a comma or commas; if it is restrictive, do not separate it from the term it modifies.**

## Subordinate Clauses and Phrases

A *non-restrictive* modifier is a subordinate clause or a phrase that does not limit or define the term it modifies. In other words, it does not *restrict* the term's meaning; if it was omitted, the meaning of the sentence might not change much. Most problems occur with clauses introduced by *who, which,* or *that,* but non-restrictive phrases may also cause difficulty. Non-restrictive modifiers are set off by commas to indicate their subordinate function in the sentence:

> Last night's audience, **which contained a large number of college students,** applauded each number enthusiastically.

> The people of India, **who have lived in poverty for centuries,** desperately need financial and technical assistance.

> Vasari's history, **hovering between fact and fiction,** is not a reliable source.

Notice that the modifiers in the three preceding sentences are not essential to the terms they modify. Although some information would be lost if they were removed, the central meaning of each sentence would not change.

A *restrictive* modifier limits or defines the meaning of a term; without it, the sentence would take on a different meaning or become difficult to understand. Since it is essential to the sentence, it is *not* set off by commas:

> He is a man **who thinks for himself.**
> Ortiz discovered many temples **which were pre-Toltec in origin.**
> The questions **that he did not answer** were the most interesting ones.

Almost all clauses beginning with *that* are restrictive. All clauses in which the relative pronoun may be omitted are restrictive (the questions *he failed to answer,* the book *I read*).

In distinguishing between restrictive and non-restrictive modifiers, the writer must carefully consider the nature of the term modified and the context in which it occurs. If the term is fully defined in itself and cannot be confused with another, the modifier that follows is non-restrictive. But if the term is vague or ambiguous without the modifier, the modifier is restrictive. Compare the function of the modifier in each of these passages:

> Children **who can't swim very well** should stay off the diving board.
> Children, **who can't swim very well,** should stay off the diving board.

> Last month I read a novel and a biography. The novel, **which especially appealed to me,** was written by Hugh Hood.

Last month I read several novels and a biography. The novel **which especially appealed to me** was written by Hugh Hood.

While in Rome, I took photographs in the vicinity of St. Peter's. The square, **designed by Michelangelo,** is perfectly symmetrical.

While in Rome, I took photographs of squares designed by Michelangelo, Bernini, and Borromini. The square **designed by Michelangelo** is perfectly symmetrical.

A good test to apply in distinguishing between restrictive and non-restrictive modifiers is to read the passage aloud. If your voice drops slightly in pitch and you hesitate briefly before and after the modifier, the modifier is probably non-restrictive and requires commas. If you read the passage smoothly without a pause, the modifier is probably restrictive and needs no commas.

**11.3**

## Appositives

Appositives—nouns or noun equivalents that extend the meaning of a preceding expression—are usually non-restrictive modifiers and are set off by commas:

Thomas Malthus, **author of the first serious study of population growth,** foresaw one of our greatest modern problems.

We visited Queenston Heights, **the site of a crucial battle in the War of 1812.**

Notice that such appositives, like other non-restrictive modifiers, must be set off by *two* commas when they occur in the middle of the sentence.

Restrictive appositives and those used as part of a person's name require no commas (close apposition):

I thought the question referred to Lewis **the novelist** rather than to Lewis **the politician.**

William **the Conqueror** invaded England from Normandy.

▶ **EXERCISE**

The following sentences contain both restrictive and non-restrictive modifiers. Punctuate each sentence appropriately. If the sentence makes sense either way, explain the difference in meaning between the restrictive and the non-restrictive modifier.

*Example:* The alligator which was often hunted for its hide is in
danger of becoming extinct.
*Correction:* insert commas after *alligator* and *hide*

1. The wall which was built by Hadrian served its purpose for many years.
2. Abraham Lincoln sometimes called "The Great Emancipator" has become a symbol to many groups which crave independence.
3. Diamonds which are synthetically produced are more perfectly formed than natural diamonds which have serious flaws.
4. American movies that are exported abroad are popular in countries that have no movie industry of their own.
5. The French chef whose accomplishments are well known is eagerly sought by expensive restaurants and hotels.
6. Cockfighting outlawed by the authorities still takes place in areas where the police seldom turn up.
7. The oboe which is a woodwind instrument is played by means of a reed inserted in the mouthpiece.
8. The early settlers who were exposed to severe winters and who expected Indian attacks usually constructed forts many of which can still be found.
9. Drunk drivers who are responsible for many traffic fatalities obviously do not consider the value of human life.
10. The common belief that science can solve everything is another example of the naive optimism that most people are prey to.

## 11.4 COMMAS TO SET OFF INTERRUPTING AND PARENTHETICAL ELEMENTS

A word, phrase, or clause that interrupts the movement of a sentence is usually set off by commas or other appropriate marks. Whether or not the degree of interruption is sufficient to require commas depends on tone and emphasis. Such commas are usual in edited English:

> In part, **no doubt,** such demands reflect the hardening of opinion against Soviet policy in Europe.—J.A. Corry, "Free Trade in Ideas"

> I spoke, **I remember,** on *The Value of Imbecility in Education.* It was more or less the same kind of talk that I had given at Port Arthur under the title *Our National Heritage.*—Stephen Leacock, "No Vote of Thanks"

> Failure, **after all,** is the sugar of life: the more lumps you take, the sweeter you are.—Eric Nichol, *A Scar is Born*

To decide whether or not to set off short phrases with commas, read the passage aloud with the kind of emphasis you want to give it. If your voice drops and you pause slightly before and after the phrase, commas should be used. If the phrase seems to run naturally into the rest of the sentence, probably no commas are necessary:

> Machines are useful, **of course,** in doing complex calculations.
> Machines are **of course** incapable of what we call creative thought.

## Adverbs that Compare or Contrast

Adverbs that relate what is being said to some preceding idea (*however, therefore, consequently, too, also*) are generally set off by commas when they occur within a sentence:

> When in good shape, **moreover,** Paul has been known time and again to jump up in the air, kick both caulked feet against the ceiling, and come down again on a chalked mark.—J.D. Robins, "Paul Bunyan"
> How, **then,** may the pronunciation of Canadian English be characterized?—Mark M. Orkin, *Speaking Canadian English*

**11.4**

When such words appear at the beginning of a sentence, they may or may not be followed by a comma, depending on the emphasis desired and the rhythm of the sentence:

> **Thus** the way was cleared for further explorations.
> **Nevertheless,** work did not always proceed according to plan.

When a clause beginning with such an adverb is joined to a preceding clause, the *semicolon* must be used, since these words are not conjunctions. They are sequence signals, which relate ideas in various ways but do not join them grammatically (see 12.1, page 160, Semicolons Between Clauses Linked with a Conjunctive Adverb):

> Business recessions take place periodically; **however,** they are generally short-lived.
>
> The natives are incredibly poor; **moreover,** they have little hope of bettering their lot.

When adverbs that closely modify the verb or the entire sentence (*perhaps, so*) begin the sentence, they should not be followed by a comma. Similarly, conjunctions are part of the clauses they introduce and should not be set off from them:

> **Perhaps** a solution can still be found.
> **But** the average Canadian cannot afford such luxuries.

## Weak Exclamations

Weak exclamations (*well, oh, say*) and *yes* and *no* sometimes occur as modifiers, particularly at the beginning of a sentence.

They are conventionally separated from the sentence they modify by commas:

> **Well,** not much can be done about it now.
>
> **Yes,** times have changed.
>
> That was a difficult climb, **eh**?
> I'd much rather eat cauliflower than, **say,** beets or carrots.

### Names in Direct Address

Names which occur as interrupters in direct address are also set off by commas:

> I firmly believe, **fellow citizens,** that justice will prevail.
> It seems to me, **George,** that your attitude is poor.
> **Workers of the world,** unite!

## 11.5 COMMAS TO SEPARATE ITEMS IN A SERIES

### Words, Phrases, or Clauses in a Series

A comma is the mark ordinarily used to separate co-ordinate words, phrases, or clauses in a list or series:

> He affected a nicely greying mustache and goatee, leather patches on the elbows of his houndstooth jacket, an ascot around his neck, a battered old pipe in his hand.— *Maclean's*
>
> We were taught how to sit gracefully, how to walk, how to converse politely.

Although usage is divided, most writers prefer to use a comma before a connective joining the last item in a series:

> The twisted features, the soft coloring, and the design of the whole mask were so blended as to produce an effect between terror and comedy.—Douglas Leechman, *Native Tribes of Canada*
>
> He couldn't decide whether to visit London, Paris, or Rome.

In some informal writing, especially in newspapers, this final comma is omitted if no misinterpretation is possible. However, because there is quite often the possibility of misreading, it's generally better to use a final comma:

> At the rock concert we heard Blackberry Wine, Golden Gate Bridge, Red Eye and the Bull Dogs. [Is Red Eye and the Bull Dogs one group or two?]

If each of the items in a series is joined by a conjunction, commas are ordinarily omitted. The following sentence illustrates two series without connectives:

> It doesn't mean that our great corporations or cartels or combines are necessarily sinister and morally debauched and without any social responsibility.—Arthur L. Phelps, "Christmas This Year (1949)"

See also 12.1, page 161, Semicolons to Separate Elements Containing Other Marks.

## Co-ordinate Adjectives

**11.5**

Commas are used to separate adjectives in a series when they modify the same noun. Since each performs the same function, such adjectives are called *co-ordinate*. In a co-ordinate series each member could sensibly be joined by *and* instead of a comma, or the order of modifiers could be reversed:

> Never did man talk as **dark, robust, dynamic, bespectacled** Robert Charbonneau talks.—W.E. Collin, "On Writing in French Canada"

Commas are not used when the adjectives are arranged so that each one modifies the entire following expression. Such items cannot be joined by *and* or reversed in order:

> She made a **tasty** [] **Hungarian** goulash.
> He spoke longingly of the **good** [] **old** [] **prewar** days.

Notice that a comma is never used between the last adjective in a series and the noun it modifies.

▶ **EXERCISE**

In which of the places marked with brackets would you insert a comma? In which do you consider a comma optional? Not appropriate?

a. If a man can write a better book [1] preach a better sermon [2] or make a better mousetrap [3] than his neighbors [4] though he builds his house in the woods [5] the world will make a beaten path to his door.—Ralph Waldo Emerson

b. Put your trust in God [1] my boys [2] and keep your powder dry.
 —attributed to Oliver Cromwell

c. When I was a child [1] I spake as a child [2] I understood as a child [3] I thought as a child: but when I became a man [4] I put away childish things.—1 Corinthians

d. Professor Tillman [1] author of several books [2] gave a series of lectures on the depression.

## 11.6 COMMAS TO SEPARATE FOR CLARITY

Commas tend to keep distinct the constructions they separate and should be used wherever necessary to prevent misreading. They are useful in the following situations:

1. When the subject of a clause may be mistaken for the object of a verb or preposition that precedes it:

   As far as I can **see, the results** have not been promising.

   When the rains are **over, the fields** are ploughed in preparation for planting.

2. When a word has two possible functions, a comma can guide the reader in interpreting it properly. Words like *for, but,* and *however,* for example, may be used in several ways:

   The surgeon's face showed no emotion, **but** anxiety and a little nervousness must have been hiding behind that impassive mask. [. . . showed no emotion but anxiety . . .]

   Sharon was thoroughly embarrassed, **for** her parents treated her like a child. [. . . was thoroughly embarrassed for her parents . . .]

   **However,** I interpreted his remarks liberally and continued my work.

   **However** [] I interpreted his remarks, they made no sense.

3. A comma is sometimes necessary for clarity when one expression might be mistaken for another:

   After he broke his **hand, writing** was very difficult for him.

4. When the same word occurs consecutively, a comma may be used, although usage is divided on this:

   Whatever **is, is** right.

## 11.7 COMMAS IN CONVENTIONAL PLACES

Current practices should be followed in the use of commas in conventional places. Such commas help the reader quickly recognize distinct units of information.

**Numbers.** Commas have been conventionally used to group numbers into units of threes in separating thousands or millions (2,853 84,962 3,542,869).

In the *metric system,* **spaces,** not commas, are left between groups of three digits to the left and right of the decimal marker. The space is unnecessary if there are only four digits to the left or right of the decimal, unless such numerals are listed in a column with other numerals of five digits or more:

| | |
|---|---|
| Canada's area is 9 976 139km$^2$ | Column of numerals |
| 1 mile = 1.609 344km | 56 113.74 |
| This is the year 1978. | 9 825.36 |
| 1 cal = 4.1868J | 12 377.40 |

Spaces do not appear in such numbers as serial numbers (My car's serial number is 982101776.) or addresses (I live at 11850 Oak St.); for any such numbers follow the style of the original source.

**11.7**

**Dates.**  Commas separate the day of the month and the year:

February 8, 1928     November 21, 1975

When only the month and year are given, a comma is not necessary, although it is frequently used:

October 1929 *or* October, 1929

**Addresses.**  Commas in addresses separate cities or towns from provinces or territories and/or countries; no comma precedes the Canadian postal code (or the U.S. ZIP code); but there is a space between the second letter and the second number of the postal code:

Ottawa, Canada
Kingston, Ontario
K7L 2W3
Yellowknife, N.W.T.
Toledo, Ohio 43601

**Titles.**  Commas to separate proper names from titles and degrees:

S.R. Bonnycastle, B.A., Ph.D.
Colonel (Retired) J.M. Smithers, D.S.O., C.D.
Raven I. McDavid, Jr.

Notice that the final element in dates, addresses, and titles is followed by a comma if it falls within a sentence:

He was born on September 10, 1929, ten years before Canada entered World War II.

She was born in Paris, Ontario, and lived there ten years.

Syl Apps, Jr., followed his father into professional hockey.

**Letters.**  Commas are conventional after the salutation of informal letters (Dear Shirley, Dear Uncle Joe,) and after the complimentary close of most letters (Yours truly, Sincerely yours,). A colon is used after the salutation of a formal or business letter (Dear Mr. Miller:).

**Quotations.**  A comma is customarily used after expressions that introduce direct quotations:

> Guy Lombardo said, "Corn is always green—like money."

If the phrase interrupts a sentence in the quotation, it is set off by two commas:

> "Corn," Guy Lombardo said, "is always green—like money."

No comma is needed with very short quotations, exclamations, or phrases closely built into the structure of the sentence:

> Father always said "Time is money."
> She began to scream "Fire!" as soon as she saw the smoke.
> One famous novelist likened Canada to "two solitudes."

## 11.8 MISUSED COMMAS

*No ,*    Remove the superfluous comma at the place marked.

Students frequently use too many commas because of a mistaken notion that the more punctuation, the better. Remember that too many commas are as bad as too few, and be prepared to justify every comma you use. The most common errors in using commas are described below.

### No Comma Between Main Sentence Elements

Since a comma is a mark of separation, it should not ordinarily be used between those elements of a sentence that naturally go together: subject and verb, verb and object (or complement), preposition and object. There should be no marks where the brackets stand in the following sentences:

> SUBJECT AND VERB: Sometimes students who have attended expensive preparatory schools[ ] have trouble adjusting to large public universities.
>
> VERB AND OBJECT: I have often noticed[ ] that a person's physical characteristics may influence his personality.

VERB AND COMPLEMENT: Whenever the dogs in the kennel appeared[ ] restless or hostile, the trainer took steps to pacify them.

PREPOSITION AND OBJECT: Nothing troubled her except[ ] that her friendship with Swift was causing gossip.

## No Comma Between Two Words or Phrases Joined by *and*

Be careful to distinguish between co-ordinating conjunctions joining independent *clauses* and those joining other sentence elements, such as compound subjects or verbs. Except for co-ordinate clauses (11.1), two items joined by *and* or by one of the other co-ordinating conjunctions are not ordinarily separated by a comma. Commas would be out of place in the following compound constructions:

**11.8**

Primitive agricultural tools[ ] and bits of clay pottery were found. [compound subject]

He either talked too much[ ] or else said nothing at all. [compound predicate]

In his senior year he was captain of the football team[ ] and secretary of his class. [compound complement]

She wanted more time for study[ ] and contemplation. [compound object of preposition]

## No Comma Between Main Clauses Without a Connective

A comma alone is an inadequate mark of separation between two main clauses. If the clauses are not joined by a co-ordinating conjunction, they must be separated by a semicolon or punctuated as individual sentences. See 2.2, Comma Faults.

## No Comma with Restrictive Modifiers

A restrictive modifier is one that is essential to the meaning of the sentence (see 11.3); it should not be separated from the element it modifies by a comma. The boldface elements in the following example are restrictive and should stand as they are here, without commas:

The conenose, or kissing bug, is an insect **whose painful bite can draw blood.**

The book **that I left at home** is the one I really need for class.

## No Comma After the Last Item in a Series

A comma is never used between the last adjective in a series and the noun it modifies:

> He imagined himself as a **rich, handsome, successful**[ ] man of the world.

A comma is also not used after the last item in other kinds of lists or series:

> The acting ability of such stars as Olivier, Guinness, Plummer, and Fonda [ ] is generally acknowledged.

▶ EXERCISE

Commas have been omitted from the following passages. Copy the paragraphs, punctuating with commas wherever you think appropriate; be prepared to account for the commas you insert. The first passage is from a version of "Rapunzel," the second from *Huckleberry Finn*.

1. There was once a man and his wife who had long wished in vain for a child and at last they had reason to hope that heaven would grant their wish. There was a little window at the back of their house which overlooked a beautiful garden full of lovely flowers and shrubs. It was however surrounded by a wall and nobody dared to enter because it belonged to a witch who was feared by everybody.

2. Mornings before daylight I slipped into cornfields and borrowed a watermelon or a mushmelon or a punkin or some new corn or things of that kind. Pap always said it warn't no harm to borrow things if you was meaning to pay them back sometime; but the widow said it warn't anything but a soft name for stealing and no decent body would do it.

# 12

# Semicolons and Colons

Both semicolons and colons are strong marks of punctuation, but their functions are completely different and should never be confused; they cannot be used interchangeably. The constructions requiring each mark are well defined and relatively few, yet some students have trouble with them, particularly semicolons. The semicolon is a mark of separation; the colon, a mark of anticipation directing the reader's attention to what follows.

## 12.1 SEMICOLONS

 Use a semicolon at the place marked to separate co-ordinate sentence elements.

As a mark of separation, the semicolon is much stronger than a comma and almost as definite as a period. If the following passage is read at normal speed, the voice should fall in pitch, pausing as for a period, after *crossroad* and after *tumble-down:*

> Our haunted house was not strictly in the best haunted-house tradition. It was not a ramshackle pile standing at a lonely crossroad; it was on a street inside the town and was surrounded by houses that were cheerfully inhabited. It was not tumble-down; it was a large, well-built mansion of brick, and it still stands, good as new.
> — Frank Sullivan, *The Night the Old Nostalgia Burned Down*

The few constructions in which a semicolon is required are listed below. Notice that in all its uses the semicolon marks a separation between *co-ordinate* elements—expressions of equal rank.

### Semicolons Between Main Clauses Without an Expressed Connective

A semicolon must be used to separate main clauses that are not joined by one of the co-ordinating conjunctions (*and, but, for, or, nor, yet*):

> The penalty for not turning work in on time is a lowered grade; the penalty for not turning it in at all is failure.

These clauses are clearly separate in thought and structure and could be punctuated as separate sentences. A semicolon is used to combine such clauses when the writer considers them parts of one idea. Sometimes the second clause continues the thought of the first:

> Alfred Hitchcock was probably the first director to place *himself* at a slightly ironic distance from the action of his films; his own subtle mockery helped him confect high-gloss thrillers that serious people might enjoy without losing their sense of identity. — Jacob Brackman, "Onward and Upward with the Arts"

Sometimes the second clause presents a contrasting idea:

> But however immature they are, these lovers are not dull characters; on the contrary, they are hauntingly and embarrassingly real. — Arthur Mizener, *The Far Side of Paradise*

The use of a comma rather than a semicolon or period between main clauses without an expressed connective is considered a serious error in writing. (See 2.2, Comma Faults.)

## Semicolons Between Main Clauses Linked with a Conjunctive Adverb

A semicolon is used before conjunctive adverbs like *however, therefore, consequently,* and *nevertheless* when they occur between clauses:

> On your income-tax return you can deduct the cost of meals and lodging for business trips; **however,** you cannot deduct the cost of meals if you were not away overnight.

> And, in fact, absence of intellectual content is the mark of the sentimental genre; **conversely,** it is because of her intellect that Jane Austen is never sentimental. — Brigid Brophy, "A Masterpiece, and Dreadful"

The use of heavy conjunctive adverbs between long clauses is probably more characteristic of a formal style, as the second example above may indicate. They do appear in other places, of course, as in the less formal first example above or in the following lines from Keats' "Ode on a Grecian Urn":

> Heard melodies are sweet, but those unheard
>     Are sweeter; **therefore,** ye soft pipes, play on;
> Not to the sensual ear, but, more endeared,
>     Pipe to the spirit ditties of no tone.

Many writers use these adverbs as transitions between sentences rather than as transitions between clauses:

This is not the place to conduct a full evaluation of the biological family. Nevertheless, some of its important virtues are, nowadays, too often overlooked. — Leon R. Kass, "The New Biology"

It is no secret that organized crime in America takes in over forty billion dollars a year. This is quite a profitable sum, especially when one considers that the Mafia spends very little for office supplies. Reliable sources indicate that the Cosa Nostra laid out no more than six thousand dollars last year for personalized stationery, and even less for staples. **Furthermore,** they have one secretary who does all the typing, and only three small rooms for headquarters, which they share with the Fred Persky Dance Studio. — Woody Allen, *Getting Even*

## Semicolons with Co-ordinating Conjunctions

A semicolon is sometimes used between main clauses connected by co-ordinating conjunctions if:

1. the clauses are unusually long,
2. the clauses are not closely related,
3. one or more of the clauses contain commas, or
4. the writer wishes to show an emphatic contrast between statements:

This new variety was related, of course, to the mother dialects of the British Isles, and preserved many of the features of its forbears; but it exhibited also an increasing identity of its own during the course of several centuries. — G.M. Story, "Newfoundland Dialect: An Historical View"

Only in a modern university, for example, could large sums be spent on television equipment to make a lecture course available in many rooms; and only a modern academic would be surprised to find the television sets performing to empty seats. — Geoffrey Durrant, "The New Barbarians"

### Semicolons to Separate Elements Containing Other Marks

Semicolons are often used in lists and series to separate elements that contain commas or other marks. In the following sentence, for example, the semicolons are necessary for clarity:

Words of unknown or uncertain origin [include] *bangbelly,* a type of pudding; *callivances,* a species of white bean; *chronic,* an old stump; *cracky,* a little dog; the *diddies,* a nightmare; *dido,* a bitch; *gandy,* a pancake; *pelm,* light ashes; *shimmick,* a term of contempt for one who attempts to deny his Newfoundland origin.... — Mark M. Orkin, *Speaking Canadian English*

Notice that here, just as with main clauses, the semicolon separates *co-ordinate* elements. It is never used between elements of unequal rank, such as phrases and clauses or main and subordinate clauses.

► EXERCISE

Commas and semicolons have been omitted from the sentences below. Insert the appropriate punctuation.

1. In the summer she visited Munich Heidelberg Frankfurt and Salzburg and in early fall she went on to Albania Greece and Egypt.
2. The weather was hot humid and miserable all day however a west wind cooled the air after dark.
3. Orchestra rehearsal begins at seven she will be there even though she needs to study.
4. The storm knocked out the electricity consequently we could not read or watch television.
5. She knew her parents were worried about her accordingly she called in to let them know she was all right.

## 12.2 COLONS

 Insert a colon at the place marked, or change the misused colon.

A colon is a mark of anticipation, directing attention to what follows:

> Sciences normally begin in a state of naïve induction: they come immediately in contact with phenomena and take the things to be explained as their immediate data.—Northrop Frye, "The Function of Criticism at the Present Time"

Students sometimes confuse colons and semicolons, but their functions are entirely different. The distinction is simple: a colon introduces or indicates what is to follow; a semicolon separates co-ordinate elements. The following passage illustrates the correct use of both marks (as does the sentence of the text above):

> The community that gathered round each country church soon came to have an organic unity about it: the parish became the natural subdivision of the countryside, comprehending most of the life of its people; their social occasions, their religious occasions, their marryings, their buryings and their business went on within its bounds, and often within earshot of the church bell.—A.R.M. Lower, *Colony to Nation*

## Anticipatory Use of Colons

A colon may be used after a main clause to indicate that a list, an illustration, or a summation is to follow:

> Needless to say, there are many slang terms native to Canada, quite a number of them relating to the sports arena: *deke, chippy, homebrew, import, rink rat.*—W.S. Avis, "The English Language in Canada"

> Understanding this, we can appreciate the overtones of meaning and the wealth of verbal history behind the use of *chair* in such sentences as: ... "Since the president of the firm was absent for the meeting, the vice-president took the *chair*"; or "The voting was even, but the casting vote from the *chair* was in favor of the motion."—P.D. Drysdale, "What's in a Dictionary"

The colon is used as an anticipatory mark only after grammatically complete expressions. Do not use a colon between verbs and their objects or complements, or between prepositions and their objects:

**12.2**

> COLON: He visited the following cities: Moncton, Quebec, and Sarnia.
> NO COLON: He visited Moncton, Quebec, and Sarnia. [objects of verb]

> COLON: The string section consists of four instruments: violin, viola, cello, and bass.
> NO COLON: The four instruments in the string section are violin, viola, cello, and bass. [complements of verb]

## Colons Between Main Clauses

A colon may be used between two main clauses when the second clause is an illustration, a restatement, or an amplification of the first:

> His opposition was never a match for him: neither in men nor in organization did the Liberals approach him.—A.R.M. Lower, *Colony to Nation*
> I was impractical: I wanted to marry a poet.—Lillian Hellman, *Pentimento*

## Colons Before Quotations

A colon is generally used between an introductory statement and a grammatically complete quotation, especially if the quotation is more than one sentence:

> Here is a well-known verse from *Ecclesiastes:* "I returned and saw under the sun, that the race is not to the swift, nor the battle to the

strong, neither yet bread to the wise, nor yet riches to men of understanding, nor yet favour to men of skill; but time and chance hap-
peneth to them all."—George Orwell, "Politics and the English
Language"

The saying of a cynical friend flashed suddenly across my mind: "A
saint may be nothing but a whitewashed sepulchre and the charity
of the philanthropist a mere cloak for the pride of humility."—
James A. Roy, "Brother Andre"

When a short quotation is built closely into a sentence, it may be
preceded either by a comma or by a colon, depending on how it is
introduced:

As Alexander Pope said, "A little learning is a dangerous thing."

She reminded him of the words of Pope: "A little learning is a dangerous thing."

## Colons in Conventional Places

A colon is customary in the following places:

1. After an expression introducing examples or a large body of
   material (as after *places* in the preceding sentence).
2. Between hours and minutes expressed in figures: 11:30
3. In formal footnotes and bibliographies:

   Between volume and page: *The Canadian Forum,* 98:295
   Between chapter and verse of the Bible: Matthew 4:6
   Between the title and subtitle of a book: *China: A Modern Enigma*

4. After the formal salutation in a letter:

   Dear Sir:       Dear Professor Jones:

See page 182 for use of capital letter after colons.

▶ EXERCISE

Either find and copy from your reading or write sentences according
to the directions below:

1. a sentence with a colon preceding a list of information or examples
2. a sentence with a colon between two main clauses
3. a sentence with a colon before a quotation

# Dashes, Parentheses, and Brackets

Dashes, parentheses, and brackets are all used to separate interrupting elements from the main thought of the sentence. Dashes are ordinarily used when the interruption is abrupt or emphatic; parentheses are used when the interruption is an aside or explanatory remark; and brackets are conventionally used when an editorial comment interrupts quoted material.

**13.1**

*/--/*

## 13.1 DASHES

*/--/* Use a dash or dashes to set off the expression marked.

Dashes are used to set off parenthetical expressions and abrupt interruptions in thought. The dash is a useful mark of separation, but since it is a more emphatic way of setting off elements than either commas or parentheses, it should not be used to excess or in places where another mark (or none) would be more appropriate. On the typewriter a dash is made with two unspaced hyphens; there should likewise be no space on either side of the dash, between it and the words it separates.

Dashes are customarily used in the situations shown below.

1. To set off parenthetical expressions and abrupt interruptions:

   > In reality, the whole idea of a specifically feminine—**or, for the matter of that, masculine**—contribution to culture is a contradiction of culture.—Brigid Brophy, "Women Are Prisoners of Their Sex"

2. To mark sharp turns in thought:

   > He praised Ann's intelligence, her efficiency, her good taste—**and then proposed to her sister.**

   > He is a humble man—**with a lot to be humble about.**

3. To enclose parenthetical elements (usually to give greater emphasis to elements that could also be set off with commas):

   > Still we do condemn—**we must condemn**—the cruelties of slavery, fanaticism, and witch-burning.—Herbert Muller, *The Uses of the Past*

> With our love of record keeping—doubtless a mark of our business society—the origin of almost everything is known or easily discoverable.—Jacques Barzun and Henry Graff, *The Modern Researcher*

For clarity, dashes are sometimes used instead of commas to set off parenthetical elements that have internal punctuation. Note that *two* dashes are necessary to enclose a parenthetical element that falls in the middle of a sentence.

4. To set off an expression that summarizes or illustrates the preceding statement:

> He founded a university, and devoted one side of his complex genius to placing that university amid every circumstance which could stimulate the imagination—beauty of buildings, of situation, and every other stimulation of equipment and organisation.—Alfred North Whitehead, "The Idea of a University"

5. To serve some special uses:
   a. To precede a credit line, as at the end of the quoted passages in this book.
   b. After introductory words that are to be repeated before each of the lines following:

> We pledge—
> To uphold the Monarchy.
> To obey the laws of Canada.

   c. To separate questions and answers in testimony:

> Q.—Did you see him?
> A.—No.

   d. To indicate interrupted dialogue (usually *two* dashes separated by a space are used):

> "Well, I had always assumed that— —"
> "I don't care what you assumed," John snapped.

## 13.2 PARENTHESES

  Use parentheses to enclose the expression marked.

Parentheses are curved marks used chiefly to enclose incidental or explanatory remarks as shown below.

1. To enclose incidental remarks:

> Her young man was a gifted carver, who had been sent out into the desert by the cruel pharoah **(pharoahs were always cruel—of this I was positive)** in order to carve a giant sphinx for the royal tomb.—Margaret Laurence, "The Mask of the Bear"

2. To enclose details and examples:

> For seven long years **(1945–1952)** austerity was the key word in British economic life.
>
> The changes can be seen by comparing the profits made before 1929 **(upper diagram)** with those made after 1929 **(lower diagram).**

3. To enclose figures or letters used to enumerate points:

**13.2**

> The main questions asked about our way of life concern **(1)** the strength of our democracy, **(2)** our radical practices, **(3)** our concept of modern economy, and **(4)** the degree of materialism in our culture.

No punctuation marks are used before a parenthetical statement that occurs within a sentence. If a comma or period is needed after the parenthetical material, it is placed *outside* of the *closing* marks:

> There is talk with music (tapes and records), talk with film and tape (movies and television), talk with live public performance (demonstrations and "confrontation").—William Jovanovich, "A Tumult of Talk"

When the parenthetical statement comes between sentences, the appropriate end punctuation is placed *inside* the closing mark:

> If we could get off by ourselves on a continental island, far away from the wicked Americans, all we should achieve would be to become a people like the Australians. (And even then the American goblin would get us in the end, as he is getting the Australians.)—Frank H. Underhill, "Notes on the Massey Report"

## 13.3 BRACKETS

[/]  Use brackets to set off any insertion in quoted material.

Brackets are used to insert brief editorial comments and explanations in material quoted from other writers:

> Lest it be thought that I am exaggerating, listen to Mencken: "The impact of this flood **[of common-speech, non-fashionable American-isms]** is naturally most apparent in Canada, whose geographical proximity and common interests completely obliterate the effects of English political and social dominance." — Eric Partridge, *Slang Today and Yesterday*

Comments or directions may be bracketed in conversation or in other quoted material to show that the speaker didn't actually say the enclosed words:

> For the first few minutes the practised speaker, therefore, fills in time with his "Thank you" to the chairman introducing him.... Then come his formal salutations, "Mr. President, honored guests **[if there are any]**, ladies and gentlemen." — *Amy Vanderbilt's Complete Book of Etiquette*

The Latin word *sic* (meaning *thus* or *so*) is sometimes inserted in brackets within quoted material to mark an error in spelling, usage, or fact that appeared in the original:

> The author's next letter was headed "St. John **[sic]**, Newfoundland, Oct. 6, 1854."

Since many writers feel that the insertion of *sic* to mark the errors of others is more snobbish than scholarly, the practice has declined in recent years.

In this book, brackets are used with examples of writing to enclose words that might better be left out of a sentence, to suggest an improved expression, and to comment on a construction. These special uses are illustrated below:

> At the end of an hour and a half we arrived at **[the spot where]** the red flag **[was situated]**.
>
> He looks **similar to [like]** his father.
> **Most** fishermen are optimists. [adjective, modifying *fishermen*]

Occasionally, brackets are used for parenthetical material that falls within parentheses — thus ( [ ] ) — but such constructions are awkward and can usually be avoided. Consult the preceding section to be sure that you don't confuse the normal uses of parentheses and brackets; See 13.2, Parentheses.

▶ EXERCISE

In each numbered space in the following sentences, which mark of punctuation would you consider most appropriate: a comma, a semicolon, a colon, a dash, or a parenthesis? Is punctuation necessary in all cases? If more than one choice is possible, list the marks in order of your preference.

a. Let us begin by looking [1] at the two countries where population pressures are most severe [2] India and Pakistan.

b. The finalists in diving were [1] Wilkins [2] U.S.A. [3] and Boyes [4] Canada [5] no one else had qualified.

c. To Ahab the white whale became an obsession [1] even Starbuck [2] the first mate [3] could do nothing to shake him out of it.

d. Reisman divides behavior into two major classes [1] inner-directed [2] directed toward pleasing the self [3] and other-directed [4] concerned with pleasing others [5].

e. The Edsel was [1] the most carefully planned and lavishly promoted new car in automobile history [2] but it was a total failure.

f. Someone [1] was it Carlyle [2] ironically used a truss factory [3] as a symbol [4] of modern [5] industrial progress.

**13.3**

$$[/]$$

g. Some industries have established good relations with their unions by increasing benefits [1] vacations, insurance, pension plans [2] but many manufacturers feel that there is only one permanent solution to their chronic labor problems [3] increased automation.

h. The key word in the essay [1] *faction* [2] is carefully defined by the author at the beginning [3] then he goes on to explain [4] what forms it may take.

i. An audience is basically one of three things [1] although various mixtures are also possible [2] friendly, hostile, or indifferent.

j. When Cadwallader quit talking [1] the chairman snorted [2] tugged at his ear [3] and spoke [4] "If you ladies and gentlemen [5] there were no ladies present [6] believe that I will support this recommendation [7] then you have lost your minds."

# Quotation Marks, Ellipses, and Italics

In general the more common punctuation marks—periods, question marks, commas, semicolons, and so on—indicate intonation and degrees of interruption that would occur if the material was read aloud. They show how the writer wants the words grouped together for meaning and emphasis.

The three marks discussed in this section—quotation marks, ellipses, and italics—are somewhat different in purpose. They are visual guides that tell the reader at a glance such things as whether the words are a writer's own and whether they are being used in a special way. Compare the following pairs of sentences:

> He said I was a fool. [He accused the *writer* of being a fool.]
> He said, "I was a fool." [He called *himself* a fool.]
>
> He spoke of Watson's moral decline. [the moral decline of Watson]
> He spoke of Watson's *Moral Decline.* [a book by Watson]

Although quotation marks, ellipses, and italics are used less often than other punctuation, it is important to know how to use them correctly. They are often necessary in writing that is likely to contain references to the writing of others.

## 14.1 QUOTATION MARKS

 Make the quotation marks and accompanying punctuation conform to conventional usage.

Quotation marks are necessary to set off direct speech and material quoted from other sources. They are also used around some titles and around words used in special ways.

Usage varies, but double quotations (" ") are the usual marks in Canadian publications. Students should follow this convention, using single marks (' )—made on the typewriter with apostrophes—only for a quotation within a quotation (see p. 172). Whether double or single, quotation marks are always used in *pairs,* before and after the quoted material.

## Quotation Marks to Enclose Direct Discourse

Statements representing actual speech or conversation are enclosed by quotation marks. The following passage illustrates typical punctuation for direct discourse. Notice not only the quotation marks but the punctuation used with them:

> When we got home, Cathy asked, "Did you win the game?"
> David said, "We sure did! I got four goals, and we won 8 to 5."
> "And Bob had a hat trick," Mindy added. "You should have seen him skate."

In dialogue the words of each speaker are normally indented like paragraphs, as in the example above. But when short speeches or statements are quoted to illustrate a point in exposition, they are usually included in the relevant paragraph:

**14.1**

> Some of the constructions were typically Cree or Ojibwa. I have heard, "Bye me I *kaykatch* [nearly] killed it two ducks with wan sot." That would be pretty good Cree translated literally into that language. Again, "John James Corrigal and Willie George Linklater were sooting in the marse. The canoe went *apeechequanee*. The watter was sallow whatefer but Willie George kept bobbin up and down callin, 'O Lard save me.' John James was on topside the canoe souted to Willie and sayed, 'Never mind the Lard just now Willie, grab for the willows.' "—S.O. Scott, "Red River Dialect"

Only *direct discourse,* which represents the actual words of the speaker, is enclosed by quotation marks. *Indirect discourse,* which gives the substance of what the speaker said but not his exact words, is *not* enclosed in quotation marks:

DIRECT DISCOURSE: The coach said, "Get in there and fight."
INDIRECT DISCOURSE: The coach told us to get in there and fight.

DIRECT DISCOURSE: "At the present time," the premier replied, "I haven't made up my mind about the bill."
INDIRECT DISCOURSE: The premier replied that he had not yet made up his mind about the bill.

## Quotation Marks Around Quoted Material

Words taken directly from another writer or speaker must be clearly set apart, either by quotation marks or by some other conventional typographic device such as setting them in reduced type. Whether a writer is quoting a phrase or several paragraphs, he should make certain that he follows the exact wording and punctuation of his source.

**Short quotations.** Quotation marks are used around quoted phrases and statements that are included within the body of a paragraph. The quoted material may be worked into the structure of a sentence or may stand by itself:

> Another immortal pun is Eugene Field's comment on the actor Creston Clarke that "he played the king as though he were in constant fear that somebody else was going to play the ace." — Max Eastman, *The Enjoyment of Laughter*

> While Iago, for example, is gulling Roderigo, he scoffs at him with superb disdain: "I have rubb'd this young quat almost to the sense / And he grows angry" (*Othello*, 5.1.11–12). — Maurice Charney, *How to Read Shakespeare*

**Long quotations.** When quoted material is relatively long—more than one full sentence from the original source or more than four lines in your paper—it is usually indented and single-spaced but not enclosed in quotation marks:

> A British member of Parliament, A. P. Herbert, also exasperated with bureaucratic jargon, translated Nelson's immortal phrase, "England expects every man to do his duty":
>
>> England anticipates that, as regards the current emergency, personnel will face up to the issues, and exercise appropriately the functions allocated to their respective occupational groups.
>
> — Stuart Chase, *The Power of Words*

**A quotation within a quotation.** Use single quotation marks around quoted material that appears within a quotation which is itself enclosed in double marks:

> If they depended solely on economic theory to guide them, they would be in the position of the man John Williams mentions: "About the practical usefulness of the theory, I have often felt like the man who stammered and finally learned to say, 'Peter Piper picked a peck of pickled peppers,' but found it hard to work into conversation." — C. Hartley Grattan, "New Books"

In the rare instances when a third quotation occurs within a second, double and single marks are alternated, like this:

> In the next passage he gives an example of Mill's uncontrolled temper: "Mill attacked Beaton with a poker after reading his comment that 'A work of genius is not, as Mr. Mill says, "a spontaneous out-

> flowing of the soul"; it is the product of intellectual discipline, a
> quality Mr. Mill notably lacks.'"

Such a proliferation of quotation marks is confusing and can
usually be avoided, either by indenting and single-spacing the
main quotation or by paraphrasing some of the material:

> In the next passage he gives an example of Mill's uncontrolled temper,
> telling how Mill attacked Beaton with a poker after reading his com-
> ment that "A work of genius is not, as Mr. Mill says, 'a spontaneous
> overflowing of the soul'; it is the product of intellectual discipline, a
> quality Mr. Mill notably lacks."

**Quoted verse.**  A phrase or portion of a line of verse may be
built into a sentence and enclosed by quotation marks, as is this
phrase from *Romeo and Juliet:*

**14.1**

cc

> "A plague on both your houses" was the general attitude toward the
> parties in any conflict, no matter what the outcome. — Percy Finch,
> *Shanghai and Beyond*

If the quoted passage extends over several lines of the poem, it is
best to line it off exactly as it appears in the original, single-spaced
and indented. Quotation marks are unnecessary:

> Milton opens *Paradise Lost* by announcing that he will write
>
>> Of Man's first disobedience, and the fruit
>> Of that forbidden tree whose mortal taste
>> Brought death into the World. . . .

If two or three lines of verse are incorporated into a paragraph, the
passage is enclosed in quotation marks and the line breaks are
indicated by diagonal lines (/):

> Milton opens *Paradise Lost* by announcing that he will write "Of
> Man's first disobedience, and the fruit / Of that forbidden tree whose
> mortal taste / Brought death into the World."

## Quotation Marks Around Titles

Quotation marks are used to set off the titles of brief compositions
published as part of larger works, as single poems, essays, short
stories, and articles. The titles of books and the names of
newspapers and magazines are italicized:

> *The Oxford Book of English Verse* includes only two poems by Oliver
> Goldsmith: **"Women"** and **"Memory."**

> Judith Blake and Kingsley Davis have contributed an article titled

**"Norms, Values, and Sanctions"** to *The Handbook of Modern Sociology,* edited by Robert E. L. Faris.

See 14.3, Italics, and 30, The Reference Paper.

A few titles are neither set off by quotation marks nor underlined for italics: the Bible, Old Testament, the British North America Act, the Canadian Tire Catalogue, the Regina Telephone Directory (or any other catalogue or directory).

## Quotation Marks to Set Off Words

Words used in some special way within a sentence are often set apart by quotation marks or by italics (underlining).

**A word used as a word.**    A word used as a word or as an example rather than for its meaning (that is, as a *citation form*) is preferably italicized. Older custom enclosed such forms in quotation marks:

> The English borrowed *pork* and *beef* from French.
>
> I have trouble typing *artificial* and *expectation.*
>
> People often confuse the meanings of "allusion" and "illusion."

**Apologetic quotes for slang and colloquial expressions.**    In serious writing, an expression associated with unedited or colloquial forms of English is sometimes put in quotation marks to show that the writer knows it is not considered appropriate in formal usage:

> The disheartening outcome of recent international conferences has convinced some of our statesmen that certain nations consider us as little more than "fall guys."

The trouble with apologetic quotes is that they focus the reader's attention on the expression and make him wonder why the writer chose to use it. If you think a word or phrase is right for what you are saying, it's best to use it without apology.

When a real or imaginary person is frequently referred to by his or her nickname, it is not set off by quotation marks:

> Joey Smallwood    Rocket Richard    Kate Reid    Huck Finn

In general writing there is seldom any need to use apologetic quotes around a word or expression. If the word is appropriate, use it without quotation marks. If it is not, use another.

**Words used derisively.**    Sometimes a writer may use quotation marks around a term to show that it is being used derisively or sarcastically:

This remarkable piece of "art" consists of a large canvas covered with mud and old bus-transfers.

She was so "genteel" that she avoided any reference to the human body.

It's generally better to try to make the tone of the whole passage derisive rather than to rely too much on quotation marks.

## Quotation Marks with Other Punctuation

The following conventions govern the use of other punctuation with quotation marks:

1. Commas and periods are always placed *inside* the closing quotation mark:

   "Yes," Roger agreed, "it's too late to worry about that now."

   Her watch case was described as "waterproof," but "moisture-resistant" would have been more accurate.

2. Semicolons and colons are placed *outside* the closing quotation mark:

   This critic's attitude seems to be "I don't like any movie"; on a few occasions, though, he has said kind words for a travelogue or a documentary film.

   Fully a third of the railway passengers were what trainmen call "deadheads": people who ride on passes and never tip.

3. Question marks, exclamation points, and dashes are placed inside *or* outside the closing quotation mark, depending upon the situation. They come *inside* when they apply to the quotation only:

   Mother looked at me and asked, "Why do you say that?"

   He gave me a skeptical look which seemed to mean "Look who's talking!"

   Terrence interrupted, "No, listen to this — " and proceeded to recite a poem none of us had ever heard before.

They are placed *outside* the closing quotation mark when they apply to the entire statement:

   Who was it who said that "good guys finish last"? [The whole sentence is a question.]

   And to top it all off, she refers to her automatic dishwasher as "essential equipment for gracious living"!

End punctuation marks are never doubled. If a quotation ends your sentence, the end punctuation within quotation marks also indicates the end of the sentence:

> This lack of response is, of course, an action from Laura, which forces him to a further question, "You got any objections?"—Brian Meeson, "The Language of Public Performance"

Notice that no period is added after the final quotation mark, even though the sentence is a statement, not a question. Occasionally it is necessary to use double marks *within* a sentence to avoid a possible misreading, as in the following sentence:

> Immediately I am reminded of other locutions with the same metallic flavour: "This really turns me on, you know?", and, "Man, she turns me off" (which isn't an action by "her", exactly, nor yet a response by "me").—Michael Hornyansky, "Is Your English Destroying Your Image?"

▶ **EXERCISE**

Write sentences according to the directions below.
1. a sentence that includes the names of two poems.
2. a sentence that includes a short quotation from something you have read.
3. a sentence in which you identify a speaker and the speaker says something as direct discourse.
4. the sentence above converted to indirect discourse.
5. three sentences giving dialogue between two speakers as direct discourse.
6. the three sentences above converted into indirect discourse.

## 14.2 ELLIPSES

**/···/**   Use an ellipsis to indicate any omission in quoted material.

A punctuation mark of three spaced periods, called an ellipsis (plural: *ellipses*), indicates that one or more words have been omitted from quoted material. If an ellipsis comes at the end of a sentence, the sentence period (or other end punctuation) is retained, and the three periods of the ellipsis follow it. There is no space between the last word and the end punctuation:

There are those ... who fear the ignorance of the people of Upper Canada; I ... stand more in dread of rulers who are virtually independent of them....—William Lyon Mackenzie (1826)

... my roots are entirely Canadian. I'm as Canadian as you'll ever find. Whatever that means.—Donald Sutherland

To indicate that an entire paragraph or more or an entire line or more of poetry has been omitted, a full line of ellipses is used:

That's my last Duchess painted on the wall,
Looking as if she were alive.... [two words are omitted here]
................. [two lines omitted]
Will 't please you sit and look at her?
                        —Robert Browning, "My Last Duchess"

Ellipses are sometimes used, especially in narrative, to indicate interruptions in thought, incompleted statements, or hesitation in speech, as in this description of the dying words of John Wilkes Booth, the assassin of President Abraham Lincoln:

**14.2**

/.../

Water was poured into his mouth. He blew it out feebly, opened his eyes and moved his lips to shape the words: "Tell ... mother...." Then he fainted again. When he came to, he finished his sentence: "Tell ... mother ... I ... died ... for ... my country."—Eleanor Ruggles, *Prince of Players*

## 14.3 ITALICS

*Ital*    Underline the word or expressions marked to correspond to the conventions for using italic type.

Words are set off or emphasized in most published works by printing them in slanting type called *italics*. In handwritten or typed papers, such words are underlined:

The article first appeared in Saturday Night and was

reprinted in The Fredericton Gleaner.

### Italics for Titles

The names of newspapers and magazines and the titles of books, plays, films, and other complete works published separately are conventionally italicized (or underlined):

|                        |                             |
| ---------------------- | --------------------------- |
| *Maclean's*            | *The Toronto Star*          |
| *The Diviners*         | *The Kingdom of Canada*     |
| the novel *Execution*  | *Hamlet,* Act III           |
| *The Senior Dictionary* | the movie *Ben Hur*        |
|                        | Dante's *Divine Comedy*     |

Titles of articles, short stories, poems, and other short pieces of writing that are part of a larger work are usually enclosed in quotation marks:

Atwood's "Further Arrivals" is a poem in *Literature in Canada.*

See 14.1, page 173, Quotation Marks Around Titles, and 30, The Reference Paper.

The names of specific ships, trains, and so on are put in italics:

He was an officer in HMCS *Athabasca.*
She took a cruise on *Princess Patricia.*
The *Royal Scotsman* was a famous locomotive.

## Italics for Words and Phrases Used as Examples

Words used as words or as examples rather than as parts of a sentence should be italicized or set off by quotation marks: (See also 14.1, Quotation Marks to Set Off Words.)

A few slang terms move into the general language: *crestfallen* and *mob* are examples; some live a long life as slang, never becoming quite respectable; *dough* for "money" is over a hundred years old, and *boozing* goes back to the 1500's.—P.G. Penner and Ruth E. McConnell, "What's the Usage?"

## Italics for Foreign Words

Words from foreign languages that have not been absorbed into English should be italicized, not set off by quotation marks:

In Antiquity every tree, every spring, every stream, every hill had its own *genius loci*, its guardian spirit.—Lynn White, Jr., "The Historical Roots of Our Ecological Crisis"

Its own natural bird, too, it had, *die goldene pawe,* the golden parrot, winging its way to the ghetto from lands remote....
—A.M. Klein, "The Yiddish Proverb"

Foreign expressions that would ordinarily be underlined for italics include terms like *coup d'état, Weltschmerz, deus ex machina, mañana.* In most books and formal writing, the accents and other marks are used.

Scientific names of plants, insects, and so on are also italicized:

The highbush cranberry (*Viburnum opulus*) is also called the mooseberry.

Words taken from other languages that are now widely used in general English are not underlined or otherwise set off:

| | | | |
|---|---|---|---|
| bourgeois | debut | laissez-faire | sputnik |
| chalet | debutante | prima donna | status quo |
| chic | fiancée | slalom | vice versa |

Although dictionaries usually designate words that are now anglicized (have become part of the English language) and those that are not, their usage tends to be conservative. If you are certain that an expression marked "foreign" is familiar to your readers, you need not underline it.

**14.3**

*Ital*

Abbreviations of the less common Latin words and phrases used mainly in reference works are sometimes italicized, but Latin abbreviations in general use are not:

e.g.    et al.    etc.    ca.    i.e.    vs.    viz.

## Italics for Emphasis

Italics are used in printed material to indicate an emphatic word or stressed statement:

Since we cannot have our fill of existence by going on and on, we want to have *as much life as possible* in our short span. — Susanne K. Langer, "Man and Animal: The City and the Hive"

Italics should be used sparingly for emphasis. When used excessively or with words that do not deserve stress, this device may strike a reader as affected.

▶ EXERCISES

1. Write sentences following the directions below:
   a. a sentence in which you quote two lines of a poem.
   b. a sentence in which you use quotation marks to set off a single word.
   c. a sentence in which you quote something you have read with ellipses to indicate that you have omitted something.
   d. a sentence that includes a word or phrase italicized for emphasis.

2. All the quotation marks and indentations have been removed from the following passage from a short story. Rewrite the passage, using

quotation marks and indentations to show dialogue and changes in speaker.

They do say, Mr. Adams said to Old Man Warner, who stood next to him, that over in the north village they're talking of giving up the lottery. Old Man Warner snorted. Pack of crazy fools, he said. Listening to the young folks, nothing's good enough for *them*. Next thing you know, they'll be wanting to go back to living in caves, nobody work any more, live *that* way for a while. Used to be a saying about Lottery in June, corn be heavy soon. First thing you know, we'd all be eating stewed chickweed and acorns. There's *always* been a lottery, he added petulantly. Bad enough to see young Joe Summers up there joking with everybody. Some places already quit lotteries, Mrs. Adams said. Nothing but trouble in *that*, Old Man Warner said stoutly. Pack of young fools.

—Adapted from Shirley Jackson, "The Lottery"

# Capital Letters, Hyphens, and Apostrophes

Capital letters, hyphens, and apostrophes are convenient signals that writers are generally expected to use. These signals are not, however, just habits: writing in which capitals are improperly used may seen sloppy or affected to readers; words incorrectly hyphenated may be difficult to read, and can cause faulty modification; misuse of apostrophes often makes the writer seem careless.

## 15.1 CAPITAL LETTERS

*Cap*  **Capitalize the marked word; be consistent in the use of capital letters.**

*lc*  **Write the marked word with a lower-case (small) letter.**

Most uses of capital letters are standard conventions; writing in which capitals are used inconsistently or unconventionally may focus attention on the wrong words and interrupt the natural flow of thought.

The following sections describe the most frequent uses of capital letters. A complete listing of all forms is obviously impossible. Consult a recent dictionary or style manual if you are in doubt as to whether a particular word requires a capital.

## Capitals to Mark Units of Expression

Capital letters are used to draw the reader's attention to the beginning of a statement or to individual words in titles.

**First word of a sentence.**  Capitalize the first word of every sentence or expression punctuated with an end stop (period, question mark, or exclamation mark):

Has the change helped? Not much. The reason is obvious.

**First word of a line of poetry.**  In traditional verse style, the first word of each line is capitalized:

> Full many a gem of purest ray serene,
>   The dark unfathomed waves of ocean bear;
> Full many a flower is born to blush unseen,
>   And waste its sweetness on the desert air.
> > — Thomas Gray, "Elegy Written in a Country Churchyard"

**First word of a quotation.**    The first word of a direct quotation that is in itself a complete sentence is capitalized:

> He said, "The future of humanity cannot be left to chance."
> "The crisis is here," she said. "We must act now."

But no capital is used when the quotation is fragmentary or built into the structure of the sentence, or when the second part of a quoted sentence is interrupted by an expression such as *he said:*

> According to the advertisement, it was the "most spectacular picture of the year."

> "The argument is based," he said, "upon a false premise."

**In parentheses.**    A complete sentence enclosed in parentheses is always capitalized when it stands alone, but when enclosed *within* another sentence, it usually is not:

> The broadcast, sponsored by a local store, was frequently interrupted by lengthy commercials. (Apparently the sponsor doesn't believe that silence is golden.)

> Fitzhugh was the member of a prominent family (his mother was the granddaughter of Sir Thomas Wyatt) and was received in the highest circles.

**After a colon.**    A complete sentence standing after a colon is not usually capitalized when the connection with the preceding clause is close:

> Indeed, if Galileo had not been so expert an amateur theologian he would have got into far less trouble: the professionals resented his intrusion. — Lynn White, Jr., "The Historical Roots of Our Ecological Crisis."

The sentence after the colon is sometimes capitalized if it is distinctly separate or if the writer wants to give it emphasis:

> Quite a few teachers in the departments of science would tell the student: We scientists deliver the laws of nature to the philosopher, who has to interpret them. — Philipp Frank, *Relativity: A Richer Truth*

**In titles of written material.** The first word, the last word, the principal parts of speech (nouns, pronouns, verbs, adjectives, and adverbs), and prepositions of more than five letters are capitalized in the titles of books, magazine articles, themes, and so on:

*Land of the Silver Birch*  *The Loved and the Lost*
*Pottery Through the Ages*  *Ox Bells and Fireflies*

*I* **and** *O*. The pronoun *I* and the exclamation *O* are always capitalized to prevent their being read as parts of other words:

> Give a man a girl he can love,
>  As **I, O** my love, love thee. . . . –James Thomson, "Gifts"

The exclamation *oh* is not capitalized unless it stands first in a sentence.

**15.1**

*Cap*

## Capitals for Proper Nouns and Their Derivatives

The names of specific people, places, and things, and the words derived from them are conventionally capitalized (Karl Marx—Marxism; Africa—African sculpture; Lent—Lenten menu). Examples of the most frequent types of proper nouns are given in the following sections.

 In a few cases, words originally derived from proper nouns have dropped the capital in the course of frequent use (*pasteurized milk, jersey cloth, french fries*). Usage differs about the capitalization of others (*diesel, levis*). Up-to-date dictionaries provide a guide in such matters, as do the practices of current publications.

**Names and titles of people.** A person's name or nickname is capitalized:

 William Lyon Mackenzie  Nellie McClung  Gordie Howe
 Laura Secord      Mindy     Mike Pearson

A title should be capitalized when it is used as part of a person's name, but not when it is used as a descriptive term. A few titles of high rank are usually capitalized whether or not the officeholder is named: the Prime Minister (of Canada), the Pope, the Queen of England, the Chief Justice of the Supreme Court. Titles referring to a position or an office rather than to the specific person holding it are not capitalized:

| Capitals | No capitals |
|---|---|
| Professor Townsend | Francis Townsend is a professor. |
| Sergeant David Moore | A sergeant maintains discipline. |
| Judge **R.A.** Snow | She was appointed judge. |
| The Captain of *Skeena* assembled the crew. | The captain of a ship is in full command. |
| The Queen addressed the opening session of Parliament. | England has had several queens. |

Names of family relationships are usually capitalized when used with a person's name or when used as proper nouns standing for the name. They are not capitalized when used as common nouns or when preceded by a possessive:

| Capitals | No capitals |
|---|---|
| Grandma Seton | She is a grandmother. |
| Aunt Sarah | My aunt's name is Sarah. |
| I showed Mother the card. | I showed my mother the card. |
| Whatever Father said, we did. | His father was demanding. |

**Names of groups.**   Names referring to racial, national, linguistic, political, or religious groups are capitalized:

| | | | |
|---|---|---|---|
| Negro | German | Liberal | Catholic |
| English | Italian | Conservative | Jew |
| French | Pole | New Democrat | Moslem |
| Israeli | Indian | Creditiste | Baptist |

Names of social and economic groups are not capitalized (except occasionally for stylistic emphasis):

the middle class     the intelligentsia     the bourgeoisie

**Names of organizations.**   Names and abbreviations of business associations, clubs, political parties, and other organizations are capitalized:

Canadian Manufacturers Association (**CMA**)
International Order of Foresters (**IOOF**)
Front de Liberation du Québec (**FLQ**)
Canadian National Institute for the Blind (**CNIB**)

**Names of places.** Words that designate specific geographical divisions or particular places and areas are capitalized:

| | | |
|---|---|---|
| Asia | Ghana | Hyde Park |
| European | Albertan | Cabbagetown |
| Latin America | Victoria | Third Avenue |

When the names of directions are used to identify geographic areas, they are generally capitalized. When they merely indicate direction, they are not:

| Capitals | No capitals |
|---|---|
| the old West | west of Suez |
| a Southerner | a southern exposure |
| the Far East | eastern Manitoba |

**15.1**

*Cap*

**Names of institutions.** The names of specific public and private institutions and their divisions and departments are capitalized. Names that apply to a whole class of institutions are not:

| Capitals | No capitals |
|---|---|
| Toronto Public Library | a public library |
| Ontario Health Ministry | public health problems |
| Smith Falls High School | our high school |

Names of government departments are generally capitalized although some newspapers have discontinued the practice:

Department of National Defence    Treasury Ministry

Specific high-school, college, or university courses are capitalized; general subjects are not, except for language courses:

| Capitals | No capitals |
|---|---|
| Modern French Literature | literature |
| Advanced Narrative Writing | composition |
| Chemistry 101 | chemistry |

**Names of specific objects.** Names of specific objects, such as ships, planes, structures, famous documents and artifacts, and brand-name products are capitalized:

| | |
|---|---|
| *HMCS Nipigon* | the Ambassador Bridge |
| the *Ocean Limited* | Brock's Monument |
| Chevrolet | Magna Charta |

**Names of units in time.** Capitalize words designating specific periods, events, months, days, and holidays:

| | | |
|---|---|---|
| the Stone Age | the Norman Conquest | Thursday |
| the Renaissance | the Battle of Waterloo | Labor Day |
| the June Ball | January | |

Names of seasons are not generally capitalized:

| | | | | |
|---|---|---|---|---|
| winter | summer | spring | fall | autumn |

**Sacred names.** References to deities and to sacred texts are capitalized. Pronouns referring to the Christian Trinity are also usually capitalized:

| | | |
|---|---|---|
| God | Holy Ghost | Talmud |
| Genesis | Bible | Koran |
| Virgin Mary | New Testament | Buddha |

**Abstractions.** Such abstractions as ideas, qualities, or conditions may be capitalized, especially in formal and sentimental writing, to show that they are being discussed in some ideal or absolute state. Sometimes abstractions are personified, particularly in poetry:

> Throughout recorded history, Man has responded to the challenge of Nature.

> The pursuit of the Good Life is a persistent human preoccupation.

In general writing, capitalized abstractions are seldom appropriate. College students should confine them to formal papers of critical analysis or philosophical theory and follow the practices found in readings assigned in the course for which the papers are written.

**Distinguishing proper and common forms.** Some words can be spelled either with or without capitals. It is important to distinguish between these forms because they often have different meanings:

| Capitals | No capitals |
|---|---|
| a Conservative (a member of the Conservative Party) | a conservative (one who believes in tradition |
| a Liberal view (of the Liberal Party) | a liberal view (of a moral issue) |
| Orthodox beliefs (of the Greek Orthodox Church) | orthodox beliefs (conventional) |
| Catholic sympathies (of or with the Catholic Church) | catholic sympathies (broad; universal) |
| Romantic poetry (of the Romantic Period) | romantic poetry (concerning romance or love) |

▶ **EXERCISE**

In the sentences below, all capital letters have been replaced by lower-case letters. Supply capitals and any other necessary marks wherever you think they are appropriate.

1. added opposition leader joe clark: "this is no time to show weakness."
2. the town of belmonte, perched atop a rocky hilltop in northern portugal, is dominated by a giant stone cross, a ruined castle and the roman catholic church of the holy family.
3. french choreographer maurice bejart had a difficult time casting his ballet rendition of goethe's faust.
4. life's little dilemmas department: the hilarious instalment of the odd couple that you've always wanted to see is being rerun tonight on channel 11 at precisely the same time that channel 5 is featuring the latest episode of the king of kensington.

**15.1**◀

*Cap*

## 15.2 HYPHENS

*Hyph*  **Insert or remove the hyphen between the marked words to conform to current usage.**

Hyphens are used to connect two or more words used as a single expression (*heavy-hearted, will-o'-the-wisp*) and to keep parts of other words distinct (*anti-inflation*).

Hyphens are needed in some instances to prevent misreading (*un-ionized*) or to differentiate between the same words used in different ways (a *drive in* the evening, a *drive-in* theatre). But generally they are used as a matter of convention (*brother-in-law, hocus-pocus*).

In printed matter the use of hyphens varies considerably: relatively few hyphens are found in newspapers and magazines; more are found in formal writing. The important thing to look for in proofreading is consistency. If an expression is hyphenated the first time it occurs, it should be hyphenated throughout.

This section lists the most common uses of hyphens. See also 22.2, Spelling and Word Division.

### Hyphens in Compound Words

A hyphen is used between two or more words considered as a single unit in certain expressions, as discussed below.

**Names for family relationships.** Some compound names for family relationships are hyphenated; others are not:

> HYPHENATED: father-in-law, great-grandfather, sister-in-law
> ONE WORD: stepson, stepmother, grandfather
> TWO WORDS: half brother, second cousin

**Compound numbers.** A hyphen is used in numbers from twenty-one to ninety-nine. Fractions are hyphenated except when the fraction already contains a hyphenated number:

> thirty-three                   four-fifths of a box
> one hundred twenty-eight       one-half inch
> twenty-first birthday          one thirty-second of an inch

**Compounds with** *self.* Most group words beginning with *self* are written with hyphens ( *self-contained, self-pity, self-support, self-government*); some words beginning with *self* are written as one word: *selfsame, selfless, selfhood.* Consult an up-to-date dictionary to find out which form is preferred.

**Standard compound nouns.** A number of compound nouns are regularly written with a hyphen: *bull's-eye, city-state, jack-o'-lantern, secretary-treasurer.* Other similar compounds are written as one word, that is, in block (*beeswax, newsprint, policyholder*) or as two words (*intelligence test, labor union, shipping point, water cooler*).

Since practice is likely to vary with many such compounds, the hyphen is often optional. Where no misreading is apt to arise, some writers would omit the hyphen. Nevertheless, block forms are increasingly common, especially where the first element of the compound carries a heavier stress than the second. When in doubt, consult an up-to-date dictionary.

## Hyphens in Group Modifiers

When two or more words act as a closely linked modifier immediately before another word, they are often hyphenated to suggest the close relationship:

> **gray-green** eyes      a **nineteenth-century** poet
> a **well-kept** lawn      an **all-out** effort

A hyphen should always be used to prevent a possible misreading:

> a **slow-motion** picture      a **pitch-dark** room
> a **navy-blue** uniform      some **reclaimed-rubber** plants

When the first word of a group modifier is an adverb ending in -*ly*, no hyphen is used after it:

richly deserved praise    openly antagonistic attitude

Compound modifiers formed with present or past participles are usually hyphenated when they precede a noun:

a **good-looking** man    a **well-planned** attack

Such phrases are not usually hyphenated in other positions:

Her father was good looking.    The attack was well planned.

Long phrases or clauses used as modifiers are hyphenated:

**15.2**

*Hyph*

. . . and he offers dramatic recitals about guerrillas (whom he didn't meet) and possible ambushes (which he didn't find), all of it pretty much in the **gosh-we-could-even-hear-the-guns-in-the-distance** school of war reporting. — G. Barrett, "Korean Scenario"

This practice is commonest in informal writing.

## Hyphens with Prefixes

Hyphens are used after certain prefixes to follow convention or to prevent ambiguity. Consult an up-to-date dictionary.

1. Between a prefix and a proper name:

pre-Renaissance       post-Confederation
anti-Communist        un-Canadian
ex-Premier Bourassa   pro-German

2. Between some prefixes that end with a vowel and a root word beginning with a vowel, especially if the root word begins with the same vowel:

re-elected    semi-independent    re-ink    pre-exist

Practice varies at present with respect to certain words beginning with a prefix that is followed by a similar vowel:

co-operation    cooperation    coöperation
re-establish    reestablish     reëstablish

For such words, the best policy is to be consistent in any given piece of writing.

3. To avoid confusing words of similar shape but different meaning; in speech, the prefix of such words is stressed:

to **re-cover** a sofa (to *recover* from an illness)
to **re-sort** buttons (a seaside *resort*)

Stressed prefixes occur in terms like *ex-wife, all-Canadian, do-gooder, Pan-African.*

## Suspension Hyphens

The suspension hyphen is often used to carry the modifying expression from one word over to the next:

Two-word forms first acquire the hyphen and later are printed as one word. Quite frequently the transition is from the **two-** to the **one-word** form, bypassing the hyphen stage.

## Unnecessary Hyphens

Don't hyphenate a term that is currently written as a single word or as two words. Even if your dictionary lists as alternatives such old-fashioned forms as *to-night* and *post-man,* use the first or preferred form. Here is a brief list of words that students are sometimes tempted to hyphenate:

| One word | Separate words |
| --- | --- |
| anybody (pronoun) | all right |
| basketball, baseball, football | class president |
| bookkeeping | grade curve |
| footnotes | high school |
| himself, myself, ourselves | "How do you do?" |
| nevertheless | motion picture |
| outdoor | no one |
| outwit | press agent |
| overlooked | report card |
| roundabout | school days |
| semicolon | single file |
| taxpayer | six o'clock |
| timetable | tax rate |
| today, tomorrow | water pressure |
| throughout | weather office |
| weatherman | |

▶ EXERCISE

Indicate which of the following expressions should be written as separate words, which should be one word, and which should be hyphenated. The words in parentheses indicate the sense in which the expression is intended.

a lot (of work to do)           non communist
base ball                       not with standing (a conjunction)

| | |
|---|---|
| dark horse | over look (to slight or neglect) |
| every one (is present) | out and out (outright) |
| flame thrower | pipe wrench |
| gilt edged | re written |
| give and take | school board |
| hydro therapy | self satisfied |
| in so far as | semi colon |
| jet black | some body (is missing) |
| left overs (food) | space craft |
| man hunt | ten word (telegram) |
| man of war (a ship) | three quarters (of an inch) |
| may be (perhaps) | un Canadian |
| never the less | where abouts (at what place) |

**15.2**

## 15.3 APOSTROPHES

*Hyph*

 Insert an apostrophe where it belongs in the marked word, or take out the unnecessary apostrophe.

An apostrophe (') is used in contractions, to mark the plural form of some expressions, and to indicate the possessive case of nouns. Although it is a minor mark that seldom affects the reader's interpretation of a statement, its omission or misuse is noticeable.

### Apostrophes in Contractions

Contractions are an attempt to represent the rhythms of speech in written discourse. They are appropriate in dialogue, informal writing, and nowadays in much general writing. Although they are used from time to time in this handbook, remember that many teachers, editors, and readers think that contractions are out of place in formal writing and academic papers.

When a contraction is appropriate in writing, an apostrophe is used to indicate the omission of one or more letters:

| | | | |
|---|---|---|---|
| can't | I'll | it's (it is) | wasn't |
| don't | I'm | o'clock | we're |
| haven't | isn't | shouldn't | won't |

Notice that *till* (as in "from morning till midnight") is *not* a shortened form of *until* and no apostrophe is used with it.

An apostrophe is used with dates from which the first figures are omitted (the class of '59, the gold rush of '98). Normally, in formal writing, dates are written in full.

## Apostrophes with Possessive Case Forms

An apostrophe is used with the singular and plural forms of nouns and indefinite pronouns to mark the genitive case:

| | |
|---|---|
| John's car | children's games |
| Victoria's parks | your parents' permission |
| a stone's throw | anybody's guess |

An apostrophe is *not* used with the possessive forms of the personal pronouns *his, hers, its, ours, yours, theirs:*

the city and **its** suburbs     these seats are **ours**

See 6.2, Forms of the Possessive, and 7.3, Possessive Pronouns.

## Apostrophes for Plurals of Letters and Figures

An apostrophe may be used before an *s* to indicate the plurals of figures:

the early 1900's [*or* 1900s]
several size 16's [*or* 16s]
An apostrophe is normally used to indicate the plurals of citation forms and letters of the alphabet:
There were three *and's* and two *but's* in that sentence.
There are two *s's* and three *a's* in Saskatchewan.

## Apostrophes for Letters Dropped in Representing Speech

An apostrophe is commonly used to indicate the omission of sounds in representing speech:

"Then comes harvest, and that is proper hard work—mowin' and pitchin' hay, and reapin' and bindin' grain, and potato-diggin'...."—T.C. Haliburton, "The Blowin' Time"

It is unnecessary in representing speech to indicate all such omissions; too many apostrophes make for difficult reading.

▶ EXERCISE

In the two paragraphs below, capital letters, apostrophes, and hyphens have been omitted. Insert them where you think they are appropriate.

1. i arrived at eau clair in late april with my wife, who had joined me at the end of spring training. we rented a single room with a tiny kitchenette on the second floor of an old two family house. it disturbed me that, unlike most baseball wives, carol knew nothing about the game to which i had devoted my life. she took her cues solely from my enthusiasms and despairs. whenever i pitched decently — a rarity — i had to tell her so, and then she would smile and say, "thats nice, dear." when i was knocked out of the box in the first inning and she saw my dejection, she commiserated with me: "well, its certainly not your fault. its hard to do good when you only play a little bit. . . . why doesnt your manager let you play as much as the other pitchers?" — Pat Jordan, *A False Spring*

2. it had been established that the girl had been strangled at about three oclock in the morning. mrs. agnew had declared that she had heard some one moving around the girls apartment shortly before that time, and later had heard someone with a slow heavy step going along the hall. she had looked out the window; a heavy set man had gone down the street. he didnt walk like a negro, he didnt look like a negro. as far as she was concerned he certainly wasnt a negro. — Morley Callaghan, *The Loved and the Lost* (Macmillan, Laurentian 9, p. 213)

**15.3**

# Abbreviations and Numbers

Abbreviations and numbers are useful and appropriate in technical, business, and legal documents, as well as in some specialized instances, such as reference works and scholarly footnotes. In most general writing, however, words and figures are usually written out. This chapter discusses the conventions followed in using abbreviations and numbers in most general writing.

## 16.1 ABBREVIATIONS

*Ab*  Write in full the abbreviation marked or, if an abbreviation is appropriate, change it to the correct form.

Dictionaries list most current abbreviations, either as regular entries or in a separate section, but they don't indicate when these forms should be used. The following sections discuss the kinds of abbreviations that are appropriate in formal and general writing as well as some forms that should not be used. If you are in doubt whether a particular abbreviation is appropriate, you will usually do better to avoid it.

### Abbreviations for Titles, Degrees, and Given Names

The courtesy titles *Dr., Mr., Ms., Mrs.,* and *Messrs.* are always abbreviated when used with proper names, as are *Jr.* and *Sr.: Mrs.* Lester H. Holt, *Mr.* Claude C. Sampson, *Jr.* The convenient *Ms.,* used as a courtesy title equivalent to *Mr.* in addressing a woman without regard for her marital status, must remain an abbreviation, since it was devised as an abbreviation and does not stand for any word. Academic degrees are also generally abbreviated: *M.A., Ph.D., LL.D., M.D., D.D.S.* If a degree or honorary title is added after a name, it is the only title used:

> William Carey, **M.D.,** *or* **Dr.** William Carey [not *Dr.* William Carey, *M.D.*]
>
> James T. Holloway, **Esq.,** *or* **Mr.** James T. Holloway [not *Mr.* James T. Holloway, *Esq.*]

In formal writing, titles like *Reverend, Professor, General, Senator, Admiral* are usually written out in full. In most other styles, they may be abbreviated *if* the first name or initials of the person are used:

| **Standard forms** | **Forms to avoid** |
|---|---|
| The Reverend James T. Shaw | The Rev. Shaw |
| The Reverend Mr. Shaw | Rev. Shaw |
| Rev. J.T. Shaw | The Reverend delivered a sermon. |
| Professor John Moore | Prof. Moore |
| Professor Moore | John Moore is an English Prof. |
| Prof. John R. Moore | |
| General Williams | Gen. Williams |
| Gen. John Williams | The Gen. was given a new command. |

**16.1**

*ab*

Spell out given names (sometimes called Christian names) or use initials. Avoid such abbreviations as *Geo., Thos., Chas., Wm.:*

> George Thompson *or* G.F. Thompson [not *Geo.* F. Thompson]

*Saint* is almost always abbreviated when it is used with a name:

> **St.** Francis, **Ste.** Catherine, **SS.** Peter and Paul, Sault **Ste.** Marie

> (Note: **St.** John's, Nfld., but Saint John, N.B.)

## Abbreviations for Agencies and Organizations

If a government agency or other organization is known primarily by its initials (or by some other shortened name), the writer should generally use the familiar abbreviation rather than the full name:

| CBC | CHR | CNIB | CTV Network |
|---|---|---|---|
| DBS | NDP | OHIP | RCMP |
| UIC | CMHC | IODE | *GPO Style Manual* |

Abbreviations that are pronounced as words (called *acronyms*) have become very common: UNESCO, CUPE, CUSA, NATO, DREE, NORAD.

See page 198 for discussions of the use of capitals and periods in abbreviations.

## Abbreviations for Place Names and Dates

The names of countries, provinces, months, and days are usually written out except in journalistic writing and reference works:

| Canada | Ghent, Belgium | Wednesday, November 3 |
|---|---|---|
| United States | Brandon, Manitoba | Christmas [not *Xmas*] |

Words like *Street, Avenue,* and *Boulevard* should be written out in general writing, not abbreviated as they might be in addressing a letter.

A few unusually long place names are customarily abbreviated even in rather formal writing: the *USSR;* Barbados, *B. W.I.* (for British West Indies); Aklavik, *N. W. T.*

## Abbreviations for Units of Measurement

In consecutive writing, most expressions for time, mass, volume and length are customarily written out:

| | | |
|---|---|---|
| in a second | **rather than** | in a s |
| in a minute | | in a min |
| hour | | h |
| year | | a |
| four grams | | 4 g |
| ten litres | | 10 L |
| twenty hectares | | 20 ha |
| sixty centimeters | | 60 cm |

The metric units are used in directions, recipes, references, and technical writing: 1 kg butter, 60 cm ribbon, 1 L milk and so on. No period is used with these metric units.

## Abbreviations for Scientific and Technical Terms

Some scientific words, trade names, and other expressions are referred to by their abbreviations when they are familiar to readers and would be needlessly long if written out:

DDT (in place of dichloro-diphenyl-trichloro-ethane)
ACTH (in place of adrenocorticotropic hormone)
Rh factor (**Rh**esus factor)
DNA (deoxyribonucleic acid)
FM radio (frequency modulation radio)

If an abbreviation is to be used repeatedly and may not be familiar to every reader, explain it the first time it is introduced:

The International Phonetic Alphabet, known as the IPA, . . . .
*A Dictionary of Canadianisms on Historical Principles (DCHP).* . . .

Measurements expressed in technical terms are abbreviated when they are used with figures:

Tests show the car's highest speeds to be 50 km/h [kilometres per hour] in low gear, 70 km/h in second, and 150 km/h in third.

The turntable can be adjusted to play records at either 78, 45, or 33⅓ **rpm** [revolutions per minute].

Expressions of this kind are written without periods. (Note the oblique stroke in km/h.) They are not abbreviated when used without figures:

The speed of a ship is usually given in knots rather than in **kilometres per hour.**

## Other Standard Abbreviations

There are a few standard abbreviations that are used in all levels of writing:

**16.1**

*Ab*

*a.m., p.m.*   The expressions a.m. (*ante meridiem*, "before noon") and p.m. (*post meridiem*, "after noon") are always abbreviated: 6:00 a.m., 12:24 p.m. Current usage prefers small letters for these abbreviations, but they may be capitalized.

The abbreviations a.m. and p.m. are used only in referring to a specific time:

STANDARD: He had an appointment at 3:00 p.m.
NOT: He had an appointment in the p.m.

The 24-hour clock is coming into general use. The approved form for noon is 12:00 in this system and midnight is 24:00 (or 00:00 the next day): *The sun will set today at 19:27.*

*B.C., A.D.*   These expressions are used to distinguish dates in history in reference to the birth of Christ; they are always abbreviated. B.C. means "before Christ," and follows the date; A.D. stands for *anno Domini*, "in the year of our Lord," and *precedes* the date when it is necessary to use it at all.

836 B.C.     A.D. 76     A.D. 1984 (usually 1984 only)

**Commonly used Latin expressions.** English has absorbed a number of Latin expressions that are conventionally abbreviated. The following are in common use and should not be italicized:

cf.      *confer*—compare (with another source)
e.g.     *exempli gratia*—for example
etc.     *et cetera*—and so forth (never *and etc.*)
i.e.     *id est*—that is

Many writers prefer the English equivalents for these and similar expressions. In student writing, the overworked catchall *etc.* should be avoided. It is best to use *and so forth* (*and so on, and the like*) or rephrase the list, introducing it with *such as* or a similar qualifier. See also 30.8, page 437-438; Abbreviations in footnotes.

**The ampersand.** In student writing the ampersand (&) should not be used as a substitute for *and* unless it appears in an expression or title that you are copying: *Quill & Quire, Clarke Irwin & Company, Limited.*

## Capitals with Abbreviations

Abbreviations are capitalized when the words they stand for are capitalized or when the abbreviation represents a title:

> IODE (Imperial Order Daughters of the Empire)
> CAHA (Canadian Amateur Hockey Association)
> RCR (Royal Canadian Regiment)
> St. Matthew, St. Thomas Aquinas
> 32 degrees C (Celsius)

When an abbreviation stands for words that would not be capitalized if they were written out, no capitals are needed unless the abbreviation begins a sentence.

## Periods with Abbreviations

A period should be put after the abbreviation of a single word and usually between the letters of abbreviations for longer terms:

| | | | |
|------|------|------|-------|
| p. | doz. | P.Q. | c.o.d. |
| ch. | Lt. | B.A. | Ph.D. |
| Nov. | hp. | e.g. | P.S. |

Usage is divided about the punctuation of abbreviated names made of two or more letters written as a unit. Some publications prefer periods (*R.M.C., C.B.C.*), but a growing number are using the solid form (*RMC, CBC*), especially when the abbreviation is generally used instead of the full name. Some dictionaries list optional forms. It doesn't make much difference which form you use as long as you are consistent throughout your paper.

When an abbreviation falls at the end of a sentence, only one period is used: He owned a hundred shares of C.G.E.

## 16.2 NUMBERS

*Num* Follow conventional usage for words or figures for numbers; be consistent in the treatment of numbers.

There are few firm rules about using figures or words for numbers occurring in most writing. In general, books and magazines write out all numbers through one hundred and also larger numbers that can be written in two words (*six thousand, three million*). This style is usually appropriate for college papers and for most other kinds of general and formal writing. Newspapers and magazines generally use figures for all numbers over ten, and some scientific and technical publications use figures exclusively.

**16.1**
*Ab*

> GENERAL AND FORMAL: four, ten, fifteen, ninety-four, 114, 2000, 22 500, thirty thousand, five million [but usage varies]
> INFORMAL: four, ten, 15, 94, 114, 2000, 22 500, 30 000, 5 000 000 (or 5 million)

There are a few special situations (described in the section following) in which figures are always customary. In other cases, use the form that is appropriate not only for your readers but also for your material. In general, write out all simple two-digit numbers and round numbers that can be easily read; use figures for numbers that cannot be written in two words and for series of numbers that are to be compared:

> WORDS APPROPRIATE: He shot three quail and one rabbit.
> FIGURES APPROPRIATE: The next ship unloaded 1500 kilograms of king salmon, 460 kilograms of chinook salmon, and 100 kilograms of crab.
> WORDS APPROPRIATE: Five votes were cast for the class president's proposal, twenty-one against it.
> FIGURES APPROPRIATE: In Ontario we sold 10 547 units; in Alberta, 17 003; in Quebec, 10 750. Our share of the national market was 87.2 per cent.
> WORDS APPROPRIATE: If I had ten dollars for every time I've broken one of my resolutions, I would have at least a thousand dollars by now.
> FIGURES APPROPRIATE: Dresses in the $25–$35 range were selling well, those from $36–$50 fairly well, and those over $50 hardly at all.

Whichever form you use, be consistent. Don't change needlessly from words to figures or from figures to words in the same piece of writing:

> INCONSISTENT: When I was 15, I thought anyone over thirty-five was old.
> CONSISTENT: When I was fifteen, I thought anyone over thirty-five was old.

## Conventional Uses of Figures

Figures are customarily used in all the following situations:

1. Dates are always written in figures except in formal social correspondence, such as wedding invitations. The forms *1st, 2nd, 3rd,* and so on are sometimes used in dates, but only when the year is omitted:

   October 10, 1976    Oct. 10, 1976    October 10    October 10th

2. Hours are written in figures before a.m. or p.m.; they are spelled out before *o'clock:*

   | | | |
   |---|---|---|
   | 7 a.m. | 18:00 hours (metric usage) | twelve noon |
   | 11:35 p.m. | one o'clock | twelve midnight |

3. Mathematical and technical numbers, including percentages:

   | | |
   |---|---|
   | 3.141 59 | longitude 74°02′E. |
   | 99.8 per cent, 99.8% | .410 gauge shotgun |

Except in dates and street numbers, a space is used to separate thousands, millions, and so on, although it may be omitted in four-digit figures:

   1365 (or 1 365) years    8 393 624    17 016

4. Page numbers and similar references:

   | | |
   |---|---|
   | pp. 183–86 | page 12 |
   | chapter iv | Genesis 39:12 |
   | Ch. 19 | Act III, scene iv, line 28 (III, iv, 28) |

5. Sums of money, except sums in round numbers or, in formal style, sums that can be written in two or three words:

   | **Figures** | **Words** |
   |---|---|
   | a bargain at $4.98 | two thousand a year |
   | The British pound was once worth $4.85. | a dollar a litre |

6. Street numbers (with no spaces between thousands):

> 2027 Fairview North     Apartment 3C, 1788 Grand North

7. Statistics and series of more than two numbers, especially when the numbers are to be compared:

> The survey showed that the class contained 24 Liberals, 18 Conservatives, and 12 New Democrats.

**Plurals of figures.** The plural of a figure is written either with 's or s:

> Six nines: six **9's**, six **9s**     By tens: by **10's**, by **10s**

**16.2**

*Num*

**Numbers at the beginning of sentences.** These numbers are written out unless they are dates:

> Two to 3% of loading and up to 10% is common and 20 to 30% in specially surfaced papers. . . .—"Paper Manufacture," *Encyclopaedia Britannica*

> 1960 was a year of devastating drought in China.

## Arabic and Roman Numerals

Arabic numerals (1, 2, 17, 96) are used in almost all cases where numbers are expressed in figures. Roman numerals, either lower case or capitals (i, ii, cxlvi; I, II, CXLVI), are occasionally used to number outlines, chapters, acts of a play, or formal inscriptions. Lower-case roman numerals are used to number the front matter of a book, pagination in Arabic numerals beginning with the body of the book.

In Roman numerals a small number preceding a larger is to be subtracted from the larger (ix = 9, xc = 90). The following table shows the common Roman numerals (lower-case):

| 1 | i | 10 | x | 50 | l | 200 | cc |
|---|---|---|---|---|---|---|---|
| 2 | ii | 11 | xi | 60 | lx | 400 | cd |
| 3 | iii | 15 | xv | 70 | lxx | 500 | d |
| 4 | iv | 19 | xix | 80 | lxxx | 600 | dc |
| 5 | v | 20 | xx | 90 | xc | 900 | cm |
| 6 | vi | 21 | xxi | 99 | xcix | 1000 | m |
| 7 | vii | 30 | xxx | 100 | c | 1500 | md |
| 8 | viii | 40 | xl | 110 | cx | 1066 | mlxvi |
| 9 | ix | 49 | xlix | 199 | cxcix | 1979 | mcmlxxix |

## Cardinal and Ordinal Numbers

Figures indicating number only are *cardinal numbers:* 1, 2, 3, 72, 135. The numbers indicating order (*first, second, seventeenth*) are *ordinal numbers.* Except in routine enumeration, ordinals should be spelled out rather than abbreviated to *1st, 2nd, 17th.*

Since the ordinals can be either adjectives or adverbs, the forms ending in *-ly* (*firstly*) are unnecessary and are now rarely used.

▶ **EXERCISE**

Read the following sentences carefully, keeping in mind the principles stated in the preceding section. Rewrite faulty sentences, making whatever changes are necessary. Since there are cases where there's a choice in usage, remember that one of the principles of using numbers and abbreviations is to be consistent:

1. When we arrived at the theatre on Yonge St., we found that the evening's performance would start an hr. late.
2. The University recently added 2 new members to its faculty—Jos. Blumenthal, MA, and Mary Persons, Doctor of Philosophy.
3. Six members of the RCMP conferred recently with Canada's U.N. Representative at his office in N.Y.
4. Fifty-five to 60% of U. of T. students approved the 02:00 curfew; about 30% were violently opposed.
5. His monument to St. Francis, a remarkable piece of sculpture, weighed over 2500 lbs. and rivalled his monument to Saint Peter.
6. P. 237 of the manual lists the home addresses of Members of Parliament & p. 298 lists their Ottawa addresses.
7. On Dec. 23 CBC will dramatize the most celebrated Xmas story of recent times—"The Christmas Carol" by Chas. Dickens.
8. Dr. Roscoe Caries, D. D. S., reported that in an experiment involving two thousand and forty-four children, tooth decay was not significantly reduced.
9. Lee had 4 sisters (ranging in age from sixteen to 31 yrs.) and a widowed mother.
10. After 10 months the RCMP finally tracked Groark to Fergus, Ont. where they found him suffering from d.t.'s in the barn of the Rev. John Gantry.

# Spelling

*This recommendation of steadiness and uniformity* [in spelling] *does not proceed from an opinion that particular combinations of letters have much influence on human happiness; or that truth may not be successfully taught by modes of spelling fanciful and erroneous. . . . Language is only the instrument of science, and words are but the signs of ideas; I wish, however, that the instrument might be less apt to decay, and that signs might be permanent.* — Samuel Johnson

 Correct the spelling of the marked word.

**16.2**

*Num*

For college and university writing, and for much other writing, this text recommends edited English, as typical in Canada. One purpose of editing is to make the use of language consistent, so that, for example, if a writer uses the word *co-exist* seven times in an essay, it will always be spelled in the same way. Another purpose of editing is, if it does not interfere with some purpose of the writer, to eliminate errors and unconventional usages. One feature of language that often requires careful editing is spelling.

Sometimes people talk about spelling as if it were some monstrous and unnatural act. It isn't that, but it isn't always easy. Some people spell well; others do not. Accurate spelling doesn't appear to have any direct connection with good writing. But good edited writing is characterized by accurate spelling. Out of regard for yourself and for your reader, you should make certain that whatever you write is as free from error as possible. You want your reader to see the same word that you intended to write, and your reader is entitled to expect that you will follow the conventions of spelling. Misspelled words seldom interfere with meaning, but they may distract the reader from what you are trying to say, or, worse, lead him or her to assume that if you don't care about your spelling, you don't care about what you are saying.

## 17.1 OVERCOMING SPELLING PROBLEMS

English spelling would be easier if each sound used in speaking were represented by a single letter or even by a combination of letters. But the way a word is pronounced and the way it is spelled do not always match. The same letter or combination of letters may represent a variety of sounds, as does the *a* in *fare, hat, many, lay, far, war, human,* or the *ou* in *though, bough, enough, through.* And one sound may be represented in a variety of ways: b*ee*, bel*ie*ve, prec*e*de, s*ea*, mach*i*ne. As a further complication, a number of English words are written with silent letters: lam*b*, *p*sychology, *k*nife, r*h*ythm, *w*rote. Others, called *homonyms*, sound alike but are spelled differently: *meat, meet, mete; sight, site, cite; write, right, rite; peace, piece.*

Obviously, absolute correctness in spelling is not easy to achieve in English. Most mistakes can be avoided, however, if you are willing to take the time and effort necessary

1. to learn the spelling of difficult words,
2. to use the dictionary when you are in doubt, and
3. to proofread what you have written.

## Eliminating Careless Mistakes

Carelessness undoubtedly accounts for the majority of misspelled words in student papers. It may result from too rapid writing (as in papers written in class) or from failure to proofread the finished copy carefully. Typical examples of careless misspelling are *their* for *there, to* for *too, who's* for *whose, it's* for *its, fourty* for *forty*—basic words that you learned before entering high school. Most people make careless mistakes when writing rapidly, but conscientious writers eliminate them by proofreading.

Accurate proofreading requires careful word-by-word reading. If you have difficulty checking your own writing, try following each line with a pencil point, so that you have to look at every word separately. Some people find it helpful to read their papers aloud, pronouncing each word distinctly. Any method is useful if it makes easier the obligation to be accurate as to what has actually been put down on paper.

## Using a Dictionary

If you are uncertain about the spelling of a word, consult your dictionary. The trial-and-error method of writing a word several ways until it "looks right" (*curiousity? couriousity? curosity?*) is unreliable.

For papers written outside class, it is probably best to check spelling in *revision*. If you stop to look up the spelling of every doubtful word while you are writing a first draft, you may lose the flow of thought or interrupt the sentence movement. Put a check in the margin or over the word as you are writing; then when you are ready to revise, look up each word you have marked.

## Learning to Visualize Words

People who do a good deal of reading tend to be better spellers than those who read little, for seeing a word on the printed page tends to fix it in the mind. Sometimes, however, we learn to recognize a word in reading without noticing how it is spelled. Very few Canadians, for example, ever learned to spell the last name of Nikita Khrushchev, the former Soviet premier, though they saw it in their newspapers every day for years. Many people have a similar problem with such common English words as *occasion, occurrence,* and *precede.* When you meet a new word—or when you have to look up a familiar word—look at it carefully, noticing each syllable, and try to fix it in your mind for future use.

**17.1**

*Sp*

## Writing Practice

If you are willing to take the time, you can often get the spelling of troublesome words straight in your mind by writing them until you spell them right without hesitation. It sounds like a tedious process, but probably worth the time if it enables you to become comfortable with words so that you can use them. If you are uncertain about the spelling of *embarrass,* for example, write or type the word ten, twenty, or more times, in its various forms, until the spelling becomes automatic: *embarrass, embarrassed, embarrassment, embarrassing.*

Separate into syllables words that you find difficult to spell (consult your dictionary for the proper divisions). Stress those letters or combinations of letters that trouble you:

| | |
|---|---|
| em baR Rass | par aL Lel |
| oC Ca sion al ly | preJ U dice |
| o MiT Ted | rep E ti tion |
| op tI mist | sep A rate |

It helps to say the word as you write it, either aloud or to yourself. The combination of (1) seeing a word letter by letter, (2) writing it carefully, and (3) pronouncing it will overcome most spelling problems.

## Learning New Words

Learn to spell new words as you meet them, especially in your courses. A new or unfamiliar expression is of little use in writing until you can spell it with confidence. Make a note of the words you may have to use in essays, reports, or examinations. Underline key words in textbooks and observe their spelling on the blackboard. Then write them out in syllables, pronouncing them as you do so:

| | |
|---|---|
| ba cil lus | Gen ghis Khan |
| bi par tite | me tath e sis |
| car bon if er ous | pro pri e tar y |
| de men tia prae cox | u ni cel lu lar |

When instructors in various courses complain that their students can't spell, they are usually referring either to very common words or to words that make up the essential vocabulary of their subject.

## Keeping a Spelling List

You can help yourself in proofreading if you will keep a list of words you have misspelled or that you have trouble spelling. The words should be spelled correctly and should be easy to find so that you can refer to them when proofreading your papers. The purpose of such a list is to prevent the same mistakes from occurring in one paper after another. When the same word occurs more than once in your list, mark it in some way that will call it to your attention.

## 17.2 COMMON SPELLING ERRORS

The following list contains one hundred words frequently misspelled in student papers. Each word is divided into syllables so that you can see more clearly how it is put together.

| | | |
|---|---|---|
| ac com mo date | ap pear ance | bus i ness |
| ac quaint ed | ar ti cle | change a ble |
| a cross | ath let ics | choose |
| a gree ment | at tend ance | com par a tive |
| all right (two words) | be lieve | con ceive |
| al read y | ben e fit ed | con science |
| a nal y sis | Brit ain | con tin u ous |

de ci sion
def i nite
de **gen** er ate
de scrip tion
de vel op
din ing room
dis ap pear ance
dis ap point
dor mi to ry
em bar rass
en vi ron ment
e quip ment
ex ag ger ate
ex ist ence
ex treme ly
fa mil iar
fas ci nate
for eign
for mer ly
for ty
gram mar
height
hin drance
im ag i nar y
im me di ate ly
in ci den tal ly
in de pend ent

in tel li gent
ir re sist i ble
judg ment [*or* judge ment]
knowl edge
lei sure
li brar y
lik a ble
main te nance
man u fac tur er
mis spelled
mo not o nous
mys te ri ous
nec es sar y
no tice a ble
oc ca sion al ly
oc cur rence
o mit ted
op por tu ni ty
par tic u lar ly
pas time
per form
pre ced ing
prej u dice
priv i lege
prob a bly
pro ce dure

pro nun ci a tion
pro por tion
psy chol o gy
quan ti ty
re ceive
re fer ring
rep e ti tion
re sem blance
sched ule
sec re tar y
seize
sep a rate
sim i lar
soph o more
suc ceed
sym pa thize
tem per a ment
tend en cy
there fore
trag e dy
tru ly
un doubt ed ly
un til
u su al ly
val u a ble
writ ing

**17.2**

You may find this list useful in testing your spelling ability and in checking and correcting errors in your papers. A spelling list of your own, however, will be more profitable to study than lists made by others, because it will help you to concentrate on your individual problems.

## Errors Caused by Faulty Pronunciation

Although faulty pronunciation is not a major cause of misspelling, it is responsible for some very common mistakes:

| Correct spelling | Misspelling |
|---|---|
| **a**th **let** ics | ath**a**letics |
| priv **i** lege | priv**l**ege |
| en vi **ron** ment | enviro**m**ent |
| mis chie **vous** | mischie**vi**ous |
| **pre** scribe | **per**scribe |
| dis **g**ust | dis**c**ust |
| re **mu ne**r a tion | re**num**eration |

Pronounce each syllable to yourself when writing longer words (*ac-com-pa-ny-ing, par-tic-u-lar-ly, stud-y-ing*). Also notice that many longer words contain letters that are neutralized or lost in speech: tem-per-*a*-men-tal, ac-ci-den-*tal*-ly, lab-*o*-ra-to-ry.

## Omission of Final -ed

One of the most common spelling errors is the omission of *-ed* at the ends of words. This sometimes occurs because of analogy to speech, where the *-ed* sound often is lost in rapid conversation by assimilation to the following sound. To catch such errors in writing, you will have to rely on your eye rather than your ear. There are three principal trouble areas:

**In verb forms.** Regular verbs form their past tenses and past participles by adding *-ed*. Be careful not to drop these letters, especially before words beginning with *t*, like *to*. *Used to* and *supposed to* are commonly misspelled:

> I **used to** [not *use to*] misspell words.
> He is **supposed to** be [not *suppose to* be] an authority.

**In verbal modifiers.** The past participle is often used as a modifier (*stewed prunes, raised platform*). Here too the tendency in pronunciation is to drop the *-ed,* and many such shortened forms have become established: *grade school, oilcloth, cream cheese, roast chicken.* Others are sometimes found in print but are debatable: *bottle beer, whip cream, advance headquarters.* In college and university papers, use only shortened forms that are generally accepted. In less formal writing, more latitude is allowed, but dictionaries, current written practice, and appropriateness to the paper should serve as guides.

**In modifiers from nouns.** Adjectives are often formed by adding *-ed* to nouns: *long-haired, heart-shaped, two-faced.* When the *-ed* is dropped in such forms—a growing tendency in current English—the result is a noun modifier (see 6.4): *king-size bed, hard-surface road, high-heel shoes.* Established forms like these are appropriate in all writing. It's usually better, however, to keep the *-ed* (as in *advanced courses, middle-aged, old-fashioned*) unless you have seen the form without the *-ed* in edited English.

## Confusion of Words That Sound Alike

Be careful not to confuse words of identical or similar sound. It is easy when writing rapidly to put down *their* for *there, its* for *it's, maybe* for *may be*, but conscientious writers will check their finished work closely for errors of this sort. Substituting one form for another may suggest an idea that the writer did not intend:

> Psychiatric treatment changed Bobby from a withdrawn, unhappy child to a normal, happy boy **excepted** by his group.

The following pairs of words are often confused in writing. See if you can distinguish between them.

**17.2**

| | | |
|---|---|---|
| accept–except | conscience–conscious | personal–personnel |
| advice–advise | coarse–course | principal–principle |
| affect–effect | credible–creditable | quiet–quite |
| aisle–isle | desert–dessert | stationary–stationery |
| allusion–illusion | its–it's | than–then |
| birth–berth | lead–led | their–there |
| capital–capitol | loose–lose | to–too |
| choose–chose | passed–past | weather–whether |
| cite–site | peace–piece | who's–whose |

▶ **EXERCISE**

Make up sentences that will illustrate clearly the differences in meaning in the paired words above.

*Examples:* Everyone *except* Sam *accepted* the invitation.
*It's* difficult for the leopard to change *its* spots.
The ceremonies will be held *whether* or not the *weather* is fair.

## Separate Words and Combined Forms

Observe the distinctions between expressions that are written as one word and those written as two. These forms frequently need to be checked in revision:

> **all ready** [adjective phrase]: The girls were at last **all ready** to leave.
> **already** [adverb of time]: It was **already** dark when they arrived.

> **all right** [adjective phrase, conventionally written as two words]: The seats seemed **all right** to me. (The forms *alright* and *alrite* are not accepted in edited usage.)

> **all together** [adjective phrase]: We were **all together** at the depot.
> **altogether** [adverb, meaning wholly]: That's **altogether** another matter.
>
> **a while** [noun]: They talked for **a while.**
> **awhile** [adverb]: Can't you stay **awhile** longer?
>
> **may be** [verb phrase]: He **may be** the next mayor.
> **maybe** [adverb, short for *it may be*]: **Maybe** you'll have better luck next time.

Certain phrases may be mistakenly written as one word through analogy with other forms or because they are often run together in speech:

> The assignment was **a lot** more difficult than I expected. [not *alot*]
>
> The judge **threw out** his testimony. [not *throughout*]
>
> The puppy was always there at his owner's **beck and call.** [not *beckon call*]

## 17.3 SPELLING TROUBLESOME PLURALS

### Nouns Ending in -y, -o, or -f

Nouns ending in -*y* following a vowel form the plural regularly by adding -*s* (*toys, bays, joys, monkeys*). But nouns ending in -*y* preceded by a consonant change *y* to *i* and add -*es:*

| | | |
|---|---|---|
| apology, apologies | curiosity, curiosities | library, libraries |
| company, companies | ferry, ferries | study, studies |

*Exception:* In forming the plural of proper names, the -*y* is retained and -*s* added: all the *Kellys,* both *Marys.*

Nouns ending in -*o* preceded by a vowel form the plural by adding -*s* (*folios, studios, tattoos*). If the final -*o* is preceded by a consonant, the plural is usually formed by adding -*es,* but a few nouns add -*s* only:

| | | | | |
|---|---|---|---|---|
| echoes | potatoes | | pianos | sopranos |
| heroes | tomatoes | But: | solos | tobaccos |
| cohoes | vetoes | | banjos | Eskimos |

A few nouns ending in -*o* add either -*s* or -*es* to form the plural: *cargos, cargoes; hobos, hoboes; zeros, zeroes.* Because no rule can be given for adding -*s* or -*es,* a writer must either memorize the plurals or consult a dictionary.

Nouns ending in -*f* or -*fe* often form the plural regularly (*be-*

*liefs, chiefs, fifes, roofs*). But some common words ending in *-f* form their plurals by changing *-f* to *-ves:*

| | | |
|---|---|---|
| calf, cal**ves** | knife, kni**ves** | self, sel**ves** |
| half, hal**ves** | leaf, lea**ves** | thief, thie**ves** |

The plural of a few nouns ending in *-f* may be either *-s* or *-ves: elfs, elves; hoofs, hooves; scarfs, scarves; wharfs, wharves.*

## Group Words and Compound Nouns

Most compound words and group words form their plurals by adding *-s* to the last word of the group, whether the expression is written as one word or two:

| **Singular** | **Plural** |
|---|---|
| baby-sitter | baby-sitters |
| cross-examination | cross-examinations |
| major-general | major-generals |

**17.3**

But when the significant word is the first term (as it often is in hyphened compounds), that word is the one made plural:

| | |
|---|---|
| daughters-in-law | passers-by |
| men-of-war | courts-martial |

The plural of nouns ending in *-ful* is made by adding *-s* to the last part of the word: two *cupfuls,* three *tablespoonfuls.*

## 17.4 SOME PRINCIPLES OF SPELLING

Chaotic as spelling is in English, some principles are helpful for spelling common words. Listed below are guides to spelling that you have probably heard before. If you *know* that you know them, you might better spend your time on some other aspect of writing. But if you aren't quite certain about these general principles, review them and perhaps consult the spelling section in the front pages of a dictionary for detailed information.

### Final *-e*

Words ending in silent *-e* generally retain the *-e* before additions (called *suffixes*) beginning with a consonant (*-ment, -ly, -some, -ness*), but drop the *-e* before additions beginning with a vowel (*-ing, -able, -ous, -ary*).

### -e retained before a consonant:

| | |
|---|---|
| arrange–arrangement | nine–ninety |
| awe–awesome | require–requirement |
| definite–definitely | shape–shapeless |
| hope–hopeless | spite–spiteful |

**Exceptions:**

argument    awful    **duly**    ninth    **truly**

### -e dropped before another vowel:

| | |
|---|---|
| argue–arguing | imagine–imaginary |
| arrive–arrival | shape–shaping |
| conceive–conceivable | value–valuable |
| grieve–grievous | write–writing |

*Exceptions:* In a few words, -e is kept before a vowel to avoid confusion with other forms or to indicate pronunciation:

| | | |
|---|---|---|
| dye | dyeing | (compare *dying*) |
| singe | singeing | (compare *singing*) |

Words ending in -ce or -ge retain the final -e before additions beginning with *a, o,* or *ou* (so that the final -c or -g will not suggest the "hard" sound):

| | | |
|---|---|---|
| changeable | noticeable | unmanageable |
| courageous | outrageous | vengeance |

## -ie- and -ei-

The familiar jingle learned by most schoolchildren is helpful in spelling -ie- and -ei- words: "Write *i* before *e* except after *c,* or when sounded as $\bar{a}$ as in *neighbor* and *weigh.*"

**Words with -ie-.** Words with -ie- are more common than words with -ei-. The typical sound of -ie- is $\bar{e}$:

| | | | |
|---|---|---|---|
| achieve | chief | grievous | niece |
| believe | field | hygiene | siege |

Other -ie- words are *mischief, sieve,* and *view.*

**Words with -ei-.** After *c,* and also to spell the sound $\bar{a}$, -ei- is generally used:

| | | | |
|---|---|---|---|
| ceiling | perceive | eight | reign |
| conceive | receipt | freight | vein |
| deceive | receive | neighbor | weigh |

The long $\bar{e}$ sound is spelled *-ei-* (rather than *-ie-*) in a few words: *either, leisure, neither, seize, weird.* Other sounds spelled *-ei-*: *counterfeit, foreign, height, heir.*

## Doubling the Final Consonant

Double the final consonant before a suffix beginning with a vowel (*-able, -ed, -er, -ing*) with (1) words of one syllable ending in a single consonant after a single vowel (*brag, hit, sit*) and (2) with words of more than one syllable, ending the same way and accented on the last syllable (*commit, forget, prefer, occur*).

**17.4**

| One-syllable words | | | Words of more than one syllable | | |
|---|---|---|---|---|---|
| bat | batter | batting | commit | committed | committing |
| grip | gripping | gripped | control | controllable | controlled |
| pin | pinned | pinning | occur | occurrence | occurred |
| spot | spotty | spotted | omit | omitted | omitting |
| wet | wetter | wettest | prefer | preferred | preferring |

The consonant is *not* doubled (1) in words with two vowels before the final consonant (*daub, daubing; keep, keeper; spoil, spoiled*), or (2) in words ending with two consonants (*help, helped; peck, pecking; lurk, lurked*), or (3) when the accent of the lengthened word shifts to an earlier syllable (*infer', in'ference; prefer', pref'erable; refer', ref'erence*).

Usage is divided about doubling the final consonant of some words not accented on the last syllable, but Canadians generally prefer the forms having doubled consonants:

| | |
|---|---|
| bias–biassed | quarrel–quarrelling |
| counsel–counselled, counsellor | travel–traveller, travelled |
| diagram–diagrammed | worship–worshipped, worshipping |
| kidnap–kidnapping, kidnapper | |

## Final *-y*

A final *-y* preceded by a consonant regularly changes to *i* before all suffixes except those beginning with *i*:

| | |
|---|---|
| body–bodies | happy–happiness |
| busy–business | lonely–loneliness |
| carry–carried, carrying | marry–marriage, marrying |
| duty–dutiful | mercy–merciful |
| easy–easily | study–studious, studying |
| envy–envious | Tory–Tories |

Final -*y* preceded by a vowel remains unchanged when a suffix is added:

| | |
|---|---|
| boy–boys, boyish | enjoy–enjoyable, enjoyment, enjoying |
| delay–delayed, delayer | play–playful, playing, played |

See also 17.3, Spelling Troublesome Plurals

## -cede, -ceed, -sede

Only one word ends in -*sede: supersede.* Only three end in -*ceed: exceed, proceed, succeed.* All other words of this sort end in -*cede: precede, recede, intercede, secede,* and so on.

## -able, -ible, -ance, -ence

Words with these endings should be carefully checked for correct spelling. Those ending in -*able* (such as *advisable, desirable, improbable, suitable*) are much more common than those ending in -*ible* (such as *audible, divisible, horrible, visible*). But since no English rules govern the spelling of these endings, and each has a similar neutral vowel in pronunciation, the individual words should be looked up in a dictionary whenever there is doubt. The same is true for words ending in -*ance, -ant, -ence,* and -*ent* (such as attend *ance,* confid *ence;* defend *ant,* exist *ent*).

## 17.5 VARIANT SPELLINGS

For a number of historical reasons, many English words have two spellings in current use, for instance, *whiskey, whisky; storey, story* (of a building); *extol, extoll; skilful, skillful.* A good dictionary indicates which is the more usual by placing that form first (as *expellant* or *expellent*). Secondary spellings that are archaic or rare will be given at the end of the entry, as will variants having much less currency than the form or forms given as entry-words.

A student should make a habit of using the word given first (as *judgment* rather than *judgement*), but he must remember that the editors are presenting as preferable the form used in the speech community the dictionary is intended for, as the United Kingdom (British usage), the United States (American usage), or Canada (Canadian usage).

As explained briefly in the prefatory Article entitled "Canadian English" (p. xvii), Canadians have special spelling dilemmas as a result of being exposed to two strongly influential patterns of spelling, British and American. As a result, Canadian usage in spelling certain words and classes of words is divided. Nevertheless, an overall norm has been established for many of these matters so that Canadians as a group have their own preferences in spelling. In some words, they use spellings similar to the British pattern in others to the American pattern.

This Canadian way of spelling, largely followed in printed matter, slavishly follows neither the British nor the American way. This being the case, Canadian dictionaries are much more reliable than any others for Canadian writers of English. Unfortunately, there are very few such dictionaries so that Canadians often buy dictionaries not specifically intended to reflect usage in Canada. Convenience, cost, and tradition all play a part in the current state of affairs.

**17.5**

The best guide to appropriate spelling is, then, a Canadian dictionary. If another must be used, then the student should know what he is using and make allowances for the intent of those who compiled the dictionary he is using for reference. In most situations, either of two possible current spellings may be used; the important point is to remain consistent in using the chosen form throughout any one piece of writing. Thus one may choose *honor* or *honour, centre* or *center, plough* or *plow* as long as he spells those words (and any others in the same class) in a consistent way; thus if he chooses to spell *honor* with *-or,* he should also spell *labor, color,* and so on in the same way.

Certain words are not at all commonly used in Canadian writing; these should be avoided, as *ax, adz, catalog, check* (for *cheque*), *connexion, gaol,* and many more. On the other hand, *draft* or *draught, mold* or *mould, medieval* or *mediaeval, program* or *programme, plow* or *plough,* and so on are widely met with in Canada, where certain spellings are preferred because of their associations; *defence* (not *defense*) is the traditional spelling in government circles, as in the *Department of National Defence.* And *Inuit* (not *Innuit*) is gradually displacing *Eskimo* in official circles. Finally, many French words having accents in the spelled form ( *Québec, Montréal, Parti Québécois*) are nowadays accepted when used in English contexts.

Simplified spellings such as *thru* for *through, enuf* for *enough, thoro* for *thorough, nite* for *night,* and so on are not acceptable in edited English anywhere.

For the spelling of proper names (the British *Labour* Party; the Center for Applied Linguistics) and for direct quotation (Prime Minister Winston Churchill described it as "a *humourless* situation"; President Carter said he would "give the bill the *ax*"), the spelling of the original should be used; but in normal circumstances, Canadian forms should be used.

▶ **EXERCISES**

1. This exercise should help to fix some of the general principles of spelling in your mind. Copy the words in each of the following groups, making the additions or changes indicated:

   a. Supply *-ei-* or *-ie-* as required for correct spelling:

   | all- -d | counterf- -t | fr- -ght | n- -ther | th- -r |
   | bel- -ve | for- -gn | l- -sure | s- -ze | w- -rd |

   b. Add *-ed* to the following verbs to show whether the final consonant is doubled or not. If there is a choice of forms, indicate both of them:

   | bargain | clot | drop | quarrel | travel |
   | bias | ship | differ | refer | occur |

   c. Add *-ing* to each of these words, making any necessary changes in the root form of the word:

   | become | control | endure | hurry | use |
   | centre | dine | hope | prove | write |

   d. Change each of these words to an adjective ending *-ous:*

   | continue | courtesy | glory | mischief | sanctimony |
   | courage | dispute | grieve | outrage | |

   e. Add *-able* or *-ible* to the following words, changing letters wherever necessary to conform with accepted spellings:

   | accept | contempt | enforce | repair | train |
   | advise | digest | justify | sense | |

   f. Add *-ance, -ant* or *-ence, -ent* to these words, making any other necessary changes:

   | ascend | confide | depend | maintain | vigil |
   | compete | defend | exist | resist | |

2. Copy the following paragraph, correcting the misspelled words. Feel free to consult a dictionary. You may first wish to see how many mistakes you can find and correct without a dictionary.

The principal that every great man is a national tradgedy is easily defensable. It is difficult to co⋯ ⋅ that strong, independant men will not irresistably impose upon tneir countrymen their own exagerated eccentricities and prejadices. Napoleon, for example, beleived that he had a definate destiny to succede, a "star" guiding him personaly and France to great heighths. He did not dream of any hinderance from the other nations of Europe. His plans were to seperate them one by one and to seize all power and priveledge. Only Britian refused to acommodate itself to his grandiose schemes.

# PART TWO

## Practices in Composition

# Discovering What You Have to Say

*If I put down something, that thing will help the next thing come, and I'm off. If I let the process go on, things will occur to me that were not at all in my mind when I started. These things, odd or trivial as they may be, are somehow connected. And if I let them string out, surprising things will happen. — William Stafford, "A Way of Writing"*

All of us have things to say, although often we don't know it. What we have to say is not always at the front of our minds, fresh, compelling, ready to be said. More often than not we have to discover what it is, learn about it, and watch it take first one shape, then another. This means exploring the world we're in, testing our personal resources, weighing our judgments and our whimsy, and evaluating our information.

From the start, whether you are in a composition course or doing some work that requires writing, you can expect to spend more time in thinking and hunting than you do in writing a complete draft of your paper. Of course, there is no *requirement* that you do some thinking and hunting. It is possible to write without doing much exploratory thinking, but what comes out will usually be a pale reflection of the thinking someone else has done.

"Bad writing" is often bad because it is anonymous writing; it has no character. It is a gathering and reporting of conventional thoughts and conventional phrasings that do not *reveal* the writer; anyone might have written the same thing. Good writing begins only when you have learned to trust yourself as a source of information, pleasure, and insight for others by accepting the responsibility of knowing yourself and learning to say what it is that uniquely connects you with a subject. Good writing begins when you undertake to think over your experiences, learning all that they signify, and expressing yourself in words that you have made your own. Good writing begins only when you make what you write *yours*.

## 18.1 FINDING AND EXPLORING WHAT YOU HAVE TO SAY

Some years ago, C. Day Lewis commented on his own writing: "I do not sit down at my desk to put into verse something that is already clear in my mind. If it were clear in my mind, I should have no incentive or need to write about it, for I am an explorer, not a journalist, a propagandist, or a statistician.'' Later in the same passage, he went on to say that ''often I have gone some way with the poem before I am able to grasp the theme which lies hidden in the material that has accumulated.'' He is talking about writing poetry, to be sure, but what he says gives a clue to most other forms of writing as well. There's no reason to expect that you already know everything you will say when you sit down to write. You'll have to search for it. And when you find it, it may be a chameleon: it may change color while you look at it.

Ancient rhetoricians called this process of searching *invention,* and it's a good word to use. It comes from a Latin verb, *invenire.* Meanings given to this verb include

1. to come upon, or find;
2. to fabricate mentally, to create or devise in the mind.

Both actions are important in the time before you write. *Invention* is a name for the processes by which you come upon, or *meet,* your own experiences, the things you know, and the things other people know; and you *make* something out of them in your mind by discovering how they mean something to you and how they can be fitted together to delight and inform others.

**18.1**

*Plan*

## Examining a Situation for Possible Subjects

Often, of course, the situation you are in will determine what subjects you will write about. If you are in business, you must answer your correspondence. If you are in a laboratory, you must report your findings. If you are in a history class that requires three book-reports on specified books, you must turn in the papers. Topics for writing may develop out of discussions in your composition class. Your composition teacher may assign a specific topic for you to write about. But even if you are given a specific topic to write about, your thinking hasn't been done for you.

The problem is that having a topic doesn't always make it possible for you to write, or give you a reason for writing. If you are assigned a topic such as "My Last Summer Job" or if you choose for yourself a topic such as "A Freshman Views the Energy Crisis," you still have to determine what you have to say and why it is worthwhile to say it. You have to learn what the subject calls for from you and what kinds of resources are available for treating the subject. You have to think about how the material can be most usefully presented to a particular audience, and about how you can be yourself, do justice to a subject, and meet an audience honestly. So, even if the topic is given, your thinking has not been done for you.

And if you're left free to choose for yourself what you will write about, a lot of thinking and searching is plainly still before you. Sometimes, given the freedom to choose their own topics, writers accept whatever ideas first come to mind, or use materials already available to them without thinking them through. Consider this essay, written in a freshman composition-class:

### My Theatre Experience

I worked at a theatre before coming to university. When my parents started managing the drive-in, they drafted me to do the odd jobs there.

While working in the cafeteria, box-office, and the projection booth, I met many new people. I found that people come to a movie for different reasons. One man said that he came to get away from his wife and kids. Many boys and girls came to have dates. A few people, however, actually came to watch the movie.

At the drive-in, I felt different emotions because of the actions of my customers. One lady aroused my indignation when she claimed that her son, who was six feet in height, was under twelve years of age. A boy eleven years old does not have to pay admission; therefore her son was admitted free. I was amused when one boy tried to hide in the back floor of a car, under a quilt, while the driver drove into the theatre. I am aware of such tricks, and the boy was caught. One girl caught her slacks on the barbed wire while climbing over the fence at the back of the theatre. I helped her off the fence, and I sold her a ticket. She never came over the fence again.

I experienced new and enlightening experiences at the theatre. At the drive-in, I found that real people are often more entertaining than people in the movies.

It's easy enough to see why a writer would decide to use this topic. Not everyone works in a drive-in theatre; in fact, few do. Drive-in theatres have been the butt of many jokes, the occasion for many stories about cultural patterns and practices among the young. A writer can safely assume that writing about work in a drive-in theatre from first-hand experience is a subject not too many other writers are going to use. But even if a topic seems obvious and ready-made, it still deserves some searching and investigating.

The author of this essay has made a start. He knows where his subject is, and he has put some things on paper. But he doesn't appear to have looked at his experiences very closely, nor has he shown the drive-in experience as it belongs uniquely to him. We're left wondering about what's *really* different about working in a drive-in, about who the "new people" are, about just exactly what makes people more entertaining than movies, about that girl hanging on the fence. We don't know what all of these things signify to the author: we don't know exactly how he sees them, or how they've entered his life. The essay needs more time spent in remembering episodes and practices and reflecting on what they mean.

When a subject is given to you, you still have exploratory work to do. If you are free to choose your own subject and if you choose one that seems to be obvious, you still have exploratory work to do. Likely to be still more troublesome are those occasions when you are free to write on your own subjects, and none at all comes into your mind.

When that happens, you have the whole world before you, and that's sometimes the same as having nothing at all before you. There are so many possibilities that it's almost like having no possibilities at all. You're called upon, in this situation, to understand and write about your own private and unique view of some part of the world, and to combine multiple and varied impressions into a personal interpretation. What do you do? How do you get started?

**18.1**

*Plan*

## Collecting Your Impressions

**Keeping a journal.**    One thing you can do that may help you with your writing requires daily attention over a long period of time. Some composition teachers may require you to *keep a daily journal;* if your teacher does not, you might try on your own. What we're suggesting is that you commit yourself to making daily entries in some kind of journal. The entries may be words, phrases, sentences, paragraphs, essays, poems, bits and pieces. The point is to record in some way things that matter to you or puzzle you or cause you to wonder. Put down what you see and learn and feel and know. A journal can get you in the habit of expressing yourself on paper.

To make a journal work as it should, you need to make daily entries: saving up for a week and writing a group of entries won't give you an account of what you were conscious of on *different* days. Don't be hesitant in making journal entries, and don't imagine that every entry should be something important. If a song you hear on the radio moves you, write about the song and try to say why and how it moved you. If something goes sour in one of your classes, try to figure out what it is by recalling what different people said and did.

**Making abstractions concrete.**    A second thing you can do requires some practice, and could be a part of your journal. Try writing concrete phrases and sentences that locate and embody the abstract ideas and impressions that come to you. The purpose in doing this is for you to get in the habit of putting your ideas and impressions into quite specific settings or quite specific terms, as in the following examples:

> EASE AND RELAXATION: an unhurried visit to the National Art Gallery in Ottawa.
>
> FEAR: the whirring of a bat when you can't see it; the taste of brass in your mouth after an out-of-control car just misses you.
>
> COMFORT: some good, fresh pipe-tobacco and some exciting books on a Friday evening with the weekend still ahead.
>
> ANXIETY: a message to call home without any indication of what it's all about.

Practice in creating particular scenes and terms to accompany ideas and impressions may help you avoid falling back on standard phrasings and clichés when you are trying to put yourself on paper. (See also 23.4, Concrete and Abstract Words.)

Neither the journal nor this practice in making knowledge concrete guarantee that you will always find good subjects to write about. Both may help by letting you see which way your thoughts and impressions are likely to run, which topics are likely to appear and reappear in journal notes, and which kinds of topics seem to matter to you most.

**Seeing patterns and connections.**    There are some other things you can do to help discover what you're going to write about and to help in thinking about subjects that are assigned. The questions and observations that follow may help you see patterns and connections in your own ideas and impressions, and to relate these patterns to things around you.

1. Do you notice which things seem to recur in your experience? Actions, attitudes, emotional reactions, and other experiences may never be *exactly* repeated, but there are likely to be recognizable likenesses and patterns among your experiences. If there are, they may help you to find a subject, or to see an assigned subject in a new way.

2. How do you look at your experiences? What do you focus on? How and when does your focus change? When you first

entered your composition class, did you see and hear individuals, or did you respond to the class as a whole? How do you
look at it now? Shifting your focus from long range to close
range, looking at one part, then at another, then at both in
relation to each other enables you to see and know what's
around you, and what happens when your focus shifts.

3. How do your experiences differ from others? How varied is
your experience? How do the things you are familiar with
appear to other people? Answering questions like these may
also help you understand your own ideas and impressions
and learn what there is in them that has significance for you.

4. What can you learn about an idea, an event, or an experience
by looking at it in three different ways? If you regard a subject
as something fixed, you can examine its parts. If you regard
your subject as changing and dynamic, you may see the relationships among the parts. Or, your subject may be part of a
larger context, and you may want to see how it fits into this
larger scene.

5. What is there in your experience that can be shared with
another? Can you find a way of presenting your experience
that will make it possible for another to share? How can you
use the knowledge and values that others have so as to connect
them with you and your subject?

**18.1**

*Plan*

Once again, you should note that asking and answering these
questions does not guarantee that you will always find good
subjects. They may help you to think about what you know and
feel and to discover what's there that has significance. Without
extensive exploration, it is possible for you to write competently.
We think it likely, however, that *good* writing won't occur until
something matters enough that the writer feels the need to speak
out.

## Limiting Your Subject

There is seldom any danger that the subject you select will be too
narrow. It is large subjects, such as "Canadian Foreign Policy,"
"The Aims of Higher Education," and "The Role of Women in
Contemporary Society" that lead to difficulty. On such ambitious
subjects, most writers can only repeat commonplace judgments
and empty generalities, and after writing a paragraph or two, they
find that they have nothing more to say.

Limit the subject you select so that you can develop it fully in the
required number of words. Most college and university essays are
short—a thousand-word essay filling only one newspaper column.

Because even ten thousand words would not be enough to cover most large subjects ("Justice," "Crime Prevention," "Forestry"), break down such subjects into topics you can handle. "TV Police Stories," for example, might be limited to "The Effect of TV Police Stories on Children." But since there are many children and several programs about police, you might write a more interesting paper and offer more interesting judgments by focussing specifically on your little brother and TV police stories. The suggestions we made above about ways of looking for subjects are also ways of limiting your subject—the more specific you are in asking about a subject, the narrower your final topic is likely to be.

It is best to concentrate on a single, well-defined aspect of the subject rather than on the subject as a whole:

| **General subject** | **More specific topic** |
| --- | --- |
| Voting as an obligation of citizenship | Arousing student interest in voting |
| Sportsmanship | How sportsmanship differs in tennis and baseball |
| Pollution control | The efficiency of pollution control devices on cars |

As you gather information, your topic may change slightly—and it may continue to change through all the preliminary stages of your thinking. The important thing to remember at first is to keep the topic specific and to avoid lapsing into a general approach.

At this stage of thinking about your subject, jot down on paper every idea that occurs to you, whether you are sure you will use it or not. One idea often suggests another and better one, and may help you to reshape or clarify your thesis (see page 228). After a reasonable amount of reflection, you will usually have more than enough material to write a paper of the assigned length.

▶ **EXERCISE**

Here is a list of general subjects. For each one, narrow the subject to a well-defined aspect that could be a specific topic for a paper: *campus fashions, academic architecture, prestige symbols, modern heroes, school discipline, current music.*

## Some Ways of Thinking About Your Subject

There are some particular ways of thinking about subjects that may help you discover what is most interesting or useful or valuable in them. Asking some or all of the questions below may help you recall information that you already have about your subject, or call your attention to information that you need but do not possess; some may help you see some principle illustrated in your subject.

The first set of questions may be useful to you as you first begin thinking about your subject and also after you have developed a specific proposition, or thesis, and are seeking a way to explain it.

1. What can you learn by *definition?* To what class does your subject belong? How does it differ from other members of the same class? Can definition help you determine just what your main point is? If you have determined what your main point is, does definition give you a way of organizing your discussion?

2. Will *comparison* with something you know well help you understand your subject? Can you detect similarities in your subject and one or more other things? Does detecting differences between your subject and a similar thing help you understand your subject? Does your subject differ in degree from similar things?

3. Studying *relationships* may tell you something about your subject and show you a way to organize your discussion. How is your subject connected with a cause? How and why did your subject come to be? Is your subject to be studied as an effect of some causes, or as a cause of later effects? What are the antecedents of your subject? What consequences are likely to follow from your subject? With what ideas or things is your subject incompatible? Are there ideas that are contradicted by your subject?

4. Is there expert *testimony* about your subject that you can call on? Are there laws, principles, precedents, or other kinds of testimony that will help you understand your subject and validate it to others?

**18.1**

*Plan*

Suppose, for example, that the general subject of *sportsmanship* interests you. Perhaps you're interested in athletics, or perhaps you've just seen an episode of bad sportsmanship, or perhaps you've simply wondered why people behave differently in games. The questions mentioned above may help you discover how to discuss sportsmanship or to find what needs most attention. If you set out to define sportsmanship, a first step is to determine what class of things it belongs to. Is sportsmanship a *virtue,* a *mark of civility,* a *quality,* a *social disguise for aggression?* The problem of defining sportsmanship, in other words, may get to be so important that you decide that this is your subject and you don't have to look further. Each of the sets of questions above may lead to a specific way of writing about sportsmanship.

Another set of suggestions lies in seven relationships that give coherence to discussions. If these relationships are put in the form of questions, they may give you some additional ways of inquiring into your subject:

1. With what is your subject *co-ordinate?* What can be linked to your subject by *and?*
2. From what is your subject *observably different?* What can be linked to your subject by *but?*
3. What can be cited as a *cause* for your subject? What can be linked to your subject by *because* or *for?*
4. What can be cited as a *result* of your subject? To what conclusions does your subject lead? What can be linked to your subject by *therefore* or *so?*
5. What are the *alternatives* to your subject? What can be linked to your subject by *or?*
6. What does your subject *include?* What examples, narratives, episodes can be linked to your subject?
7. What *sequences* exist within your subject? Is your subject part of a larger sequence?

To see how these questions might work, go back to the sample subject that started off as "TV Police Stories," then became "The Effect of TV Police Stories on Children," and finally became "TV Police Stories and My Little Brother." If you say "My little brother watches all of the TV police stories *and . . . ,*" when you finish the sentence in your own way you'll probably have to name some other things he does that are like watching the police stories. If you say "My little brother watches all of the TV police stories *but. . . ,*" when you finish the sentence you'll probably find yourself talking about ways your little brother is different from other children who watch these programs. If you ask what sequences there are in your little brother's actions, that may lead you to discuss how he behaves after watching the programs, or the ritual he goes through to get ready to watch the programs.

These two sets of questions and suggestions can be used in two ways: first, as guides to thinking about your subject *before* you have settled on a central thesis you wish to develop, and second, as guides to developing and organizing your work *after* you have arrived at a central thesis.

## A Checklist for Finding a Subject and Locating Material

### For Help in Finding a Subject

1. Keep a journal and record ideas and information.
2. Practise making abstractions concrete.
3. Look for patterns and connections:
   a. What things recur in your experience?
   b. How do you look at things? When and why does your focus change?
   c. How does your experience differ from that of others?
   d. What do you learn when you look at an experience or possible subject as fixed? as changing and dynamic? and as part of a larger context?
   e. What can you share with someone else?

### For Help in Thinking About a Subject

1. What can you learn by definition?
2. Will comparison reveal something about the subject?
3. What kind of relationships does your subject have with other things?
4. Is there testimony available about your subject?
5. What can be linked to your subject by *and?*
6. What can be linked to your subject by *but?*
7. What can be linked to your subject by *because* or *for?*
8. What can be linked to your subject by *therefore* or *so?*
9. What can be linked to your subject by *or?*
10. What does your subject include?
11. What sequences occur in your subject?

**18.1**

*Plan*

## Locating a Thesis

When you have gone far enough in your thinking and planning to select a specific topic, and you know pretty well what position you take toward it, it is often helpful (and sometimes necessary) to compose a *thesis statement*. This definite statement of the main point or central idea of your paper is useful for three reasons:

1. it will help you see just where you are going and why;
2. it will give you a single focus for the development of your topic;
3. it will help you select the material you will use in the paper.

Usually a single declarative statement, the thesis statement should normally be either a simple or complex sentence, though dependent modifiers can be added: if the thesis statement has a *single* main clause (as in simple and complex sentences), then you are directed to keep one dominant idea as the centre of attention in your paper.

The thesis statement is not the topic of your paper or its title; it is a sentence that answers the question "What is the main idea that I am trying to present to the reader?" A statement of the central or controlling idea of a paper titled "The Honor System" might read "The honor system works only as well as the students want it to work" or "The honor system at this school is popular with the faculty but not with the students." In a paper explaining a process or activity, the thesis statement might be "Learning to play the violin demands patience as well as talent" or "Performance is more important than appearance when you are buying a used car."

Writing a thesis statement requires you to stop and think about the materials of your subject and to decide what is important or interesting. The essay "My Theatre Experience" (see p. 220) might have been given direction and focus by a good thesis statement. The author, with some thought and digging in his memory, might have written several essays about his theatre experience. Consider some of the possibilities:

1. Since the writer indicates that he did many odd jobs around the theatre, an essay could have developed on the behind-the-scenes operation of a drive-in theatre.
2. The writer remarks that he "met many new people" and that "people come to a movie for different reasons"; an essay might have developed on the types of people who attend drive-in movies or on the reasons people have for attending or on the significance of drive-in movies as entertainment.

3. The writer "experienced different emotions"; an essay might have developed on the range of emotional responses he experienced and how he adjusted to them.
4. The writer might have written an informal essay on amusing episodes at a drive-in theatre.
5. The writer might have developed an essay on the erratic, often unseemly behavior of people at drive-in theatres.

Suppose that a little thought leads the writer to choose the fifth possibility. Perhaps the first is so familiar to the writer that it is no longer very interesting. The possibilities listed second above probably require some interviews and some gathering of attendance statistics that the writer can no longer do. Perhaps the third and fourth possibilities don't seem important enough to tell about. But the fifth possibility is a good one, the writer thinks; here is a chance to write about the way people behave in the dark when they think no one is watching, at least no one they know ("People in the Dark," incidentally, wouldn't be a bad title). But just deciding on the fifth possibility doesn't give the writer a direction or focus. Writing a thesis statement requires that the writer decide what the central thought is to be and say it in a single sentence. Consider some possible thesis statements from the fifth suggestion above for a new essay on experience in a drive-in theatre.

**18.1**

*Plan*

> My experience working in a drive-in theatre taught me that people behave differently in the dark, resorting to trickery, deceit, and foolishness.
>
> I learned from my work in a drive-in theatre that public manners and private manners are not the same.
>
> Darkness seems to make people do things they would not do in the broad light of day.

At this point, a thesis statement is still tentative, and further thinking and planning may suggest changes. But each of these thesis statements suggests definite ways to get started on developing the paper. (See also 21.1, Using Sentences to Control Direction.)

▶ **EXERCISE**

Each of the following topics has a thesis statement that can lead to an interesting paper, but some of the points listed do not have any bearing on the controlling idea and should be changed or eliminated. Arrange the ideas in groups that belong together, eliminating or changing them as necessary.

1. *Salmon Fishing:* Salmon fishing is a thrilling and inexpensive sport.

   a. Requires skill
   b. Prizes offered for biggest fish
   c. Equipment need not be expensive
   d. Boats can be rented cheaply
   e. Salmon fight to the last breath
   f. Fraser and Restigouche Rivers two of the best locations
   g. Conservation efforts have paid off
   h. Baked salmon is a delectable dish
   i. How the Indians prepare salmon
   j. No thrill equals that first strike.

2. *Regulating Children's TV Habits:* Although some TV programs are undesirable, parents should not regulate what children watch.

   a. There are some excellent educational programs
   b. Developing good judgment depends on practice in choosing
   c. TV often takes place of baby-sitter
   d. Children want to watch what playmates watch
   e. Some TV programs bad for immature minds
   f. Children resent too much discipline
   g. Outdoor exercise also important
   h. Free play of curiosity develops intellect
   i. Violence fascinates children
   j. Overprotection in youth produces distorted ideas of reality

## Using Available Resources

Two kinds of resources—what we might call *private resources* and *public resources*—should be considered in developing a paper. Some subjects require one, some the other, some both.

**Private resources.**   For some papers that you will write you already know enough to treat the subject well. Your own experience will provide subjects and material for many of your essays: what you have done in school and out, the jobs you have held, your hobbies, the people you know, the places you have visited, and the courses you are taking. Consider this brief list of topics and see how many you could write on from your own experience:

| | |
|---|---|
| Overcoming Self-Consciousness | Considerations in Buying a Car |
| A Job I Disliked | |
| Advice to a High-School Student About to Enter the University | A Successful Amateur Play |
| Living Within a Budget | Building a Record Collection |
| | How to Play Basketball |

You need not feel that a paper based upon your personal experiences will be boring to others. Some beginning writers are afraid that their own experiences have been too limited, or that their opinions and attitudes are too commonplace to be of interest to anyone but themselves. But much published material is based upon incidents and attitudes that are in no way unique or sensational ("Making Your Hobby Pay," "The Most Unforgettable Character I Have Met," "Diary of a City-Bred Farmer"). If you are interested in what you have to say, your readers probably will be too. A fresh and lively account of the experiences of a baby-sitter is more readable than a dull description of a journey up the Amazon.

If you are far enough along in your thinking and planning to formulate a thesis, you will be able to tell whether or not your present knowledge, opinions, and attitudes are sufficient material. For papers based on personal experience, ask yourself as many questions as you can think of about the subject. If you are going to explain how a person should apply for a job, recall and analyse your own experiences in looking for work. How did you find out what jobs were available? How did you decide which jobs to apply for? Did you apply in person or by letter? If you were not hired, what were the probable reasons? What mistakes, if any, did you make either during an interview or in your letter of application? If you were going to apply for another job, would you go about it in the same way?

**18.1**

*Plan*

A similar analysis will help you gather material for papers presenting personal opinions or attitudes. If you decide to enumerate the qualities of a good teacher, think of two or three of your teachers who were outstanding and try to discover what qualities they had in common: a sound knowledge of their subject? a genuine interest in students? a willingness to help the slower students? fairness in grading? a sense of humor? You could extend your analysis by considering also one or two teachers who were definitely unsatisfactory, to see what qualities they lacked.

**Public resources.**   Not all papers can be written entirely from personal opinion or experience. Many subjects call for information that must be gathered by reading, by observation, or through personal interviews. Some subjects will demand thorough research and formal presentation. Others may require only the addition of your casual reading as support. Still others—such as some of the interpretive essays you will be asked to do in English courses—may require that you gather additional information (for example, information about literary techniques), even though the paper is going to be an informal expression of your response to meaning in something you have read. It is quite permissible to use knowledge from casual reading for any occasion that requires it—not as in a formal report with documentation, but as the natural supplement to what you wish to say.

In using outside resources to develop material for a paper, read critically, and think about what you read. Be careful to distinguish between verifiable *facts* (the cost of living index in Saskatoon and in Halifax) and *opinions* (the reasons for the rise of separatism in Québec). On controversial subjects, read and weigh the opinions on all sides of the question before arriving at a firm opinion of your own.

Make the effort to understand and assimilate material from published sources before using it in a paper. Instead of copying an author's words, think about the ideas he is expressing. Do you agree or disagree with them? Why? Proper acknowledgment should always be made for borrowed material—in a footnote if the paper requires formal documentation, or informally if the situation warrants it—as for the quotations opening the sections of this handbook. (See 30.8, Documenting the Paper, for details on using materials from printed sources.)

▶ EXERCISE

See what possible subjects you can find in a daily newspaper. For each subject you find, make some rough notes on what you might be able to do with the subjects, and indicate what kinds of resources you might need to draw on. Try finding subjects in each of these features from the newspaper: *front-page stories, editorials, regular feature-columns, and "fillers."*

## 18.2 THE MEETING PLACE OF AUTHOR, SUBJECT, AND AUDIENCE

Some kinds of writing you may do for your own sake—diaries, notes, and the like. Some kinds of writing you may do for the sake of the subject—laboratory reports, case histories, meditative explorations. Often, however, an audience of some kind is waiting, and you must find a just and happy balance among the material and arguments available on a subject, the interests, needs, and peculiarities of an audience, and your own character. You must be true to yourself, do justice to a subject, and earn an audience.

## The Writer's Position

If you imagine yourself, a subject, and an audience at the three points of a triangle, you'll be able to visualize some of the problems in determining where to stand. If you stand too close to your subject, you may forget the need of sharing it with an audience. If you stand too far from your subject, you may not see it clearly. If you stand too close to your audience, you may get to sounding too chummy. If you stand too far from the audience, you may seem remote and aloof.

It is possible—even common—for a writer to be so busy at winning the audience that the subject and even the writer are given scant service. Good writing requires honesty of the writer—an honest, serious approach to the subject and to the audience, and an honest critical understanding of his or her own capabilities. None of us is complete in what we write, for no one can say all there is to be said on any subject; the demands of space and time, the interests and patience of our readers, and the inadequacies of our own character and knowledge make it unlikely that what we write can ever express an entire truth. But that does not mean that our piece of writing is by definition a poor thing. Indeed, it is the character of good writing that it is a single, limited voice speaking in order to think things out.

**18.2**

*Plan*

Before you begin writing the first draft of a paper, you must discover where *you* stand with regard to your subject and to your audience. Have you engaged yourself in the subject enough to make it interesting to others? Have you weighed it to give it worth? What position will you take toward your subject in presenting it to your audience? Must you address the audience in strictly logical and impersonal fashion? Or does the subject justify a more emotional presentation? Or should you concentrate rather on the impression of yourself that will emerge through your writing? Can you combine these tactics in such a way that you and your audience will come together and share an idea?

## Adjusting to the Audience

As you are planning a piece of writing, you may need to keep in mind the interests and needs of a particular audience. It is easy, of course, to forget your readers and to think only about your subject in some of the writing you will do as a student. The announcement of an assigned subject does not necessarily give you a purpose for writing; and unless you *discover* a purpose and relate it to your audience, even a dutiful fulfilment of the assignment will amount to little. If there is an audience for your work and you ignore it, your work is in vain, no matter how correct.

It is difficult, when you are writing alone at night, for example, even to think of an audience. The easiest thing to do is to get the paper written without bothering about an audience; but when you write something, somebody reads it. When you are writing for a class, it's easy to assume that your teacher is your only audience. Often it is better to write for your class, or for people who read habitually, or for people like yourself, or for an ideal audience of readers who are willing to set aside their own views and heed what you have to say.

One way to get in the habit of thinking about your audience, if your assignment permits it, is to specify a particular audience for what you are writing and indicate at the first of the paper who the audience is: "Those of you who are partial to TV police stories may never have thought about their effect on a twelve-year-old boy."

If the subject you are dealing with is controversial, and if both you and your audience are likely to have intense feelings about the matter, you may have particular problems in finding the right approach to an audience. On matters we care deeply about, where feelings and emotions are taut—politics, ethical practices, conservation and ecology, personal relationships, social, professional, or sexual, for example—we have difficulty hearing each other, and we're not always likely to listen to logic. How can we meet an audience in such a situation? There is no easy way.

One thing you can do, if you encounter this situation, is to move over into the shoes of your audience. You can begin by looking at the issue at hand from your audience's view. You can, for example, try to describe something as another person might see it—some scene or object, say, that is displeasing to you but pleasing to another. Or you can try to impersonate another and write an explanation or argument as the other person would.

You can still be authentically yourself and yet open to others. You can acknowledge opposing views and work to understand them. If people disagree with us, it's usually because they see good in a different way, and we can try to see it as they do, without sacrificing our own views. It takes times and patience to search for the space where you and an audience can be together, but that is a courtesy we owe each other.

The following chapter will discuss in more depth some of the rhetorical approaches that may help you plan your writing so that your subject most effectively reaches your audience.

▶ **EXERCISE**

For this exercise, if possible, use a paper you have already written.
The first two or three paragraphs will probably be enough to work with.

1. Rewrite the opening paragraphs as they might be if you were farther
   from the subject physically or more remote from it emotionally.
2. Rewrite the opening paragraphs as they might be if you were
   physically much closer to your subject or emotionally closer to or
   more involved with it.
3. Rewrite the opening paragraphs as they might be if you were more
   impersonal toward your audience.
4. Rewrite the opening paragraphs as they might be if you were more
   familiar with your audience.

**18.2**

*Plan*

# What Writing Will Let You Do

*No writer has ever lived who did not at some time or other get stuck.*
*—Jacques Barzun, "Calamophobia, or Hints Toward a Writer's*
*Discipline"*

The preceding chapter suggested some ways of exploring for a subject and discovering a subject's potential, and discussed some of the problems and possibilities in establishing a way of looking at a subject and an audience. The chapter ended with an account of a kind of triangular relationship among a writer, his or her audience, and a subject. This chapter will take up where that chapter left off.

Writers do get stuck sometimes. They can lose track of their subject, or become too wrapped up in the sound of their words and forget the substance, or meet any of a hundred different obstacles. But there is one great blessing available to you when you write: You don't have to invent everything for yourself. Customary practices in different kinds of writing—indeed, the very existence of different kinds of writing—give you resources to draw upon. Other writers have written before you; their exploration and practice will often help to show you ways of doing things. The preceding chapter stressed *your* resources, your thinking and exploration, as means of discovering what you have to say. This chapter suggests that other writers, by their practices in different kinds of writing, also offer resources to you.

One way to see the nature of different kinds of writing is to return to that triangular relationship and to start with a simple diagram representing the chief elements in writing. (In the following paragraphs we are calling on the work of James Kinneavy in *A Theory of Discourse* for help in differentiating among kinds of writing.) We'll put these chief elements in connection with each other so as to suggest their interaction in writing. This triangle connects the chief elements—author, subject, audience. The pointing lines inside are meant to suggest something about the nature of different kinds of non-literary writing.

In many kinds of writing the author is dominant; the writing is by the author and, in many ways, for the author. As line 1 in the diagram shows, this kind of writing leaves the author and returns to the author. It may be called *expressive writing,* for the author's need to express appears to be the primary motive in such writing.

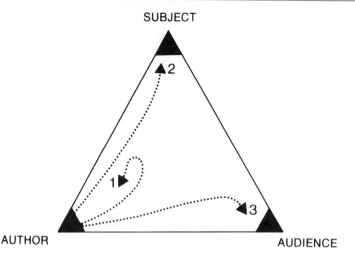

You should note two things about *expressive writing*. First, there are many different kinds of *expressive writing*. Personal letters, diaries, and journals often seem intended chiefly as personal expression; some descriptive writing is the author's account of learning to see. Some expository and argumentative writing turns out to be *expressive writing* when the author, instead of seeking to explain or to persuade, uses the occasion for meditative purposes to work out personal thoughts about a subject. Second, expressive writing offers some opportunities and sets some limits that other kinds of writing don't. You are probably free, for example, to write more informally than you might otherwise and to use looser forms of organization. On the other hand, you may not be free to enter into a technical discussion of something that has taken your interest. You are your own prime object of attention in this kind of writing; you must first of all be honest with yourself.

But in other kinds of writing, the subject deserves primary attention, and you must get out of the way. As line 2 indicates, some writing is focussed on the subject, with the author and any possible audience fading into the background. Kinneavy calls this kind of writing *referential writing;* it refers to something outside the author. Many business letters are *referential writing,* as are most reports, including book reports, laboratory reports, and other class reports. Most answers on essay examinations and most writing about literature are forms of *referential writing.* You don't have the same kind of freedom in this kind of writing that you

**19**

*Writ*

might with *expressive writing;* the subject must be dealt with, and that may require tighter organization, more technical use of language, and closer control of your own opinions. But you need not think of *referential writing* as only limiting; sometimes it is a great advantage to get outside yourself and plunge into the exploration of a subject.

In other kinds of writing, which Kinneavy classifies as *persuasive writing,* the audience seems to be the proper target of attention. Many forms of writing wish not to express an author's views or to explain a subject, but rather to move or to persuade an audience. Sermons belong to this group, and so do letters of recommendation, critiques, all forms of argument, and some kinds of public letters, for example, letters of protest. Writing of this type may make particular demands on you; it may require close, lucid reasoning that an audience can easily follow, and sure, specific evidence that will support assertions. Most troublesome of all—it will require you to be believable in a way not demanded by *expressive writing* or *referential writing.*

The particular writing tasks you will face both in school and out of school may each have special needs, forms of organization, and styles. This general scheme of organization— *expressive writing, referential writing,* and *persuasive writing*—is a reminder that the language you use, the style you use in sentences and paragraphs, the forms of organization you depend on, the relationship you establish among yourself, your subject, and your audience, may vary according to what the writing you are doing needs to do. It makes a difference in the way we talk and write whether we are talking about ourselves, some subject outside ourselves, or to an audience. Speakers and writers sometimes go astray when they forget what they are supposed to be doing. We've all been in classrooms where teachers have become so involved in their subject (referential discourse) that they have forgotten their audience of students (requiring persuasive discourse). We've all heard salesmen and politicians so intent on selling themselves to us (persuasive discourse) that they have forgotten to learn very much about their subject (requiring referential discourse).

The terms we've been using— *expressive writing, referential writing,* and *persuasive writing*—are useful because they are a reminder of these relationships in writing among an author, a subject, and an audience. They are not, however, the only terms that can be used to discriminate among different kinds of writing. In the following sections we'll use another set of terms to discuss some of the special problems and opportunities of different kinds of writing: *exposition, argumentation, description, and narra-*

*tion.* The two sets of terms are related, although the latter set is more traditional and less concerned with relationships. Argumentation is persuasive writing. Exposition is usually referential writing, although a writer might explain (write exposition) in order to express himself or herself. Description and narration are often referential, but they may also be expressive. But in any case, knowing what others have done in these modes of writing—knowing what is possible—is a way of learning what you can do when you set out to write.

## 19.1 EXPOSITION

The purpose of exposition is to *inform* your readers, to carry their knowledge of something beyond its present point, to help them understand a situation or a process, to give them information about an idea or belief. It ranges from the explanation of small personal matters ("How to Select a Summer Wardrobe") to complex scientific treatises ("The Effect of Ultraviolet Light on Steroids").

**19.1**

*Exp*

Skill in exposition is essential in all school work. You will probably do more expository writing, where you inform your reader or explain a point of view, than any other kind of writing. Most of the reading required in school, except in literature courses, is also expository. Increasing skill in expository writing, then, is a major aim of composition courses.

### Gathering Information

Whatever your subject and whatever the length of your paper, you will have to exercise judgment in deciding what resources to use and in gearing your information to your particular audience and situation. (See 18.1, Using Available Resources, and 30.0, The Reference Paper.) Some of the short expository papers you will be assigned as a student can be based entirely on your own knowledge and experience. Other papers will require that you gather and evaluate information from various sources in order to develop your subject adequately.

Even when you base your paper on a personal experience, such as building a boat or working in a drive-in theatre, you may find it useful to add to your information by reading in the library or by talking to people who have had similar experiences. It is a good idea in planning such a paper to make a list of points about which your memory is hazy or about which you lack adequate information. Then, to fill in the gaps, you can extend your observations or read what others have reported about the subject.

For typical information papers on subjects such as "The Canadian Senate" or "Devices for Controlling Air Pollution," you will usually need to consult a variety of printed sources—books, magazines, newspapers—to find information you cannot gather first-hand.

## Relating Specialized Information to Your Reader

In gathering and selecting additional facts to use in an expository paper, be particularly careful to consider your audience. If you are writing a paper for a group of bridge fanciers, you probably need not define terms like *point count* and *slam* or explain how a *finesse* is made, since your readers would be familiar with such fundamentals. But if you are writing on bridge for an English class, you cannot expect the typical student to have this knowledge; to make sure that your audience understands, you must take the time to insert brief definitions or explanations. If you do not, the whole paper may be puzzling or even incomprehensible to general readers. Remember that you are writing the paper in hopes of telling them something new, of adding to their knowledge in an area where they do not have your background. Put yourself in their place: what words or ideas might be unfamiliar to them? How can you explain these things so that they will understand them?

The following passages show effective and ineffective ways of relating specialized information to general readers:

INEFFECTIVE: There are various ways to bridge the gap from one solo to the next. The trumpeter may play a series of riffs accompanied only by the rhythm section. This is probably the most common method.

EFFECTIVE: There are various ways to bridge the gap from one solo to the next. Probably the most common method is for the trumpeter to play a series of short, conventional jazz phrases, called "riffs," accompanied only by the rhythm section—piano, bass, and drums.

INEFFECTIVE: If the bleeding becomes severe or there is a chance of infection, you may have to cauterize the wound.

EFFECTIVE: If the bleeding becomes severe or there is a chance of infection, you may have to cauterize the wound by searing it with a piece of metal that has been held over a flame until it is red hot.

## Documenting Your Information

When your own observations form the basis of the paper, be sure to tell the readers why you consider your statements to be fairly authoritative. Otherwise they may not be sure how much value to attach to them. Somewhere near the beginning of the paper, state the circumstances under which you gathered your facts:

> Since I was sixteen, I have spent my summer vacations working in a local department store, first as a stock clerk and later as an assistant display manager. During that time, I have become familiar with the typical organization of a large retail store. . . .

> My home is only nine miles away from the Blackfoot Indian reserve, and I have had many opportunities to meet and talk to members of the Blackfoot people. . . .

> In gathering examples for this paper, I spent ten hours listening to radio programs featuring rock-and-roll records and copied down the lyrics of a dozen of the current favorites. . . .

When you incorporate published material into your paper, be sure to reproduce it accurately and to credit the sources, whether you quote them directly or not. It is not honest to offer someone else's experiences or observations as if they were your own. In a research paper, credit is given formally by means of footnotes (30.8, Documenting Your Paper), but in a general paper mention may be made informally. The following are some typical examples of how such acknowledgments can be handled:

**19.1**

*Exp*

> Franklin Soames, the author of *Zapotec Culture,* found that. . . .

> At a recent medical convention, H. L. Matthews, the noted urologist, was quoted as saying. . . .

> But according to Morris Wolfe, in a recent article in *Saturday Night.* . . .

Sources which have been used extensively may be given in a note at the beginning or at the end of a paper:

> Much of the material for this paper was taken from Donald Creighton, *Dominion of the North* (Toronto: Macmillan, 1957).

▶ **EXERCISE**

Look for several pieces of expository writing and bring them to class for discussion. Notice in particular how much detail different writers use, how writers convey specialized information, how much time they spend on different parts of their subject. Try to find selections that illustrate different relationships between the writer and the subject (involved? dispassionate? aloof? distant? close?). Explanations are likely to occur in many interesting places; look at the labels of jars and cans, the owner's manual that comes with some appliances or a car, a popular magazine for crafts and mechanics, textbooks, a book on how our language developed, the jacket commentary for a record album.

## 19.2 ARGUMENTATION

Whereas the purpose of exposition is to *inform* your readers, the purpose of argumentation is to *convince* them. The two kinds of writing have much in common, and both are based on facts or impressions gathered from various sources. But expository writing simply *presents* information, while argumentative writing *uses* it to support or test a belief. A paper describing current fashions in clothing, the social habits of bees, or the history of the fur trade invites the readers to share the writer's knowledge of the subject; a paper attacking campus rules for dress, on the other hand, expresses an opinion and tries to convince the reader of its validity. Like exposition, argumentative writing ranges widely, from matters close at hand ("Down with Large Classes") to those of major public concern ("Let's Get Rid of the Senate").

### Locating the Argument

An argumentative paper *proposes* something. Whether it calls for action or simply asks for the recognition of a point of view, it centres on a proposition that the writer must be prepared to prove.

An argument from a proposition, as Edward P. J. Corbett has said in *Classical Rhetoric for the Modern Student,* is similar to a factual report in that it can ordinarily be judged as true or false; but a statement of fact is not in itself an occasion for argument, since presumably facts can be checked. An argument is also similar to a statement of opinion, in that it represents a judgment the writer has made; but an opinion is not an occasion for argument unless it is based on *facts* instead of mere preference, for only then can its validity be proved.

In planning a persuasive paper, you must take the time to formulate your proposition carefully. As your thesis statement, your proposition gives direction and unity to your argument. Ordinarily it needs to be simple—composed ideally of a single subject and a single predicate. If you argue, for example, that "The municipal government must be put into new hands on election day and reformed to keep provincial and federal agencies from encroaching on local authority," you have, by using a double predicate, introduced two arguments, both of which must then be proved.

You should find the suggestions in 18.1, Locating a Thesis, helpful in formulating an arguable proposition.

### Using Resources and Evidence

When we state our opinions in informal situations, we often give little or no evidence to support them: "John is a reckless driver";

"The cost of living is going up every day"; "Divorce is the main cause of juvenile delinquency." This vagueness does not mean that we have no good reasons for so believing, but simply that our reasons are usually known and accepted by our listeners. On occasions when our opinions are questioned, we may attempt to support them with facts drawn from our experience and reading: "John had two accidents last month, and he always drives too fast." "Steak is up sixty cents a pound, and a refrigerator costs almost twice as much today as it did six years ago." "Psychologists say that emotional stability depends on a secure family life." Such evidence is considered acceptable or even convincing in informal situations, usually because the listener's personal regard for the speaker lends some weight to the evidence.

In writing, however, the relationship with your audience is far more impersonal; authority must rest much more on the facts themselves. Readers who know neither John nor you will want to know what kind of accidents John had and who was at fault; they will wonder whether "too fast" means in excess of speed limits; they may suspect that "always" is an exaggeration. Before accepting your opinion in regard to the relation between divorce and delinquency, they may want to hear what psychologists say in their own words, to be sure you are not misinterpreting their remarks or ignoring opposed opinions.

**19.2**

*arg*

The more facts supporting your opinion that you can gather from experience or from the written statement of others, the more reason you can give your readers to accept that opinion. You will probably not be able to present absolute *proof*, but the greater the weight of your evidence, the more probable it will seem to them that your belief is the best one.

## Types of Arguments

Some traditional kinds of argument may suggest certain ways of thinking about your material that will lead you to the evidence you need. One is the *argument from nature*. Not long ago on a western campus a young man who wished to call attention to inadequacies in the campus guidebook petitioned to have his name placed on the ballot in an election for winter carnival queen. He maintained that he was eligible on the grounds that the guidebook stipulated only that candidates should be students under twenty-one; sex was not mentioned in the body of the rules. The young man's petition was denied through an argument from nature. Pointing out that the rules came under the heading "Eligibility requirements for winter carnival queen," his opposition seized on the meaning of the word *queen*—by nature a female—to deny his eligibility. An argument from nature may be developed by a number of techniques: by defining the nature of a thing; by studying the meanings attached to the key words in a proposition; by classifying the subject in order to establish a frame of reference in terms of which it can be discussed.

People cannot always agree on the nature of things, of course, and for that reason they have often turned to other kinds of argument. The *argument from analogy* brings a subject and argument into a reader's knowledge by suggesting its similarity to something better known, as in the fairly common — but usually ineffective — analogy of government and business. The evidence you bring to this kind of argument must show that the comparison is both significant and accurate.

The *argument from consequence* enforces a proposition by examining cause and effect, antecedent and consequence. This is a useful kind of argument, but it is limited by the fact that human affairs are not ordered by certain laws of causality. Poverty *sometimes* breeds crime; prolonged tyranny *frequently* leads to revolution; honesty is *occasionally* rewarded. Before expressing an opinion about the outcome of some course of action, or about the cause of some event, make sure that the weight of evidence lends probability to your statement.

The *argument from authority* depends upon the testimony of respected persons, the authority of institutions, the weight of important documents. This is probably the least popular of the traditional kinds of argument, for most audiences prefer to feel that the truth is *discovered* in the course of an argument, rather than that it has been *pronounced* by authority.

## Taking the Argument to Your Audience

Whatever kind of argument you use, and those above are only samples, remember that your readers have some confidence in their own intelligence and judgment and are likely to resent a writer who attempts to make up their minds for them. (See the discussion of author-audience relationships in 18.) State your facts as specifically as possible — so that your readers can check them for themselves if they want to — and give your reasons for whatever conclusions you draw. Compare the following statements for effectiveness:

> VAGUE: A few years ago, the president of a large company said that taxes were too high.
>
> SPECIFIC: In a speech to the Kingston Chamber of Commerce on April 14, 1974, Oscar Winslow, president of the Winslow Paint

Company, said, "Corporation taxes today are so high that they are destroying business incentive.

VAGUE: In many of his newspaper articles, H. L. Mencken made slighting references to democracy. Anyone can see that he despised it.

SPECIFIC: In his articles for the Baltimore *Sun*, H. L. Mencken frequently referred to democracy in terms such as these: "the domination of unreflective and timorous men, moved in vast herds by mob emotions" (July 26, 1920); "it may be clumsy, it may be swinish, it may be unutterably incompetent and dishonest, but it is never dismal" (July 14, 1924).

In trying to persuade readers to accept your opinion, you will naturally want to gather facts that will support your position. It is not fair to your readers, however, to suggest that *all* evidence reinforces your belief. They may be familiar with contrary evidence; even if they are not, its absence may make them suspect that you are stacking the deck in your favor. In a court of law, an attorney who deliberately suppresses evidence damaging to his or her case may be disbarred from future practice. The consequences to writers are usually not so serious, but they may also lose the case.

**19.2**

*arg*

When you come across facts that do *not* support your opinion, give them as careful consideration as you do those that do. Is their source authoritative and relatively free of bias? Do they offer serious and relevant reasons to question your present opinion? Do they outnumber the facts you can find to support it? It may be that you will want to alter or modify your proposition after taking opposing facts into account. You may decide that your original opinion was wrong; many writers are unaware of the flimsy basis of their beliefs until they begin trying to substantiate them.

Even if the facts you gather do not change your opinion, it is unfair to simply discard those that fail to support it. In fact, it will strengthen your position in the readers' eyes if you frankly admit unfavorable evidence along with your reasons for being unpersuaded by it. Remember that the readers are your jury. If you have arrived at an opinion by weighing opposing evidence sensibly, they should be able to do the same.

## Testing the Argument

One way to test your argument, or to examine the argument of another writer or speaker, is to scrutinize it for flaws in reasoning and in the use of evidence. Probably the most common flaws are these:

**Hasty generalization.**  In informal situations, we often over-generalize from the facts: "She's *never* on time"; "Advertising is *only* a pack of lies." A little consideration shows us that in reality all-or-none, black-or-white situations are rare; reality is more accurately described in terms of finer shadings and degrees. Most readers are aware of this, and although they will accept and make statements like the above uncritically enough in conversations, they are suspicious of them in writing.

Be especially cautious in using terms like *all, always, everybody, nobody, never, none, only,* and *most.* Before making such all-inclusive statements, make sure that they are justified. If there are any exceptions to some assertion you make, modify your language to make it more accurate. Don't say that *all* young people want a home and family: *some* or *many* might be more accurate. Before you say that *most* early marriages end in divorce, ascertain from some reliable source whether more than 50 per cent actually do; otherwise you are not justified in using *most.* Keep in mind that the English vocabulary provides you with a wealth of qualifying terms (*some, few, often,* to name only a few) and choose those that most accurately describe the number, extent, and frequency of the facts you are asserting.

Compare these two statements for precision of expression. Both are based on the same facts (of the delinquents in the Provincial Training School, 75 per cent come from low-income families, 45 per cent have used narcotics at some time, and 20 per cent have IQ scores over 100):

> OVERGENERALIZATION: **Almost all** delinquents in the Provincial Training School come from homes **on the verge of starvation. Most** of them are **dope addicts,** and **very few** are **brilliant.**
>
> ACCURATE STATEMENT: **Three out of four** delinquents in the Provincial Training School come from **low-income homes. Almost half** of them have **at least experimented** with narcotics. **A significant minority** are **above average mentally.**

**False analogy.**  Comparison and analogy are effective means of arguing, but only if there is really a basic similarity between the compared terms. If, for example, a university administrator sets out to argue for new rules and economies in his or her school on the basis that it should be run like a business, we should probably reject that argument on the grounds that the analogy is not valid, for similarities between a business and a university seem only incidental, not essential.

**Post hoc, ergo propter hoc.**  This fallacy (literally, "after this, therefore because of this") is the fairly common one of assuming that two events or things are causally related simply because they are related in time. The young man who gets a raise a week after using a new deodorant probably owes his success to something else.

**Non sequitur.**  The label *non sequitur* ("it does not follow") applies to errors of reasoning in which the conclusion does not follow from the evidence presented. Sometimes a step in reasoning has been omitted, and the fallacy can be corrected by supplying the missing link. But sometimes the conclusion is drawn from evidence that has no bearing on the issue: that Mary Starr uses a particular toothpaste has nothing to do with its quality; that a man does not beat his wife has nothing to do with whether he is a good husband; that the army teaches useful skills has nothing to do with the wisdom of sending troops to other countries.

**Begging the question.**  This term applies to an argument that assumes the truth of what needs to be proved. A politician who argues "Our feeble municipal government, greatly in need of reform, must be placed in new hands on election day" is begging the question unless he *proves* that the present government is feeble and in need of reform.

**19.2**
*arg*

**Ignoring the question.**  This is a broad term that applies to all arguments that are irrelevant, as when a premier argues that his government is not corrupt because the provincial budget is balanced. Another way he might ignore the issue would be to resort to an *argumentum ad hominem* ("argument against the man"), attacking the integrity of his opponents rather than the charge of his own corruption. Or he might use *glittering generalities* such as "my devotion and dedication to the fine people of this province" to draw his audience into acquiescence by the weight of good words. All arguments that use emotional means to persuade an audience to arrive at a judgment without examining the evidence are ways of ignoring the question.

When you have finished the first draft of an argumentative paper, examine it carefully for flaws. Have you weighed the available evidence? Are your generalizations supported by fact? Are your inferences valid? Make sure that your argument is both honest and sound.

▶ **EXERCISE**

Look for several pieces of argumentative writing and bring them to class for discussion. In each, try to determine just what the central topic of debate is and what kind of evidence the writer uses. Notice what kind of relationship the writer works to establish with the audience. Test the argument against your own judgment and common sense and against the fallacies listed above. You may find it helpful to look at newspaper editorials, letters to editors, advertisements, television commercials (if you can get the words down on paper), graffiti, bumper stickers, political and social commentary in magazines.

## 19.3 DESCRIPTION

The purpose of descriptive writing is to enable a reader to see an object, person, or scene as you have seen or imagined it. This requires an eye for significant details as well as a knack for putting sense impressions into words. Description is often written for its own sake, as a form of artistic expression, and it may also be an important part of other kinds of writing, from long research papers to technical reports and case histories.

### Seeing Your Subject Clearly

To make a description vivid to a reader, you must first of all know where you stand, physically and mentally, in relation to the thing you are writing about. How did you see your subject? From what angle? Under the weight of what mood? How can you define your subject, distinguishing it from similar things in the same class? What makes this particular sunset, for example, different from all others?

Descriptive writing succeeds only when you show your audience the specific, identifying details of object or scene. This requires that you see it clearly yourself, that you understand what you see, and that you say *precisely* what you see, as the writer has done in this passage:

> I know how a prize watermelon looks when it is sunning its fat rotundity among pumpkin vines and "simblins"; I know how to tell when it is ripe without "plugging" it. I know how inviting it looks when it is cooling itself in a tub of water under the bed, waiting; I know how it looks when it lies on the table in the sheltered great floor-space between house and kitchen, and the children gathered

for the sacrifice and their mouths watering. I know the crackling sound it makes when the carving knife enters its end and I can see the split fly along in front of the blade as the knife cleaves its way to the other end; I can see its halves fall apart and display the rich red meat and the black seeds, and the heart standing up, a luxury fit for the elect. — Mark Twain, *Autobiography*

No two persons look at a scene in exactly the same way. What makes one writer's description more vivid than another's is the kind of details selected and the way they are arranged.

## Selecting and Arranging Details

Good descriptive writing is precise. If in describing a person you write "I first noticed this lady because she was wearing a funny hat," your description won't mean much to the reader because there are many kinds of funny hats. State in specific terms what the hat looked like: perhaps it was a black velvet beret covered with sea shells or perhaps it was a miniature merry-go-round.

Notice how lifeless the description is in this paraphrase, from which the specific expressions have been removed:

**19.3**

*Desc*

> Gabriel watched as she ran her hand over her blonde hair, as girls do in some parts of France. Her mother's hair had been black, and Chantal was not nearly as pretty as her mother had been, for she had a snub nose and a rather big mouth. Yet she was as graceful as her mother in her movements.

By way of contrast, compare the description as it was written:

> Gabriel ... watched her pass a slender hand over hair which most people called blonde but which he thought of as French-blonde because its basic chestnut was highlighted with pale-silver in a way he associated with girls of northern France. Her mother's hair had been ebony against a very white, soft skin. Chantal was not as handsome as her mother had been; her mouth was wide and her nose was somewhat snubbed, but she moved with her mother's grace and was so supple she seemed double-jointed. — Hugh Mac-Lennan, *Return of the Sphynx*

Being specific in descriptive writing doesn't mean that you should overload your sentences with adjectives and adverbs. While such words are used to "describe" or qualify other words, too many of them can be disastrous to any piece of descriptive writing. To refer to Lake Louise as "*absolutely* the *most marvellous* sight I have *ever* seen in my *entire* life" may give your readers some hint about your emotions, but it won't tell them much about Lake Louise or help them re-create your impression of it.

The details you select for a descriptive passage should contribute to a central impression. (See 27.3, Continuity in Descriptive Paragraphs.) Often a few well-selected details will give a sharper picture than a large number of ill-assorted ones, as in this quick sketch of old houses:

> Houses are like sentinels in the plain, old keepers of the weather watch. There, in a very little while, wood takes on the appearance of great age. All colors wear soon away in the wind and rain, and then the wood is burned gray and the grain appears and the nails turn red with rust. The windowpanes are black and opaque; you imagine there is nothing within, and indeed there are many ghosts, bones given up to the land. They stand here and there against the sky, and you approach them for a longer time than you expect. They belong in the distance; it is their domain. — N. Scott Momaday, *The Way to Rainy Mountain*

To give focus to a description, you may find it useful to adopt one of the methods for developing material discussed in 21.2. For example, a spatial arrangement that takes you from left to right in picturing your subject, or from high to low, or from near to far, may help you create order in your description.

Often objects attract attention to themselves and deserve to become subjects for description because of some special impression they make. Thus, an interesting way to organize description is to focus attention on the dominant impression, subordinating all else. In the following passage the impression of quiet laziness, idleness, dominates the scene:

> The Mausoleum Club stands on the quietest corner of the best residential street in the City. It is a Grecian building of white stone. About it are great elm trees with birds—the most expensive kind of birds—singing in the branches. The street in the softer hours of the morning has an almost reverential quiet. Great motors move drowsily along it, with solitary chauffeurs returning at 10:30 after conveying the earlier of the millionaires to their downtown offices. The sunlight flickers through the elm trees, illuminating expensive nursemaids wheeling valuable children in little perambulators. . . . And through it all the sunlight falls through the elm trees, and the birds sing and the motors hum, so that the whole world as seen from the boulevard of Plutoria Avenue is the very pleasantest place imaginable.—Stephen Leacock, "A Little Dinner with Mr. Lucullus Fyshe"

Good descriptive writing demands restraint and discrimination. It also takes practice to get the exact effect that you want. One way to get additional practice is to study published examples

of descriptive writing that appeal to you, observing what kinds
of details the writers use and how they present them.

▶ **EXERCISE**

Look for several pieces of descriptive writing and bring them to class for
discussion. Spend some time taking note of how many of the sentences
contain specific sensory details and impressions. Notice the arrangement in
each selection, and see if you can determine what the description is for.
Where is the writer in relation to the subject? Check advertisements, stage
directions in printed plays, passages in novels, fashion magazines, craft
magazines, textbooks, merchandise catalogues.

## 19.4 NARRATION

The purpose of narrative writing is to re-create an experience
or event, usually without expository comment. Like description,
narration depends upon particulars, but unlike description, it
moves through a time period:

> The second file was more enigmatic. It was a report on the curious
> death of the CIA station chief, Mark Henderson, who two years
> earlier had been found dead, seated in a chair in front of his
> television set. The set was still on and a half-finished meal sat on a
> tray on the table in front of him. The autopsy showed that he had
> choked on a piece of steak gristle. His body was discovered shortly
> before midnight by S who, on his way home, had happened to see
> the lights on, and stopped by. The two men were apparently more
> than professional acquaintances.—Ian Adams, *S: Portrait of a Spy*

**19.4**

*Narr*

### Point of View

The particulars of narrative writing are reported to an audience
selectively through a given point of view. Ordinarily it is neither
possible nor desirable to present every action in a sequence of
events. Rather, you should focus on those aspects of an experience
that, from your point of view, make it worth preserving.

   Most of the narrative writing you do will be presented as the
narrative of either a first-person observer or participant or of
a third-person observer. Personal narratives and autobiographical
sketches are ordinarily told in the first person, but it will depend
on the story you tell whether you present yourself as participating
or observing. In historical writing, reports, and case histories,
you will ordinarily present the action in the third person, letting
the events speak for themselves.

Whether you report an action as a participant or observer, try to focus attention directly on what went on. In the following passage the narrator draws attention to *himself* rather than to the event he is narrating:

> I was riding with a friend late one night, returning from a long weekend trip. I was extremely tired, and I am sure he was too, and as a result we weren't very observant about traffic lights. I did notice in the distance one very red blinker-light, though. I also saw a car directly in front of ours, like a slow-moving ship in a submarine's sights. I knew immediately that we were going too fast to stop, so my natural reaction was to brace myself for a crash. It seemed to me that I could hear the tires squealing for minutes before anything happened. I was surprised to find during those actually few short seconds that I was seeing a variety of vivid colors that I hadn't even noticed before. I was aware of the yellow dividing strip of the highway, and still off in the distance, the brilliant red flashes of the traffic signal. There were also the browns and greys and whites of the surrounding buildings, that I hadn't seen a few moments before, but now were things of sharp beauty.

This narrative could be tightened up, and the *I*'s made less conspicuous, by revising some of the sentences:

> Late one night I was riding with a friend. We were both extremely tired after a long weekend trip and not very watchful of the traffic lights. But I was dimly aware of one very red blinker-light in the distance. Suddenly a car loomed up in front of us, like a slow-moving ship seen through a submarine's sights. We were going too fast to stop, and instinctively I braced myself for the crash. Our tires squealed for what seemed minutes. Actually, only a second or two passed, but in that brief instant, all the color of the scene jumped into view—the bright yellow dividing strip of the highway, the brilliant red flashes of the traffic light, the browns, greys, and whites of the nearby buildings. For one sharp moment everything took on a strange and fearful beauty.

A reader will understand your experience more clearly if you concentrate on the events as they happened instead of on your feelings about them.

## Use of Tenses

In narrative writing events are typically written down in chronological order, with verbs and adverbs controlling the movement:

> . . . **After a long half hour,** the rain **eased** a bit and the clouds **rose. I relaxed** a little. **I was showing** them that a rookie **could get through. Just then,** the engine **stopped** cold. As a rule, **when** an engine **fails,**

it **will give** some warning. The water temperature **will rise,** or the oil pressure **will drop,** or there **is a knocking or clanking.** Even if it **is only for a minute or two,** it **gives** the pilot a chance **to look around** and **head for** a field or open place. However, **when** the timing gear in a Liberty engine **failed, one second** it **was roaring along** even and strong, and **the next** there **was** a tremendous silence. I **quickly twisted** all the knobs and gadgets in the cockpit, but there **was** no response, and the engine **stayed** dead. **While** my hands **were trying to restart** the engine, my neck **was stretching** and my eyes **searching** for some sort of field to **land in.** I **was surrounded** by heavily forested, sharply rolling hills. To my left **was** a cuplike basin with a small clearing. It **was** downwind, but my gliding radius **didn't allow** much choice. I **went** for it. — Dean C. Smith, "Flying by Guess and by God"

Most narrative writing uses the past tense, but the present (or "historical present") is sometimes used to create a sense of events actually happening, as in this paragraph:

Above me the clouds roll in, unfurling and smoking billows in malignant violet, dense as wool. Most of the sky is lidded over but the sun remains clear, halfway down the west, shining beneath the storm. Over my head the clouds thicken, then crack and split with a roar like that of cannonballs tumbling down a marble staircase; their bellies open — too late to run now! — and suddenly the rain comes down. — Edward Abbey, *Desert Solitaire*

**19.4**

*Narr*

Whether a narrative is written in the present or past, one tense should be kept throughout. This paragraph illustrates unnecessary and confusing tense shifts:

As I **hop** [present tense] on the city transit that will take me to the University, I notice that as always the bus is filled past capacity. As I **turned** [past] around, I saw a blind man sitting directly behind me with a dog lying at his feet. I **watch** [present] the dog, sitting there perfectly still, looking through the glass doors. Suddenly the dog **got up** [past], nudged his master, who pulled the cord above his head and with no difficulty got off the bus and proceeded up the street. I **wondered** [past] how a dog could be trained to know when to get off the bus, when to cross the street, and when to wait for a signal. Dogs seem to have more sense than some humans.

## Pacing a Narrative

Because it moves through a time sequence, narration presents some problems not found in description. Foremost among these is the problem of pacing. Whether a series of events that you are narrating covers three years, three weeks, or three hours, you cannot reproduce the entire sequence — nor should you want to, for much of the time in any sequence of events is filled with action that has no particular bearing on the experience you are relating. The problem is to pace the telling of your story so that thorough attention goes to the significant actions and less attention to actions that have less immediate impact for your narrative.

If you study any example of effective narrative writing, you will see, as Leo Rockas has noted, a balance of "remote" narration and "minute" narration. We *do* something just about all the time, but it may be that only a small portion of our doing is directed toward an end that is central to the experience we are trying to preserve in narrative. Still, if the significant actions that warrant narration are to have any context and continuity, they must be seen as part of a continuing stream of events. What you must do, then, is find a way to suggest a considerable amount of time in a relatively short space (remote narration) and so create a context for your slower, more detailed account of the significant actions (minute narration). If you are a reader of comic strips, you will remember that in a strip such as *Steve Canyon* or *Mary Worth,* the cartoonist-narrator will occasionally use a picture or two to show the characters at their regular work; but when some dramatic episode nears its climax, he may use the full strip for several weeks to present a single, climactic action. In a detective novel, two weeks of routine work may pass in a sentence, while a brief fight lasts two pages.

## Including Adequate Details

If your narrative is to come alive for your reader, you must include enough details to make it interesting and understandable. Avoid any statement that might leave the reader wondering "What?" or "Why?" or "When?" or "Who?" In this paragraph, for example, the narrator fails to tell *what* his teacher said or *why* "the results of the contest were disappointing":

> On the night of the final judging, I was so nervous I could hardly move my fingers. As I waited backstage for my turn to appear, I was sure I had forgotten the opening notes of my number completely. I began thinking of ways to escape; maybe I could faint or pretend to be violently ill. But then at the last minute my piano teacher came by to wish me luck and **said something that suddenly changed everything.** When my turn came, I played with ease and confidence. **Although the results of the contest were disappointing,** I was pleased that I had conquered one of my major enemies — stage fright.

In selecting details, choose those that illuminate or enliven significant actions. A narrative should not be loaded down with minute and unimportant details. You can usually make your point and still keep the action moving by selecting two or three lively incidents, as in this example:

> The big fisherman started pounding his fists up and down in the air. "He just doesn't mean anything to me at all," Michael said quickly. The fisherman, bending down, kicked a small rock loose from the road bed and heaved it at the hangman. Then he said, "What are you holding there, Michael, what's under your arm? Fish. Pitch them at him. Here, give them to me." Still in a fury, he snatched the fish, and threw them one at a time at the little man just as he was getting up from the road. The fish fell in the thick dust in front of him, sending up a little cloud. Smitty seemed to stare at the fish with his mouth hanging open, then he didn't even look at the crowd. That expression on Smitty's face as he saw the fish on the road made Michael hot with shame and he tried to get out of the crowd. Smitty had his hands over his head, to shield his face as the crowd pelted him, yelling "Sock the little rat. Throw the runt in the lake." The sheriff pulled him into the automobile. The car shot forward in a cloud of dust.—Morley Callaghan, "Two Fishermen"

See also 27.3, Continuity in Narrative Paragraphs.

**19.4**

*Narr*

▶ EXERCISE

Look for several pieces of narrative writing and bring them to class for discussion. Who is doing the narration? Where is he or she in relation to the action? How do you know you can trust the writer to give you an accurate account of the action? When is the pace fast? When is it slow? Look at a variety of different kinds of narration: check the sports pages in your newspaper for accounts of different hockey games and notice how the narrative of a headlined game differs from that of a game assumed to be less interesting or important. Look at a history text or at some good books on an area of history that interests you. Notice how a movie critic summarizes the action of a movie, or how *TV Guide* summarizes the action of a variety show.

The purpose of the preceding discussion of different types of writing was to indicate that any kind of writing you do sets some obligations before you. You need to know where you are in relationship to your subject and your audience, and you also need to understand your own purpose, whether it is to explain, to persuade, to describe, to narrate. The best way to meet these obligations is to spend some time and energy in serious planning before you write.

# Organizing Your Material

*Once the plan is made and the material parcelled out, then the dry skeleton of this structure should be hidden beneath a surface which is all variety and interest.* — *Herbert Read,* ENGLISH PROSE STYLE

Before you begin to write, spend some time thinking through the order in which you intend to present your material. With some subjects the material itself will determine organization. For example, narratives and papers that describe personal experiences usually follow the order of events, and an explanation of a process follows a step-by-step pattern of presentation. In descriptive writing ("A Trip Through the Agawa Canyon") the normal order may be from one point to another (leaving Sault Ste. Marie, entering the canyon, arriving at Bridal Veil Falls) or from a general impression to the specific details that give rise to it, arranged more or less in the order of prominence.

The order of presentation may require more thought with other topics, such as "A Criticism of Olivier's *Hamlet*" or "Repression and Rationalization as Defence Mechanisms." Whether you select the subject or your instructor assigns one, in most instances you will have to examine the material carefully to find the best order for your special purpose. (See 21.2, Developing Your Material, for suggestions about choosing a pattern of development.) Outlining your material is one good way to determine its best organization.

## 20.1 THE OUTLINE IN RELATION TO THE PAPER

The usefulness of an outline depends on the material in it. No matter how correct the form—in numbering, punctuation, and structure—if the outline doesn't help in writing your paper, it serves no purpose. You can make a pretty outline *after* you've written the paper if you just want to have an outline to turn in. Of course, that's a waste of your time. Outlines are useless unless you take them seriously. Outlines in themselves are no great matter. No one reads outlines for entertainment and education. There is no gold medal for the best outline of the year. What matters about outlines is that they represent a writer's care about the subject and possible readers. Taken seriously, they represent a writer's effort to think a subject through and get information and ideas together in the best relationship.

You can learn a number of things from a good outline. From the main divisions in a good outline you can estimate the number and relative length of the paragraphs in your paper, although usually the paragraphs will not correspond exactly to the headings. You can frequently construct topic sentences for these paragraphs by rephrasing or expanding the outline headings. The divisions will show where transitions are needed and suggest the kind of development that will be possible: contrast, comparison, illustration, or others. (See 27.2, Patterns of Paragraph Development, and 21.2, Developing Your Material.)

An outline should be long enough to suit your purpose, and no longer. It should be no more complex than the material demands. The number of main headings for most papers ranges from three to five. A larger number of main headings for a thousand-word paper, for example, suggests that the division is haphazard or that the organization is faulty. The same principle applies to subheadings. Outlines that run from A through J or K need revision, for no single topic ordinarily needs such minute subdivision. And except for very complex material, there is seldom any need to go beyond the third-level subheading.

**20.2**

*Org*

When you are asked to submit an outline with your paper, it should represent the plan that you actually followed. Your outline serves then as the table of contents. You may find it necessary in writing the paper to depart occasionally from your original plan; if so, make the corresponding changes in the final outline before handing it in.

## 20.2 TYPES OF OUTLINES

Four kinds of outlines are widely used: the scratch outline, the thesis-sentence outline, the topic outline, and the sentence outline. Sometimes your instructor will tell you which form to use. When you have no specific instructions, select the form that best suits your method of working and the kind of paper you are writing. In planning a long paper, especially one involving research, you will probably want to make a topic or sentence outline. For short papers and extemporaneous writing, informal notes or a scratch outline will generally serve the purpose. Even for long papers, you may find it useful to work informally for some time before committing yourself to a final, detailed plan. It is not uncommon, for example, for writers at work on long projects to draft key passages—an opening paragraph, a closing paragraph, a passage developing the central idea—and then to fit these bits of writing into a more formal plan, along with jotted notes, sentences, and other scraps of ideas. Whatever techniques you use, the important thing is to develop a plan that will guide you in writing your paper.

## Scratch Outlines

A scratch outline is a series of notes—single words or phrases—jotted down to refresh your memory as you write. An outline of this sort is useful when time is limited, as when you are writing examinations or brief papers in class. The following is a sample scratch outline for a theme on the subject "The Value of Summer Jobs":

> Earning money for clothes and school
> Sense of responsibility
> Learning to budget own time and money
> Opportunity to learn about different kinds of jobs
> Develop good work habits and maybe learn practical skills

The exact form of a scratch outline is not particularly important, since ordinarily you will be the only one who sees it. If the list is longer than five or six items, you may need to arrange the entries in some logical order (or number them) before beginning to write.

## Thesis-Sentence Outlines

If you have developed a thesis statement (page 228), you may be able to use its parts as the terms of your outline. This can be especially helpful for short papers and essay examinations. Suppose, for example, that upon arriving in class you are given an assignment to write a short theme during the class period, and that one of the possible topics is "Campus Fashions." Suppose further that your experience and observation enable you within a few moments to jot down the following ideas on this general subject:

> Something like hippie dress is still fairly common
> Straight casual dress is just as common
> There are some variations, like camp style and freaky new fashions
> Most people dress pretty much alike
> It's getting harder to tell the two styles apart

It is possible to arrange these notes as a scratch outline, as suggested above. Another moment's reflection, however, might enable you to exercise tighter control over your theme by formulating a thesis statement such as this:

> While there are some interesting variations in fashion here and there on campus, including camp and freaky fashions, the dominant modified hippie and straight casual dress, which draw closer together every day, give our campus a near-homogeneous appearance.

If you can get this far quickly, you can use the thesis statement as your outline. The sentence above, for example, could forecast a fairly brief, six-paragraph theme, each paragraph developing in sequence the structural units of the thesis statement:

> PARAGRAPH 1: a brief introduction that ends with the thesis statement
>
> PARAGRAPH 2: the interesting variations in fashion (this, judging from the form of the thesis, is an interesting but minor part of the theme)
>
> PARAGRAPH 3: the modified hippie style
>
> PARAGRAPH 4: the straight casual style
>
> PARAGRAPH 5: recent illustrations that show the two coming together
>
> PARAGRAPH 6: a conclusion on the homogeneity of style on your campus

**20.2**

*Org*

One particular advantage of this method of organizing is that you can plan the shape and emphasis of your theme by planning the shape and emphasis of your thesis statement. Your observation might lead you to revise the thesis statement above in this way:

> While the dominant modified hippie and straight casual dress (which draw closer every day) give our campus a near-homogeneous appearance, some very interesting variations have appeared here this year.

A short essay developed from this sentence would have a totally different emphasis from the one suggested above.

## Topic Outlines

The topic outline, the most frequently used kind of formal outline, is helpful in organizing papers of more than five hundred words. It consists of brief phrases or single words (not sentences) that are numbered or lettered to show the order and relative importance of the ideas.

The first thing to do is to get all your ideas down on paper.

On the subject "The Forces as a Career for Young Men and Women," your preliminary thinking might produce this rough, unsorted list of ideas:

Security
Promotion slow but steady
Many different branches appeal to different interests
Low pay
Commissioned ranks open to men and women graduates
Can't be fired
Cost of uniforms
Discipline often annoying
Frequent moves hard on serviceman's family
See interesting places and people
Social life restricted to small circle
Good retirement benefits
Annual vacation with pay
Military job-training useful in civilian careers

**Determining the central idea.**   A quick glance at the list above reveals that some points stress the advantages of a service career; others, the disadvantages. The next step then is to divide the notes into two columns:

| **Advantages** | **Disadvantages** |
|---|---|
| Security | Low pay |
| Promotion slow but steady | Cost of uniforms |
| Many different branches appeal to different interests | Discipline often annoying |
| Can't be fired | Frequent moves hard on serviceman's family |
| See interesting places and people | Social life restricted to small circle |
| Good retirement benefits | |
| Annual vacation with pay | |
| Commissioned ranks open to men and women graduates | |
| Military job-training useful in civilian careers | |

In this form the relationship between the various ideas is not shown (What is the relationship between "Promotion slow but steady" and "Many different branches appeal to different interests"?) and there is no clear balance between the two columns (Is "Security" supposed to balance "Low pay"?). In analysing the columns, however, you can see that there are two main ideas in each—the financial aspect of a service career and the living conditions that go with service life. You might then balance the notes in this way:

    I. Financial aspect
        A. Disadvantages
            1. Low pay
            2. Cost of uniforms
        B. Advantages
            1. Security
            2. Promotion slow but steady
            3. Commissioned ranks open to men and women graduates
            4. Can't be fired
            5. Good retirement benefits
            6. Annual vacation with pay
            7. Military job-training useful in civilian careers
    II. Social aspect
        A. Disadvantages
            1. Discipline often annoying
            2. Frequent moves hard on serviceman's family
            3. Social life restricted to small circle
        B. Advantages
            1. Many different branches appeal to different interests
            2. See interesting places and people

When the notes are arranged in some system, decide on a main point you want to make in your paper. "The Forces as a Career for Young Men and Women" doesn't tell what you are going to say about the subject; it is a title, not a central idea.

**20.2**

*Org*

At this stage you can see that there is more and stronger material on the financial advantages of a military career than on its disadvantages. On the other hand, the disadvantages of living conditions seem to outweigh the advantages. But assuming that you want to treat the subject fully and in a favorable light, you could frame a tentative statement of purpose: "Although there are definite disadvantages to a career in the forces, the advantages outweigh them." This statement now governs the reworking of the outline. At this stage it is still tentative and can be changed as the purpose becomes clearer in your mind.

**Revising the outline.**    With the central idea as your guide, arrange the outline so that every part of it contributes directly to the purpose of the paper. Examine each heading to see if it needs to be strengthened or elaborated upon, if it repeats or overlaps another heading, or if it is unrelated to the central idea.

In the first part of the outline "Cost of uniforms" seems to be a weak point. Aren't officers given allowances for their uniforms? Possibly "Expense of frequent entertaining" is a stronger point; if so, substitute it for "Cost of uniforms."

The financial advantages of a career in the forces seem to stand out, but looking at these entries closely, you will see that some overlap or are actually minor parts of other points. The heading "Security" obviously covers "Slow but steady promotion," "Commissioned ranks open to men and women graduates," and "Can't be fired." Closer examination reveals that "Annual vacation with pay" is an aspect of living conditions rather than of finances; it should therefore be shifted to the second main heading.

Under "Advantages" in the second main heading, the first entry, "Many different classifications appeal to different interests," seems out of place or badly phrased. Perhaps the point is that service people may be able to find jobs they like or are best fitted for.

As the plan now stands, the first part seems stronger. To make the argument more convincing, it would be a good idea to reverse the present order: begin with "Living conditions," and then end on an emphatic note—the training that the armed forces provide for other fields. After these changes have been made, and after some headings have been reworded to make them parallel in form, the final outline might be:

Thesis sentence: Although from the standpoint of finances and living conditions, there are some disadvantages to a service career for men and women, the advantages outweigh them.

I. Living conditions
  A. Disadvantages
    1. Discipline often annoying
    2. Frequent moves hard on family
    3. Social life restricted to a small circle
  B. Advantages
    1. Opportunity to find the job one is suited for
    2. Annual leaves with pay
    3. Chance to travel, to see new places, and to meet new people
II. Financial considerations
  A. Disadvantages
    1. Relatively low pay
    2. Frequent entertaining expensive
  B. Advantages
    1. Security
      a. Slow but steady promotion, including commissions for men and women graduates
      b. Permanent employment
      c. Good retirement benefits
    2. Preparation for civilian careers on retirement

The outline now can be the basis for an orderly paper that makes a definite point.

## Sentence Outlines

A sentence outline is developed in the same way as a topic outline, but the ideas are more fully expressed. Each heading is expressed as a complete sentence, usually consisting of just one main clause:

Thesis sentence: Although from the standpoint of finances and living conditions, there are some disadvantages to a service career for young men and women, the advantages outweigh them.

I. Living conditions are a major consideration in choosing a career.
   A. Service life has several shortcomings in this respect.
      1. The strict discipline imposed is often annoying.
      2. Frequent moves are hard on an officer's family.
      3. Social life is usually restricted to a small circle of army families.
   B. On the other hand, there are certain advantages to service life.
      1. The armed forces, with its wide range of occupations, give one an opportunity to find the job he or she is best suited for.
      2. There are generous annual leaves with pay.
      3. Wide travel opportunities can introduce one to new places and people.

II. Financial considerations are also of major importance.
   A. Two disadvantages are apparent.
      1. The pay is low compared to that in many civilian jobs.
      2. Officers are burdened with the cost of frequent entertaining.
   B. The advantages, however, are more striking.
      1. The armed forces offer a high degree of job security.
         a. Promotions are slow but steady, with commissions open to men and women graduates.
         b. There is almost no danger of dismissal.
         c. Retirement benefits are good.
      2. A career in the armed forces provides excellent preparation for civilian careers on retirement.

**20.2**

*Org*

Each heading is a complete sentence, and only one sentence—not two or three. All sentences are in the form of statements. All are in the same tense and reasonably parallel in structure.

The chief advantage of a sentence outline is that the ideas will have to be clear and fully thought out before they can be stated in complete sentences. For that reason, it is sometimes assigned for training in writing long formal reports such as reference (or library) papers.

► **EXERCISES**

1. Choose three of the following general subjects, narrow them to a topic specific enough for a 500-word theme, and write a scratch outline for each: *population growth, separatism, summer activities, television standards, automobile safety-standards, automation, popular myths.*

2. Write a scratch outline on any one of the following topics that appeals to you, or choose your own. When you have jotted down all your notes, frame a thesis sentence and put the notes in the form of a topic outline:

| | |
|---|---|
| Why People Watch Excavations | Speaking in Public |
| Should Physical Education Be | Unusual Place Names |
| a Required Program? | Forecasting Election Results |
| Income Is Not the Primary | I Prefer Bach |
| Goal of Education | Our Local Parking Problem |

## 20.3 STANDARD OUTLINE FORM

Numbering, indention, punctuation, and other physical aspects of outlines follow certain conventions, particularly when the outlines are to be read by someone other than the writer. When you are required to turn in an outline with your paper, use the type of outline your instructor specifies and put it in standard form.

### Numbering and Indention

Make the numbering of your headings consistent throughout. This is the typical method for numbering and indenting a topic or sentence outline:

Thesis sentence: _____

| | |
|---|---|
| _____ | (Sentence statement) |
| I. _____ | (Roman numeral for main head) |
|   A. _____ | (Capital letter for subhead) |
|     1. _____ | (Arabic numeral for second sub- |
|     2. _____ | head) |
|       a. _____ | (Lower-case letter for third sub- |
|       b. _____ | head) |
|   B. _____ | |
| II. _____ | |

The main heads (I, II, III . . .) are set flush with the left-hand margin. The subheads are indented four or five spaces in typed copy and about three quarters of an inch in longhand, or they may be indented so that they are directly under the first word of the preceding heading, as shown in this book.

When a heading runs over one line, the second line is indented as far as the first word of the preceding line:

I. The photo-electric cell, known as the "electric eye," has been put to a variety of practical uses.
   A. It is used in elevator floors to enable the elevator to stop at exactly the right level.

When you make an outline, avoid overelaborate and confusing systems. There is rarely any need to go farther than the third subhead (a, b, c . . .). Two levels of headings are often enough for a short paper.

## Punctuation and Capitalization

In a topic outline, capitalize only the first letter of the word beginning the heading (and all proper nouns), and do not put any punctuation at the end of the entry, because these headings are not complete sentences:

I. Present need for physicists
   A. In private industry
   B. In government projects
   C. In colleges and universities

**20.3**

*Org*

Punctuate every heading in a sentence outline just as you would punctuate the sentences in your paper: begin with a capital letter and end with a period. Except for proper nouns, other words in the heading are not capitalized (a heading is not a title):

I. The advantages of specialization are numerous.
   A. Students can set goals for themselves.
   B. They can obtain more knowledge about their subjects.

## Content of headings

Each heading in an outline should be specific and meaningful:

**Vague and useless**
The Profession I Want to Follow
  I. Introduction
  II. Why I prefer this work
  III. What the opportunities would be
  IV. The chances for success
  V. Conclusion

**Specific**
The Profession I Want to Follow
  I. Lifelong interest in veterinarian's work
   A. Grew up with animals on a farm
   B. Saw importance of veterinarian's work
   C. Worked with a

**Specific**

> veterinarian last two
> summers
> II. Many opportunities in
>     veterinary work today
>     A. In rural areas
>     B. In cities
> III. Worthwhile and well-
>      paid profession

Headings like "Introduction," "Body," and "Conclusion" aren't useful unless you indicate what material belongs in the sections. Instead of using general labels such as "Causes" and "Results," indicate what the causes or results are; it will save time later.

Putting headings in the form of questions or in statements that will have to be filled in later is not an efficient practice. The necessary information will have to be supplied when you write, so you might as well supply it in the planning stage:

| **Indefinite** | **Definite** |
|---|---|
| I. The Wars of the Roses | I. The Wars of the Roses |
|   A. When they began |   A. Started 1455 |
|   B. Why? |   B. Caused by rivalry between Houses of Lancaster and York |

## Dividing the Material

Generally, if a heading is to be divided at all, it should be divided into more than one part. When there is only one heading under a topic, it usually repeats what is in the topic and should therefore be included with it:

| **Unnecessary division** | **Accurate division** |
|---|---|
| The Hudson's Bay Company | The Hudson's Bay Company |
| I. Chartered by English king | I. Chartered by Charles II |
|   A. Charles II |   King of England, |
|     1. In 1670 |   in 1670 |

The heads of an outline should represent equally important divisions of the subject as a whole, and should be parallel in grammatical form and tense. In a topic outline, if *I* is a noun, *II* and *III* are also nouns; if *I* is a prepositional phrase, so are *II* and *III*. The same principle applies to subdivisions. A sentence outline should use complete sentences throughout and not lapse into topic headings:

| **Unequal headings** | **Equal headings** |
|---|---|
| Growing Roses | Growing Roses |
| I. Preparing the soil | I. Preparing the soil |
| II. Planting | II. Planting |
| III. Growing the plant | III. Watering |
| IV. Mildew | IV. Fertilizing |
| V. Insect pests | V. Spraying |
| VI. Using a spray gun | |

The subdivisions should also designate equally important and parallel divisions of one phase of the main divisions:

| **Unequal subheads** | **Equal subheads** |
|---|---|
| I. Job opportunities in Alberta | I. Job opportunities in Alberta |
|   A. Raising crops |   A. Agriculture |
|   B. White-collar work |   B. Business |
|   C. Dairy farms |   C. Industry |
|   D. Factory jobs | |
|   E. Breweries | |

Headings of equal rank should not overlap: what is in *II* should exclude what is covered in *I; B* should be clearly distinct from *A*.

**20.3**

*Org*

| **Overlapping** | **Accurate** |
|---|---|
| Ways of transporting freight | Ways of transporting freight |
| I. Water | I. Ship |
|   A. Ships |   A. Passenger ships |
|   B. Freighters |   B. Freighters |
| II. On the ground | II. Truck |
|   A. Trucks | III. Railroad |
|   B. "Piggyback" in trucks |   A. Loaded into cars |
| III. Railroads |   B. "Piggyback" in trucks |
| IV. In the air | IV. Airplane |

Whatever form of planning you do for your paper, take it seriously. Use your plan as an opportunity to see your subject and its parts, and as an opportunity to try different arrangements. Remember that any outline is tentative; you may learn a better way of planning as you proceed.

▶ EXERCISE

Check the following outlines from the standpoint of effective and useful planning. Then state specifically what you consider to be the unsatisfactory aspects of each one, in form and content. Revise the outlines accordingly:

1. Types of Canadian schools
  I. Schools open to everyone
    A. Elementary schools

      B. There are many colleges and universities
      C. Secondary or high
      D. Providing technical instruction
      E. Private schools

2. Why everyone should be able to swim.
    I. Everyone should learn to swim.
      A. As early as possible.
        1. Children have been taught as young as three years
    II. The ability to swim may save your life.
      1. never swim alone
      2. don't show off in the water
      3. Many schools require students to pass swimming tests.
        a. my experiences
        b. Red Cross lifesaving test

3. Increasing automation in industry presents many problems.
    I. Unemployment
      A. Permanent layoffs
      B. Shorter working hours
      C. Decreases job opportunities
    II. What is automation?
      A. Definition
      B. Uses
        1. Where it cannot be used
      C. There are many advantages to automation
    III. Increased leisure time
      A. Recreation
        1. Hobbies
        2. Travelling
        3. Adult education classes
    IV. New skills are required.
      A. Trained technicians
      B. The unskilled workers are laid off.
        1. Providing government benefits
        2. Providing added training
    V. Is automation here to stay?

# Writing the First Draft

*. . . The great thing is to last and get your work done and see and hear and learn and understand; and write when there is something that you know; and not before; and not too damned much after.* —*Ernest Hemingway,* DEATH IN THE AFTERNOON

*To get started, I will accept anything that occurs to me. . . . So, receptive, careless of failure, I spin out things on the page. And a wonderful freedom comes. If something occurs to me, it is all right to accept it. It has one justification: it occurs to me. No one else can guide me. I must follow my own weak, wandering, diffident impulses.* —*William Stafford, "A Way of Writing"*

When you are reasonably well satisfied with your preparations and your plans for organizing your material, it's time to begin the actual writing. You probably shouldn't expect to be completely satisfied with your preparation and planning. Even with long and careful preliminary work, you won't always have a good sense of all that you are going to say until you do the writing itself. Sometimes, when you have studied a subject and thought it out, you'll be able to lay out a plan for a piece of writing that has in it everything you wish to say in the order you wish to say it, and your own attitude toward your subject matter will already be clear. If that happens, the actual writing may be easier than usual: you may have little to do but complete your outline or plan by adding illustrations and transitions.

Often, however, even when you have thought your subject through and have a good, thorough, workable plan, you still won't have a good sense of all that's to be said: you still won't know exactly which illustrative material you may need to use to fill out parts of your plan, and your own attitudes toward the material may not be clear until you have found the words for them. It has often been remarked that we do not always know what we think until we hear what we say. Thinking and planning are not always over when you've developed a plan for your writing.

For this reason, when you are composing papers outside the classroom, it is usually best to write them out in rough draft first. Revising and copying can come later. No matter how certain you are about the material and the order of presentation, a complete first draft is important if the final paper is to represent your best work.

Up to this point, you have been dealing with ideas in abbreviated forms as notes or outline headings, even though you may have

21

*Draft*

written bits and pieces in complete form. Now you are ready to put it all down in full sentences and paragraphs, to see the whole paper as your reader will, and to make whatever changes may be necessary for continuity and effectiveness.

## 21.1 GETTING STARTED

Begin writing the first draft as soon as you have decided on the content and organization of the paper. Don't wait for "inspiration" or the proper mood: write while the ideas and information are still in your mind; an outline that you put away for three hours or three days can look cold and unfamiliar if your mind isn't still turning in the same way. For almost everyone, writing is work, and you must often begin writing when you would much prefer to do something else. If you wait until the last minute, your first draft may have to serve as your final paper, and the cracks and loose screws in it will show.

The beginning of a paper is often the most difficult part to word effectively. If you can't think of a good opening sentence, begin with some other part; if the wording of a good first paragraph doesn't come to you at once, start with a part that comes more easily. You shouldn't waste time trying to get an ideal opening; as you work, a good start will often occur to you. Many beginnings are written last. (See 21.4, Opening Paragraphs.)

Once you have broken the ice by writing two or three sentences, you'll often find it easier to go on, even without that elusive "inspiration." Writing, like many other activities, calls for a warm-up, and you may have to do a few laps and some wind sprints before you are ready to go.

As a rule, write the first draft as rapidly as you can. Your paper will have more life if you put your ideas down one after the other without pausing to worry about correctness. At this stage, you should concentrate on getting down the gist of what you have in mind. You are the only one who will see your first draft, and matters of spelling, punctuation, and wording can be taken care of in revision. (See 28.1, Revising the First Draft.)

Plan to spend at least some time at uninterrupted writing. When you are working on a paper that is too long to be written in one sitting, it sometimes helps to stop in the middle of a paragraph or a passage that is going easily and well, perhaps even in the middle of a sentence. This practice will make it easier to get started again when you come back to your work. Take time to read over what you have already written before you begin writing again.

Leave plenty of space in the first draft for making corrections and changes. There should be ample margins on both sides of the page and space between lines for insertions and corrections.

## 21.2 DEVELOPING YOUR MATERIAL

Make the first draft as complete as possible. Write down more than you will probably use in your final paper; be generous with explanations and illustrative examples. It is much easier to cut out material in revision than it is to look for more to satisfy the requirements of length or completeness of presentation. Papers that are heavy with material added at the last moment always seem disjointed. Those that have been pruned down from, say, fourteen hundred to a thousand words are likely to be more compact and to the point.

Put in any good ideas that occur to you when you are writing the first draft, even though they may not have appeared in the original plan. In this stage, an outline does not need to be followed down to the last minor subdivision. Frequently a sentence written on paper will bring to mind an aspect of the topic that you overlooked when your material was in the form of notes. If the new idea turns out to be irrelevant, it can be omitted in revision; but if it is important, you can alter your outline to include it.

**21.2**

*Draft*

### Kinds of Development

As the full paper grows from the organization plan you have decided on, it should follow the form of development that best suits the topic and that will be clearest to the reader. If you have made an unusually complete plan for your paper, the plan itself may tell you how to develop and amplify each part. Often, however, an outline or some other kind of plan will tell you what is to be in each part of your paper, not what to do with it, or how to write it out. The patterns of development discussed in the section on paragraphs (27.2) may be useful to you in developing whole papers, though adequate development of a whole paper may require a combination of different kinds of paragraphs. Which kind predominates is determined by the needs of the paper. These are some of the most commonly used types of order:

1. **Time and sequence:** describing events in the order of their occurrence. This approach is apt in narrative writing (a report of an athletic contest, an account of an incident in history) or in describing a process (the construction of a log cabin, stages in the development of a frog).

2. **Space:** describing objects as they exist within a certain area, often used in descriptive expository writing (a description of a city from outskirts to centre, of a mural from left to right).

3. **Increasing complexity:** beginning with the simple or familiar and proceeding to the more complex or unfamiliar (discussing wind instruments beginning with the toy whistle, continuing to simple recorders, and ending with orchestral instruments like the flute and oboe).

4. **Comparison and contrast:** discussing all the features of one idea or situation, then all the features of another, and ending by drawing a conclusion about the two ("Television and Newspapers As Sources of News," "Public Schools and Private Schools"). If such a plan seems to make the paper break in the middle, present a sequence of comparisons and contrasts on each major point—not all the features of public schools and then of private schools, but in some such order as this: 1. Cost of attendance, 2. Curriculum, 3. Facilities.

5. **Support:** beginning with a general statement or impression and then supporting it with specific examples, details, reasons. This method is often useful in argumentation and for such topics as "The Value of Studying Foreign Languages," "The Problems of Increasing Automation," "Freshman Composition Courses Should Be Required."

6. **Climax:** beginning with a specific fact or situation and unfolding the subject until it stands completed at the end. A paper about the development of the polio vaccine might begin with the need for the vaccine, then take up the problems facing researchers, go on to explain how solutions were found, and end with the production of an effective vaccine.

7. **Cause to effect or effect to cause:** beginning with an analysis of causes, culminating in a statement of effect, or stating the effect first, then moving to the analysis of cause. The subject should determine which pattern is better: if you are writing about your city's traffic mess, for example, you might want to describe that problem briefly at the beginning as an effect already known, then proceed to an analysis of the causes, which are probably less well known.

The working outline should represent the kind of development most appropriate to your subject. Often two kinds of development are used in combination: a narrative could follow both the order of time and that of climax; the method of support might be used effectively with comparison or climax. The essential thing is that you present your material in some sensible order.

## Controlling Direction

One way to get into your draft and develop your meaning—especially if you are having trouble starting your paper or a particular section of it—is to use a sentence to direct the development. In your opening, for example, you can use your thesis sentence to indicate the development of your theme as a whole. (See 20.2.) And in the body of your paper, you can similarly work with sentences to direct the development of each section.

Suppose that you have developed this topic outline as the basis for a paper:

**21.2**

*Draft*

The Profession I Want to Follow
Thesis sentence: I want to become a veterinarian because of my life-long interest in veterinary work, because of the many opportunities it offers, and because it is a worthwhile and well-paid profession.

  I. Lifelong interest in veterinarian's work
     A. Grew up with animals on a farm
     B. Saw importance of veterinarian's work
     C. Worked with a veterinarian last two summers
 II. Many opportunities in veterinary work today
     A. In rural areas
     B. In urban areas
III. Worthwhile and well-paid profession

The thesis sentence is a guide, directing the development of the outline and the theme. It could be used, for example, to introduce a climactic development that places increasing stress on the series of three factors.

The separate sections of the theme could also be directed by opening sentences. For example, we can assume that Section I will require at least three paragraphs. To control the relationships among them, the writer could introduce the section like this:

> Although I grew up with animals on a farm and saw the importance of the veterinarian's work, I didn't really understand all that a veterinarian does until I worked with one the last two summers.

This sentence, which might be used to open the first paragraph of the first section or might be used alone as an introduction, shows how the ideas in Section I are related and gives the writer a direction: there is a time sequence which suggests that the three paragraphs might be narrative; the last paragraph should probably get the dominant stress.

The first section closes with the idea that the writer is aware of the value of the veterinary profession. Section II, then, might open with a sentence like this:

> The needs for veterinary work are great in the country and surprisingly varied in the city.

This sentence, which makes the rural and urban needs coordinate, could forecast a balanced treatment by the method of comparison. The section would probably be developed in two paragraphs. Section III might then be directed in this way:

> Because the needs for veterinary medicine are great, the work is worthwhile; because the work is needed, the pay is good.

This balanced introductory sentence could lead the writer into a balanced, judicious paragraph stating an effect—the causes having been analysed in Sections I and II.

Sometimes a writer can also use particular patterns of paragraph development (27.2) to determine a means of expanding the material; this approach can be helpful in writing short themes. Suppose you arrive in your composition class some Monday morning to find an assignment on the blackboard for an in-class theme. One of the suggested subjects invites your response to the idea of an honor system. If you are familiar with the patterns of paragraph development, you might be able very quickly to settle on a design, a means of developing your paper. Not everyone has participated in an honor system; not everyone knows what it is. You might therefore decide that the purpose of your paper would be to explain what an honor system is. Knowing the pattern of definition, you could develop your explanation in this way:

> PARAGRAPH 1: entirely **illustration,** describing an honor system in action
>
> PARAGRAPH 2: **comparison** of honor system with similar things, such as codes of behavior in clubs
>
> PARAGRAPH 3: **contrast,** an account of how honor system is unlike other codes

The sequence of three paragraphs forms a definition: the first by illustration identifies the *term;* the second by comparison puts the term in a *class;* the third by contrast shows how it *differs* from other members of the same class. With this three-paragraph definition, you might then be able to write a fourth, concluding paragraph of evaluation.

▶ **EXERCISE**

For each of the three topics listed below, write out five sentences to show how you would develop the topic according to the suggested pattern of development, as shown in the example.

*Example: topic:* **New** artists change our musical tastes. *pattern:* time

a. In the mid-1950's, Elvis Presley changed the direction of pop music with "Blue Suede Shoes" and other hits.
b. By the early 1960's, folk musicians like Bob Dylan and the Kingston Trio brought different sounds into prominence.
c. The Beatles took the spotlight in the later '60's, and spawned an entirely "new" sound, which many other groups imitated.
d. The early 1970's found a new and "slicked-up" country sound which brought country music onto the popular music charts in a big way.
e. Many singers and groups have come and gone in the past twenty years, but it is interesting that artists like Presley and Dylan have not only been able to change with the times, but they have also helped shape and change our musical tastes.

1. *topic:* Building a new shopping centre downtown. *pattern:* space
2. *topic:* Opinion is divided on the harmfulness of marijuana. *pattern:* comparison and contrast
3. *topic:* The discovery that the world is round changed both science and everyday life. *pattern:* cause to effect

**21.3**

*Draft*

## 21.3  RELATING PARAGRAPHS IN SEQUENCE

As you write your first draft, remember that you are going to have to take a reader with you. Your individual paragraphs should represent a progressive development of the subject. If there is too wide a gap in ideas between the end of one paragraph and the beginning of the next, the reader may not be able to follow your line of thought. You must provide clear transitions.

### Showing the Connection Between Paragraphs

Connect paragraphs by linking the topic of a new paragraph with the topic of the preceding one. This is not as hard as it may sound; usually it's easy—and natural—to phrase the opening statement of a paragraph so that it grows out of what you have just said. In the paragraphs below, linking words are in boldface type:

What about the Indians? There are no Indians in the Arches country now; they all left seven hundred years ago and won't be back for a long time. But here as elsewhere in the canyonlands they left a **record** of their passage. Near springs and under overhanging cliffs, good camping spots, you may find chipping grounds scattered with hundreds of fragments of flint or chert where the Anasazi hunters worked their arrowpoints. You may find shards of pottery. At other places you will see their writing on the canyon walls—the **petroglyphs** and **pictographs.**

**Petroglyphs** are carved in the rock; **pictographs** are painted on the rock. Whether in one form or the other **they** consist of representations of birds, snakes, deer and many other animals, of human, semihuman and superhuman figures, and of designs purely abstract or symbolic. In some places you find only **petroglyphs,** in other places only **pictographs,** in some places **both.** The explicitly representational often comes side by side with the highly abstract.

In style the **inscriptions** and **paintings** range from the crude and simple to the elegant, sophisticated and subtle. **They** seem to include the work of different cultures and a great extent of time. . . .— Edward Abbey, *Desert Solitaire*

Transitions from paragraph to paragraph (and from sentence to sentence) are made here by repeating key words (*petroglyphs* and *pictographs,* linked with *records*), by pronoun references to key words (*both, they*), and by synonyms of key words (*inscriptions* and *paintings*).

## Showing the Relation to the Topic of the Paper

Whenever possible, show the relation between the paragraph and the thesis of the paper and thus keep your paragraphs going in the same direction. For example, in this discussion of the games played by primitive peoples, the author begins each paragraph by introducing a different kind of sport:

PARAGRAPH 1: Wrestling is probably universal. [four sentences follow]

PARAGRAPH 2: Races are far more common. [three sentences follow]

PARAGRAPH 3: Ball games are also widespread, but vary greatly in type. [six sentences follow]

PARAGRAPH 4: Frequently the ball games are played in a more elaborate way. [fourteen sentences follow]

PARAGRAPH 5: On the western Plains of the United States, the "hoop-and-pole game" was very popular. [six sentences follow]

PARAGRAPH 6: Compared with such sports, rope-skipping seems simple, but the Australian Euahlayi make an art of it. [two sentences follow]

PARAGRAPH 7: Polynesians lead in aquatic sports. [four sentences follow]

PARAGRAPH 8: Maori stilt-walkers raced one another across streams, and also tried to upset one another's balance. [two sentences follow] — Robert H. Lowie, *An Introduction to Cultural Anthropology*

## Transition Paragraphs

For major transitions, such as from one main section of a long paper to another, a brief paragraph (sometimes just one sentence) will often serve to prepare readers for what is coming next. Notice the middle paragraph below:

> But nothing in that end of town was as good as the dumpground that scattered along a little runoff coulee dipping down toward the river from the south bench. Through a historical process that went back, probably, to the roots of community sanitation and distaste for eyesores, but that in law dated from the Unincorporated Towns Ordinance of the territorial government, passed in 1888, the dump was one of the very first community enterprises, almost our town's first institution.
>
> More than that, it contained relics of every individual who had ever lived there, and of every phase of the town's history.
>
> The bedsprings on which the town's first child was begotten might be there; the skeleton of a boy's pet colt; two or three volumes of Shakespeare bought in haste and error from a peddler. . . . — Wallace Stegner, *Wolf Willow*

Ordinarily, the subject matter of successive paragraphs is so closely related that separate transition paragraphs are not needed, and in short papers they are usually out of place.

**21.4**

*Draft*

## 21.4 OPENING PARAGRAPHS

The first paragraph of a paper usually has two functions: to introduce the subject and to catch the reader's interest. Plan your paper so that you can get into your subject as quickly as possible. The shorter the paper, the more direct your beginning should be.

If, after finishing your first draft, you find that you have written an obviously weak beginning, see if the second or third sentence, or even the second paragraph, may not provide a better starting point. Often the first few lines of writing are simply a warm-up, and the paper actually begins a few sentences later.

## Effective Openings

No matter what you are writing about, the beginning of your paper should catch the readers' interest and get them into the subject. Some of the ways to accomplish this are discussed below.

**A statement of purpose or point of view.**    This should not be a mechanical statement ("In this paper I am going to give you my reasons for majoring in political science.") or a flat rewording of the assignment, but a natural lead into the topic:

> When I decided to enter the university, like most freshmen I had only the vaguest notion of what subject I intended to major in. But now after two terms of haphazardly chosen course-work, and after a good deal of self-analysis, I have decided that **there are at least four good reasons why I should major in political science.**

If your purpose is to discuss one aspect of some general subject, the first paragraph can make the limits of your paper clear:

> The Great Lakes are among the major lake systems of the world. Through the centuries many large cities have grown up along their perimeter as people recognized their value for inland navigation, water supply, and recreation. Pollution of their waters by industrial wastes has also inevitably increased through the years, until now it presents a serious threat. **The pollution problems in Lake Erie are typical of those of the Great Lakes area as a whole.**

**A definition.**    If your paper deals with some subject which has a variety of meanings for different readers, it is good to make your definition clear at the outset. There is no need to start with such a trite statement as "According to the *Gage Canadian Dictionary,* a hobby is 'something a person especially likes to work at or study apart from his main business.'" Try a definition that fits your own approach to the subject:

> A hobby, as I see it, is an activity that takes up most of your spare time and all of your spare money. At least that has been my experience since I became interested in photography. . . .

**An important fact.**    One of the quickest and clearest ways to open a paper is with the statement of an important fact that will lead to the general topic. This is a natural opening for a narrative and can also be good for a discussion of ideas:

> The retail price of beef has nearly doubled between last August, when it averaged $1.20 a pound, and last week, when it averaged $2.02 a pound. Prices are expected to continue to rise and to stay

high for three or four years.—Editorial, "Inflation on the hoof," *The Globe and Mail* (Toronto)

My cultural loyalties, like just about everyone else's in this schizoid country we call home, are confusing. I was born in the province of Quebec, a Jew, my nationality Canadian, and the demands on my heart being made by each group seem to me increasingly contrary.—Mordecai Richler, in *Maclean's*

**A reference to personal experience.**  If your subject is one with which you have had some personal experience, a reference to your connection with it provides an appropriate beginning. In an essay on the complex problems of the decline in literacy, for example, a university professor  begins in this way:

When I let it slip among ordinary company that I'm a professor of English, you can guess what the reaction is: "Oh-oh," they say with nervous smiles, "I'd better watch my language." No use explaining that I don't teach composition. If English professors hit the front page..., it's not when they have profound or brilliant ideas about literature, but when they are testily muttering that their latest crop of freshmen can neither read nor write. And the truth is, of course, that we are—we must be—concerned with language. It is the medium both of the works we study, and of our attempts to teach it. If language should decay far enough, the study of literature becomes difficult or impossible.... So I worry a good deal about language myself. And I think the most useful way to put my worries before you is to pursue that automatic reaction: "Oh-oh, I'd better watch my language."—Michael Hornyansky, "Is English Destroying Your Image?"

**21.4**

*Draft*

**A lively detail or illustration.**  A good way to arouse the reader's interest and curiosity is to begin with a lively detail—perhaps with an anecdote, an apt quotation, or an allusion to some current topic. Such material should of course be related to the subject of the paper, as is this beginning of an article on conservation:

Millions of years ago, a volcano built a mountain on the floor of the Atlantic. In eruption after eruption, it pushed up a great pile of volcanic rock, until it had accumulated a mass a hundred miles across at its base, reaching upward toward the surface of the sea. Finally its cone emerged as an island with an area of about 200 square miles. Thousands of years passed, and thousands of thousands. Eventually the waves of the Atlantic cut down the cone and reduced it to a shoal—all of it, that is, but a small fragment which remained above water. This fragment we know as Bermuda.—Rachel Carson, *The Sea Around Us*

## Openings to Avoid

The opening paragraph should mark the actual beginning of the paper and be clearly related to the subject. If it does not create interest in the subject or get it under way, it probably does not belong in the paper. These common mistakes make poor beginnings:

**Beginning too far back.**    If you are discussing the organization of the United Nations, there is no need to begin with the reasons for the failure of the League of Nations, nor is there any reason to begin a paper on Trudeau as Prime Minister with an account of his world travels. The shorter your paper, the more direct should be the beginning. A statement of the purpose or a rewording of the central idea is the simplest way to begin a paper written in class.

**An apology or a complaint.**    A statement such as this is discouraging to most readers: "Being a mere freshman, I'm afraid that what I have to say on this topic won't be of much value. . . ." Complaints are also better left unwritten: "Before I started to write this theme, I thought I could find some interesting material on it in the library, but there wasn't any. . . ." Remember that readers are interested only in the ideas that you present, not in the difficulties or disappointments you may have had while writing the paper.

**Too broad a generalization.**    "Science in the last fifty years has made more progress than any other branch of knowledge" is a generalization far too sweeping to explain or prove in a five-hundred-word or even a five-thousand-word paper. Statements such as this are likely to be more impressive to the writer than they are to the reader. Wherever possible, begin with a specific statement: "Though smaller than your thumb, an electronic device called the transistor has had a tremendous effect on radio and television sets."

**A self-evident statement.**    Avoid starting a paper with a remark so obvious that it need not be mentioned: "Canada has a great number of resorts and parks situated in many scenic localities." And resist the temptation—a good exercise, anyway, once in a while — to open your paper with some commonplace observation that gives no hint of your subject: "It has been said that the only thing constant in life is change." If you have started your paper with a self-evident remark, see if the sentence immediately following is a good beginning for your paper.

▶ EXERCISE

Revise the following opening statements so that they at least tell readers what the paper is about. Try also to make the statement lively enough to catch the readers' interest:

*Example:* In your modern world of today, personal hygiene has become very important for success in the modern complex world of business.

*Good opening:* These days, if you want to get ahead, it probably helps to look good and smell good.

*Better:* Each year, Canadians spend millions on creams, deodorants, after-shaves, soaps, and other products designed to make them look and smell good. It is a sad reality that one's success in the world is probably determined as much by grooming as it is by talent.

1. There are many topics of importance in the news these days. One of the many important topics is how we are going to control inflation.

2. I have always liked certain kinds of hobbies. One of the most interesting hobbies I enjoy writing about is training guinea pigs, which is a very interesting hobby.

3. The abolishment of the Senate and some of the reasons why I support it is the subject of this paper.

4. The morning was dark and grey. A fog enshrouded the dormitory, and reflected my mood as I approached the delicate topic of required physical education.

5. "There are two sides to every question," says the proverb. This is not so in the case of the controversy over whether or not to register handguns. Only one opinion can be substantiated with facts. According to one dictionary, a handgun is a "gun which can be held in one hand easily, usually a pistol."

**21.5**

*Draft*

## 21.5 CLOSING PARAGRAPHS

The beginning and ending of your paper—the point at which you meet your readers and the place at which you leave them—should be among the most interesting and forceful parts of your paper. Make the ending definite and emphatic, if possible—unless, of course, you are writing a paper that specifically calls for another tone, such as reverie or whimsy. Otherwise, plan your paper so that it won't trail off or leave your reader up in the air. The final paragraph should round out your discussion in such a way that the reader will know you have said all you intended to say and that you have not stopped because you were tired of writing or because time ran out. Remember that the total effect of your paper may depend largely upon the way you end it.

## Effective Conclusions

Your final paragraph should tie together the ideas you have been developing and emphasize the main point of the paper. Some suggestions for effective conclusions follow:

**A climax.** Make your final paragraph the culmination of the ideas you have been developing, or save the most important idea for the last. The concluding paragraph thus becomes the climax of the paper. A student paper of about a thousand words, which has described in detail the operation of a large used-car lot, brings all the details to a focus in this conclusion:

> This used-car lot was sponsored by an organization which sells thousands of cars a year, so it was by no means a fly-by-night affair. Although no sloppy repairs were done, and no highly crooked deals were tolerated, there was just a slight suspicion that the company was getting the best of every customer on every deal. This company, however good or bad, is representative of many similar organizations throughout Canada.

**A suggestion for action.** If you have been criticizing some situation (parking on the campus, the price of textbooks, daylight-saving time), end your paper with a positive suggestion for action, or at least a clear call for action, as in this paragraph:

> Of course the task of the [second-] language teacher is to teach a language. Nothing is justified in the language classroom that does not contribute to that end. My experience, however, has been that some reasoned introduction of pertinent general principles of language can expedite learning enough to make it a real bargain. An hour's worth of such comments scattered approximately into relevant contexts can speed the learning by two hours. But even more important than that, it can make a noticeable improvement in the quality of the students' language learning and, hence, of their communicative competence.—H.A. Gleason, "Linguistics and Language Learning"

**A summary statement.** Longer and more formal papers are sometimes concluded by restating the main points of the discussion. But for most papers written in composition courses, it is seldom necessary or advisable to summarize what has been said. The result is often a weak and mechanical ending.

## Tying the Ending to the Beginning

The final paragraph may repeat, in different wording, the opening idea. This method is useful in longer papers, both to remind the reader what the main subject is and to give it final emphasis. It is also helpful, if not overdone, in shorter papers, where the repetition of key ideas, key words, or key images may give the reader a sense of a circle neatly closing. The two paragraphs below are the opening and closing of an essay in which the author reminisces about his instructor in writing:

> When I was a freshman, *Gulliver's Travels* taught me more about writing than any other book. Other freshmen might find little to learn from it, but that is because they do not have Craig LaDriere for a teacher. . . .
>
> Freshman English is not supposed to be a source of innocent merriment. Its object all sublime is to make thought yield to words. Nobody quite learns how, but I went farther with Jonathan Swift and Craig LaDriere than ever before or since.—Francis G. Townsend, "A Freshman in Lilliput," *College Composition and Communication*

## Endings to Avoid

**21.5**

*Draft*

Avoid unemphatic, inconclusive, or contradictory endings. Here are some typical pitfalls to avoid in your closing paragraphs:

**An apology.**    Ending a paper with an apology for its shortcomings only serves to emphasize them:

> I am sorry this paper is so short, but I always have a difficult time putting my ideas on paper.

If you carefully work out your ideas before writing and then present them as effectively as you can, you will not need to apologize for your efforts.

**A qualifying remark.**    If the last sentence of a paper is an exception or a qualifying remark, it weakens everything that has been said before:

> Although I haven't answered why some people refuse to face facts, I have come to the conclusion that not facing facts may be a natural part of human nature. Of course, this can be carried to extremes.

There may be two sides to every subject, but when the purpose or scope of your paper is limited to the arguments for one side only, don't suddenly shift to the other side in your conclusion. If, for example, you have been presenting every argument you can think of in support of price controls or strict ecological legislation, don't end like this: "Of course, there is much to be said for the other side also." If you feel such a qualifying statement is necessary, make it earlier in the paper.

**Minor details or afterthoughts.**   A paper describing the role of the pitcher in baseball shouldn't end with a remark about other aspects of the game:

> Baseball is one of our favorite sports, and to spend an afternoon at Olympic Stadium watching two great pitchers battling for a victory is an exciting experience. What I have said about pitching gives you an idea what a pitcher must keep in his mind while out there on the mound, or as a substitute on the bench. **There are eight other players on the team besides the pitcher and the same can be written about each individual player and his position.**

Some concluding statements make a reader wonder whether the writer actually finished his paper or abandoned it in the middle of an idea:

> I could go on for pages describing the other interesting people I met on the ship, but the length of this paper doesn't permit it.

Instead of putting a sentence such as this at the end of your paper, round out the description fully, or if the topic is already developed sufficiently, see if the next to the last sentence wouldn't make a respectable conclusion.

## 21.6  WRITING A TITLE

Word the title of your paper so that it gives a definite and accurate idea of the subject matter in as few words as possible. A title need not mystify or startle the readers, although it may perhaps arouse their curiosity or appeal to their sense of humor. Interesting titles are always appreciated, but one that is brief, simple, and exact will serve the purpose; it is, after all, the label on the product.

A title should not suggest more than the paper actually covers. If you are discussing your tastes in music, avoid such sweeping titles as "Modern Jazz" or "Music of Today"; use instead "Music I Like" or "I Prefer Bruce Cockburn." A report on the experiences of a baby-sitter scarcely deserves the title "Child Psychology" or "The Care of Infants"; "Experiences of a Baby-Sitter" will be good enough if you cannot think of a better title.

Unnecessarily long titles are not satisfactory, especially those that merely repeat the assignment: "An Experience in Childhood That Left a Lasting Impression on Me." The thesis sentence of your paper is not intended to serve as a title. Instead of writing "Reading Taught by Sound Should Replace Sight Reading," name the subject: "Reading by Sound."

The title is not part of the paper, and it should not be referred to by a pronoun in the first sentence. If you want to mention the title in your opening, rephrase it slightly.

| **Unsatisfactory** | **Satisfactory** |
|---|---|
| Becoming a Citizen | Becoming a Citizen |
| This is not a difficult process in Canada. . . . | It is not difficult for an immigrant to become a citizen of Canada. . . . |

▶ **EXERCISE**

Below are four sample beginnings and endings from student papers. For each one, write two or three sentences criticizing the writing, including the title, if necessary. (Point out effective writing, too.) Then, pick two and rewrite them yourself.

**21.6**

*Draft*

*Example: Beginning paragraph from a paper called "Good Policy or Bad"*

Since I myself have never been outside of Canada, it would be foolish of me to think I can make any useful suggestions about Canada's Latin American policy. However, I have read about recent events in the Caribbean and South America with great interest, and, if you will bear with me, I would like to comment at some length on our present policy.

*Critique:* (1) The writer doesn't complete his thesis statement until the last two words of the paragraph. (2) The writer needlessly emphasizes his own weaknesses, which turns off the reader. (3) The title might be too general.

*Rewrite:* Recent events in the Caribbean and South America have stirred up a great deal of interest in the press about Latin America. It seems to me that we should take this opportunity to re-examine our country's role in these events, and perhaps our entire Latin American policy.

1. *Beginning paragraph from a paper called "Modern Chicken Farming"*
   The world today is not what it was fifty years ago. Just think of all the amazing technological changes that have taken place. The automobile has replaced the horse and buggy; radio and television have revolutionized communications; modern medicine has conquered disease. And in 1945 the atomic age was born. Chicken farming, too, has changed drastically from what it was in 1920. I would like to describe some of those changes in the pages that follow.

2. *Closing paragraph from a paper called "What a Liberal Education Means to Me"*

But the greatest value of a liberal education is a personal one; it goes beyond politics and economics. Besides helping the individual to live in his world, it helps him to live with himself. Liberal studies stimulate a love of reason and a flexible, inquiring attitude toward the great questions of mankind. They keep the mind strong and alert and stimulate a well-rounded intellectual development which is as essential to a full life as physical development. A liberal education, in the deepest sense, is an education for life.

3. *Closing paragraph from a paper called "The Population Explosion"*

All the statistics indicate that the future is bleak for the human race if the population explosion is not checked. Food, water, and other essential resources are even now inadequate. Living space is dwindling fast. Of course the picture may not be as dark as it looks. Maybe science will find a solution before long, or maybe the explosion will just taper off.

4. *Closing paragraph from a paper called "Population Pressures"*

An architect recently suggested that cities could be built in the sea to house the extra millions. They would consist of concrete buildings like silos attached to pontoon islands, and could extend as far below the water as they do above. People who lived on the lower levels could then watch the fascinating underwater world through their living-room windows! People have never even begun to exploit the sea and know very little of its hidden wonders.

# Using a Dictionary

*There was a time when the meaning of language presented no problem, when it was a simple matter, upon being challenged as to meaning, to call to witness the dictionary. But in our age of universal skepticism, we have come to know that dictionaries are not depositories of eternal meanings of language. Dictionaries are made by ordinary human beings, who have collected data from—of all people—you and me, the general users of the language.—James E. Miller, Jr.,* WORD, SELF, REALITY

While it certainly is more reliable than any single one person, a dictionary is not a supreme authority to be quoted in settling all arguments about the meaning, pronunciation, and spelling of words. Although modern dictionaries aim to record the ways in which terms are actually used, none can possibly be a complete record. The pioneer lexicographer Samuel Johnson concluded long ago that it was foolish for a man to attempt to "embalm his language." But the notion still persists that a dictionary is—or should be—a code of law for language use.

For this reason, there has been considerable debate, and some heated argument, about whether a dictionary should *prescribe* or *describe* language use. Some people want a dictionary to tell us which pronunciation is right, which meaning is proper, which use of a word is correct.

Other people, including the editors of many dictionaries, declare that dictionaries are not intended to dictate use of language. Since almost any rule that a dictionary could offer to govern pronuncia-tion or definition would have originated in observation of how people at some time in the past actually pronounced and defined words, if a dictionary sets out to be a system of law, the editors would be converting the *habits* of some past time into *rules* for the present.

The editors of most recently published dictionaries want to *register* how the language is used. To that end, many offer a variety of acceptable pronunciations for many words, with no effort to dictate what is "best." Some editors, too, have begun to omit usage labels—which indicate that some words are *informal* (or *colloquial*) or *slang*—on the ground that the correctness or appropriateness of a word can seldom be determined out of context.

Contexts (the situations in which words are used) change, and language changes. The changes are not always good, and it's understandable that we might sometimes wish for an authority to

**22**

*Dict*

stop changes that are not good, such as those in which a unique or precise meaning of a word is lost. But changes often *are* good: our language has for centuries, for example, been enriched and enlarged by the addition of words from other languages.

Since language changes—sometimes for the worse, probably more often for the better—a dictionary cannot control, but simply record the way it is actually used. The standards for determining what good language is rest in other hands (see Introduction).

## 22.1 SELECTING A DICTIONARY

A good dictionary, though not a final authority, is a basic reference tool for every student. Dictionaries answer questions about the meanings, spellings, origins, and pronunciations of words. They also give information about the grammatical forms of words (plurals, past tenses) and about idiomatic constructions (what preposition, for example, is commonly used with a particular noun or verb). Many also give usage notes explaining divided or non-standard usage (as the "double negative") and information about synonyms, doublets, and so on. One of the most valuable habits a writer can acquire is checking a dictionary for the meaning and spelling of words.

Dictionaries differ in size and purpose, but certain criteria apply in evaluating any dictionary for general use. First of all, it should be up to date. New words and expressions are continually coming into the language (*acrylic, ambience, détente, Francophone, Anglophone, mainstreeting, psychedelic*) and old words are always being used in new senses (a *crash* program, an advertising *flyer*, a publicity *handout*). Even spelling and pronunciation can change with time (*judgment, judgement; ab'dəmən, abdō'mən*). In addition, most dictionaries are somewhat encyclopedic, including information about prominent people and places. There are always new names to be added (*Sadat, Namibia*) and new facts to be recorded.

In an effort to keep their entries up to date, most dictionaries make limited changes every few years. Check the copyright dates before you buy a dictionary to find out when it was last revised. You might also want to look up some words that have recently come into use to see if they are included.

In evaluating a dictionary, you should also consider the quality of its editing. A good dictionary of current English is not simply an updating of earlier editions; it reflects the research and judgment of a large staff of experts who record and analyse hundreds of thousands of examples of words in actual use. It is the responsibility of the lexicographer to make certain that the language has been sampled adequately and that all the most common uses of even uncommon words have been found. Then all new evidence must be carefully evaluated, some being discarded and some carefully edited. The result should be a concise yet reliable description of the words current in the language. Whatever "authority" a dictionary has, then, depends on the scholarship, discrimination, and judgment of its editors.

## Dictionaries for General Use

The most complete descriptions of contemporary English are to be found in the various "unabridged" dictionaries. Though not practical for desk use, these large dictionaries are invaluable for reference, and at least one of them is available in every library of consequence. All English unabridged dictionaries are American, the best-known being *Webster's Third New International Dictionary* (the most complete record now available); *The Random House Dictionary of the English Language;* and the *New Standard Dictionary of the English Language.*

For everyday use, however, "college-size" dictionaries are more practical for college and university students. Among the best American dictionaries of this category are *Webster's New World Dictionary of the American Language;* the *Random House Dictionary,* College Edition; *Webster's New Collegiate Dictionary;* and the *American Heritage Dictionary.* Worthy of special attention is *Funk & Wagnalls Standard College Dictionary,* which gives more attention to Canadian words than the others; the Canadian Edition includes a great deal of lexical and other information pertaining to Canada, though it is still substantially American in content. Of comparable quality are two British dictionaries: the *Concise Oxford Dictionary* and the *Longman Modern English Dictionary;* both give considerable attention to Americanisms, very little, as yet, to Canadianisms.

Canada does not yet have either an unabridged or a purely Canadian college-size dictionary of her own. Nevertheless, there is an up-to-date and reputable general work in the "desk-dictionary" category: *The Gage Canadian Dictionary* (*GCD*)—also known as *The Senior Dictionary* in the graded Dictionary of Canadian English series, which includes *The Junior Dictionary* and *The Intermediate Dictionary.* Although it is somewhat less inclusive than most of the dictionaries mentioned above, the *GCD* is highly suited to Canadians, for it is intended to record usage in Canada, an objective not sought by American and British dictionaries.

**22.1**

*Dict*

## Special Dictionaries

The general dictionaries—abridged and unabridged—are supplemented by a number of specialized dictionaries that may be consulted for information not to be found in general works.

**Historical dictionaries.**  Good general dictionaries are based in part upon scholarly dictionaries of international repute. *The Oxford English Dictionary,* twelve volumes and a *Supplement,* 1888-1933—more recently supplemented by four additional volumes (1972-)—is a historical dictionary of the words and idiomatic phrases of the English language. It traces the various forms and meanings of each word, giving the date of its first appearance in recorded English and illustrative quotations from writers to show its typical use at various times in its history (a dozen or more columns are sometimes devoted to a single word). In many kinds of study, it is a basic tool for research. *The Shorter Oxford English Dictionary* (two volumes) is an abridgment of the larger work and somewhat easier to use.

*The Dictionary of American English* (four volumes), made on the same plan as the *Oxford,* gives the history of words as they have been used by American writers from 1620 to 1900. *A Dictionary of Americanisms* (two volumes) gives the history of words that originated in the United States and brings the record of American English down to 1944.

*A Dictionary of Canadianisms on Historical Principles* (1967) provides "a historical record of words and expressions characteristic of the various spheres of Canadian life during the almost four centuries that English has been used in Canada." Also available is an abridgment entitled *A Concise Dictionary of Canadianisms* (1972).

**Dictionaries in special subjects.**  Dictionaries of slang, usage, and other specialized language uses are available, and most special fields have dictionaries of their specialized vocabularies. It would be useful to know the titles of those for fields you may intend to enter. For these and other sources of information, familiarize yourself with the reference shelves in the library.

## 22.2 LEARNING TO USE YOUR DICTIONARY

Dictionaries differ not only in the information they include but in the way they present it, and the best dictionary in the world will be of little value to you unless you know how to read and interpret the information it provides. Before using a new dictionary, read

## Sample Dictionary Entries

1. Entry word
   —spelling and
   syllabication
2. Pronunciation
   respelling
3. Part-of-speech
   labels
4. Inflected forms
5. Definitions and
   illustrations
6. Restrictive labels
   or phrases
7. Etymology
8. Run-on entries
   —derived forms
9. Synonym list
   or synonym study
10. Usage note

**burn¹** (bėrn) v. **burned** or **burnt, burn·ing,** n. —v. **1** be on fire; be very hot; blaze; glow. **2** set on fire; cause to burn. **3** destroy or be destroyed by fire: *burn old papers.* **4** injure or be injured by fire, heat, or an acid: *He burned his hand on the hot iron.* **5** make by fire, by a heated tool, etc.: *His cigar burned a hole in the rug.* **6** feel hot; give a feeling of heat to: *His forehead burns with fever.* **7** be very excited or eager: *burning with enthusiasm.* **8** inflame or be inflamed with anger, passion, etc.: *burn with fury.* **9** give light: *Lamps were burning in every room.* **10** sunburn; tan. **11** use to produce heat or energy: *Our furnace burns oil.* **12** produce, harden, glaze, etc. by fire or heat: *burn bricks, burn lime.* **13** in chemistry, undergo or cause to undergo combustion; oxidize. **14** in nuclear physics, make use of atomic energy (from uranium, thorium, etc.). **15** cauterize. **16 burn down, a** burn or be burned to the ground. **b** decrease in fuel or heat. **17 burn oneself out,** use oneself up physically or mentally; exhaust one's store of energy, ambition, etc. **18 burn out, a** destroy by burning. **b** cease to burn; become extinct. **c** burn the inside of: *The warehouse was burned out.* **d** drive (a person) out by fire. **19 burn up, a** consume: *This car burns up the gasoline.* **b** *Informal.* make or become angry.
—n. **1** an injury caused by fire, heat, or an acid; a burned place. **2** a sunburn; tan. [coalescence of OE *beornan* be on fire and OE *bærnan* consume with fire]
—**burn′a·ble,** adj.

**Syn.** v. **1** flame. **2** ignite, fire. **4** Burn, scorch, sear = to injure or be injured by fire, heat, or acid. **Burn,** the general word, suggests any degree of damage from slight injury to destruction by fire, heat, or acid: *The toast burned.* **Scorch** = to burn the surface enough to discolor it, sometimes to damage the texture, by heat or fire: *The cigarette scorched the paper.* **Sear** = to burn or scorch the surface enough to dry or harden it, by heat, fire, or acid, and applies particularly to burning the tissues of people or animals: *Wounds are cauterized by searing.*

☛ **burn.** The past tense and past participle of *burn* are either *burned* or *burnt. Burnt* is usual when the participle is used as an adjective: *The partially burnt papers gave them little help in solving the mystery.* Verb: *They hastily burned all the old letters before they left.*

**burn²** (bėrn) n. *Scottish.* a small stream; creek; brook. [OE *burna*]

**burn·er** (bėr′nər) n. **1** the part of a lamp, stove, furnace, etc. where the flame or heat is produced. **2** any thing or part that burns or works by heat: *Some stoves are oil burners; others are gas burners.* **3** a man whose work is burning something: *a charcoal burner.* **4** in a jet engine, a combustion chamber. See **jet** for diagram. **5** a lamp used to burn the paint off a surface.

**burn·ing** (bėr′ning) adj. **1** glowing hot; hot. **2** vital; urgent. —**burn′ing·ly,** adv.

**burning glass** a convex lens used to produce heat or set fire to a substance by focussing the sun's rays on it.

**bur·nish** (bėr′nish) v. n. polish; shine. [ME < OF *burniss-,* a stem of *burnir* make brown, polish < *brun* brown < Gmc.] —**bur′nish·er,** n.

**bur·noose** or **bur·nous** (ber nüs′ or bėr′nüs) n. a long cloak with a hood, worn by Moors and Arabs. [< F *burnous* < Arabic *burnus*]

**burn·out** (bėrn′out′) n. **1** a failure due to burning or extreme heat. **2** in aerospace: **a** the dying out of the flame in a rocket engine as a result of its fuel being used up or intentionally shut off. **b** the time or position when such dying out occurs.

—Homograph
Idioms
Homograph
Derived forms
Noun phrase, or two-word compound
One-word compound

**22.2**

the front matter carefully. It will explain the organization of entries, the method of indicating pronunciation, the use of restrictive labels, and the meaning of abbreviations and symbols used in the definitions and etymologies. Then look carefully at a page of entries to see how words and phrases are handled. Test your understanding of the pronunciation guide by using it to pronounce some familiar words. Look through the table of contents to see what sections of information your dictionary provides in addition to the main alphabetical list of words. You may find a short grammar of English, a short history of the English language, a discussion of punctuation, a table of signs and symbols, a list of colleges and universities, and a guide to the preparation of manuscript copy.

A little time spent in learning to use your dictionary can make it immensely useful to you. The following sections describe the kinds of information found in most dictionaries; the sample entries on page 291 show how one dictionary presents this information, but most dictionaries are very similar.

▶ EXERCISE

To help you familiarize yourself with your dictionary, write out the following information about it, for discussion in class or to be handed in.

1. The title, the name of the publisher, and the most recent copyright date. This date may be found on the back of the title page.
2. A list of the sections following the introduction and preceding the dictionary entries (such as "How to Use the Dictionary," "A Guide to Pronunciation," "Usage Levels").
3. A list of the material in the appendix (if any), such as "Signs and Symbols," "Biographical Names," "Colleges and Universities."
4. Do the words appear in one alphabetical list or in separate lists (for biographical names, geographical names, abbreviations, and so on)?
5. Are derived forms (*cynical* and *cynicism* from *cynic*, for example) listed separately as main entries in the alphabetical list, or are they listed under the base form?
6. Do the etymologies come at the beginning or at the end of an entry?
7. The order of the definitions of the words. Does the older meaning or the current meaning come first in words such as *cute, ghastly, shrewd, liquidate, souse* (noun), *recession, sheriff, reeve, umpire?*

## Spelling and Word Division

Develop the habit of using your dictionary to check the spelling in your papers. If you are unable to find a word because you are uncertain of one of the beginning letters, try to think of other possible spellings for the same sound. (Is it *gibe* or *jibe?*) Remember that dictionaries give the spelling not only of the base form of a word but also of distinctive forms—the principal parts of verbs, the plurals of nouns, the comparative and superlative forms of adjectives and adverbs—that are in any way irregular.

Your dictionary may give two spellings for a word when usage is divided (*hemoglobin—haemoglobin; adviser—advisor*). Use the spelling that the editors have indicated is the more common one. (The method of listing variants and of indicating their relative currency will be explained in the front matter.) American and British dictionaries are not always helpful for Canadians. (See the comments at 17.5, "Variant Spellings.")

Dictionaries divide words into units (usually corresponding to spoken syllables) by means of small dots or spaces: *de·mar·ca·tion, de light ful.* This device will enable you to see each part of the word clearly and to notice if you have omitted or transposed any letters. In writing, divide a word at the end of a line only where your dictionary shows a division and never divide words pronounced as one syllable (as *clipped*). The word *reorganization,* for example, has five possible places for division: *re·or·ga·ni·za·tion.* Not all dictionaries divide every word in exactly the same way, but by following the practice of any good dictionary, you will avoid such careless blunders as dividing *bedraggled* into *bed-* and *raggled.* See also 17, Spelling, and 28.2 Manuscript Form.

**EXERCISE**

What information do you find in your dictionary on the spelling of these pairs of words? Are the spellings interchangeable? If so, which form would you use and why?

| | |
|---|---|
| aesthetic—esthetic | gaol—jail |
| carat—karat | ketchup—catchup |
| catalog—catalogue | licorice—liquorice |
| draft—draught | sac—sack |
| favor—favour | traveling—travelling |

**22.2**

*Dict*

## Pronunciation

Because English spelling is not consistently phonetic (there are over 250 ways to spell the forty-odd sounds in English), dictionaries use a system of special symbols to show how words are pronounced. The word *bamboozle,* for example, might be respelled this way after the entry word: *bam büʹ zəl.* The pronunciation key at the bottom of the page will illustrate, with familiar words, the sounds represented by the symbols, (*a*), (*ü*), and (*ə*). Since the consonants (*b*), (*m*), (*z*), and (*l*) have no special marks over them, you may assume that they are pronounced in the usual way. The accented syllable in (*bam bü′ zəl*) is indicated by a heavy stress mark. Phonetic spellings also indicate secondary stress, when appropriate, usually by a lighter mark (′). Since the system for showing pronunciation varies somewhat from dictionary to dictionary, you should study carefully the explanatory notes in the front of your own book before attempting to use its pronunciation key.

Dictionaries often list two or more pronunciations for a word when usage is divided. Although the first pronunciation is usually the more common one, it is not necessarily "preferred," and you should use whichever pronunciation is customary in your own community.

▶ **EXERCISES**

To familiarize yourself with the pronunciation key in your dictionary, write out the following exercises:

1. What pronunciations does your dictionary list for each of these words? Is the first pronunciation given the one you hear most frequently? If not, tell how it differs, including the stress (accent):

| address | creek | gratitude | pianist |
| adult | culinary | herb | poesy |
| Celtic | drama | implacable | research |
| coupon | gibberish | leisure | Oedipus |

2. How is each of these words pronounced when used as a noun? As a verb?

| confine | escort | impact | misuse |
| conflict | exploit | import | refuse |
| consort | ferment | | |

## Meaning

Dictionaries are perhaps most important for what they tell us about the meanings of words. To a reader, a dictionary is useful for finding the meanings not only of unfamiliar words but also of familiar words used in new senses. To a writer, dictionary definitions are most useful for checking the meanings of words about which he is uncertain.

Dictionaries begin each definition, or group of definitions, with an abbreviation showing whether the word is being defined as a noun (*n.*), adjective (*adj.*), verb (*vb.*), or other part of speech. Sometimes, verbs are distinguished as being transitive (*v.t.*) or intransitive (*v.i.*). This information is important, for words usually have different meanings in different grammatical contexts. Sometimes the meanings are closely related (for example, the meanings of *advance* as a verb, a noun, or an adjective) but sometimes they are completely different (the meanings of *fly, plant,* and *court* as verbs or as nouns).

In looking for the meaning of a word in context, therefore, you must ordinarily isolate the right group of definitions before you can find the particular meaning you are looking for. Then you should look over all the definitions included in that group. Some dictionaries give the oldest meaning first and others the most common current one. Often, however, you will be looking for a more specialized meaning that comes later in the entry. At the end of the entry, or at the end of a group of definitions for one part of speech, you may also find one or more idioms listed.

In using dictionary definitions, you should keep two general principles in mind:

1. A dictionary does not *require* or *forbid* a particular meaning or use of a word; it merely *records* the most common ways in which a word has actually been used. Therefore, you must exercise judgment in deciding whether a particular word will be appropriate in a particular context.
2. A dictionary definition is for the most part a record of the *denotation,* or specific meaning, of a word; at best, it can only suggest the *connotation,* or suggestive qualities, which varies with context and with use. (See 23.1.) In general, it is better not to use a word until you have heard it or read it in context and know at least some of its connotations.

**22.2**

*Dict*

▶ **EXERCISES**

1. Answer the following questions by referring to the definitions given in your dictionary:

   a. In what kind of writing would it be appropriate to use the word *gimmick?*
   b. In what profession would the word *dolmen* most likely be used?
   c. Where would you be most likely to hear the word *legato?*
   d. When a woman *rests on her laurels,* what is she doing?
   e. Which of the following expressions would be underlined in a paper to indicate they belong to a foreign language?
      quid pro quo   de facto   sarong   apartheid   toccata   vice versa

2. Consult your dictionary and choose the best definition for the italicized word in each of these sentences:

    a. At ten he became a printer's *devil.*
    b. His *fellowship* expired at the end of the year.
    c. Luther objected to the sale of *indulgences.*
    d. The entrance fee was *fixed* at twenty dollars.
    e. She has extremely *catholic* reading tastes.
    f. They soon discovered that the resort was a *white elephant.*

## Areas of Usage and Special Labels

Some words (or particular meanings for some words) are labelled in a dictionary as *dialectal, obsolete, archaic, foreign, informal* (or *colloquial*), *slang, Cdn., Brit., U.S.,* or are identified with some particular activity, field or region — *medicine, law, astronomy, music, hockey, Newfoundland, Maritimes.* Words that are not labelled in a dictionary are considered part of the general vocabulary.

Usage labels can serve as rough guides, but you should bring your own observation to bear on individual words. Certainly you would ordinarily avoid words marked *obsolete* or *archaic,* but many words that carry no label (*albeit, perforce*) would be equally out of place in most college writing. On the other hand, many words marked *Dial.* or *Informal* (such as *highbrow*) might fit perfectly well into both informal and general English. The label *colloquial,* used for *informal* in some dictionaries means simply that a particular usage is more characteristic of conversation than it is of writing. The labels *Cdn.* or *U.S.* mean that the usage is associated with those countries rather than with other parts of the English-speaking world.

Most dictionaries of the English language include frequently used words and expressions from foreign languages. Some dictionaries indicate that such terms are generally considered foreign by indicating the language, as *German, Latin* or (It.), (Gk.). Others use an identifying mark, such as a dagger or an asterisk, before all foreign-word entries. Such labels are useful because they help distinguish between words that are now considered part of the English vocabulary (*chalet, aria, junta*) and those that are still considered distinctly foreign (*dolce far niente, Weltanschauung, ibidem*) and must be underlined in a paper. (See 14.3 Italics for Foreign Words.)

▶ EXERCISE

Answer the following questions by consulting the *grammatical infor-mation* given in the dictionary entry for each word:

1. What is the past participle of *shear?*
2. What is the past tense of *bear* in the sense of *carry?*
3. What does *feign* mean when it is used intransitively?
4. What does *gull* mean when followed by a direct object?
5. What is the plural of *ghetto?*
6. What is the plural of *stratum?*

## Synonyms and Antonyms

Most dictionaries list words of similar meaning (*synonyms*) with the basic or most comprehensive word of a group and explain how these various related words differ slightly in meaning, especially in connotation. Sometimes the entry for a word will also list an *antonym,* a word of opposite meaning, as *cowardly* would be an antonym for *courageous.*

There are several specialized books containing lists of related words: *Webster's Dictionary of Synonyms,* Fernald's *Standard Handbook of Synonyms, Antonyms, and Prepositions,* Soule's *A Dictionary of English Synonyms, Webster's Collegiate Thesaurus,* and Roget's *Thesaurus.* The *Thesaurus* is probably the most widely used book of synonyms, but since it does not give definitions, its chief use is to remind writers of words they recognize but do not use regularly. If you find words that appear to be appropriate but you are not completely sure, check their definitions in a dictionary.

## Etymology

**22.2**

*Dict*

A dictionary not only tells how a word is used and pronounced but also gives its origin, or *etymology.* Sometimes the etymology is merely a notation of the language from which the word was borrowed (as *decor* is from French and *Gestalt* is from German) or a statement of how it was coined. But often the etymology is fairly complicated; the development of the word *advance,* for example, can be traced back through Middle English to Old French and finally to Latin. The explanatory notes at the front of your dictionary include a discussion of etymology and a key to the abbreviations and symbols used on tracing a word's origin.

Knowing how a word originated will often help you understand and remember it. Knowing that *philanthropy,* for example, comes from the Greek words *philein* (to love) and *anthropos* (man) may help fix its meaning in your mind. Beyond this, it may help you figure out other unfamiliar words by analogy (*philology, anthropocentric*).

Etymologies often illustrate how word meanings have changed from their original to their present use and are interesting as records of human thought and experience.

▶ **EXERCISES**

1. Consult the *etymologies* in your dictionary to answer the following questions:

   a. What is the origin of these words?

   | | | |
   |---|---|---|
   | sandwich | assassin | lecture |
   | robot | okra | semester |
   | farm | radish | geology |

   b. Which of the following words have retained most or all of their original meanings? Which have retained some? Which none?

   | | | |
   |---|---|---|
   | bigot | fiasco | pilot |
   | curfew | neat | silly |
   | feeble | pedigree | tragedy |

2. The following questions can be answered by finding the needed information in the dictionary. In some cases, this information will be found under the appropriate entry-word; in others, special sections at the back or front of the dictionary must be consulted.

   a. Write sentences using the words shown below. Be sure your sentences distinguish among the similar words put together as sets:

   deviate – digress – diverge – swerve
   slim – thin – slender – skinny
   fictitious – legendary – mythical
   giggle – titter – snicker – chuckle
   latent – potential – dormant

   b. Give antonyms for the following words: *authentic, chaste, devout, futile, verbose.*

   c. Who was John Huss? When did he live?

   d. What was Camelot?

   e. Where are lemmings found?

   f. When was Napoleon Bonaparte born?

   g. What is a pronghorn?

   h. What does IPA stand for?

   i. What does the symbol B/L mean in business and commerce?

   j. Of what country is the cordoba the monetary unit?

# The Meaning of Words

*Respect for the word—to employ it with scrupulous care and incorruptible heartful love of truth—is essential if there is to be any growth in society or in the human race.—Dag Hammarskjöld,* MARKINGS

*A word is dead*
*When it is said,*
*Some say.*
*I say it just*
*Begins to live*
*That day. —Emily Dickinson*

We usually take for granted that we know the meanings of the words we use, except when there is a question of accuracy (*infer* or *imply?*) or of appropriateness (*boss* or *supervisor?*). But if you are to use the words that will best convey your meaning, you need to do more than simply accept and use the first words that come to mind. You need to take an active interest in words as words. What gives a particular word its special meanings in different situations? In what different ways can a word be used? How will others take the words you use? Words have many possible meanings. If you are to choose those that best serve your purpose, you need to know first what the choices are.

**23**

## 23.1 WORDS IN CONTEXT AND SITUATION

Words do not actually have "meaning" until they are used in speaking or writing. Then their meaning derives partly from the *context,* or the words around them, and partly from the *situation* in which they are used, which involves the attitudes and purposes of either a speaker and listener or a writer and reader.

It is easy to see how the context limits the meaning of a word. A word like *deck, run, fly,* or *match* can be used in several senses, but usually in a particular sentence it can have only one meaning:

> Tomorrow we'll take a **run** up to the lake.
> You will have to **run** to catch the train.
> Frowning, she noticed the **run** in her stocking.
> McKay scored the third **run** after two were out in the seventh.

He did a **run** of scales and decided that was enough practice.
When the store opened on the morning of the sale, there was a **run** on leather goods.

The situation in which a word is used also helps clarify its meaning. The word *bill* in "The bill is too large" would mean one thing if the speaker were trying to identify a bird and another if he were discussing family finances. A writing situation includes at least a topic of discussion, a writer, and a potential audience. The writer must use words that are not only appropriate to the topic but also those that will help the reader know the writer and see the writer's world.

▶ **EXERCISE**

The meaning of a word often depends on the context in which it is used. Write two sentences using each of the following words to show how the meaning of the words can change as they move from one context to another: *realize, studio, elevation, pitching, cup, book, stack, feedback.*

## Denotation: The Core of a Word's Meaning

When we think first about the meaning of words, we usually think of their *denotation,* what they have come to represent as a result of the ways they have been used. This is the meaning that dictionaries usually record and try to define for us. The thing that a word refers to or suggests is called its *referent.*

Some kinds of words have more definite denotations than others because their referents are more limited or more exact. Depending on their definiteness, words may be classified into three groups:

1. **Concrete words,** words that name specific people, places, or objects, are the most exact in meaning: *Wilfrid Laurier, Lake Erie, my bicycle, the library, reindeer, a Boy Scout knife.*

2. **Relative words,** words that describe qualities, are less definite than concrete words and frequently depend for their meanings on the situation or on the writer's past experience with a term: *hot, pretty, honest, angry, silly, impossible.* In Toronto, a *tall* building might refer to any structure over twenty storeys, but in a city with no skyscrapers, *tall* might refer to any building higher than five storeys.

3. **Abstract words,** words that refer to general concepts—acts, situations, relationships, conditions—are the least definite: *reasoning, citizenship, education, intelligence, culture, ob-*

*jectives, art.* Since these words have a range of reference (think of all the activities that may be included in *education,* for example), rather than a specific referent, they are more difficult to use precisely than concrete words. (See also 23.4, Concrete and Abstract Words.)

## Connotation: The Power to Suggest Meaning

Most words have been used by so many different people in such different circumstances for such different purposes that they have acquired associations and suggestions that go beyond their denotation. The word *twilight,* for example, has been used so often in association with melancholy or romance that we sometimes don't think of it as a time of day. And someone has suggested that the word *nightingale* could lose all its suggestion of beauty and be merely the name of a bird only to a tone-deaf ornithologist. This set of qualities that words have acquired from their expanded use is called *connotation.*

Very often the chief difference between words of closely re-lated denotation is in their connotation. Both *inexpensive* and *cheap* refer to low price, but *cheap* may also connote poor quality; *average* and *mediocre* both refer to the middle of a range, but *mediocre* suggests dispraise; *belief, faith, creed, dogma* all refer to ideas held, but they differ widely in suggesting how they are held. It is easy to see why some students of language say that there are no true synonyms.

Dictionaries try to suggest the shades of meaning that words may have, but the best way to discover the connotations of a word is to observe how it is actually used in current writing and speech. The connotative value of a word often changes over time. *Sly,* for example, once meant *skilful,* but as generally used now, it would fit into the same context as *devious* or *tricky;* it may even suggest *criminal* or, sometimes, *lecherous.* Words like *genteel* and *bucolic* have lost their favorable connotation as the values they represent have lost much of their appeal. Certain words, usually those whose referents arouse widely ranging responses, are extremely variable in connotation: *pop art, radical, socialism, jazz.* When you use such words, be cautious, making sure that your attitude is clear to your reader and that you are being fair to your subject. Words with highly emotive connotations, such as those associated with prickly controversies, may create special problems.

In such situations, the view of the whittler who sat in the town square may be instructive. This man, widely known for his uncannily realistic carvings of birds, when asked how he managed

**23.1**

*Mng*

to achieve such realism in his carvings, said, "Well, I just whittle off all the wood that don't look like a bird." When you use words that have high emotive power, you may have to whittle away all the meanings that you do not want to express. This may mean taking the time to define, to set limits to what you are trying to say, to establish clearly how you want to use the words. Any potential readers you have are real people, too, and they are at liberty to take your words in any way they wish unless you have shown them the limits of meaning that you have in mind. If you refer to a co-educational dormitory, for example, some people will read in suggestions of immorality and infer a sharp decline in moral values, *unless* you take pains to define the nature of a co-educational dormitory as you wish them to see it.

▶ EXERCISE

The connotative value of words is very important in determining their use: for example, you might say "I am *plump;* you are *heavy;* he is *fat";* three different pictures emerge. Arrange the following groups of words into columns, according to their connotation: favorable, neutral, or unfavorable.

1. student, scholar, bookworm
2. stubborn, firm, pigheaded
3. counterfeit, replica, copy
4. racy, obscene, blue
5. unusual, bizarre, unique
6. tolerant, flexible, wishy-washy
7. caustic, penetrating, sharp
8. reserved, aristocratic, snobbish
9. buffoon, wit, comic
10. officer, policeman, fuzz
11. svelte, skinny, thin
12. literary artist, hack, writer

## 23.2 FAIR WORDS AND SLANTED WORDS

Your readers don't always see things as you see them, or know them as you know them, just as you don't see and know things as they do. If you want your readers to see and know things as you do, at least for a moment, you have to show them where you are, how you have positioned yourself. Words chosen carefully for their connotative value can help you show your readers what your attitude is toward your subject. A fair and balanced presentation of your position is entirely appropriate. Sometimes, however, writers attempt to manipulate the emotions of their readers by using words chosen to influence the readers' responses in one way or another. This practice—intentional or otherwise—is called *slanted writing*.

## Words Used Fairly for Effect

It is not possible to speak or write in completely neutral, objective language about anything that has fully engaged our interest. To write well about a subject, we must care about it enough to take a position or make a judgment concerning it.

In factual as well as in imaginative writing, interest, liveliness, and effectiveness depend greatly on the successful use of connotation. Our awareness of all the values that words have enables us to represent our subject precisely, to address our audience with a varied and appealing style, and to show where we stand in relation to our material. Fairly used, words with apt connotative value give *shape* and *texture*—as opposed to *slant*—to what we say.

Observe the power of suggestion in this passage:

> In schools and universities, sensitivity sessions, the linking of hands..., mutual strokings, deep breathing ..., and the communion of pot, have all been experimented with and in their turn abandoned in the search for some more immediate, less difficult, and more deeply unifying medium than mere human speech.—Geoffrey Durrant, "The New Barbarians"

**23.2**

*Slant*

Deeply concerned about the erosion of English studies, the author uses connotation, irony, and shock to win support for his view that recent trends in educational practice must be re-assessed. The term *sensitivity sessions* suggests that such sessions are indulged in by the insensitive; the sexual images—expressed in ironically formal terms—suggest titillating but aimless and unproductive activities; and *communion of pot* suggests minds high on something other than the desire for learning. The slanting here is powerful and clearly intentional. Thus the point is fairly and effectively made that the merits of *human speech* as a *unifying medium* have been neglected and that it is high time due emphasis were given to teaching the art of using language effectively.

## Slanted Words

The story is told of a harvester of enormous appetite who shortened the legs of the dining table on the side where he sat so that the food would slide toward him for instant availability. By exploiting the suggestive power of words, writers can similarly tilt arguments and meanings in their favor.

Sometimes slanting occurs only because writers, in their enthusiasm, allow words that are too intense to intrude in statements presented as fact. To say "All television programs are designed for the twelve-year-old mind" is to allow a personal distaste for television programming to displace good sense. Too often *all* or *most* are used for *many,* or a superlative is used when a less extreme word is called for, or *only* or *nothing but* is used to the exclusion of other possibilities.

Much unfair slanting occurs in statements of opinion where a writer, knowingly or not, assumes that he or she is the only reliable authority. There is no slanting in a simple statement of one's likes or dislikes ("I can't stand these people with their long hair"). But the same opinion stated as a general fact in slanted wording ("Long, stringy hair and freaky clothes are signs of decadence") implies that the writer expects the reader to share that opinion without thinking about it.

Just as writers who unfailingly trust themselves as the only reliable authority are apt to slant their writing, so are writers who, in their enthusiasm for their own position, fail to consider more than one possibility. The following passage is from an essay in which the author argues that destroying the wilderness and its resources is a perfectly natural and appropriate human activity:

> The trumpeting voice of the wilderness lover is heard at great distances these days. He is apt to be a perfectly decent person, if hysterical. And the causes which excite him so are generally worthy. Who can really find a harsh word for him as he strives to save Lake Erie from the sewers . . . , save the redwoods from the . . . highway engineers, save the giant rhinoceros from the Somali tribesmen who kill those noble beasts to powder their horns into what they fondly imagine is a wonder-working aphrodisiac?
>
> Worthy causes, indeed, but why do those who espouse them have to be so shrill and intolerant and sanctimonious? What right do they have to insinuate that anyone who does not share their passion for the whooping crane is a Philistine and a slob? From the gibberish they talk, you would think the only way to save the bald eagle is to dethrone human reason.—Robert Wernick, "Let's Spoil the Wilderness"

Unexamined assumptions (wilderness lovers are hysterical) and unsubstantiated assertions (they speak gibberish) are the source of much slanting. For this reason, many of the most serious

instances of slanting come in writing on social or political problems, especially when the words reflect prejudice. This type of
slanted writing can be objected to on at least four grounds:

1. it doesn't accurately represent the situation being discussed;
2. it suggests that the writer is at best quite careless of what he or
   she says and at worst willing to distort the facts for his or her
   own purposes;
3. it stands in the way of an intelligent and constructive approach
   to problems that affect the public interest;
4. it is likely to antagonize the reader (unless similarly prejudiced)
   and so prevent clear communication.

Slanted writing, which is often clever and sometimes funny, does
not always stress loaded words. The gentle ridicule that emerges
from the following passage is largely implied by the asides and the
tone:

> ... the Trudeau aides, seeking as always to humanize his image
> before a working-class audience, suggested that he toss in a topical
> reference to Hank Aaron. Who *is* Hank Aaron? Well, ahem. It was
> explained that he is a baseball player who at the moment is set to
> surpass Babe Ruth's home-run record. *Who* is Babe Ruth? Well,
> er, ahem, it was explained with some rolling of eyes, who Babe
> Ruth was. So came the speech and there was the prime minister,
> exhorting the voters not to give up on the Liberals because even
> Hank Aaron is allowed three strikes and ... Hank Aaron was soon
> to break the home-run record of "Baby" Ruth. —Allan
> Fotheringham, in *Maclean's*

**23.3**

▶ EXERCISE

Practise shifting connotations by rewriting the first three paragraphs in
two newspaper editorials so as to illustrate slanted writing. Bring to class
some slanted passages from newspapers or magazines.

## 23.3 CHOOSING THE RIGHT WORD

*ₐ ᵧ* Replace the marked wrong word with one that
accurately conveys your intended meaning.

In most factual prose, words should be used in their established
forms and senses; if they are not, the reader may be misled or

confused. A sentence such as "The scene *provoked* his imagination" (in which *provoked,* commonly meaning "angered," is inaccurately used instead of *stimulated*) interferes with communication. In revising your papers, check any words that you are unsure of, especially those that are not part of your regular vocabulary. Be particularly alert to words that are easily confused.

## Distinguishing Words of Similar Spelling

In English there are many pairs of words that closely resemble each other in sound or spelling but have quite different meanings: *moral* and *morale, personal* and *personnel, historic* and *historical.* When writing hastily, you may accidentally substitute one word for another, but you can easily eliminate such errors by proofreading your work and by referring to a dictionary when necessary. When words of identical pronunciation, called *homonyms,* are confused in writing, the mistake may be called a spelling error (*bear* for *bare; there* for *their*). But your instructor is likely to label it WW (wrong word) if he or she suspects that you may not know the difference in meaning (*principal* for *principle; affect* for *effect*).

The following words are very often interchanged in writing. If you are not sure of the distinction between them, use your dictionary, or the glossary of usage on page 464:

| | |
|---|---|
| accept – except | detract – distract |
| adapt – adopt | formally – formerly |
| affect – effect | human – humane |
| allusion – illusion | mantle – mantel |
| censor – censure | persecute – prosecute |
| cite – site | precede – proceed |
| complement – compliment | principal – principle |
| conscientious – conscious | respectful – respective |
| credible – creditable – credulous | stationary – stationery |

▶ EXERCISE

Write sentences using the words listed above. Be sure that your sentences show clearly the differences in meaning.

## Distinguishing Words of Similar Meaning

Word errors most frequently occur because the writer has failed to distinguish between words of similar meaning. A synonym is a word having *approximately* the same meaning as another:

angry — annoyed — indignant
frank — candid — blunt
multitude — throng — crowd — mob
strange — peculiar — quaint — bizarre

A few words have identical meanings and are therefore inter-changeable (*flammable—inflammable; ravel—unravel; toward—towards*). But most synonyms, while they refer to the same idea or object, differ somewhat in denotation or connotation and thus cannot be substituted for each other without affecting the sense or tone of the statement. One term may be more formal than another (*coiffure—hair-do*); more specific (*tango—dance*); more precise (*charitable—kind*); or more personal (*dad—father*).

Usually it is not the more subtle distinctions between closely related words that cause trouble (*necessary—indispensable; intrinsic—inherent*), but the failure to distinguish between common words in different contexts:

> The mysteries of the unknown arouse curiosity that must be **fulfilled.** [for *satisfied*]

> We may expect food consumption to increase everywhere because of the **growth in people.** [for *increase in population*]

The only way to avoid such errors is to notice how words of similar meaning are used in various contexts. Connotation as well as denotation should be considered. Notice, for example, how unexpected the last word in this statement is:

> In the 1890's, Dawson City was a gathering place for prostitutes, cardsharps, confidence men, thugs, and other **scamps.**

**23.3**

*Scamps* might be quite appropriate in referring to mischievous children, but the term is conspicuously out of place in this company. Moreover, certain synonyms are too heavy or too flippant for the context:

> The water was rougher past the next bend, and we had **difficulty circumventing** the rapids. [too formal: had *trouble getting around* would be more appropriate]

> I enjoyed studying Plato, because among other things I **got the low-down on** what is meant by a Platonic friendship. [too informal: *learned* would be better]

But remember the principle of appropriateness. There are special situations in which such incongruities might be useful. T.C. Haliburton (Sam Slick) and Mark Twain, for example, could, by mixing different kinds of language, get comic effect from the incongruity.

Writers sometimes use strings of fanciful synonyms to avoid

repeating the same expression for an idea or object (*cats, felines, furry beasts, tabbies, nine-lived creatures*). Such "elegant variations" are pretentious and are usually more confusing than simple repetition. Readers expect key words to be repeated when they cannot be replaced by pronouns (*cats . . . they*). Factual synonyms (*these animals*) are also unobtrusive and will seldom strike the reader as repetitious.

## Distinguishing Words of Opposite Meaning

Some words that have contrasting or wholly opposite meanings are frequently confused, probably because the writer associates them mentally but has reversed their meanings. Among the most common antonyms or near antonyms are the following. Make sure that you know their meanings.

| | |
|---|---|
| concave — convex | inductive — deductive |
| condemn — condone | infer — imply |
| explicit — implicit | prescribe — proscribe |
| famous — notorious | subjective — objective |
| former — latter | temerity — timidity |

Confusing such pairs may result in your saying the very opposite of what you intend. Half-knowing a word is often more dangerous than not knowing it at all.

▶ EXERCISE

Write sentences using the words listed above. Make sure that your sentences show clearly the difference in meaning.

## Learning New Words

Although many word errors are caused by confusion or carelessness, it's easy to use the wrong word (or settle for the almost-right word) simply because you do not know another one. Very many papers are likely to deal with complex ideas and precise distinctions that may demand a larger vocabulary than the student has needed in the past.

It has been estimated that children enter first grade knowing about 25 000 words and add 5000 every year, so that they leave high school with a vocabulary of perhaps as many as 90 000 words. The average vocabulary of college and university graduates is about twice this size. These estimates are for *recognition* (or *passive*) vocabulary, words understood in reading and listening.

One's *active* vocabulary, the words actually used in writing or speaking, is considerably smaller.

Most people use only about a third as many words as they recognize. Thus, an obvious way for you to enlarge your working vocabulary is through conscious exercise. In making an effort to say precisely what you mean you should search not only among the words in your active vocabulary, but also among those you have learned to recognize. Frequently we find new words in reading (*cybernetics, rhetoric, apartheid*) and learn their meanings from the context or from a dictionary. Using these words in writing or speaking helps to make them more readily available for future use.

It is sometimes possible to guess the meaning of a word by knowing its parts. Many scientific words, for example, are formed with suffixes and roots from Greek or Latin:

| | | |
|---|---|---|
| mono- (one) | -graph (writing, written) | poly- (many) |
| bi- (two) | bio- (life) | macro- (large) |
| tele- (at a distance) | photo- (light) | micro- (small) |

Since the combined meanings of the parts may only approximate the meaning of the whole, however, it is usually safer to use a dictionary and learn the entire word.

Ordinarily, we learn and remember words not for their own sake but for the meanings they represent. We have a good stock of words in the fields that interest us because facts and ideas are retained chiefly in verbal form. Thus, anything that extends the range of your ideas or experiences will help to enlarge your vocabulary. The typical college or university course adds to a student's vocabulary several hundred new words and new meanings for familiar words.

**23.3**

When you meet a new word that is likely to be useful, learn it accurately at the start—its spelling and pronunciation as well as its usual meaning. Students quite often have trouble in their courses because they only half know the specialized words essential to a subject. Using these words in conversation, when they are appropriate, or in reviewing course work with another student will fix them in your mind so that you can use them easily and accurately in examinations, papers, and class discussions.

▶ EXERCISES

1. The first word that comes to mind is not necessarily the best one, even if it means *approximately* what you intend. Read each of the following sentences carefully and choose the word in parentheses that most *exactly* expresses the intended meaning.

a. The latest statistics (dispute, refute, rebuke) his claim that the economy is expanding.
b. In time Einstein (convinced, persuaded, showed) most physicists that his theory was correct.
c. Most cities have laws that (stop, deter, prohibit) littering.
d. We stopped in our stroll on lower Mill Street to (give, donate, contribute) some money to a blind man.
e. The remarks at the end of his speech (implied, inferred, insinuated) that he had some financial support for his plan.

2. Examine the diction in the following sentences to determine whether some words are misused. If so, rewrite the faulty sentences, supplying more exact or more appropriate words. Be prepared to explain why you made each change.

a. Within the next few days the assassin gained considerable renown.
b. I do not like to be around him, for his perpetual pessimism aggravates me.
c. A student who is writing a research paper should compulsively read through the leading works devoted to his subject.
d. If we adopt the plan, how will the changes in procedure effect the goals?
e. I found this poem extremely obtuse, and even after struggling over it for hours with a dictionary and an encyclopedia, I could not decipher many of its illusions.

# 23.4 CONCRETE AND ABSTRACT WORDS

Words can be classified according to the nature of their referents as *abstract* or *concrete* (p. 300). Abstract (general) words refer to ideas, qualities, acts, or relationships. Concrete (specific) words refer to definite persons, places, objects, and acts. This list demonstrates the differences between the two kinds of words:

| Abstract (general) | Concrete (specific) |
| --- | --- |
| institution | King's College |
| work | running a bulldozer |
| men's organization | Lion's Club |
| a politician | the mayor of Vancouver |
| food | cheesecake |
| an educator | my history teacher |
| creed | Westminster Confession |

Often a word cannot be classed as abstract or concrete until it is read in context:

ABSTRACT:  Honest labor never killed anyone. [a generalization about all labor]

CONCRETE:  In the GM contract dispute, labor seeks a five-cent per hour wage increase. [in the context, a specific reference to the United Automobile Workers]

## Effective Uses of Concrete and Abstract Words

Concrete words are essential in discussing situations, incidents, and processes that are based upon personal experience or direct observation: impressions of people or places, discussions of plans for the future, explanations of the writer's attitudes or interests. Abstract words, on the other hand, are usually necessary in discussing general ideas ("The Intangible Values of Education"), for summarizing facts or stating opinions, or for analysing theoretical problems ("Is Specialization in Education Undesirable?").

Abstract words are more characteristic of formal than of general or informal English and are best used by writers with a good deal of experience in handling ideas. In this passage, for example, the writer uses very few concrete words, yet the meaning is clear to anyone who is interested in jazz:

> Some of the most brilliant of jazzmen made no records; their names appeared in print only in announcements of some local dance or remote "battles of music" against equally uncelebrated bands. Being devoted to an art which traditionally thrives on improvisation, these unrecorded artists very often have their most original ideas enter the public domain almost as rapidly as they are conceived to be quickly absorbed into the thought and technique of their fellows. Thus the riffs which swung the dancers and the band on some transcendent evening, and which inspired others to competitive flights of invention, became all too swiftly a part of the general style, leaving the originator as anonymous as the creators of the architecture called Gothic. — Ralph Ellison, "The Charlie Christian Story"

**23.4**

*abst*

But broad ideas can also be discussed in concrete terms. For example, the passage below is from an essay on Christian social values, an abstract idea:

> Next winter at a theatre meeting that I had instituted on Sunday evenings, we had one evening devoted to public health. The City Health Officer gave a lecture on how disease could be prevented. This was illustrated by means of moving pictures which showed how the fly developed, how it flew from the decaying refuse to the sugar bowl or from a spitoon to the baby's feeding bottle. It was a horrible exhibition—one saw snakes all night after it; but it was tremendously effective. Even the poor foreigners who could not

understand English could understand the pictures. But my church friends were shocked. Here was I, a minister of the Gospel, who had degenerated until I was running a moving picture show in a theatre on Sunday evenings!—J.S. Woodsworth, "Thy Kingdom Come"

When Shakespeare in Sonnet 73 wrote about the sad longing associated with the loss of what we love, he didn't use abstract words, but rather presented images of autumn, twilight, and a dying fire, concrete images that suggest ending, loss, and longing. When Keats told of his excitement when he discovered Homer's works, he didn't write about *excitement stimulation, amazement, discovery,* or other abstractions; instead, he pictured specific situations where such excitement would occur:

Then felt I like some watcher of the skies
  When a new planet swims into his ken;
Or like stout Cortez when with eagle eyes
  He star'd at the Pacific—and all his men
Look'd at each other with a wild surmise—
  Silent, upon a peak in Darien.

—"On First Looking into Chapman's Homer"

Generalization is appropriate—even necessary—when a writer must summarize a large body of facts. This is frequently done in short papers on general subjects, where the writer's primary concern is to survey briefly the available facts and explain their significance. The important thing in such cases is to choose general words that *accurately* summarize the specific details examined, without distortion or unnecessary vagueness. A student writing a paper on conservation, for example, might run across this passage:

In the seven years from 1883 to 1890 the New South Wales Government was forced to spend not less than £1,543,000 in its attempt to control the scourge, and today rabbit control both in Australia and in New Zealand is a financial load upon every community. Many methods of eradicating this pest have been attempted. In Western Australia more than 2000 miles of fencing was erected at a cost of almost £500,000, but after it was all up it was found that some rabbits were already on the other side of the fence! Unfortunately, incidental to the compulsory use of poison for rabbits, there has been a very great destruction of wildlife as well as livestock, and phosphorus poisoning, employed for rabbit control, has been one of the principal causes of death among the marsupials and native birds.— Fairfield Osborn, *Our Plundered Planet*

In writing the paper, the student might effectively generalize from these facts as follows:

> Attempts to limit the rabbit population in Australia and New Zealand have been costly and destructive of other animal life.

It is perfectly proper to use abstract words when the material calls for them, if they can be used accurately and clearly. But writing on almost any subject gains force through the use of specific words. It is usually more convincing to generalize at the beginning or end of a paper, on the basis of a number of specific facts, than it is to pile up generalities throughout.

## Excessive Use of Abstract Words

*Abst* **Replace the marked abstract expression with one that is more specific.**

The most common fault in the wording of many student papers is a fondness for abstract terms where concrete words would be more meaningful and certainly more interesting. Even if an assigned topic is so worded that it seems difficult to discuss in specific terms ("The Importance of Education," "What Democracy Means"), a paper can be reasonably factual, concrete, and convincing if it is written in words that represent the writer's own experiences and beliefs.

Some students make the mistake of believing that the more general the expression, the more convincing and impressive it is. Others mistake the use of abstract words for intellectual discipline. The use of a general or indefinite expression where a concrete one would fit is annoying to readers:

**23.4**

> I began to participate in all of the different aspects of college pleasure.

*Abst*

We don't know if the writer began to drink, to study, to play bridge, to attend concerts, to sleep late, or to do all or none of these.

The excessive use of abstract words can become an unfortunate habit in writing. Some students never take *physics, history, economics,* or *French;* instead, they encounter *various interesting courses of study;* instead of attending, say, Simon Fraser, they attend *an institution of higher learning;* they do not play *golf, bridge, tennis,* or *baseball,* but *participate in various recreational activities.* Few traits of style are less convincing than the unnecessary use of vague, abstract terms for ideas that could better be expressed concretely.

▶ **EXERCISES**

1. The sentences below are general statements, and they may be somewhat vague. Rewrite each of them so that they use more concrete

words and name more specific things. Don't worry about the length of your sentences—think instead about making them as specific as you can.

a. City noises are sometimes raucous and distracting.
b. Individuals who live in an urban metropolis can engage in more leisure activities.
c. Fuel conservation will require some changes in our way of living.
d. More people now are interested in keeping fit.

2. Sometimes you may need to generalize without citing specific information. Keep track of the information in each of the items listed below and then write out your generalization from each:

a. one week's daily weather reports in a local newspaper
b. one episode of a soap opera
c. any three hours of listening to the same disk jockey on a radio station you are familiar with
d. the letters to the editor in any three days' issues of a local newspaper

# The Effect of Words

*Words are sounds, and written words are the musical score of meaningful sounds.... Those same symbols are given to us ... to influence people. All we need do is choose them wisely and use them imaginatively. The person to whom you are writing will respond to some words while remaining indifferent to others. How can you expect to energize a reader into doing what you want him to do if you write stale and flat words in uninspired sentences? Mark Twain is quoted as saying: "The difference between right words and the almost right word is the difference between lightning and the lightning bug."* —The Royal Bank of Canada Monthly Letter.

Words occur in sentences, and sentences occur in paragraphs and compositions. If they are to convey to a reader the meaning you desire, words must be used accurately in context. They should be appropriate to the purpose and tone of the composition: the individual words should fit the subject; they should sound like the writer; and they should be understood by the intended reader.

Because you can't judge the effect of words out of context, you must rely on your own judgment in choosing words that will tell your meaning and reveal your attitude toward your subject. A dictionary is a useful guide to meaning, but it is of little help when it comes to putting proper words in proper places.

In the absence of specific guidelines, there are three things you can do to help make your word choice more effective. First, you can choose more thoughtfully from the range of your own present vocabulary the words that best suit your purpose. A good part of the time when we are writing or speaking, many of us just accept and use the first words that come along. Often we already know words that would be more precise and appropriate than the first ones we think of. Second, you can sharpen your judgment by paying closer attention to the language around you—the language of your classmates, your instructors, your parents, the people you hear speak on television and radio—and noticing the differences in usage that you hear and read. Third, you can read widely to familiarize yourself with the range and variety of writing. All written English is a bank you might draw on.

**24**

*Wds*

## 24.1 FORMAL WORDS

We may call a piece of *writing* formal, even if its vocabulary is largely from the range of general English, when its sentences are unusually complex, its organizational patterns tight and demanding. We call *vocabulary* formal if it ranges much beyond the characteristic spoken vocabulary, from words slightly more characteristic of writing than of speaking to such specialized words as *moribund, graduand, genotype,* and *zymurgy.*

## Appropriate Use of Formal Words

In using formal language, you run the risk of sounding remote from your subject and from your reader. Unless you are at ease with formal words, you also run the risk of seeming affected. But some situations demand and deserve the precision of good formal usage. Some things cannot be said easily, or at all, otherwise. If the nature of your subject requires a formal vocabulary, as the following passages do, use it:

> The solid character of [David] Helwig's work, in terms of his syntax, his particular observation, his persistent moral awareness, has always been one of its main attractions.... If we note in addition Helwig's emphasis on reason, on moderation, on the plain moral dimension of human experience, we may conclude that [he] is closer to the spirit of Jonson's classicism than to that of many recent poetic movements.—D.G. Jones, in *Queen's Quarterly*

> Through the centuries (if not millennia) during which, in their retelling, fairy tales became ever more refined, they came to convey at the same time overt and covert meanings—came to speak simultaneously to all levels of the human personality, communicating in a manner which reaches the uneducated mind of the child as well as that of the sophisticated adult. Applying the psychoanalytic model of the human personality, fairy tales carry important messages to the conscious, the preconscious, and the unconscious mind, on whatever level each is functioning at the time.— Bruno Bettelheim, *The Uses of Enchantment*

Formal words are appropriate to writers and speakers who use them easily and naturally and to situations that require them for precision. Increase the number of formal words in your vocabulary whenever you can, but use them only when they are necessary, not to translate ordinary matters into "big words."

## "Big Words"—Stilted Language

*Big 9f* **Replace the stilted word or words with words from the general vocabulary.**

In *Modern English Usage,* H.W. Fowler remarks that sometimes "We tell our thoughts, like our children, to put on their hats and coats before they go out." Noting that "the less of such change there is the better," he adds, "there is nothing to be ashamed of in *buy* or *see* that they should need translating into *purchase* and *observe;* where they give the sense equally well they are fit for any company and need not be shut up at home."

"Big words," as the term is used here, are any and all expressions that are too heavy or too formal for the situation. Such words sound stilted, whether they are short or long, common or uncommon. A typical fault of inexperienced writers is the use of big words in a misguided effort to sound learned:

> It is difficult to filter out one specific cause for a social problem. Most often there are many minute factors interrelated and closely corre-lated. Our conception of a social problem today possesses more magnitude than that of two or three decades ago. We now consider the world as a unit rather than an aggregation of component entities.

Ideas are easier to understand and are more convincing if the wording is natural. It should be exact, not inflated beyond the requirements of the subject or the expectations of the reader. The language of the sentences just cited, for example, might be simpli-fied as follows:

> A social problem can seldom be traced to a single, specific cause. Today we are much more aware of the complexity of social problems than we were twenty or thirty years ago, for we have come to see that all societies are interrelated.

**24.1**

*Big W*

Writers are most likely to use stilted language when they are not certain what attitude they should take toward their material or toward their readers. They may use inflated diction because they wrongly believe that certain papers should be as formal and impersonal as possible, or that big words will impress the reader, or that inflated diction is humorous ("a fair damsel garbed in the mode of the moment" instead of "a fashionably dressed young woman").

An extreme use of big words is sometimes called *gobbledygook* —inflated diction that seems to have lost all contact with the matter being discussed. Writing full of such jargon is often found in print today, especially in specialized journals and government publications, but this does not make it good English. Here is what James Thurber had to say of such language:

> Great big blocky words and phrases bumble off our tongues and presses every day. In four weeks of purposeful listening to the radio and reading the newspapers I have come up with a staggering list, full of sound and fury, dignifying nothing: "automation," "roadability," "hummature," "motivational cognition" (this baby turned up in a

> series of travel lectures and was never defined), "fractionalization," "varietism," "redesegregation," "additive," "concertization" (this means giving a concert in a hall, and is not to be confused with cinematization or televisionization). . . . Ization is here to stay. It appeals to bureaucrats and congressmen because of its portentous polysyllabification. Politicians love it the way they love such expressions as "legislativewise." Lord Conesford, stout defender of the Queen's English, recently paraphrased Churchill's "Give us the tools and we will finish the job" by Washingtonizing it like this: "Supply us with the implements and we will finalize the solution of the matter." — James Thurber, *Alarms and Diversions*

The remedy for too many big words is simple: Read aloud what you have written, preferably some time after you have written it; if you find the language markedly different from what you would use in conversation, look at the words carefully to see whether you can find simpler and clearer synonyms.

The trouble with gobbledygook is that people who talk and write that way get to thinking that way. The journal *College English*, in an effort to bring gobbledygook to public attention, began in 1974 a continuing series of articles on "public doublespeak." Each article in the series records instances, often from political life, of public gobbledygook. Each year an announcement is made of the worst examples that appeared during that year; these announcements are usually publicized by newspapers and television.

## Technical Words

In writing intended for a general audience, unfamiliar terms not made clear by the context should be defined or explained. Technical terms or unfamiliar expressions that often need explaining include

1. scientific terms (*isotope, lobotomy, gneiss*) and other expressions restricted to a specialized activity (*a cappella, heroic hexameter, escrow, chiaroscuro, farinaceous, binary*);
2. words used in special senses rather than in the usual way (the *spine* of a book, to *justify* a line of type, the *recorder* as a wind instrument, a *frog* as a fastener for a jacket);
3. words and phrases not customarily used by most people (*lex talionis, leitmotif, eisteddfod, de trop*).

You should not use an inexact or wordy expression in place of a necessary technical term. If, for instance, the subject of a paper is "Mountain Climbing," it is better to define and use a word like *piton* than to say "those little metal gadgets that ropes are tied to." Do not use unfamiliar words just to show off, but use and explain those that are essential to your subject.

Often a simple definition or explanation can be worked into the sentence where the technical term is introduced, as in the following examples:

> The ability of the heart to function depends primarily on the state of the heart muscle, or myocardium, as it is technically known.

> In the study of rhetoric we are first to consider *inventio,* or what we now refer to as the problems of pre-writing.

> In cold weather the Inuit wear mukluks (fur boots) and parkas (short fur coats with fur hoods).

As a rule, do not simply quote a dictionary definition, which may be too narrow, but compose one that fits the style and scale of your own paper. Compare a dictionary definition of *oligarchy* with this description of the term:

> I mean by "oligarchy" any system in which ultimate power is confined to a section of the community: the rich to the exclusion of the poor, Protestants to the exclusion of Catholics, aristocrats to the exclusion of plebeians, white men to the exclusion of colored men, males to the exclusion of females, or members of one political party to the exclusion of the rest. A system may be more or less oligarchic according to the percentage of the population that is excluded; absolute monarchy is the extreme of oligarchy. — Bertrand Russell, *The Impact of Science on Society*

**24.1**

*Big 24*

The crucial thing in defining a term is to give an adequate description of the way *you* are using it, with details and concrete illustrations to clarify the meaning.

▶ EXERCISE

Rewrite the following passages in clear and effective English.

1. *From a student composition:* Our high school was eminently well equipped for various recreational pursuits. For those of sportive inclinations, there was the capacious gymnasium, which resounded to multitudinous roars whenever our champions engaged a challenging contingent.

2. *From a professional journal for teachers:* This film demonstrates the progress of an idealized date, from the ideational impetus to the request, acceptance, the dating experience itself, and the final leave-taking, in the process raising some significant questions regarding dating and suggesting partial answers as discussional guides.

3. *From a letter to the editor:* Is the love of monetary remuneration such that it acerbates all else into obliviousness? Can we not conjure into our configurations and substratums of consciousness some other destination than the all-mighty dollar?

## 24.2 INFORMAL WORDS

Informal words include those marked *informal,* or *colloquial,* in dictionaries and most of those marked *slang.* They are part of general English but may not be appropriate to all kinds of writing.

### Appropriate Use of Informal Words

Informal words are often appropriate in discussions of informal or humorous situations, and activities such as sports. They are also sometimes fitting in discussions of more important topics, where the language is typically general English. You will find such words used, without apology or quotation marks, in many reputable publications. Note the boldface words and phrases in the passages below:

> Even so, these two bits of intellectualistic slang are preferable to certain other clichés so commonly heard as to be allowed to befoul the language almost unnoticed. No study is **worth its salt** unless it is *in depth;* no memorandum can be taken seriously unless it is a *position paper;* and everyone is **at sea** until he is *orientated.* — Russell Lynes, "Dirty Words," *Harper's*

> On the other hand, **shrinks** don't like small cities—the isolation sometimes **gets to them.** [One] is moving now to Toronto, where he plans to make $250,000 a year **shrinking Bay Street tycoons.**— "Inside Track," *Saturday Night*

If you are tempted to apologize for informal words by putting them in quotation marks, ask yourself whether they are genuinely appropriate. If they are, use them without apology, but if not, replace them with words from the general vocabulary.

### Inappropriate Use of Informal Words

*fnf* Change the informal expression to one that is more general.

It is disconcerting to a reader to encounter an informal expression in relatively formal writing:

The displaced persons in Europe experienced many **tough breaks** after the end of the war. [more appropriate: *hardships*]

The natives believe that they can expiate certain offenses against tribal customs by **throwing a feast.** [better: *giving a feast*]

In formal writing, informal words not only indicate a shift in variety of usage but may also suggest that you've grown careless toward your subject:

When Desdemona failed to produce the handkerchief, Othello began to suspect that she **wasn't on the level.**

Be particularly careful about certain expressions so widely used that you may not realize (until the slip is called to your attention) that they are considered informal rather than general usage:

Plays of this sort are seldom seen **in our neck of the woods.**

Malcolm Lowry had **a funny habit** of writing long, rather complicated sentences.

▶ EXERCISE

Listen to the conversations of people around you and take note of occasions when you and they fall back on inappropriate or inaccurate informal words in place of more precise words. Record such instances on paper for discussion in class.

## 24.3 LIVE WORDS AND DEATH MASKS

**24.2**

*Inf*

Good writing, whether factual or fictional, captures a reader's interest and holds attention; other writing, concerned with similar facts or ideas, may strike a reader as lifeless and boring. In either instance the wording may be correct enough, but in the more enjoyable and memorable reading, the words are fresh and direct:

Multi-coloured kites bounced in the skies over the Heath. Lovers strolled on the tow paths and locked together on the grass. Old people sat on benches sucking in the sun.—Mordecai Richler, "Playing Ball on Hampstead Heath"

Supper was a young squirrel who had nevertheless achieved an elder's stringiness, roasted in foil on the embers, and a potato baked in the same way.—John Graves, *Goodbye to a River*

The search for fresh and direct expression does not require that you should strain obviously for effect, by searching for unusual expressions or words, any more than it requires that you should use eccentric punctuation or unconventional sentence structure. It does mean that you should take an interest in the freshness of your expression and that you should take sufficient time and thought to put aside *death masks* in favor of live words.

We have used the expression *death masks* as a general name for several kinds of words and expressions, including worn-out terms, euphemisms, incongruous figures of speech, or currently over-worked expressions. A *death mask* is a casting made of someone's face just after death—and that seems to have little to do with words. Yet two ideas are brought together in the term to describe the effect of some words: they are dead, for they lack vitality and freshness; they hide or mask meaning. A euphemism, for example, is lifeless language, and it hides the writer's meaning, masking it as something else. Several varieties of death masks are discussed in the following sections.

## Vogue Words

We naturally use words that are in current use. All of us from time to time resort too easily to "vogue words," words that our society has currently adopted as signals of value. *Meaningful* is such a word; *dialogue* is another, and *ambience* is a third. These words and others like them come into popular use in a number of ways, and then suddenly they are everywhere. The problem is that when we start using words and phrases such as "the bottom line," or "relevant," or "scenario," then the vogue words begin to take the place of thinking, and we use them automatically.

Other vogue words can be listed: *game plan, flat out, lib* (short form of *liberation*), words with *-in* (*work-in, love-in, sit-in*), *raunchy, gut feeling, pick up on, get it together,* and certain words ending in *-wise* (*profitwise, timewise*). A useful activity would be for you to list the vogue words you hear or read.

## Trite Expressions

*Trite*    Replace the trite expression with one that is fresher or more direct.

Trite expressions, or clichés, are pat phrases so familiar that, given the first words, we can usually finish the expression without thinking:

This is going to hurt me more _____ .
He is down but not _____ .
Gone but _____ .
It isn't the heat but _____ .

Try to avoid the following overworked expressions; they occur constantly in student papers:

| Cliché | Comment |
| --- | --- |
| according to Webster | Did Webster write the dictionary you are using? |
| history tells us | A dubious personification, one that often leads to empty generalizations. |
| the finer things of life | Name two or three. No matter what they are — a good pipe, a Beethoven quartet, a cheesecake — they'll be more convincing to the reader than this nebulous phrase. |
| last but not least | Is the last item or fact *never* of least importance? |

The problem with trite expressions is that you can use them without thinking. They are there in the air, and you can fill a gap on your page by plucking one. They are part of a community language; using them easily becomes habitual. But when you use trite expressions, they replace your own words and thoughts, and so they mask your own meaning.

Figurative language (24.4) adds interest to writing when it is fresh and appropriate, but stale comparisons and personifications only serve to bore the reader. It will not make anything seem cooler, hotter, or neater if you describe it as *cool as a cucumber, hot as a two-dollar pistol,* or *neat as a pin.* Here is a short list of trite figures of speech; you can probably think of many similar expressions:

**24.3**
*Trite*

| | |
| --- | --- |
| quick as a wink | at the drop of a hat |
| lost in thought | a watery grave |
| sly as a fox | run like a deer |
| rotten to the core | like a shot from a cannon |
| white as snow | brave as a lion |
| in a nutshell | Mother Nature |
| darkness overtakes us | spreading like wildfire |
| commune with nature | bull in a china shop |
| the rat race | the crack of dawn |

Similarly, many quotations have lost their vividness through overuse:

| | |
| --- | --- |
| a sadder but wiser man | all the world's a stage |
| stone walls do not a prison make | water, water, everywhere |

There are many fresh, vivid, less-quoted lines, if you wish to enliven your writing with quotations.

When you find yourself using overworked expressions, look at them closely to see if they actually mean anything to you; usually you will decide that they really mean very little, and you will make your point another way.

## Euphemisms

A euphemism is a polite and often affected expression used in place of a more common term which the user fears might be offensive. Euphemisms are often used in conversation out of consideration for the listener's feelings: a teacher might tell parents that their child is *slow* or *exceptional* rather than *dull* or *stupid;* a salesperson is more likely to tell a customer that she has a *problem figure* than that she is *overweight* or *fat.* But although euphemisms are often necessary in social situations, they ordinarily sound evasive or affected when they are used in writing:

| Euphemistic expression | Direct expression |
|---|---|
| a reconditioned automobile | a used car |
| underprivileged, disadvantaged | poor |
| senior citizens | old people |
| halitosis | bad breath |
| unmentionables | underwear |
| expecting | pregnant |
| pass away | die |
| lay to rest | bury |
| our statement apparently has escaped your attention | you haven't paid your bill |
| preferred customers | customers who pay their bills regularly |

▶ EXERCISE

The sentences below contain clichés and trite expressions. Rewrite them in more direct language or, if you can, in fresh figurative language.

1. If he wins the election—and he may—we are all up the creek without a paddle.
2. Silence reigned supreme among us as the principal gave us a piece of his mind.
3. When he got to the campus post office and found his failure notice, it was a bitter pill to swallow.
4. Armed to the teeth with notes and coffee, he started to work on his research paper.

5. The chairman nipped the squabble in the bud and got the discussion down to brass tacks.
6. Each and every man should take out life insurance so that his loved ones will be well provided for when he goes to his eternal reward.
7. I told him straight from the shoulder that his work was no longer acceptable.
8. If it didn't mean showing my hand too soon, I would tell the newspapers that I intend to throw my hat in the ring.
9. A teacher is called upon to render services beyond the call of duty time and time again. His unselfish devotion to the youth of Canada goes a long way toward making this a better world to live in.
10. The investigators didn't leave a stone unturned in their relentless search for the fugitive from justice.

## 24.4 FIGURES OF SPEECH

Figures of speech are expressions of comparison, personification, or association that are used to intensify statements or to make them more expressive and vivid, usually by shifting from the ordinary uses and meanings of words. This is a literal, non-figurative statement:

> The fewer words a person uses, the more quickly his or her meaning will be understood.

The same idea can be expressed in a more memorable way by a well-chosen figure of speech:

**24.4**
*Fig*

> . . . meaning is an arrow that reaches its mark when least encumbered with feathers.—Herbert Read, *English Prose Style*

Notice how the use of well-chosen figures of speech enlivens this description of a spot on the British Columbia coast:

> Among the grim conifers, forever fighting to survive and forever doomed, the smooth limbs of maples search for the light, spreading jagged leaves to the sun, like supplicating hands, and in the bottom lands beside the streams the alders leap up overnight, with white-mottled bark, hand-painted. High in the coastal mountains the gray boles of yellow cedar are as antiseptic in their emanation as the smell of a hospital. Down in Saanich, which the evergreen forest has not yet discovered, there are old oaks, with crooked arms, running across the hillsides like frightened gnomes.—Bruce Hutchinson, ''The Trees''

The use of figurative language is not limited to purely descriptive passages or to "literary" subjects. You will find figures of speech used freely and effectively in such diverse material as financial articles, literary criticism, advertising copy, sports writing, and political discussions. The chart on page 327 defines some of the more common types of figurative expressions.

### Effective Figures of Speech

*Fig*    **Change the figure of speech to an expression that is more appropriate to your subject and your style; avoid inconsistent figures.**

Although figures of speech, if they are fresh and perceptive, clearly have an appeal, they are *not* mere ornaments. Indeed, when they seem to be ornaments, we can usually conclude that they are used unnaturally and ostentatiously. If they are vivid and natural, they make writing attractive, but they can accomplish much more than this.

Each kind of figurative language has its special uses. Metaphor and simile, for example, can enlarge our perception and understanding of a subject, and can say much in little space. If a writer says, "The old cowpuncher's parenthetical legs were covered by worn, brown chaps," we gain from the metaphor a pretty clear picture of the cowboy's shape; some notion of his age and the amount of time he has spent on a horse; and some insight into his character and the writer's attitude toward him (the choice of metaphor suggesting a familiar, even comic treatment). We can learn something about a subject in one area by the light cast on it from language of another area, much as we do in reading parables and allegories, which, in a sense, can be considered extended metaphors.

For these reasons, figurative expressions should be in keeping with your subject and your style, and they should be accurate enough to contribute to the meaning. Expressions that are too strong or that strive too hard to be picturesque only confuse or irritate the reader:

> As fall comes in with its gentle coolness, Mother Nature **launches her chemical warfare,** changing the leaves into their many pretty colors.

> My grandfather's barn was **like a medieval fortress shrouded in legend.**

Straining for unusual expressions seldom results in effective writing. The figures to use are those that actually come to mind

## Types of Figurative Language

HYPERBOLE: Deliberate exaggeration for interest and emphasis.

> It was a day **to end all days.**
> He's the **greatest** second baseman **in the world.**

IRONY: Use of a word or phrase to signify the reverse of its literal meaning.

> For Brutus is an **honourable man.** . . . Shakespeare, *Julius Caesar*
> That's just **great.** [expression often signifying disgust]

LITOTES: An assertion made by the negation of its opposite.

> Hemingway was **not a bad writer.**
> Rome was **no mean city.**

METAPHOR: Implied comparison between two unlike things, often used to show some unexpected likeness between the two.

> . . . . Out, out, **brief candle!**
> **Life's but a walking shadow,** a poor player
> That struts and frets his hour upon the stage
> And then is heard no more. . . . Shakespeare, *Macbeth*

METONYMY: Substitution of an associated word for what is actually meant.

> Suited to the **plough,** he sought to live by the **pen.**

ONOMATOPOEIA: Use of words to create a sound appropriate to the sense.

> It was a hot day in late July when I sat with Uncle Miles at Belting beside the **strippling ream.** The deliberate Spoonerism was Uncle Miles's, and it did seem to express something about the stream that rippled beside us as we sat on the spongy grass. — Julian Symons, *The Belting Inheritance*

OXYMORON: Coupling contradictory terms.

> At eleven, she **enjoyed the fright** of reading *Dracula.*
> Life is a **bittersweet** experience.

PERIPHRASIS: Substitution of a descriptive phrase for a name, sometimes of a name for a descriptive phrase.

> Be true to the **red, white, and blue.**
> Hockey gave us the **Big Train** and the **Rocket.**

PERSONIFICATION: Attribution of human qualities to non-human or abstract things.

> They turned and waved, and then the jungle **swallowed** them.

SIMILE: Stated comparison between two unlike things (see *Metaphor*).

> My mistress' bosom **is as white as the snow, and as cold.** — Joseph Addison, *The Spectator*

SYNECDOCHE: Naming a part when the whole is meant, or naming a whole when a part is meant.

> The poor man had twelve **mouths** to feed.
> **Calgary** plays **Montreal** for the Grey Cup.

**24.4**

*Fig*

when you are trying to give an exact account of the subject. They should be fresh, if possible, but, even more important, they should fit their context and sound natural.

## Consistent Figures of Speech

A figure of speech should not begin with one kind of image and switch to another wholly unrelated one. These *mixed metaphors,* as they are usually called, often present a ludicrous, confused image instead of the fresh insight the writer intends:

> The nineteenth century **became a door** opened by some of the braver authors, through which many of the earlier ideas of writing for children, which had been **crushed or discarded, again sprang to blossom,** and spread into the many branches of children's literature that we have today.

If you can look at your own writing with some degree of objectivity, you can usually determine whether a figure is consistent or not. Sometimes an expression that seemed very vivid at the moment of writing proves, upon rereading, to be confusing or even ridiculous.

▶ **EXERCISE**

The critic I.A. Richards has speculated that we use figurative language more than we are aware. He maintains that we can barely get through three sentences without it. Try checking out this claim in any magazine you have handy. Go through an article or two, copying the figurative language that you find. Try classifying it according to the types of figures listed in the chart on p. 327.
*Example:* There were nine *hands* on the ranch (synecdoche) who tended the cattle and also the fields of wheat that *rippled like waves* (simile) in the wind.

# Sentence Length and Economy

*It is as important for the purpose of thought to keep language efficient as it is in surgery to keep tetanus bacilli out of one's bandages.—Ezra Pound,* LITERARY ESSAYS

Good sentences are varied in length and in pattern. Sometimes they are leisurely, unfolding slowly and gradually rounding out an idea; sometimes they are direct and emphatic. They may be balanced, or curt, or loose. They may be accumulating, piling up facts or ideas or observations to achieve a meaning, or they may be discriminating, distinguishing grammatically among facts and ideas and observations to state a meaning. In other words, they are as different as people.

The stylistic qualities of sentences are matters of choice rather than of rule. You can write short, grammatically correct sentences almost indefinitely, but if you wish to say what cannot be said in that way—to expand your meaning or to vary it—then you must use other more complex grammatical constructions in order to express what you want to say in an effective way. Remember that reading first-draft sentences critically and revising them can be extremely important in developing a good style.

This chapter is about the stylistic features of sentence *length,* including economy of wording. Chapter 26 considers the variety of forms, or *patterns,* that sentences may take to communicate meaning.

## 25.1 SENTENCE LENGTH AS A MATTER OF STYLE

Written sentences may vary in length according to your purpose, the way in which you typically express your ideas, and the type of material you are presenting. Longer sentences generally occur in rather formal discussions of complex ideas, shorter ones in rapid narrative, simple exposition, and other general writing.

Sentence length varies somewhat according to the fashion of the times. Early nineteenth-century writers built their ideas into sentences that often averaged thirty to forty words. Current writing uses somewhat shorter sentences, averaging between twenty and thirty words. These figures are only estimates, of course; individual sentences may vary greatly in length.

There is no special virtue in either long sentences or short ones. More important is the total effect of a passage in which the sentences are characteristically long or short. In the following paragraph by a well-known writer, the sentences are noticeably shorter than average for professional writers. The average length is just over fifteen words, and six of the thirteen sentences have fewer than fifteen words. Yet the form seems appropriate enough for its time and place.

> July 3, 1943
> We received a letter from the Writers' War Board the other day asking for a statement on "The Meaning of Democracy." It presumably is our duty to comply with such a request, and it is certainly our pleasure.
>
> Surely the Board knows what democracy is. It is the line that forms to the right. It is the don't in don't shove. It is the hole in the stuffed shirt through which the sawdust slowly trickles; it is the dent in the high hat. Democracy is the recurrent suspicion that more than half of the people are right more than half of the time. It is the feeling of privacy in the voting booths, the feeling of communion in the libraries, the feeling of vitality everywhere. Democracy is a letter to the editor. Democracy is the score at the beginning of the ninth. It is an idea that hasn't been disproved yet, a song the words of which haven't gone bad. It's the mustard on the hot dog and the cream in the rationed coffee. Democracy is a request from a War Board, in the middle of a morning in the middle of a war, wanting to know what democracy is. — E. B. White, "Democracy." From *The Wild Flag* (Houghton–Mifflin); © 1943 E. B. White. Originally in *The New Yorker*. Reprinted by permission.

But in another essay, White uses somewhat longer sentences (average length, twenty-two words) with a more leisurely tempo:

> I would rather train a striped zebra to balance an Indian club than induce a dachshund to heed my slightest command. For a number of years I have been agreeably encumbered by a very large and dissolute dachshund named Fred. Of all the dogs whom I have served I've never known one who understood so much of what I say or held it in such deep contempt. When I address Fred I never have to raise either my voice or my hopes. He even disobeys me when I instruct him in something that he wants to do. And when I answer his peremptory scratch at the door and hold the door open for him to walk through, he stops in the middle and lights a cigarette, just to hold me up. — E. B. White, "Dog Training," *One Man's Meat*

Length alone is seldom as important as variety and appropriateness, and your ability to use the form, long or short, that best suits your purpose and your material will give variety and liveliness to your writing.

There are times, especially when you first start writing, that you may be tempted to keep sentences short. It's safe: punctuation errors and other troubles may be less likely to show up in short sentences. The world around you may sometimes seem to show you evidence that short statements are the characteristic form of human utterance. The opening lines of newspaper stories are often filled with short sentences. Radio disc jockeys often speak in a staccato rhythm of short sentences. Television commercials and magazine ads and billboards depend almost exclusively on short, presumably forceful statements.

Don't be too cautious, and don't be too quickly convinced by the apparent frequency of short statements. There are some things that cannot be said briefly. There are times when a leisurely accumulation of insight and observation in a sentence will let you be more thorough, more honest. John Erskine, the novelist, remarked some time ago that "When you write, you make a point, not by subtracting as though you sharpened a pencil, but by adding." As you add to sentences, more often than not they become more specific. Start with a basic sentence, for example:

> The girl sat in the chair.

The statement is generalized. The girl is given no identity, nor is the chair; the manner of sitting is not specified. But consider what happens when we add to the statement:

> 1. The small girl sat in the big chair.
>
> 2. Quiet and thoughtful, the small girl sat curled in the big, brown, high-backed chair.
>
> 3. Quiet and thoughtful, the small girl sat curled in the big, brown, high-backed chair, her legs tucked under her, a book in one hand, a cup of coffee in the other.
>
> 4. Quiet and thoughtful, lost in what she was reading, the small girl sat curled in the big, brown, high-backed chair by the record player, her legs tucked under her, a book in one hand, a cup of coffee in the other.

**25.1**

With each addition, the scene is more clearly specified.

Here an interesting paradox occurs: *by adding you take away.* Consider the sentence *The girl sat in the chair.* Since you give no identity or distinguishing marks to the scene, readers are at liberty to see the girl and the chair according to *their own* experiences. As you add specifying details to the sentence, making it more clearly a scene from *your* experience, you gradually subtract from your readers' visualization of the scene and make it possible for them to see it as you do. With each addition, the texture of detail in the sentence becomes richer. Many ways of adding to your basic sentences are open to you:

1. you can make the subject, the verb, or the complement compound;
2. you can insert appositives into the subject-verb-complement structure;
3. you can use verbals or verbal phrases;
4. you can use noun clauses for the subject or the complement;
5. you can use adjective clauses to modify the subject or the complement;
6. you can use adverb clauses to modify the verb;
7. you can add adjectives, adverbs, or prepositional phrases.

With each addition — and there are others that you can devise by reviewing the section on the grammar of sentences — it is also possible to begin rearranging the sentence.

▶ EXERCISE

Five short sentences appear below. Rewrite each one of them in two different ways, adding constructions as suggested below:

*Example:*    The singer looked surprised.

*Revision 1:* The singer, a woman no longer young, looked surprised.
*Revision 2:* The singer, looking surprised, turned toward the orchestra behind her.
*Revision 3:* The singer, tall and stately, looked surprised.
*Revision 4:* The singer, who is best known for her recordings of Schubert, looked surprised.
*Revision 5:* The singer looked surprised when the bassoonist called out to her.

1. The third baseman hit a double.
2. Mrs. Merriwether took the job.
3. The book is interesting.
4. The class inspired her.
5. Joe fell.

## 25.2 SENTENCE LENGTH AND MEANING

Rewrite the passage marked to eliminate choppy or stringy sentences and to show the relationship of ideas.

Appropriate sentence length is determined less by the number of words in a sentence than by what a sentence contributes to the total meaning of a paragraph. Self-evident or extremely obvious statements contribute nothing to writing:

> These scientific theories came into being only after definite steps had been taken.

Of course definite steps were taken. This statement is so general that one could substitute for *scientific theories* almost anything that comes to mind—the Peace Bridge, the United Nations, a formal dance, or a term paper.

## Choppy (Too Short) Sentences

Some sentences say too little because a simple idea has been broken up unnecessarily into two or more statements, as in this example:

> I took my first course in mathematics at Riverdale High School. This was first-year or elementary algebra.

Most readers will not feel any need to invest their time in these individual sentences, which might better be combined:

> I took my first course in mathematics, elementary algebra, at Riverdale High School.

A succession of very short sentences tends to give a piece of writing a halting, jerky effect. Such sentences also impede the flow of thought, for they fail to show how ideas are related:

> We arrived at the recruit camp that afternoon. We were divided up. We were sent to barracks. They were reserved for recruits. The barracks were old. The floors were scrubbed almost white. Vague scars of cigarette burns marked them. I wondered how many wars had brought recruits here.

The choppy movement of this passage gives an effect the writer did not intend. The passage could be made smoother by combining related statements:

**25.2**

> When we arrived at the recruit camp that afternoon, we were divided up and sent to the old barracks reserved for recruits. The floors were scrubbed almost white, but the vague scars of cigarette burns marking them made me wonder how many wars had brought recruits here.

Short sentences are useful in various writing situations—in dialogue, for emphasis, for creating a feeling of rapid action or of tension—but you must exercise judgment if you are to use them successfully. In the following passage, for example, the writer's intention was probably to convey a feeling of excitement, but the breathless style defeats this purpose because it goes on too long and has no variety in sentence pattern:

> It was my senior year in high school. Our basketball team had won the trophy the year before. This year the team was considered even stronger. Nearly every member of the pep club was seated. It was the final game. We had come all the way through the tournament without a defeat. This game would determine which team would be the champion. I looked toward the end of the gym. The referees were talking. They, too, were excited. Would that starting gun never go off! My hands were clammy. My cheeks burned.

Examine closely any passage in your own writing that contains a noticeable number of consecutive sentences under eighteen words. Try reading the passage aloud to see whether it conveys the effect you intended or whether the writing is simply hasty.

## Stringy Sentences

Avoid stringing together (with *and, but, so, and then*) statements that should be written as separate sentences or as subordinate elements. Sentences carelessly tacked together in this manner are not only monotonous to read but lose all their emphasis because every idea seems to be of equal importance:

> About fifty feet away I saw a buck deer running for safety **and so I** knelt on my right knee **and then** I brought the rifle to my right shoulder. He was still running, **so I** fired one shot at him, **but I** missed, **but** he stopped and looked at me, **and then** I had a much better target to shoot at.

Reading such sentences aloud should reveal their weaknesses and help you to revise them for better organization:

> About fifty feet away I saw a buck deer running for safety. Kneeling on my right knee and bringing the rifle to my shoulder, I fired once, but missed. He stopped to look at me, providing a much better target.

Stringy sentences often result from linking too many main clauses together (*Most people know that our agricultural system is the world's best* and *they have grown to expect great things from this system,* and *they should*). The cure lies in cutting down the number of co-ordinating conjunctions (*and, but, so*) and in subordinating ideas of lesser importance.

## Relating Ideas Clearly

Avoid combining unrelated ideas in the same sentence. If there is a relationship between the ideas, so that they can reasonably be combined, show what it is. Don't leave it to your reader to puzzle out:

> As Byron is the poet of youth, it is appropriate that the new and completely reset edition of his poems should be published on March 1. [What is the relation between *youth* and the date of publication?]

> Nassau has a delightful climate that attracts hundreds of tourists every year, and some historians think that Columbus landed in this area in 1492. [If there is any relationship between Nassau's climate and Columbus, it should be stated.]

Sentences that are haphazard or contain contradictions can be improved by clarifying the intended relationship:

> HAPHAZARD: There is no evidence to support the fact that her marriage to another writer may have had some influence on her style.
>
> REVISED: Although her marriage to another writer may have had some influence on her style, there is no evidence to support this.
>
> HAPHAZARD: I consider *The Old Man and the Sea* one of the literary masterpieces of our time, but many people have disliked Hemingway's other novels.
>
> REVISED: Even those who have disliked Hemingway's other novels are likely to enjoy *The Old Man and the Sea*, which I consider one of the literary masterpieces of our time.

A sentence should be constructed so that the most important idea receives greatest emphasis; the relationship of other ideas can usually be shown in subordinate constructions. See also 26.2, Subordination to Control and Clarify Meaning, and 26.4, Sentence Emphasis.

**25.2**

▶ EXERCISE

Rewrite the following passages, paying special attention to clarifying the meaning and to eliminating ambiguities and contradictions.

1. My high-school days are over and I realize I cannot turn back time, so I must now make the best of my future. Now that I am continuing my education, I am also trying to improve on the mistakes I made in high school. One by one I am ironing out the deep wrinkled problems and solving them.

2. There is a lot of evidence that great scientific discoveries do not happen by chance, but usually involve thinking on the part of the scientist.

3. There are two major factors that help a person mature, heredity and environment. Although my heredity was good, my environment was a different matter. The friends I had were by no means juveniles, nor were they scholars. Since I spent most of my spare time with my buddies, I adopted the same habits they had concerning studying. We did not excel or fail in school, but we could have done a lot better.

4. As time passes, many complexities in our environment result from scientific and technological advancements which create new branches in every field of activity, thus causing the youth of today to seek out a more thorough education.

5. The body goes through certain changes between youth and old age, whether a person realizes it or not.


## 25.3  AVOIDING WORDINESS

*wdy*  **Make the marked sentence or passage less wordy and more direct.**

Achieve sentence economy by wording statements so that their meaning can be grasped by the reader without unnecessary effort. No one likes to listen to a speaker who talks too much and says too little, and no reader likes to cut a path through a tangle of useless words or constructions to get at a relatively simple idea. Phrases, clauses, or other constructions that use many words to say what can be said more directly are called *circumlocutions*.

Practising sentence economy does not always require stripping your sentences down to the bare minimum, as you might in composing a telegram or writing a classified ad. The shortest words and simplest constructions are not always the most economical, for they may fail to convey your exact or complete meaning. Economy of expression requires rather that you state your ideas in the most accurate and direct way possible.

Often it is possible to make a statement more direct by reducing a sentence or a clause to a phrase or a single word:

**The snow lay like a blanket.** It covered the countryside. [two sentences]

The snow, **which lay like a blanket,** covered the countryside. [One sentence contains the other, which has been reduced to a clause.]

The snow covered the countryside **like a blanket.** [One sentence contains the other, which has been reduced to a phrase.]

The snow **blanketed** the countryside. [One sentence contains the other, which has been reduced to a single word.]

One way to tighten sentence form is to eliminate unnecessary and ineffective verbs and their modifiers:

WORDY: He crawled slowly over the river bank, looking for the flint chips which would mean that he had found a campsite.

REDUCED: He crawled slowly over the river bank, looking for flint chips marking a possible campsite.

The two verbs that can most frequently be eliminated without any loss of meaning are *be* in its various forms and *have:*

WORDY: **He is a native of the prairies** and knows the value of water conservation.

MORE ECONOMICAL: **A native of the prairies,** he knows the value of water conservation.

WORDY: A few of the fellows **who were less serious** would go into a bar **where they would have** a steak dinner and a few glasses of beer.

MORE ECONOMICAL: A few of the **less serious** fellows would go into a bar **for** a steak dinner and a few glasses of beer.

WORDY: **There is** only one excuse **that is acceptable,** and **that is** "I have a class this hour."

MORE ECONOMICAL: **Only one excuse is acceptable:** "I have a class this hour."

If a number of your sentences begin with *There,* try to revise some of them so as to express the idea in a more direct way:

WORDY: **There are two plays in our anthology,** and I like them both.

MORE DIRECT: I like both plays in our anthology.

WORDY: **There is a suggestion box** in almost all big business houses where employees may put ideas.

MORE DIRECT: Most big business houses provide suggestion boxes for their employees.

**25.3**

*Wdy*

While a writer's style and the general movement of the entire composition determine to a large degree whether shorter or longer constructions are more appropriate, the careless habit of consistently using two or more statements where one would be just as effective should be avoided in all styles of writing.

▶ **EXERCISE**

Rewrite the following paragraph, tightening it whenever possible by substituting words and phrases for clauses; eliminate all unnecessary words:

There were so many things to do and the summer was so short. We could go and chase rats in the barn, which was a dangerous and slightly sickening enterprise; we could teach a kitten how to play circus. We could climb to the roof of the corridor where we could watch the ducks file out to the pond, and crack dry mirthless jokes to one and another. We could help with the cider press, where all the apples with a rotten spot, those that had been claimed and contended for by the yellow jackets, disappeared into the hopper and gushed out the sides in a seethe of liquor that was brown and bubbly. There were so many things to do and the summer was so short.

## 25.4 REMOVING DEADWOOD

*Dead* Revise the marked sentence or passage to eliminate deadwood.

*Deadwood* is a term for a particular kind of wordiness: lazy words and phrases that clutter up a statement without adding anything to its meaning.

Anyone acquainted with violin construction knows that the longer the wood is seasoned, the better **the result will be as far as** the tone of the instrument **is concerned.**

Empty expressions like those in boldface above are excess baggage and do nothing to further communication. They often find their way into first drafts because they come to hand so readily, but you should take care to prune them out in revision. Eliminating deadwood will make a statement neater and more direct without changing its meaning in the least, as these examples illustrate (deadwood in brackets):

Every thinking person these days seems to agree [with the conception] that the world has gone mad.

Because [of the fact that] she had been ill, she missed the first two weeks of classes.

After a delay of forty-five minutes, the audience [got to the point that it] became restless and noisy.

The wordy formulas that serve as fillers in casual conversation are more noticeable and annoying in writing than they are in speech. Roundabout expressions should be replaced in revision by terms that say the same thing more directly:

| | | |
|---|---|---|
| **get in touch with** | *means* | **call** or **see** |
| **due to the fact that** | *means* | **because** or **since** |
| **in this day and age** | *means* | **now** or **today** |
| **at the same time that** | *means* | **while** |

Certain words, generally in stereotyped phrasal combinations, account for much of the deadwood found in student writing. This list, while not exhaustive, illustrates phrases built upon the most common of these words:

| Word | As Deadwood | Deadwood Eliminated |
|---|---|---|
| case | **In many cases** students profit from the research paper. | Many students profit from the research paper. |
| character | Her gossip was **of a sordid and ugly character.** | Her gossip was sordid and ugly. |
| exist | The soil conditions **that existed** in Manitoba became serious. | The soil conditions in Manitoba became serious. |
| fact | In spite of **the fact that** he is lazy, I like him. | In spite of his laziness, I like him. |
| factor | Speed is also **an important factor.** | Speed is also important. |
| field | Anyone interested in **the field of** Canadian history should take his course. | Anyone interested in Canadian history should take his course. |
| instance | **In many instances,** students write their papers just before the deadline. | Often students write their papers just before the deadline. |
| line | He always thought he would be successful **along agricultural lines.** | He always thought he would be successful in agriculture. |
| manner | He glanced at her **in a suspicious manner.** | He glanced at her suspiciously. |
| nature | She seldom talks on any subject **of a controversial nature.** | She seldom talks on any controversial subject. |
| seems | **It seems that** we have not lost a daughter, but gained another icebox-raider. | We have not lost a daughter, but gained another icebox-raider. |
| tendency | When I am supposed to be working, **I have a tendency to** clean my pipes and dawdle. | When I am supposed to be working, I clean my pipes and dawdle. |
| type | His father had an executive **type of** position. | His father had an executive position. |

**25.4**

*Dead*

These words have definite meanings in some expressions (a *case* of measles, a minor *character* in the play, a *field* of clover, and so forth), but as used here, they are superfluous.

▶ **EXERCISE**

Read the following sentences carefully, looking for roundabout expressions and deadwood. Then rewrite them into direct and economical statements.

1. In university one must put away the childish thoughts of her girlhood and begin thinking of the future that lies ahead with adult ideas and responsibilities.
2. Throughout my previous school days, I have been the type of person who hasn't had to study a great deal to get grades above those obtained by the average student.
3. One of my bigger excuses was the fact that I claimed there were too many social activities currently in progress.
4. The method used to detect the approach of other ships is radar.
5. One lady aroused my indignation when she claimed that her son, who was six feet in height, was under twelve years of age.
6. Habits can be classified into two distinct types: one is the useful, progressive, uplifting kind while the other is of the nature that deteriorates character and often damages the physical body.
7. My scholastic averages show, in my opinion, a rather distorted picture of my true knowledge.
8. I have chosen this road of higher education to reach my goal, which is that of teaching children.
9. To reach this goal I must be well educated and have a thorough understanding of my subject.
10. The income from the tourist business is an important source of revenue for people who own businesses in Prince Edward Island.

## 25.5 AVOIDING CARELESS REPETITION

*Rep.*  Eliminate the ineffective repetition of words, meaning, or sound.

Unless repeated for a definite reason, a word or a phrase should not be made conspicuous by too frequent use in the same passage.

### Effective Repetition

Sometimes repetition is essential for meaning or for sentence structure:

For three thousand years, poets have been enchanted and moved and perplexed by the power of their own **imagination.** In a short and summary essay I can hope at most to lift one small corner of that mystery; and yet it is a critical corner. I shall ask, What goes on in the mind when we **imagine?** You will hear from me that one answer to this question is fairly specific: which is to say, that we can describe the working of the **imagination.** And when we describe it as I shall do, it becomes plain that **imagination** is a specifically *human* gift. To **imagine** is the characteristic act, not of the poet's mind, or the painter's, or the scientist's, but of the mind of man. — Jacob Bronowski, "The Reach of Imagination," *American Scholar*

Intentional repetition may also be effective for emphasis:

There is no way of becoming **inaccurate** by industry, and if you deliberately try to be **inaccurate** you fail. **Inaccuracy** is perhaps the most **spontaneous** and the **freest** of **gifts** offered by the Spirit to the wit of man. It is even more **spontaneous** and more **free** than the **gift** of writing good **verse,** or that rarer **gift** which I have also written of here — the **gift** of writing abominably **bad verse;** exceptionally **bad verse;** criminally **bad verse;** execrable **verse.** — Hilaire Belloc, *On*

Some kinds of words must of course be used over and over again: articles (*a, an, the*), conjunctions (*and, but, or*), prepositions (*of, in, at*) , and pronouns (*it, that, my, which*). Because their purpose is grammatical, the constant repetition of these words goes unnoticed.

## Useless Repetition

Unintentional, unnecessary, and ineffective repetition of words is illustrated in this passage:

When I was in high school, I would take a book home once or twice a week and maybe read it two or three hours at a **time. Most of the time** I would read **most** of my homework just in **time** to have it ready before class began. It was very easy **most of the time** to read the assignment and have it prepared when my **time** came to be called upon for recitation.

Repetition of this kind is weak and clumsy, for it focusses attention on words rather than on ideas. It also suggests that the writer may be careless and unconcerned with what he or she is saying.

**25.5**

*Rep*

**Repetition of words.**    Repeat words in a passage only when you have good reason for doing so. Key words (such as the subject) may sometimes be repeated for clarity or emphasis, but less important terms should not be used more often than necessary.

POINTLESS REPETITION: The **problem** of feeding its ever-increasing population is one of India's most acute **problems.**

REVISED: Feeding its ever-increasing population is one of India's most acute problems.

POINTLESS REPETITION: Many people think **that** if a **product** is endorsed by a prominent person **that** it is a good **product** to buy.

REVISED: Many people think that a product endorsed by a prominent person is a good one to buy.

Especially to be avoided is repetition of the same word when it has two different meanings:

If I **run,** I'll get a **run** in my stockings.
If I run, I'll **tear** my stockings.

Astrology is so popular in Hollywood that many movie **stars** won't sign a contract unless the **stars** are favorable.

Astrology is so popular in Hollywood that many of the movie stars won't sign a contract unless their **horoscopes** are favorable.

**Repetition of meaning.** Adding an expression that repeats the meaning of another (called *tautology*) is one of the most common forms of unprofitable repetition. The bracketed expressions in the following sentences are a form of deadwood (25.4). They should be omitted because they merely repeat ideas that are sufficiently expressed in other words in the sentences:

In the modern world [of today], time has a meaning different from what it had when transportation was slower.

It is believed that the age of the earth is about two billion years [old].

She decided to trim the family room in bright red, but the [resultant] effect was not what she had anticipated.

Words like *color, size,* and *shape* often needlessly repeat a meaning that is already clear:

UNSATISFACTORY: His hair was brick red **in color.**
REVISED: His hair was brick red.

UNSATISFACTORY: **The length** of the locks is about two thirds of a mile **long.**
REVISED: The locks are about two thirds of a mile long.

UNSATISFACTORY: Behind the house was an enclosed court which was rectangular **in shape.**
REVISED: Behind the house was an enclosed rectangular court.

The abbreviation *etc.* (*et cetera*) means "and so forth." To write "*and* etc." is equivalent to saying "and and so forth." Avoid this non-standard expression; and avoid *etc.* in formal writing.

**Repetition of sounds.**   A sound should not be made conspicuous by careless repetition. The cumulative effect of certain suffixes like *-ly, -ment,* and *-tion* may be evidence of weak style:

> The concept of such sanctuary immunity unquestionably predominantly influenced the enemy to enter into the conflict.

> Written permission of the administration is required for reregistration of those students who are on probation.

Alliteration—the repetition of the same sound at the beginning of words in a series—is out of place when it attracts attention to the words at the expense of the ideas:

> I am looking for a shop that still has pleated pants for poor and paunchy professors.

> He then made himself comfortable in a rather rickety rattan rocker.

Even though your papers are not usually written to be read aloud, you should try to avoid unintentional sound patterns that may be momentarily irritating or distracting to a reader who has a well-tuned ear:

> The enemy was reported to have seized this important port, and reinforcements were hurrying up in support.

▶ EXERCISE

Revise the following sentences to eliminate clumsy or pointless repetition of words, meaning, or sounds. If the repetition in any statement seems intentional and effective, explain what purpose it serves:

1. The hazy figures in the background are vague and indefinite, and they add a sinister note to the painting.
2. The advantage of getting a broader perspective through travel is only one of the advantages of spending a summer travelling through Canada.
3. Many people live so compulsively by the clock that they have a fixed time for eating, a fixed time for bathing, and a fixed time for everything but enjoying life.
4. An application of lotion to the area of inflammation should relieve the pain.
5. Concrete and steel have both been used successfully in skyscraper construction, but buildings of concrete must have much thicker walls at the lower levels than those of steel. On the other hand, concrete has a far greater decorative potential than steel.

**25.5**

*Rep*

# Sentence Variety, Control, and Emphasis

*There is a natural emphasis in his style, like a man's tread, and a breathing space between the sentences.—Henry David Thoreau,* WALDEN

You can write just by putting down the words, phrases, and sentences that come to mind most easily, but most of us can't write *well* that way. Good writers don't always accept the first words that occur to them, or the first sentences that take shape on their papers. The construction of sentences can be arranged and rearranged, and you can gain some control over the sentences you write and emphasize your meaning to help ensure your reader's understanding.

## 26.1 SENTENCE VARIETY

*Var*    **Vary the sentence patterns in the marked passage to avoid monotony or to make your meaning clearer or more emphatic.**

Often when we are reading good writing, we don't notice the sentences and we are unaware of their patterns. But if the patterns become monotonous, either in length or in arrangement, then we are likely to notice and react unfavorably, even irritably. An easy variety and flexibility customarily pleases us more and lets us move without vexation from sentence to sentence, as in this passage:

> Not every student can be educated to the same degree of literacy, though my own long experience has taught me what a great deal can be achieved with what may seem to be unpromising human material. But the teacher must have a clear notion of what he is trying to do ..., and be constantly imaginative and inventive in his methods. English is by no means an obsolete industry. It is an industry which has been suffering from a good deal of confusion about what products it is trying to make and about what its workers are supposed to be doing. Its genuine and proper products should be as valuable and as necessary as ever.—F.E.L. Priestly, "English: An Obsolete Industry?"

This paragraph is readable and understandable at least partly because the movement is easy and natural, with variety in sentence structure. The five sentences begin, in order, with a negative adverb, a conjunction, a subject, and the last two with a pronoun; length ranges from eight words to thirty-six words. The first sentence is an observation from experience; the second, opening with the conversational conjunction, states a critical reaction; the third states a position; the fourth qualifies the third; and the last sounds a note of optimism.

## Varying Sentence Beginnings

When several consecutive sentences begin the same way — with a noun subject, for example — the passage is likely to be monotonous and to lack impact:

> **Meteorology** has made many advances in recent years. **Weather observation balloons** have been developed to gather data from the upper stratosphere. **Time-lapse photography** has improved the study of cloud formations and patterns. **Barometric instruments** of greater sensitivity are widely used. **Radar** is useful in detecting the approach of storms and precipitation.

Sentence beginnings can be varied and made more interesting by occasionally starting with a modifier — a word, phrase, or clause — as in this passage from an essay on Paul Bunyan:

> **The vogue of the Paul Bunyan stories among the men of the woods** is probably past, with the changing type of woodsman, and the changing conditions of working and living. **If this is true, then** we owe a debt of gratitude to those who are collecting them. **As collected in books, the tales,** like old folk songs without their tunes, must in the main be lifeless things, except to those of us who can from old experience reconstruct their settings and hear the old raconteurs at the telling; **but even so,** there is enough life in them to justify richly their preservation. **They** represent, perhaps as nothing else does, the spirit of the **men of the woods** in those days.
> — J.D. Robins, "Paul Bunyan"

**26.1**

*Var*

To begin sentence after sentence with the same kind of modifier is no less monotonous, of course, than to begin every sentence with the subject. Deliberately inserting or shifting modifiers to gain variety is a makeshift or affected practice, hence an ineffective one. The emphasis you wish to make and the general movement of the passage should determine your sentence beginnings.

### Varying S — V — O Order

A less common means of varying sentence patterns is changing the usual order of subject-verb-object or subject-verb-complement in declarative statements. This is called *inversion:*

> Supplementing the guitars and drums are a solo cello, a ragtime piano, an Indian sitar, sound effects of barnyard animals, and a complete symphony orchestra. — Peter Schrag, "Facing the Music"

But except in questions and requests, inversion should ordinarily be used only when the words put first really deserve special emphasis by withholding the subject. Inversion used solely for variety may have painful results, as in this reversal:

> A garden city, with one of the most delightful climates in the world, is Victoria.

### Loose and Periodic Sentences

Sentence patterns may also be varied by using both loose and periodic sentences.

**Loose sentences.**    In a loose sentence the main statement comes first, followed by subordinate elements that explain or amplify or alter its meaning. This pattern is the one most commonly used both in speech and in writing, for writers characteristically make points by adding information. Notice especially the second, third, and fifth sentences in this passage:

> Montreal this winter is the colour of a gray and white cat. It is furry like a cat, too, thick with snow-dusted trees and vegetation along the undulating flank and haunches of Mount Royal. Its factories hum and its traffic often snarls and the crowds along the sidewalk are thicker than fleas trying to escape extinction. Everyone is in a hurry, but less from exuberance than because it is a long-standing tradition in Montreal to be late for everything except hockey games. We blame our tardiness on overcrowded trams, on motorists who persist in their Gallic right to be individuals, on the fact that nearly everyone is working too hard. Certainly there has never been so much lettuce to be picked or more Montrealers busy gathering it. — Hugh MacLennan, "Letter from Montreal"

One particular kind of loose construction, called *prolepsis* in early rhetoric texts, can be useful. *Prolepsis* is the expression of a general statement, which is then followed by amplifying details:

> Once on the mound, he was a most unlikely looking pitcher, slouching, tangle-footed, absent, with the aspect of a lost goose.

> Modern homes have lost a tempo they once had—urban activities speed them up, television governs some hours, and separation from relatives and neighbors leaves them alone.

Such a construction can set the subject for a paragraph or short essay, determine its content, and act as an outline. The second sentence above, for example, could be amplified in an essay that had three key parts, each fully illustrating one of the three factors listed.

Loose, or *accumulating,* sentences are an interesting reflection of the writer. As you add to a sentence, amplifying and specifying your meaning, you show yourself in the *process of thinking.*

**Periodic sentences.**    A periodic sentence, however, is more often than not the statement of *completed thought.* Much less common both in speech and in writing, a periodic sentence is one in which the main statement is not completed until the end or near the end of the sentence:

> And around the sunken sanctuary of the river valley, stretching out in all directions from the benches to become coextensive with the disc of the world, went the uninterrupted prairie.—Wallace Stegner, "Quiet Earth, Big Sky"

Although periodic sentences occurred frequently in writing before this century, they are now much less common than loose sentences. They require planning beforehand and are more typical of a formal than of a general style. The very fact that periodic sentences are not widely used, however, gives the pattern all the more value as a means of achieving emphasis.

When you are framing a periodic sentence, make certain that the suspension is not awkward or unnatural, as it is in this example:

**26.1** ◀
*Var*

> The reader will probably agree after reading this essay **that Pearl Buck's example** of the woman who, after being married for a number of years and raising a family, gradually loses interest in most of her former outside activities, **is true.**

## Varying Kinds of Sentences

If you discover in scrutinizing your first draft that you have written an essay in which most of the sentences have the same kind of clause structure, you should consider combining, dividing, or reshaping your sentences. Quite aside from the question of variety, different kinds of sentences — simple, compound, complex — are ordinarily necessary for meaning and for emphasis.

Sometimes a question or directive makes an effective variation from the usual declarative sentence:

> Is "painfully clear" an evasion of the too political "perfectly clear?" Certainly it is an example of the meaningless adverbial sludge which clogs inflated editorial writing.—Maurice S. Elliot, "Respecting Our Organs"

> You know, because you felt the pain in your own flesh, that evening when the police shot your son. Is it necessary to feel pain in our own flesh before we really know? More and more, I think that it probably is.—Margaret Laurence, "Open Letter to the Mother of Joe Bass"

Questions and commands can be effective if they serve a legitimate purpose, but like other sentence patterns they should not be used solely for the sake of variety. Unless the answer is self-evident ("Who would trade freedom for tyranny?"), don't raise a question without answering it. Never conclude a paper with a pointless, blunt question such as "What do *you* think?"

▶ **EXERCISES**

1. Make loose sentences by adding to the five simple sentences or independent clauses below. Try to add at least three additional units to each, as in the example.

   *Example:* It was a depressing day.
   *Loose sentence:* It was a depressing day, with black clouds obscuring the sun, a cold wind whipping through the trees, and even the birds hiding from the weather.

   a. This house is your dream house.

   b. The eastern third of China is the core of the nation.

   c. Railways played an important part in building Canada.

   d. The student council listened attentively.

   e. "Liberation" can mean a lot of different things.

2. Make periodic sentences by completing the sentences started below, as in the example.

   *Example:* After he found the candlestick on the rug,
   *Periodic sentence:* After he found the candlestick on the rug, and after he learned that the fingerprints were not those of the dead

woman, and after he found the scratches on the lock, the inspector became convinced that this was a case of murder.

a. When the sun went down

b. After finals were over for the seniors

c. Although regular class-attendance is important

d. While others might need lots of money

e. If you have followed the map carefully up to this point

# 26.2 SUBORDINATION TO CONTROL AND CLARIFY MEANING

*Sub* Show the intended relationship between ideas by using appropriate subordination, or correct the faulty subordination.

By bringing related ideas together, you give continuity to your writing and signal the direction of your thinking to your reader. But even when ideas are so closely related that they belong in the same sentence, they do not necessarily deserve equal weight. You must decide, in every case, how contributing ideas can best be arranged around a major idea, or how minor points can best accumulate to help make a major point. This means that every sentence should be *composed*.

An indiscriminate clustering of ideas in a sentence or paragraph is a disservice to the writer, to the subject, and to the reader. Ideas are *not* all the same: some are antecedents to others, some are conditions of others, some are less important than others. If you fail to show the relationship of one idea to another—whether in a single sentence or in a series of sentences— you may be informing your readers, in effect, that all your ideas are equally important or that you are too lazy to bother making your meaning clear:

**26.2**

*Sub*

> FAILURE TO SUBORDINATE: I worked hard and I turned out a first-rate manuscript, and I missed my deadline and my publisher was angry.
>
> IDEAS EFFECTIVELY RELATED: Although I worked hard and turned out a first-rate manuscript, my publisher was angry because I missed my deadline.

In the first version, four sentences are presented, and all are treated equally. In the revised version, the writer shows how the four are related. One of the statements was chosen as dominant ("my publisher was angry"). One was reduced and rewritten as a cause ("because I missed my deadline"), and the other two are presented as contrary conditions.

Subordination serves writers in several ways. You can put minor ideas into grammatically dependent constructions in order to stress your major point in an independent construction. And at the same time, if you are judicious, you can precisely relate the major and minor ideas. The key statements in the following passage occur at the first of each sentence. Because the author does not move slowly toward his main points but chooses typically to announce them directly at the start of each sentence, the sentences have a kind of incessant beat, the key point coming first, to be followed by contributing but subordinate statements. The sentences shaped in this way make a rhythm appropriate to this account of the defeat and desolation of a people:

> The last of the Sioux war chiefs now became a reservation Indian, disarmed, dismounted, with no authority over his people, a prisoner of the Army, which had never defeated him in battle. Yet he was still a hero to the young men, and their adulation caused jealousies to arise among the older agency chiefs. Crazy Horse remained aloof, he and his followers living only for the day when Three Stars would make good his promise of a reservation for them in the Powder River country. Late in the summer, Crazy Horse heard that Three Stars wanted him to go to Washington for a council with the Great Father. Crazy Horse refused to go. He could see no point in talking about the promised reservation. He had seen what happened to chiefs who went to the Great Father's house in Washington. . . . —Dee Brown, *Bury My Heart at Wounded Knee*

Notice especially the first, third, fourth, and seventh sentences, where the initial key point focusses on the Indians, while the subordinate elements insert white men into the narrative.

Thoughtful subordination also allows you to move easily from sentence to sentence, using dependent constructions as transitions. Notice, for example, the subordinate clause introducing the last sentence of this passage:

> When you write, you make a point, not by subtracting as though you sharpened a pencil, but by adding. When you put one word after another, your statement should be more precise the more you add. **If the result is otherwise,** you have added the wrong thing, or you have added more than was needed. —John Erskine, "A Note on the Writer's Craft"

Because grammatical constructions are important signals of meanings, you should make certain in checking your first draft that you have not put major ideas into minor constructions, or minor ideas into major constructions—a fault known as inverted or "upside-down" subordination. See also 3, Subordinate Clauses and Connectives, especially 3.5, Faulty Subordination.

## 26.3 PARALLELISM

*Paral*
*(//)* Make the sentence elements marked parallel in form.

Ideas of equal value in a statement can be made parallel; that is, they can be expressed in the same grammatical form. Putting co-ordinate ideas in parallel constructions shows the reader that you regard two or more things as related and equal in importance; the *appearance* of parallel passages is a signal that they are closely related. Parallelism also helps the reader see in which direction the statement is going and makes for smoother writing, since it helps prevent unnecessary shifts in person and number and in the tense and mood of verbs.

### Elements in Series

Words, phrases, and clauses in series are best stated in parallel form. The boldface words in the following sentence are parallel because each is the object of the preposition *with:*

> His mind was filled with artistic **projects, schemes** for outwitting his creditors, and vague **ideas** about social reform.

The compound predicates in this sentence are also parallel:

> His dramatic attempt to take over the conduct of his own case **alienated** him from his counsel, almost **broke up** the trial, and probably **helped** to cost him his life. —Joseph Kinsey Howard, *Strange Empire*

When co-ordinate ideas are not stated in parallel form, the statement is likely to seem awkward and unpolished:

**26.3**

*Paral*
*(//)*

> NOT PARALLEL: We were told **to write** in ink, **that we should** use but one side of the paper, and **we should** endorse our papers in the proper manner. [an infinitive phrase and two clauses]
>
> PARALLEL: We were told **to write** in ink, **to use** but one side of the paper, and **to endorse** our papers in the proper manner. [three parallel infinitive phrases]

A preposition or a conjunction should be repeated between the items of a series when necessary for clarity:

> PREPOSITION NOT REPEATED: These problems are currently of great concern **to** the school system, teachers, and many parents.

CLEARER: These problems are currently of great concern **to** the school system, **to** teachers, and **to** many parents.

CONJUNCTION NOT REPEATED: The opposing citizens argued **that** the increased tax rates were exorbitant and the **school board** should find some other way to raise the money.

CLEARER: The opposing citizens argued **that** the increased tax rates were exorbitant and **that** the **school board** should find some other way to raise money.

## Elements Being Compared or Contrasted

Elements that are compared or contrasted through the use of pairs of conjunctions such as *either . . . or, neither . . . nor, not only . . . but* (or *but also*) are usually clearer and more emphatic when they are stated in parallel constructions:

This is the life of a musician in which are recorded **not only the events** of his life, **but also details** of all his works, which are analyzed and described fully.—Lionel McColvin, *The Wonderful World of Books*

Since readers expect similar constructions to follow pairs of conjunctions, they may be momentarily confused or sidetracked if the pattern is shifted:

SHIFTED: You may go to the ski jump either by special train or a chartered bus may be taken.

PARALLEL: You may go to the ski jump either by special train or by chartered bus.

SHIFTED: He admired the premier not for his integrity, but because of his political cunning.

PARALLEL: He admired the premier not for his integrity, but for his political cunning.

Making related ideas parallel is one of the jobs of revision. Similar forms for similar ideas help hold a sentence together.

## Balanced and Antithetical Sentences

When parallel constructions, especially clauses, are noticeably equal in length and similar in movement, the sentence is called *balanced*. Balance is useful for emphatic statements, for comparing and contrasting ideas:

He was no more willing to change these views than he was to stop drinking whisky. And he was known as a man with a powerful thirst.—Ramsay Cook, *Saturday Night*

The best model of the grand style simple is Homer; perhaps the best model of the grand style severe is Milton. — Matthew Arnold, *On Translating Homer*

When contrasting clauses occur in parallel constructions in a single sentence, the sentence is called *antithetical*. Such a construction fittingly emphasizes a striking or important contrast:

You may eat without danger our canned food, fresh and hot, from your own campfire, but you will drink in peril the dirty water, polluted and foul, from the nearby stream.

Antithetical sentences can easily be overused, but they are occasionally effective to mark turning points in an essay—the first half of the sentence pulling together what precedes, the contrasting second half foreshadowing what follows.

▶ **EXERCISE**

Rewrite the following sentences, eliminating unnecessary words and making related elements parallel in form.

1. I wrote because it amused me, and I enjoyed correcting the work, too.
2. The town turned out to be hard to reach, a bore, and very chilly in the evening.
3. The squirrel in our front yard is a playful sort, and who mocks us from his tree.
4. He slogged his way through his homework, and finished off his notes, then turning on the TV.
5. The house was charming and a real buy, but it was not near enough public transportation nor quite large enough for our family.
6. People who have not been to the Yukon ask questions about the prices, how cold it gets in winter, and what is worth seeing.
7. I am tall and bald and have an ungainly gait.
8. This report is exceptionally complete and a fine example of concise writing.

**26.4**

*Emph*

## 26.4 SENTENCE EMPHASIS

*Emph*    **Rewrite the marked passage so that the position and expression of the ideas will show their relative importance.**

In composing your sentences, you should help your reader to see your ideas in the same relative importance as you do—to distinguish among the most important, the less important, the incidental. Although the emphasis given to particular ideas depends in large part upon the way the whole paper is put together, from the beginning to the final paragraph, individual sentences can weaken or strengthen this effect. The sentences in the following paragraph, for example, are unemphatic because they are haphazardly constructed. They are wordy, the beginnings are weak, and the endings are unemphatic:

> There are some interesting points about contemporary Canadian life in "The Mobile Society" by Herbert MacAdoo. Some of the things he notes are the paradoxes in it. The way a person often reduces his independence by relying more on mechanical devices is one example the author gives. A man may actually become the machine's slave instead of its master, as he thinks he is.

To make the statements more forceful and concise, the writer might have revised the sentence structure in this way:

> In his essay "The Mobile Society," Herbert MacAdoo points out some of the paradoxes in contemporary Canadian life. He notes, for example, that increasing reliance on mechanical devices often reduces a person's independence. Thinking he is the machine's master, he may actually become its slave.

## Emphasis by Position in the Sentence

Important ideas can be stressed by putting them in emphatic positions in the sentence. In longer statements, the most emphatic position is usually at the end, the next most emphatic position at the beginning:

> It is obviously demanding the impossible in any existing society to ask that all individuals in it should be **so linked and united.** But freedom of expression, and other freedoms as well, can have only a precarious existence where the bulk of the people are not **so linked and united.** Thus freedom of expression has been best safeguarded in countries like Britain with a **profound sense of national unity.**— J.A. Corry, "Free Trade in Ideas"

Sentences—particularly those that introduce or sum up the main points of a topic—should end strongly. Statements that are qualified by a phrase or a word at the end are usually weak:

UNEMPHATIC: The work at the mill was hard and often dangerous, but the mill hands didn't complain, or at least very seldom.
IMPROVED: The work at the mill was hard and dangerous, but the mill hands seldom complained.

UNEMPHATIC: These songs are dull and unoriginal, with few exceptions.

IMPROVED: With few exceptions, these songs are dull and unoriginal.

Because the main statement is not completed until the end, periodic sentences are frequently more emphatic than loose sentences:

LOOSE: Sociology 101 should interest every thoughtful student with its discussion of the theoretical as well as the practical aspects of human behavior.

PERIODIC: Sociology 101, with its discussion of the theoretical as well as the practical aspects of human behavior, should interest every thoughtful student.

A particular kind of periodic sentence, the *climax* sentence, directs the reader through phrases and clauses arranged in ascending order to the most important element at the end:

We shall fight on the beaches, we shall fight on the landing-grounds, we shall fight in the fields and in the streets, we shall fight in the hills; we shall never surrender. — Winston Churchill, Speech following Dunkirk, 1940

Sentences that begin with *There is* or *There are* tend to be unemphatic as well as wordy; frequent use of these constructions will make your writing seem flat and uninteresting.

FLAT: There were several people who objected to the commission's plan.

IMPROVED: Several people objected to the commission's plan.

## Emphasis by Separation

Ideas can be emphasized by setting them off from other parts of the sentence with strong internal punctuation — semicolons, colons, or dashes (12 and 13):

It is one thing to read *Time;* it is another to pronounce the words correctly. — E. B. White, *Quo Vadimus?*

I regret above all the mind insensitive to humour and word-play of all kinds—not just the reflex groan at a bad pun, but the total inability to grasp a good one.—Michael Hornyansky, "Is Your English Destroying Your Image"

**26.4**

*Emph*

When the ideas warrant it, the most emphatic separation is into individual sentences:

Adolescence is a kind of emotional seasickness. Both are funny, but only in retrospect. — Arthur Koestler, *Arrow in the Blue*

## Emphasis by Repeating Key Words

Statements can be made emphatic by repeating important words or phrases:

> His highest hope is to **think** first what is about to be **thought,** to **say** what is about to be **said,** and to **feel** what is about to be **felt.** — Bertrand Russell, *Unpopular Essays*

In your reading, you will sometimes see a word or phrase repeated deliberately for effect at the beginning of consecutive clauses or sentences:

> Vimy was more than a battle. It has become for Canada a **symbol.** It is a **symbol,** as were many other and even bloodier battles, of the courage and the self-sacrifice of Canadian men. It is also a **symbol** of the coming of age of Canada as a nation, a nation which was brought to birth in the emotion of that time with a unity sealed by blood. — Lester B. Pearson "Vimy — Fifty Years After"

This kind of rhetorical repetition is often found in political speeches. Occasionally a word or phrase may be repeated at the end of consecutive clauses, as in Psalm 136, where each verse concludes "for his mercy endureth forever." In the hands of a skilled writer, these techniques can be highly effective, but they should be used very sparingly, and only when a serious subject can be honestly and appropriately conveyed in the deliberate manner they suggest.

Effective (and intentional) repetition should be distinguished from careless repetition, as discussed in 25.5.

## Emphasis by Mechanical Devices

The least effective way to emphasize ideas is by underlining or capitalizing words, by setting them off in quotation marks, or by using emphatic punctuation marks (!!!). Certain kinds of advertising rely heavily on such devices:

> "Oh, of course," you may reply, "it's just a matter of calories." But IS it? Suppose you had to choose between a larger glass of orange juice and half a sirloin steak? You would probably reach for the orange juice. Actually, *the steak would give you 15 times as many ENERGY-stimulating calories. Yet the total number* of calories in each is roughly the same! So, you see, it ISN'T "just a matter of calories." It's the KIND of calories that makes the big difference.

In college writing, mechanical devices for emphasis should ordinarily be avoided; the wording of the statement or its position in the sentence should give it the emphasis it deserves.

▶ EXERCISE

Rewrite the following sentences so that the important points are correctly emphasized.

1. Television programs today are very adolescent in content, at least most of them.
2. There were two magnificent volcano peaks which towered over the valley.
3. Theoretically, the plan seemed flawless; its results, however, were disastrous.
4. Students on the campus were completely unaware that under the abandoned stands of Stagg Field scientists had produced, through concentrated day-and-night effort under rigid security precautions, the first controlled atomic chain reaction.
5. There is something the average voter doesn't realize—that his ONE vote really *can make a difference;* in fact, it can change the outcome of the WHOLE ELECTION!
6. Thumbing frantically through his calendar and clutching his registration cards in his sweaty hands while he stands in line is the typical freshman.
7. Sculpture is an excellent hobby, although it can be expensive and not everyone has the skill to pursue it.
8. Outside his office there were several customers waiting and they insisted there were other matters they had to attend to.
9. The recent civil defence drill—like all the preceding ones—showed that public apathy toward survival methods is immense.
10. Many juvenile delinquents (you'd be surprised *how* many) have parents who refuse to try to *understand* them.

**26.4**

*Emph*

# Paragraphs

*If a paragraph is to make its proper contribution to the whole paper, it must do something. . . . [It] must first of all make a point—convey an idea or impression.—Porter G. Perrin, "Writer's Guide and Index to English"*

A paragraph can be taken as a form of punctuation. The indention of the first line of a paragraph tells your reader that you're taking a new step, shifting attitude, turning to a new feature of your subject, looking at some part of your subject in a different way. If a piece of writing shows a mind at work, then paragraph indentions are the major signs that let a reader follow the mind's movement. But at the same time that it separates units of thought for reading ease, a good paragraph is smoothly integrated into the paper as a whole. Indeed, this coherence is achieved by providing clear transitions and emphasis for key points. These features of paragraphs are explored in Chapter 21, Writing the First Draft, which discusses the use of paragraphs to control the direction of a paper, techniques for relating paragraphs in sequence, and the special character of paragraphs that open or conclude a paper. This section is concerned with the general problems of paragraph development and paragraph continuity.

## 27.1 PARAGRAPH DEVELOPMENT AND LENGTH

*¶ dev* **The marked paragraph is not adequately developed. Add enough explanation or illustration to make the central idea clear and complete.**

In a well-developed paragraph the central meaning is clear and complete. Some ideas can be fully expressed in a few simple statements; others may require from a hundred to two hundred words or more of explanation or illustration in order to be complete.

### Underdeveloped Paragraphs

The effect of underdeveloped paragraphs is illustrated by the following student narrative of a trip:

> Two years ago I took my first trip up the British Columbia coast. On this cruise there were only forty-five passengers. I learned from the steward that the usual number of weekly passengers ranged from seventy-five to two hundred.
>
> The fruit basket in each cabin was filled daily with apples, oranges, and other kinds of fruit. Since meals were included in the price of the ticket, we could choose anything we wanted from the menu without worrying about the price.
>
> We arrived at our first port, Ocean Falls, on a rainy day. We were told that the ship would be there for about four hours unloading cargo and that we could go ashore if we so desired. After taking a good look at the town, I decided that I would very much prefer to be on board ship.

These paragraphs don't work well because they raise questions that the writer fails to answer: Why were there so few passengers on this trip? (This should be explained in the first paragraph or else not mentioned.) What is the point of the second paragraph, which jumps so abruptly from the introductory statements? the abundance of food? how cheap it was? how much the writer enjoyed it? Some statement is needed at the beginning of this paragraph to link it with the preceding one and to express the main idea ("Because there were so few passengers, we were offered more food than we could eat...."). The third paragraph leaves the reader wondering what Ocean Falls looked like, what unpleasant things the writer saw that made him prefer to stay on his ship. Three or four explanatory sentences would have cleared up this point and would have made the paragraph more interesting.

The following paragraph is similarly underdeveloped. It is too brief to convey adequately the writer's ideas:

> People have been faced lately with many different ideas and systems of government. Each has tried to win the majority to its side, frequently by force or by unscrupulous propaganda. Each person thinks of himself or herself as being representative of the majority.

This paragraph could be improved by listing some specific examples after the second sentence (Communism in Angola? monarchy in Spain?) and by using a separate paragraph to explain the third sentence.

**27.1**

¶ dev

A good way to avoid underdeveloped paragraphs is to explore all your ideas fully in the first writing, putting down everything that occurs to you. If the paragraph turns out to be too long or to contain irrelevancies, it is easy enough to trim it in revision. To do the reverse—to fill out an underdeveloped paragraph with details and explanations—takes much more time. (See 21, Writing the First Draft.)

## Typical Content of Paragraphs

No rule exists that says a paragraph *must* do this, or that, or the other. Paragraphs may have one sentence or many. One paragraph may state a point and amplify it with explanation and illustration. Another paragraph may be nothing but illustration of a point made in a preceding paragraph. A whole series of paragraphs may contain only episodes and illustrations to explain an earlier point.

Still, it is probably reasonable to say that *most* fully developed paragraphs are composed of three kinds of statements:

1. **General statements** in a paragraph may range from attitudes and opinions (This is the better plan; You are wrong) to large generalizations (Everyone needs some form of artistic expression; Prison conditions are in desperate need of reform). General statements may also appear as *restatements,* where a general statement is put into different words for clarification; *summary statements,* where ideas already introduced are brought together, and *conclusions,* where material previously presented leads to a new judgment.

2. **Specific statements** are generally subtopics of a general statement. In a paragraph opening with the general statement "This is the better plan," the specific statement that followed might be something like "It has three particular advantages." Specific statements may often be used for one of the following purposes:

   **to expand,** where a sentence amplifies and explains a general idea already expressed;

   **to define,** where a sentence gives the meaning of a word or words in another sentence;

   **to qualify,** where a sentence restricts the meaning of a general statement already made;

   **to concede,** where a sentence acknowledges facts or ideas contrary to a statement already made;

   **to refute,** where a sentence introduces some kind of evidence contrary to a statement already made;

   **to evaluate,** where a sentence makes some judgment about a statement already made;

   **to identify a cause or result,** where a sentence states what produced the event described in a previous sentence, or what resulted from it.

(For what is said here, we are indebted to Richard L. Larson's study of paragraphing.)

**3. Details** are particular observations and facts (He is eleven years old; This violet is a Blue Akey; In two years the city's population increased by 11 460) and summaries of facts (All day the planes had been running late). Details may be offered for several purposes:

to **particularize,** where sentences give the specific facts or details implied in a more general statement;

to **exemplify,** where sentences illustrate what is meant by a previous statement;

to **describe,** where sentences give details to help the reader visualize an object, person, or scene;

to **narrate,** where sentences show actions or events in series, in order to particularize a previous statement;

to **support,** where sentences offer evidence for a previous statement;

to **compare or contrast,** where sentences explain something already said by comparing it or contrasting it with something else.

Generalizations and statements of opinion are most convincing when supported by details, because details can usually be checked for accuracy. Most effective writing, in fact, is made up largely of *details,* with occasional *general statements* to hold them together and show their meaning, and with occasional *specific statements* to direct the reader's attention. The following short paragraph contains all three of these elements:

[General statement:] There are not many good critics for an art, but there have been almost none for the modern theatre. [Specific statement to expand:] The intellectuals among them know little about an operating theatre and the middlebrows look at plays as if they were at a race track for the morning line-up. [General statement:] It is a mixed-up picture in many ways. [Detail to support:] One critic who wrote that *The Little Foxes* was a febrile play later called it an American classic without explaining why he changed his mind. — Lillian Hellman, "Theatre," *Pentimento*

**27.1**

*¶ dev*

Whatever the purpose of a paragraph is, its full development often depends on adequate use of both details and general statements. An *expository* paragraph, for example, is a unit of facts (details) and ideas (general statements) that serves *to explain.* In the following passage, a doctor explains the nature of coronary thrombosis, a disease unfamiliar to many readers:

The diagnosis of "heart disease" is feared by all of us, and not without reason. As long as the heart beats there is hope, but we all realize that if the heart stops beating we will die.

The ability of the heart to function depends primarily on the state of

> the heart muscle or myocardium, as it is technically known. Our existence, therefore, depends largely on the state of the blood vessels that bring nourishment to the myocardium—the coronary arteries. The heart can, of course, be damaged by other disease processes. For instance, the heart may fail because it is irreparably damaged by an infection as in rheumatic disease, or by poisons, or toxins, as in diphtheria.—William A. R. Thompson, M.D., "Coronary Thrombosis," *Today's Health*

The first paragraph makes contact with the reader's common knowledge and concern. The second begins the actual exposition, explaining the meaning of the technical word *myocardium* and rapidly adding other facts that expand the reader's understanding of coronary thrombosis.

An *argumentative* paragraph is a unit of facts (details) and ideas (general statements) that serves *to persuade*. The paragraphs below occur early in an essay discussing the status of women and urging revision of the attitudes that cause women to be treated as not-quite-human. The first paragraph opens with a general statement. The second sentence repeats the point in a more specific statement. Then the last three sentences (a general statement and two amplifying statements) offer a contrary view. The short second paragraph reiterates with supporting general statements the view given at the end of the first paragraph. The last paragraph is made up chiefly of details illustrating the view already announced:

> The first thing that strikes the careless observer is that women are unlike men. They are "the opposite sex"—(though why "opposite" I do not know; what is the "neighbouring sex"?). But the fundamental thing is that women are more like men than anything else in the world. They are human beings. *Vir* is male and *Femina* is female: but *Homo* is male and female.
>
> This is the equality claimed and the fact that is persistently evaded and denied. No matter what arguments are used, the discussion is vitiated from the start, because Man is always dealt with as both *Homo* and *Vir*, but Woman only as *Femina*.
>
> I have seen it solemnly stated in a newspaper that the seats on the near side of a bus are always filled before those on the off side, because, "men find them more comfortable on account of the camber of the road, and women find they get a better view of the shop windows." As though the camber of the road did not affect male and female bodies equally. Men, you observe, are given a *Homo* reason, but Women, a *Femina* reason, because they are not fully human.—Dorothy Sayers, "The Human-Not-Quite-Human"

Developing paragraphs by full use of details removes a frequent worry of beginning writers—"getting the required length." The bulk of the space in most papers should be taken up with specific details, with occasional general statements to interpret or summarize their meaning.

▶ **EXERCISE**

Select one paragraph from each of three articles in a magazine, or from different magazines. Copy the paragraphs, numbering each sentence as you do so. Then determine what each sentence in each paragraph does and how it is related to the rest of the paragraph. Write down your observations in a phrase or two, numbering them to correspond to the sentences.

## Topic Sentences

Both the clarity and completeness of a paragraph can often be enhanced by stating its main idea in what is called a *topic sentence:* a key sentence to which the other statements in the paragraph are related. The topic sentence typically comes at the start of the paragraph, as in this example:

> **A faith is not acquired by reasoning.** One does not fall in love with a woman, or enter the womb of a church, as a result of logical persuasion. Reason may defend an act of faith — but only after the act has been committed, and the man committed to the act. Persuasion may play a part in a man's conversion; but only the part of bringing to its full and conscious climax a process which has been maturing in regions where no persuasion can penetrate. A faith is not acquired; it grows like a tree. Its crown points to the sky; its roots grow downward into the past and are nourished by the dark sap of the ancestral humus. — Arthur Koestler, *The God That Failed*

Another method is to work *toward* the topic sentence, using it as a summary or a conclusion for the details in the paragraph, as in this passage from the New Testament:

> Behold the fowls of the air: for they sow not, neither do they reap, nor gather into barns; yet your heavenly Father feedeth them. Are ye not much better than they? / Which of you by taking thought can add one cubit unto his stature? / And why take ye thought for raiment? Consider the lilies of the field, how they grow; they toil not, neither do they spin: / And yet I say unto you, That even Solomon in all his glory was not arrayed like one of these. / **Wherefore, if God so clothe the grass of the field, which to day is, and to morrow is cast into the oven,** *shall he* **not much more** *clothe* **you, O ye of little faith?** — Matthew 6:26–30

**27.1**

¶ dev

There is no rule requiring topic sentences to be either first or last. They may appear in the middle of a paragraph, and they may appear both first *and* last, as when a writer returns at the end to his or her main point.

The purpose of a topic sentence is twofold:

1. to help the writer focus his or her ideas on one central thought to which every statement in the paragraph is directly related,
2. to make it easier for the reader to see what the paragraph is about, by specifically stating its controlling idea.

Topic sentences are most typically found in expository and argumentative writing, but often even in descriptive paragraphs a single sentence will state a dominant impression that is borne out by the remaining sentences. (See also 27.2, Inductive and Deductive Development.)

▶ EXERCISE

In the sample below, the first sentence is a topic sentence, and each following sentence in some way refers to it. Study the example, and then write similar paragraphs from the topic sentences provided.

*Example:* One popular linguistic myth is that people living in technologically unsophisticated cultures speak primitive languages. / But the languages of native Canadian Indians such as the Cree, the Ojibway, or the Sarcee of Alberta are as complex in syntax and phonology as English or German. / The many languages of Africa, also, are just as rich and complicated as any language in the Indo-European family. / Even the Ainu—one of the most primitive people discovered thus far—prove to have a language that is capable of expressing the most subtle thoughts and needs of the speakers. / If there is such a thing as a "primitive" human language in existence anywhere on earth, the burden of proof now rests with those who glibly equate mechanization with linguistic superiority.

1. I can think of five reasons why I should be elected to Parliament.

2. A car is still a necessity in our society.

3. What do students want from a post-secondary education?

## Appropriate Paragraph Length

Remember that a fully developed paragraph should embody a clear-cut division of the topic. A paragraph indention is a mark of separation, indicating to the reader that one stage in the development of the topic has been completed and that another is about to begin.

A paragraph that attempts to cover more than one stage of the topic should be divided:

> About three years ago when I started my final year in high school, a neighbor who was the captain of the local Naval Reserve unit paid me a visit. He started talking about the wonderful possibilities the Reserve had to offer—training in radio, electronics, and other technical subjects. Evidently he must have been a good recruiting officer, for after he had talked for an hour, I fell for his argument and joined, thinking I might learn something. I did. [**Next sentence starts a new stage of the topic.**] After a few drill parades, I was able to draw some conclusions about this outfit and my place in it. All the fancy talk I had heard was just propaganda, for as soon as I got my uniform, they hustled me down to the naval dockyard. From then on, for a year, I spent most of my weekly drill parades scrubbing the harbor craft while the Petty Officers stood around talking about sports and women. Occasionally they would look busy when they saw an officer coming, but most of the time they loafed while I worked.

Since the discussion of recruiting clearly stops with "I did," the next sentence should begin a new paragraph.

Perhaps a more common fault of inexperienced writers is breaking up related statements into too many paragraphs. This practice distracts the reader and gives the writing a choppy effect:

> The day of the game finally arrives and the first thing you do is look out the window to check on the weather.
>
> As the paper predicted, it is a beautiful sunny morning with very little wind—real football weather. You try to pass the morning by reading about the game, while you are counting the hours and the minutes until the game starts.
>
> Finally you start for the game, only to find the nearest parking lot over a mile from the stadium. You begin the long walk across the campus, joining the thousands of people all as eager as you are, all hurrying in the same direction.
>
> As you pass the impressive Gothic buildings, memories of your undergraduate days come back to you, and you wish for a moment at least that you were back in school again.

**27.1**

¶ dev

The first two paragraphs concern the morning of the game and should be written as one; the last two paragraphs also deal with one topic—the trip to the stadium—and should similarly be combined.

To get an idea of how your paragraphs compare in length with those of experienced writers, examine some articles in several recent publications. Beginning writers generally write paragraphs averaging from forty to seventy-five words, but as they learn to develop their ideas more fully their paragraphs approximate those in books and magazines—seventy-five to a hundred words. Paragraphs in newspapers are usually considerably shorter, but they are deliberately abbreviated for fast reading and are not typical of general writing. Ordinarily, if there are more than two or three indentions on a single page of one of your papers, you should look at your writing carefully to determine whether or not you have separated things that belong together in the same paragraph.

This does not mean that a short paragraph is automatically a poor one: even a one-sentence paragraph can sometimes be used to good effect. Thus, a rather brief sentence conveys an ironic comment and hence deserves to stand alone as the second paragraph of the following passage:

> I have yet to see direct influences from James Joyce, but I am absolutely certain that he will turn out to be a very influential Canadian critic indeed, if a Canadian critic is a man who influences Canadian writing.... I suspect Earle Birney of coming under the spell already.
>
> And, of course, there is always Sir Walter Scott, who remains the great model of many of us, both in verse and in prose.
>
> But in spite of these guides and signposts, some of us are beginning to feel that there are things which have to be said about Canada to Canadians, which need methods not exactly covered by any of these exemplars: not even Sir Walter Scott.—Lister Sinclair, "The Canadian Idiom"

In the next example, so much is packed into a single long sentence that it also qualifies as a good paragraph:

> In short, French Canada had no future: its past could be left to archaeologists and historians, its present would be dealt with by assimilation, aided along, in Sir John A. Macdonald's joking phrase, by "immigration and copulation."
>
> As late as 1942, B.K. Sandwell admitted in *Saturday Night* that "a great many English Canadians" had expected the French Canadians "to be Anglicized if not Protestantized, and are now surprised and distressed when confronted with very strong evidence that they are not."
>
> Since 1960, some of these attitudes have changed....—Ramsay Cook, in *Saturday Night*

Single-sentence paragraphs that serve as transitions between one part of the discussion and another are fairly common in papers that have several main divisions. The one-sentence paragraph below is used to shift from the discussion of a technological development to a judgment of the development:

> ... There are already cryptic advertisements in the Personal columns of literary magazines, urging the purchase of electronic headsets for

the training and regulation of one's own brain waves, according to one's taste.

You can have it.

Not to downgrade it. It is extremely important, I know, and one ought to feel elated by the prospect of taking personal charge, calling the shots, running one's cells around like toy trains. . . . — Lewis Thomas, *The Lives of a Cell*

The real test of paragraph length is not the number of words or lines but rather the answer to these questions: Why was indention necessary? Should any one of the paragraphs be written as two, for clarity and emphasis? Are two so closely related that they should be combined? Appropriate paragraph length follows almost automatically from effective paragraph development.

▶ **EXERCISE**

Take a good sampling of the length of paragraphs in your textbooks and in two or three magazines that you read. Take special note of paragraphs that are unusually long or short; how do you account for the atypical length?

# 27.2 PATTERNS OF PARAGRAPH DEVELOPMENT

Much of the labor of writing consists of managing general statements and details, arranging them in sequences that move toward a point, or support a point, or move toward a transition, or achieve some other effect.

**27.2**

*¶ dev*

## Inductive and Deductive Development

The two basic patterns for developing the main idea in a paragraph are *deductive development,* supporting a main point made at the beginning of the paragraph, and *inductive development,* moving toward a main point at the end. Deductive and inductive development are often referred to as the methods of *support* and *climax.* A deductive or support paragraph will, as you can see, often have its topic sentence at or near the beginning. An inductive or climax paragraph will often have its topic sentence at or near the end.

In the following inductive paragraph, the early sentences provide the data on which the conclusion — the last sentence — is based:

> Ignorance feeds on itself. Children asked to choose, as indeed they sometimes are, between a visit to a library or a visit to a shopping mall, will and do undoubtedly choose the latter. Are they in school, by compulsion, to make such choices? There are entire worlds closed to them which they have a right to encounter, but these are left unrealized. One could understand non-compulsory, non-educative, play-oriented babysitting centres. One could understand compulsory, subject-oriented learning centres where skills and information are presented to be mastered and measured. But surely one cannot understand compulsory attendance that was designed for the latter applied to the former. **Schools should be seedbeds of intellect, but in our time they are often sterile nurseries.** — Joseph Gold, "A Word to the Wise"

The more common deductive pattern, illustrated in the following paragraph, has the primary assertion or main point first, followed by supporting details:

> **Word-magic belongs to poetry. In prose it is an intrusion.** That was the view of Coleridge. It was because, among other qualities, Southey's writing was so free from the shock of the dazzling word that Coleridge held it to be the perfect example of pure prose. The modulations are so just, the note so unaffected, the current so clear and untroubled that you read on without pausing once to think "What a brilliant writer this fellow is." And that is the triumph of the art. It is an art which addresses itself to the mind, and not the emotions, and word-magic does not belong in its true armoury. — A.G. Gardiner, "On Word-Magic"

Notice that the central thought in both of these paragraphs is focused in a topic sentence, its position depending on the pattern the writer has used to develop his main idea.

## Other Patterns of Development

Some texts spell out a number of specific "methods" for developing paragraphs. The catalogue of methods usually includes deduction (support) and induction (climax) as well as these patterns:

1. **Illustration,** ordinarily another name for the overall method of elaborating a general statement by illustrative details
2. **Definition** (frequent in exposition and argument), the explanation of a term by logical definition, that is, by assigning the term to an appropriate class or species and then distinguishing it from other members of the class
3. **Comparison** and **analogy,** the explanation of a particular subject by pointing out its similarities to another subject, usually one that is better known or more easily understood
4. **Contrast,** the explanation of a particular subject by pointing out how it differs from another subject
5. **Cause-effect,** the arrangement of a paragraph according to cause-effect sequence, such as beginning a paragraph with a general statement giving a cause and filling out the paragraph with specific effects, or beginning a paragraph with a series of specific statements naming separate causes and concluding with a general statement that gives the effect
6. **Classification,** the explanation of a subject either by putting it into the class it belongs to and then examining the characteristics of the class, or by dividing the subject in order to consider its individual parts
7. **Chronological order** (characteristic of narrative writing and of expository writing concerned with explaining a process), the arrangement of events in temporal order
8. **Spatial order** (probably most characteristic of descriptive writing), the arrangement of objects in some systematic spatial sequence, as near to far, far to near, high to low

It is possible to write good paragraphs by deliberate use of any one of these patterns, examples of which may be found in books and magazines. The pattern of development in the following paragraphs is indicated in brackets:

**27.2**

¶ dev

DEVELOPMENT BY DEFINITION: Ibsen's *When We Dead Awaken* [term to be defined] is a play [the subject is classified as a *play*] about the use that the male artist and thinker—in the process of creating culture as we know it—has made of women, in his life, and in his work; and about a woman's slow struggling awakening to the use to which her life has been put. [This play is distinguished from other plays.] Bernard Shaw wrote in 1900 of this play: "[Ibsen] shows us that no degradation ever devized or permitted is as disastrous as this degradation; that through it women can die into luxuries for men and yet can kill them; that men and women are becoming conscious of this, and that what remains to be seen as perhaps the most interesting of all imminent social developments is what will happen 'when we dead awaken.'" [An authority is quoted to assist in the characterization of the play.] — Adrienne Rich, "When We Dead Awaken: Writing as Re-Vision"

CAUSE EFFECT DEVELOPMENT: The chief military weakness of the Iroquois was ... the result of ... their individualism and their total lack of discipline [statement of two related causes]. These made it difficult for them to take concerted action or make a sustained effort [effects number 1 and 2]. They were like a ship without a rudder, manned by a quarrelsome crew, able to maintain a steady course only as long as the wind remained constant and some common danger forced the crew to co-operate [effect number 3]. — W.J. Eccles, *Frontenac: the Courtier Governor*

All of these methods or patterns of development are good, but they are really nothing more than characteristic ways of thinking, operations we go through as we mull things over and work them out.

## Combining Patterns of Development

You should notice too, as you read, that the various methods or patterns of development often converge in a single paragraph. The following short paragraph illustrates process analysis by three such patterns: By *defining* a conventional internal combustion engine in the first sentence, the writer is then able to *contrast* the diesel engine with it. The explanation of the diesel engine is then further developed by telling in *chronological order* how it works:

The conventional gasoline engine functions by drawing a vaporized mixture of gasoline and air into itself, compressing the mixture, igniting it and using the resulting explosion to push a piston down a cylinder. In the cycle of the diesel, only air is drawn in; the air is then very highly compressed so that it heats up naturally. In the next stage, a very accurately timed and measured quantity of fuel is injected into the cylinder, and because of the heat of the air, the mixture explodes spontaneously, which is why the diesel is sometimes referred to as a compression-ignition engine. — Tony Hogg, "That Old-time Ignition," *Esquire*

A paragraph, like a full paper, should follow the form of development that best suits the subject and that will be clearest to the reader. See also 21.2, Developing Your Material.

▶ EXERCISE

Choose a topic from the sentences below, and write two different paragraphs from the one sentence. Choose two of the patterns discussed above.

1. Much of the character of a nation comes from its quaint customs.
2. Many people never pay much attention to the history and geography of the place in which they live.
3. Movies are worse than ever.
4. Suppose the telephone had never been invented.

## 27.3 PARAGRAPH CONTINUITY

*ℋ Con*  **Rewrite the marked paragraph to make the relationships between ideas clear.**

A paragraph represents a chain of thought: it is a series of statements that are associated in your mind and that you want the reader to see in the same relationship. The elements in most paragraphs should be related as closely as the elements in a sentence, where presumably the parts fit each other to make a whole. In the paragraph below, the relationships between successive statements are shown in brackets:

> Have you got termites? In your house, I mean. It is the newest and most fashionable house disease. [Three sentences presenting the subject.] It used to be called "ants" and no one was interested [contrast]. Also sinus used to be called catarrh. But "sinus" made the old disease under another name popular [comparison]. Last summer in the fashionable country places the talk was all about termites. [Repetition of idea in third sentence.] How so and so suddenly stepped on her floor and went right through [example of the "talk"]. And, my dear, they had to call an exterminator and it cost hundreds and hundreds of dollars to get rid of the things: the whole house was almost torn apart and they had to treat the floors with the most awful smelling stuff! [Example continued.] If you hadn't had termites, you just weren't in Society. [Repetition of idea in third sentence.]
> — Roy Chapman Andrews, *This Amazing Planet*

**27.3**

*ℋ Con*

It is not so important to be able to name the relationships as it is to make sure that they will be clear to your readers. They should not have to "read between the lines" to supply missing connections.

## Methods of Showing Continuity

The most common ways of showing continuity between statements, called *transition devices,* are the following:

1. **repetition** of an important word from a previous sentence;
2. **use of a synonym,** a different word of much the same meaning as one already used;
3. **use of a pronoun** referring to a word or idea in the preceding sentence;
4. **use of a connecting word,** an adverb or a conjunction that points out the thought relationship.

These signs of the relationship between statements are emphasized and identified in brackets in the following paragraph:

> An instructive example of the failure of a people to take advantage of available materials is afforded by the Onas of South America. **In this respect** [synonym: failure to take advantage of available materials] **they** [pronoun: the Onas] may be contrasted with the Eskimos. **Here** [adverb: connecting with preceding two sentences] are **two peoples** [synonym: the Onas and the Eskimos] living in cold environments, the one to the north, the other to the south. **The Eskimos** [repetition] have made a most satisfactory adjustment to their environment. **They** [pronoun: the Eskimos] have good houses and a complete wardrobe. **Indeed** [adverb: connects and emphasizes], **the latter** [pronoun: a complete wardrobe] surpasses that of most civilized peoples of the past. **The Onas** [repetition], **on the other hand** [connective: shows contrast with preceding statements], go practically naked, and lacking adequate shelter, seek unsuccessfully to keep warm before an open fire. **Yet** [connective: contrast] **the Onas** [repetition] hunt the guanaco, the skin of which is suitable for clothing. In trying to account for the backwardness of **these people** [synonym: the Onas], **then** [connective: result], geographic conditions are not be emphasized.— William F. Ogburn and Meyer F. Nimkoff, *Sociology*

The thought of this paragraph is a unit, and each statement follows the other clearly. You cannot start reading it after the first sentence without realizing that something has gone before. (The sentence "The Eskimos have made a most satisfactory adjustment to their environment" could begin a paragraph, but if it did, the paragraph would be about Eskimos, not about Eskimos and Onas.)

We are inclined to overlook the absence of guides to the reader in our own writing, because the relationship of ideas is already clear to us, but we notice immediately when other writers forget to show the connection between ideas. Consider how the following unconnected paragraph is improved by showing the relationship between the statements:

> UNCONNECTED VERSION: Many people today believe that objectionable movies should be censored by provincial or local agencies. The recent emphasis in films on immorality and violence is outrageous. They are undermining morals and traditional values,

according to many people. There may be some truth here. I agree with the diagnosis, but I cannot accept the cure. Censorship poses a greater threat to a democracy, in my opinion.

RELATIONSHIPS SHOWN: Many people today believe that objectionable movies should be censored by provincial or local agencies. **These critics** have been outraged by the recent emphasis in films on immorality and violence. **Such films,** according to **them,** are undermining morals and traditional values. **This** may be true. **However,** although I agree with **their** diagnosis, I cannot accept **their** cure. It seems to me that censorship poses a greater threat to a democracy **than objectionable entertainment.**

▶ EXERCISE

In the sample paragraph below, each sentence picks up a word, phrase, or idea from the preceding sentence. Using the topic sentences provided, write paragraphs following this model.

*Example:* Lots of Canadians talk about "getting in shape," but few do much about it. By "getting in shape" I don't mean taking a walk now and then or wearing a girdle. There is only one way to get in shape, and that is with regular exercise. And regular exercise means setting aside some time of the day, every day, for strenuous physical activities. Among the useful activities are jogging, push-ups, and sit-ups.

1. The road to riches is usually a muddy path, not a freeway.

2. The registration system at this institution is incredibly complicated.

3. Without the "missing link," evolution remains a theory.

## Eliminating Irrelevant Ideas

Paragraph continuity is damaged by the introduction of irrelevant and unrelated ideas. These break the chain of thought and make a paragraph seem ragged:

Among the oddities of the plant world, Venus's-flytrap is one of the most interesting. **Venus is the mythological goddess of love.** It is a carnivorous plant that catches and devours insects and occasionally even small birds. This is done by means of paired lobes that resemble the halves of an oyster or clam, **scientifically known as bivalves.** When the lobes are open, they expose a colorful interior that attracts insects in search of nectar. Once it is disturbed, the powerful lobes snap shut, and strong digestive juices go to work to break down and assimilate the body. **Some people have successfully grown these plants in their homes.**

**27.3**

*¶ Con*

The boldface statements in this example are not directly related to the subject of the paragraph, and in revision they should be omitted or transferred to another paragraph. The last sentence above, for example, might be appropriate in a paragraph telling how to grow Venus's-flytrap, but it is out of place in a description of the plant's physical qualities.

## Continuity in Descriptive Paragraphs

The details in a descriptive paragraph should give the reader a clear, unified impression. Descriptive writing is more than simple enumeration. You need to choose the most effective details and arrange them so that the more important ones stand out. The following paragraph illustrates a lack of selection and focus. Some of the sentences focus on size, direction, and appearance. Others focus on busy activity. Too much attention is given to minor details, and as a result no single impression emerges:

> We entered the Roundup Room through a curtained entrance just past the check room on a right turn. The Roundup Room was a long ell-shaped affair with the end of the ell angling off to the left. It was about two-hundred feet long and probably fifty feet wide. Along the wall on the left ran a long bar made of dark wood. Behind the bar five bartenders were busily filling orders and giving them to a dozen or so waitresses ranging in age from about twenty to forty-five. Above the bar mirror on the wall were paintings of western scenes and cartoons, like those I described on the outside of the building. Down the aisle in front of us there seemed to be a beehive of activity, with couples coming and going to the small dance floor. I say "small" because it couldn't have been more than twenty-five feet square. On our right were small tables, all filled with customers, and on the right wall, farther down, were a number of small booths. We threaded our way through the smoky haze to an empty table.

If the writer intended to emphasize the overcrowding and confusion in this room, he should have concentrated on those features and omitted or briefly summarized such unnecessary details as the shape and dimensions of the room, the paintings above the mirror, the age of the waitresses, and so on.

When you are writing a descriptive paragraph, try to include only the material, facts, or images that will contribute to a single central impression. In the paragraph below, notice that everything is excluded except what contributes to the scene of grim austerity:

> The little crowd of mourners—all men and boys, no women— threaded their way across the market-place between the piles of pomegranates and the taxis and the camels, wailing a short chant over and over again. What really appeals to the flies is that the corpses here are never put into a coffin, they are merely wrapped in a piece of rag and carried on a rough wooden bier on the shoulders of four friends. When the friends get to the burying-ground they hack an

oblong hole a foot or two deep, dump the body in it and fling over it a little of the dried-up, lumpy earth, which is like broken brick. No gravestone, no name, no identifying mark of any kind. The burying-ground is merely a huge waste of hummocky earth, like a derelict building-lot. After a month or two no one can even be certain where his own relatives are buried. — George Orwell, "Marrakech"

## Continuity in Narrative Paragraphs

When you are relating an experience, describing an incident, or summarizing the plot of a story or play, keep the action moving in one direction and avoid unnecessary interruptions. The boldface sentences in the following paragraph destroy the continuity of the narrative because they stop the action:

It was the seventh of August 1976. My friend and I were hitch-hiking from a small town in the northern part of the province. Unlike most adventurers, I did not notice the sky nor did I feel the impending danger. **I guess I don't make a very good hero. Now I must get back to my story.** After waiting by the side of the road for some time, we were picked up by two men in an old station wagon.

Later events in this narrative should show whether or not the writer is "a very good hero." This unnecessary remark not only slows down the action, but also suggests the outcome of the incident before it is unfolded.

The connection between statements in a narrative paragraph is usually simple, since it is controlled by time. Events follow each other as they happened in time or as they are imagined to have happened. The verbs usually carry this movement, and the continuity is made stronger by the repetition of the same grammatical subject from one sentence to another. Time may be emphasized and made more obvious by adverbs — *then, next, before, soon, later, presently* — or by adverbial phrases or clauses: *When he got to the corner . . . , After the last dance. . . .* The boldface verb forms and adverbs of time in the following passage show how large a part words of action and time play in giving continuity to a narrative paragraph:

**27.3**

*¶ Con*

**Slowly** the clear place on the glass **enlarged:** oval, **then** round, **then** oval again. The sun **was rising** above the frost mists **now,** so keen and hard a glitter on the snow that instead of warmth its rays **seemed shedding** cold. One of the two-year-old colts that **had cantered** away **when** John **turned** the horses **out** for water **stood** covered with rime . . . , head down and body **hunched,** each breath a little plume of steam against the frosty air. She **shivered** but **did not turn.** In the clear, bitter light the long white miles of prairie landscape seemed a region alien to life. — Sinclair Ross, "The Painted Door"

To maintain continuity in narrative paragraphs, keep the tense of verbs consistent. If you start with one tense—the past or the present—don't shift without reason to another. See also 19.4, Narration.

▶ EXERCISE

Both of the following paragraphs lack continuity. Rewrite them, making whatever rearrangements, additions, or omissions are needed to make the continuity clear.

1. My grandparents still follow many of their national customs. They have lived in Canada for more than forty years. The traditional ceremony of the eggs begins on the night before Easter, when my grandmother prepares a dozen elaborately decorated eggs. Despite her age, she still has a very firm hand. The eggs are passed from hand to hand around the table, where the whole family has gathered. My grandfather chants a prayer meanwhile. The eggs are taken outside and buried in the garden, and everyone goes to bed for the night. Then everyone takes the candle he has left lighted in his window and returns to the garden. As dawn is breaking, the eggs are dug up and placed in a basket decorated with flowers. There is a sumptuous breakfast to celebrate the successful recovery, and humanity's redemption by Christ has been acted out.

2. When I got about thirty feet out into the lake, I saw that the water was rougher than I had thought. Several large breakers hit me full in the face, and I took in too much water for comfort. There are techniques good swimmers use to avoid getting swamped by breakers, but I had never learned them because I didn't think it was important at the time. I decided to head back toward the rocks, but I couldn't see the flat shelf where I had entered. In desperation, I headed toward a jagged group of rocks nearby. Just as I got close to it and was groping for a foothold, a large breaker threw me against a sharp edge and knocked me breathless. Being thrown against rocks in rough waters is a danger many inexperienced swimmers overlook.

# Revising and Correcting a Paper

*Do not be afraid to seize whatever you have written and cut it to ribbons; it can always be restored to its original condition in the morning, if that course seems best. Remember, it is no sign of weakness or defeat that your manuscript ends up in need of major surgery. This is a common occurrence in all writing, and among the best writers.—E. B. White,* THE ELEMENTS OF STYLE

When you have finished the first draft of a paper, put it aside for a while before revising it. Most people find it difficult to look at their own writing carefully while the ideas they have tried to express are still running about in their minds. For this reason, the first draft should be written as early as possible, so that you can wait a day or two (or at least several hours) before examining it. If the assignment gives you time to write a draft and put it aside for a *week or two,* you may be astonished to discover how perceptive a critic you are when you return to it for revision.

The purpose of revision is to check major as well as minor matters: to tighten and improve the organization, the content, and the expression, as well as to correct the mechanics of your writing. You will save time and improve the quality of your writing by going over the first draft systematically, looking for specific flaws. A hit-or-miss approach to revision is likely to be a waste of time, since you may catch only the most glaring faults. The checklist on page 378 may help you keep the major points of revision in mind.

## 28.1 MANUSCRIPT FORM

 Be sure the manuscript is in the form specified.

Make a neat and accurate copy of your revised paper to submit to your instructor. Follow the directions he or she gives you for the form: the size and the kind of paper; margins and spacing; numbering of pages; endorsement. Typical manuscript form is described in the following pages.

**28.1**

## A Checklist for Revising

### Checking the Content

1. Does your paper need more or better examples and illustrations?
2. Is information in your paper clear enough so that a reader unfamiliar with the subject can understand it?
3. Are there general statements that don't have accompanying details or illustrations?
4. Can you show that every statement is directly related to the topic?
5. Have you expressed your own convictions? Are the ideas your own, or are you merely repeating ones you have often heard?

### Checking the Organization

1. Is it clear from near the beginning what the paper is about?
2. Does each paragraph clearly add something to the paper?
3. Do important ideas and statements stand out from less important ideas and statements?
4. Can you justify the order of the important statements?
5. Are all sentences and paragraphs tied together in a coherent way?
6. Is the ending clear?

### Checking the Wording

1. Are there words whose meanings you are not sure of?
2. Have you used any unfamiliar terms that need explanation?
3. Is there any unnecessary or awkward repetition?
4. Are any of your sentences too involved? Do you stumble over some passages as you read your work aloud?
5. Does the language sound like something *you* could reasonably be expected to say?
6. Have you used trite language (vogue words, phrases, or sentences) that you have often heard or read?

### Checking for Accuracy

1. Have you checked your work specifically for any errors that you have made in earlier writing?
2. Have you checked a dictionary for doubtful spellings?
3. Can you account for your punctuation?
4. If a sentence seems doubtful or confusing, have you tried to analyse it grammatically for structure and punctuation?

### Checking Again

1. Have you read the draft systematically?
2. Have you read the paper aloud at an easy, normal tempo?

## Typed Papers

If you have a typewriter and know how to use it, it is a good practice to type all papers written outside class. Typed manuscript is easier to read than most handwriting.

In typing your final draft, use unlined white 21.5cm x 28cm paper, but not onionskin, for it lets the type show through.

Type everything double spaced except long quotations and footnotes. These should ordinarily be set off appropriately and single spaced.

Follow standard conventions in typing. For the figure 1, use lower case l (not capital I). For a dash, use two hyphens with no space between the words and the dash:

`The book--a first edition--was missing.`

Check your work carefully for typographical errors. Uncorrected typing mistakes are usually considered to be errors.

## Handwritten Papers

If you cannot type, you may write the paper by hand—if the instructor concurs. Legibly written and neatly prepared, such papers are usually quite acceptable.

Use lined white paper 21.5cm x 28cm, with lines at least 13mm apart. Writing done on closely lined paper is hard to read and difficult to correct. Do not use pages torn from spiral-bound notebooks, because their rough edges stick together. Use black or dark-blue ink.

Handwritten papers should be easy to read. If a word looks misspelled or is difficult to decipher, it may be marked as an error. Handwriting that is too small puts an unnecessary strain on the eyes of the reader; handwriting that is excessively large is no less difficult to read. Try to strike a happy medium in size. If you have developed what you consider to be an individual style of penmanship, make certain that it will be as legible to others as it is to you.

## Margins and Spacing

Leave ample margins on both sides of the page. About 3.8 cm on the left and 2.5 cm on the right are customary margins in handwritten and typed papers. Leave at least 3.8 cm at the top and 2.5 cm at the bottom of every page.

Indent paragraphs uniformly. Five spaces from the left-hand margin is an acceptable indention for typed papers, and about

**28.1**

*ms*

2.5cm for those written in longhand. Don't indent any line that is not the beginning of a paragraph, even though it is the first line on a page. The last line on a page should not be left partly blank unless it is the end of a sentence or paragraph.

Don't crowd your writing at the bottom of a page. Start a new page, even if it will contain only a line or two.

## Division of Words

*Div*   Divide the marked word according to the syllabication given in a reliable dictionary.

If you leave plenty of room at the right-hand side of your page, you will not have to divide many words at the ends of the lines. It is a good idea to divide words only if writing them out or putting them on the next line would make the lines conspicuously uneven.

Words of one syllable must not be divided at all: *through, played, bright.* And avoid breaking a word if a single letter will be left at the beginning or end of a line. There is no point in dividing a word like *a-lone;* the single letter at the end of the line is less attractive than leaving space and carrying the whole word over to the next line. See 22.2, Spelling and Word Division.

Words spelled with a hyphen (*mother-in-law, self-confidence*) should be divided only at the hyphen.

## Form of the Title

The title appears on the first page of your paper. On unlined paper, place it in the centre about 5 cm from the top of the page; on lined paper, write the title on the top line. Leave a blank line between the title and first line of the text.

Capitalize the first and last words in your title and all others except short words like *and, the, a, an,* and prepositions less than six letters long:

|  |  |
|---|---|
| Breaking and Training a Horse | How Not to Become Overweight |
| The Art of Making Friends | Strength Through Community |

No period should be put after a title. However, if the title is expressed as a question or as an exclamation, it should be followed by the proper punctuation:

Why not the NDP?   Man Overboard!

Titles are not enclosed in quotation marks. Even when familiar quotations are used as titles, no marks are needed:

Blood, Sweat, and Tears     From Sea to Shining Sea

## Numbering Pages

The first page of a manuscript is not numbered. Begin with the second page, using Arabic numerals (2, 3, 4 ...) for paging. Numbers are customarily put at the top of the page in the centre— or in the right-hand corner. Make certain that the pages of your paper are in the right order before you turn the paper in.

Long tables, diagrams, charts, and other material supplementary to the text itself are usually put on separate pages, placed near the part that refers to them, and numbered consecutively with the other pages.

It is not necessary to write "more" at the bottom of each page or to put "Finis" or "The End" at the conclusion.

## Endorsing the Paper

Sign your papers as you are expected to. Include all the information that is asked for, and put it in the right order. Clear and uniform endorsement is a real convenience to the teacher who must handle the papers.

Ask your instructor how the papers should be submitted, whether folded, flat, or otherwise. Sheets should be held together by a paper clip or a staple only. Use binders only for longer papers unless instructed to the contrary.

## Proofreading

When you finish your final draft, put it aside for a while and then proofread it carefully before handing it in. No matter how perfect the finished product may appear, it will pay to give it one final check. Errors somehow creep into even the most careful writing. To find them, you will have to get away from the paper for a time so that you can look at it with a fresh eye.

**28.1**

Look for slips of the pen or typing errors, for the omission of words and marks of punctuation. And look particularly for mistakes of the kind marked on your previous papers.

## Making Corrections in the Final Copy

Changes and corrections should be kept to a minimum, particularly on important papers. When you have to make major changes in the final copy (rewording sentences, revising paragraphs), do the page over. For minor changes (spelling, punctuation, adding or striking out a word), make the corrections neatly and according to standard practices.

To add a word, use a caret ( ∧ ) and write the missing word directly above it:

```
Manuscript should ^be easy to read.
```

To strike out a word, draw a straight line through it (do *not* use parentheses or brackets):

```
Final copy should be as ~~as~~ accurate as possible.
```

To indicate the beginning of a new paragraph where you have failed to indent, write the symbol ¶ immediately before the first word of the new paragraph:

```
So ended my first day away from home. ¶ The second day. . . .
```

To correct a misspelled word, draw a line through it and write the correct form directly above. This makes a neater and more legible correction than an erasure:

```
Quality is more important than ~~quanity~~ quantity.
```

To indicate in typed copy that two letters should be reversed in order (transposed), use a curved line:

```
be⁀tween              reci⁀eve              Smith⁀'s novel
```

## Submitting Manuscript for Publication

If you are going to submit a manuscript for publication, you should type it (or have it typed) and follow the suggestions already given. Many publications have their own preferences about the form in which manuscripts should be submitted, and many will send guide sheets or samples of various kinds to writers who want to submit work.

Be sure that your name is on the manuscript. One way to identify your work is to put your complete name and address in the upper left-hand corner of the first page. It's also a good idea to put at least your last name on each page. A simple way to do this is to put it adjacent to the page number (for example: Jones, 2).

Enclose a stamped, self-addressed envelope with any manuscript you submit. Most publications will not take responsibility for returning manuscripts unless you do.

If you are serious about submitting a manuscript for publication, it's a good idea to study a reference such as *The Canadian Writer's Market.* Now in its fourth edition, the current volume includes detailed and comprehensive general advice for writers and information about various categories of magazine and book publication in Canada.

## 28.2 REVISING A CORRECTED PAPER

In composition, as in other areas of experience, you often learn by making mistakes. No matter how conscientiously you have applied yourself to a written assignment, you may find that the instructor has marked a number of corrections on the returned paper. To improve your writing skills, you must give serious attention to these corrections. Many instructors require their students to revise all corrected papers and resubmit them. But even if the instructor does not ask for revisions, it is worth your time to make a careful analysis of all correction marks and to revise or rewrite the paper accordingly. A cursory glance down the margins is not enough—if errors and weaknesses are not studied and corrected they will no doubt recur in other papers.

Some papers, of course, may contain only minor errors, requiring the change of a few words or punctuation marks on the original. Often, though, a satisfactory revision means sentences or even whole paragraphs must be rewritten or rearranged. For passages that require extensive changes, experiment with different versions. Then read the revisions through several times to determine which is the best one.

In correcting a paper, it is important to understand *why* the corrections are necessary. If the instructor's mark is not immediately clear to you, consult the correction symbol key at the front of this handbook and then read the relevant section in the text, noting the examples and comparing them with the passage marked.

Compare the original and corrected versions of the student paper reprinted on pages 384-387. This paper was used because it exhibited a variety of faults. (The most serious fault was pointed out in the instructor's overall comment: "Your general approach is vague and unrealistic. What do you actually *do* when you are studying your best?") Study the instructor's marks on the original version and determine their meaning. Then examine the changes (underlined) made in the corrected paper.

When writing a paper, you should review your *last* paper—a

**28.2**

*Cor*

*ms*

*Agr*

*//*

*awkd*

*Dm*

*//*

*No-1*
*WW*

*Sp*

"Good Study Habits"

It is important for every college student to develop good study habits. A lucky few have already developed them in high school, but for the <u>majority</u> of students the greater demands of college work *Dic* <u>requires</u> some adjustment. Good study habits <u>consist</u> primarily of two *WW* things: a mature mental attitude and appropriate physical techniques.

Going to college is a demanding full-time job, <u>and</u> students *Dic* should be prepared to spend about forty-five or more hours a week on it. Like any other job, it requires effort and concentration. Some students are indifferent toward required courses, <u>which they feel are</u> <u>uninteresting or cannot see how they are related to their chosen</u> <u>course of study</u>. Students should remember that if colleges require certain courses, usually of a general nature, this means that <u>they</u> *Ref* present basic knowledge that every educated person is expected to acquire while in college. If <u>you</u> are indifferent to such courses, <u>you</u> *Shift* are condemning <u>yourself</u> to a lopsided intellectual development, which <u>you</u> will probably regret later on in life.

<u>Whether attending class or studying at home</u>, full concentration is essential. Students sometimes complain that they do poorly in courses even though they spend many hours studying every̶day. "Studying" means inattentively running their eyes over a page between frequent distractions <u>from the radio, conversing with their roommates,</u> and daydreams. Five hours of this kind of studying is worth less than an hour of uninterrupted concentration on the material. A student who goes to a lecture without having done the assigned reading and without having reviewed his notes from the last lecture is not really in a good <u>mood</u> to acquire new information and relate it to what he already knows.

*A*
*con*

An erratic and undisciplined approach to study is usually disasterous. Many students ignore course assignments until just before an examination. Then they frantically do all the required reading in one or two nights, try to decipher sloppy, disorganized notes, and stay up all night over black coffee cramming hundreds of

Good Study Habits

It is important for every college student to develop good study habits. A lucky few have already developed them in high school, but for most students the greater demands of college work require some adjustment. Good study habits are based on two things: a mature mental attitude and appropriate physical techniques.

Going to college is a demanding full-time job, so students should be prepared to spend about forty-five or more hours a week at it. Like any other job, it requires effort and concentration. Some students are indifferent toward required courses because they consider them uninteresting or unrelated to their chosen field. They should remember that such courses are required because they provide general knowledge expected of every college graduate. Students who neglect these courses are limiting their intellectual growth and usually regret it later.

Full concentration is essential both in the classroom and in the study room. Students sometimes complain that they do poorly in courses even though they spend many hours studying every day. But to many of them "studying" means inattentively running their eyes over a page between frequent distractions from the radio, conversations with their roommates, or daydreams. Five hours of this kind of studying is worth less than an hour of uninterrupted concentration. The same principle applies to class attendance. A student who goes to a lecture without having done the assigned reading and without having reviewed his or her notes from the last lecture is not concentrating on acquiring new information and relating it to what he or she already knows.

An erratic and undisciplined approach to study is usually disastrous. Students with poor study habits ignore course assignments until just before an examination. Then they frantically do all the required reading in a day or two, try to decipher their sloppy, disorganized notes, and stay up all night over black coffee cramming hundreds of facts into their heads. The result usually is that they come to the examination not only exhausted but also con-

**28.2**

*Cor*

*awk*

facts into their heads.  The result is usually that <u>he</u> comes to the  *Shift*

examination <u>fatigued and stupefied by a plethora of chaotic data.</u>  All  *Big H*

of this could have been avoided if the student had kept up with his

assignments and had gotten into the habit of taking neat, orderly

notes which <u>were reviewed by him</u> regularly.  Studying for an examin-  *Pass*

ation should involve only glancing over his notes and readings and

planning how to organize related facts to answer the questions most

likely to be asked.

*frf*

*Log*

A student should not be afraid that his <u>room mates</u> and friends

will <u>call him a square</u> if he sets aside regular times for daily study

and refuses to be interrupted.  On the contrary, most good students

are respected by their fellow students and popular because they devote

more time to social activities than students with poor study habits.

## CORRECTION SYMBOLS

**MS**   Do not enclose titles of papers in quotes. Set them off from the body of the paper by extra space.

**Agr**   Avoid blind agreement. Despite intervening words, subject and verb must agree: *demands* (S) *require* (V).

**WW**   Choose words for their exact meaning.

**Dic**   (1) *Most* is better. (2) Use a more exact connective (than *and*) to show the relationship of ideas.

**‖**   Constructions joined by co-ordinating conjunctions should be equivalent in rank and meaning.

**Wdy**   Express ideas as directly and economically as possible.

**Ref**   Pronouns should refer clearly to a definite antecedent. The pronoun *they* might seem to refer to *colleges* or *students* as well as to *courses*.

**Shift**   Avoid shifts in person (*they* to *you* in the second paragraph, *they* to *he* in the fourth).

fused by a mass of unrelated facts. They could have avoided all this by keeping up with their assignments, making orderly notes, and reviewing their notes regularly. Studying for an examination then would involve no more than glancing over the material and mentally organizing it in terms of the questions most likely to be asked.

Students should not be afraid that their roommates and friends will make fun of them if they set aside regular times for daily study and refuse to be interrupted. On the contrary, good students are usually respected for their scholastic achievements and, because they use their time more efficiently, are usually freer to participate in social activities than are students with poor study habits.

| DM | The sentence should include the word to which the modifer refers. |
|---|---|
| ¶ con | Make sure the relationships among ideas in a paragraph are clear to the reader. |
| No , | Do not separate subject and verb by a comma: *A student* (S) *is* (V). |
| AWK | Smooth out awkward passages when revising a first draft. |
| Big W | Stilted, unnecessarily heavy language is out of place in all kinds of writing. |
| Pass | Avoid the awkward use of the passive voice, especially an unnecessary shift from passive to active. |
| Inf | Writers should be consistent in their level of usage. The informal *call him a square* is out of place in this relatively formal paper. |
| Log | Make sure the logic of a statement is clear to the reader. Devoting a large amount of time to social activities does not necessarily make a student popular; neither do good study habits. The writer's intended meaning is made clear in the revision. |

**28.2**

*Cor*

valuable resource, if you are willing to take the time to use it seriously. If your teacher has marked it thoroughly, his or her marks and suggestions may let you see what kinds of mistakes you are likely to make, where your attention is likely to wander, what you are likely to omit, what you are likely to include unnecessarily. The writer of the sample paper should be particularly concerned about the instructor's general comment on the importance of dealing directly and realistically with the subject matter. Even the corrected version of the paper, though it eliminates most of the specific faults in the original version, is pretty conventional and not very interesting.

In correcting this paper, the writer might also have observed that there are two main categories of weaknesses in the writing: faulty diction and awkward sentence construction. The instructor has called attention to poor diction in six instances: the too specific use of *the majority* for *most;* the inaccurate *consists of;* the poor connective *and;* the vague and inappropriate *a good mood;* the inflated *fatigued and stupefied by a plethora of chaotic data;* and the colloquial *call him a square.* In addition, the passages marked for sentence economy (Wdy) and awkwardness (Awk) are marred by poor word choice as well as faulty sentence construction. The writer shows no particular skill in selecting accurate, appropriate, and forceful language to express his or her ideas. If errors in diction are to be avoided in future papers, he or she will have to become more alert to other writers' use of words, consult the dictionary frequently, and study first drafts critically to eliminate wordiness and pretentiousness.

The instructor has also marked several passages for sentence and paragraph weaknesses. The second paragraph concludes with two long, clumsy sentences (Wdy). The third paragraph lacks continuity (con), because the student has omitted certain words and expressions necessary to indicate connections and transitions between ideas. The fourth paragraph contains two jumbled, awkward sentences (Awk). In the corrected version, the student has made each of these passages more clear and direct and has gained valuable practice in expressing the ideas as economically as possible. To avoid sentence weaknesses in future papers, he or she should practise reading the sentences and paragraphs aloud to see whether they are difficult to follow, repetitious, or ambiguous. And to assure continuing improvements, the student should become more alert to sentence patterns used by other writers, particularly in published material.

Even so, writers who analyse their errors and revise their papers as carefully as the writer of the sample paper did will soon find that even their original drafts are improving.

▶ **EXERCISES**

1. Mark up the following student essay as if you were the instructor, write a helpful terminal comment, and assign the paper a grade. Compare your suggestions and evaluations with others in the class.

"The Farmers and Food Prices"
   When people complain about high food prices, the blame always ends up in the farmer's lap. "Those farmers are making a fortune and we're almost starving!" I hear people say. Well, I can tell you that the farmers do not make a fortune, and that compared to any other workers, farmers are overworked, underpaid, and have jobs with the most risk and least security.
   Labor unions have decreed that laborers can work no more than forty hours a week without being paid overtime, which is time-and-a-half. And if you ask a laborer to work on Sundays or holidays, they get double-time. But the farmers have to work every day, often from sunup to sundown (which in the summer is over fourteen hours). Cows must be milked everyday, Sundays and holidays included. And when the crops are ripe, the farmer's must work to harvest them seven days a week until all are in. There is no forty-hour week, no overtime, no double-time, for farmers.
   Laborers have unions which negotiate wage contracts for them. Members of the most powerful unions get longevety and cost-of-living raises yearly. But farmers get paid what the food processors feel like paying them. They cannot strike for higher wages. The only thing they can do is withhold their crops from the market until prices rise to where they think they should be. But if they do that, people think their just being greedy, when really their only doing what laborers are doing, trying to get a living wage.
   If you asked a laborer to work at a job where all the products he works on, through no fault of his own, can disintegrate over night and where he will get no pay if this happens, he will just laugh at you. But farmers do just that. They must work to get out a product which may or may not materialize, depending on purely outside influences, particularly inclement weather. If there is a too-wet spring, they cannot plant in time. If there is a too-wet fall, the harvest is delayed or sometimes even ruined. If there are shortages of gasoline or fertilizer, farm work will be held up. The farmers are at  − the mercy of the elements and the various chemical shortages that can happen at any time.
   So, its not the farmers who make a killing while your food bill goes up. Any money they make can never fully pay them for the risk they take and the hard work they do day in and day out, year after year.

**28.2**

*Cor*

2. Rewrite one of your own recent papers, paying particular attention to the comments of your instructor.

# Practical and Vocational Writing

*Though often letters, speeches, and reports must be written in a hurry and, because of the countless considerations that clear writing involves, are bound in some way to fall short of the full intended meaning, conscientious people will always regret this necessity and arrange their affairs as far as possible to avoid it — Robert Graves and Alan Hodge,* THE READER OVER YOUR SHOULDER

*I keep cautioning my students and anyone who will listen to me not to use the jargon of trades, not to use scientific language, because they're going to be out of date the day after tomorrow — Katherine Anne Porter,* WRITERS AT WORK

Sometimes we hear woeful tales of the non-human language used in business and professional writing and in specialized writing assignments in school. Sometimes the stories are true:

> The parent of a high-school pupil received this message from the school principal concerning a special meeting on a proposed new educational program:
>
> "Our school's cross-graded, multi-ethnic, individualized learning program is designed to enhance the concept of an open-ended learning program with emphasis on a continuum of multi-ethnic, academically enriched learning using the identified intellectually gifted child as the agent or director of his own learning. Major emphasis is on cross-graded, multi-ethnic learning with the main objective being to learn respect for the uniqueness of a person."
>
> The parent wrote the principal:
>
> "I have a university degree, speak two languages, including French, and read four others; I have been to a number of county fairs and three goat-ropings, but I haven't the faintest idea as to what the hell you are talking about. Do you?"

Often in specialized assignments and in writing associated with business and professional work, writers depend upon ritual phrases and standardized patterns of organization. Some businesses and professions, indeed, expect writers to conform to standard practices long established and widely used in vocational writing. And to be sure, if a writer has to answer 122 letters inquiring about the same market item, it is clearly more convenient and economical to use a form letter.

Still, whatever can be recommended for writing in general can also be recommended for particular forms of practical and professional writing. The vocabulary should be accurate, and the spelling should be orthodox. Even if you are going to use organizational patterns developed by someone else (as in some report writing or business correspondence), you don't have to stop thinking. Your language should be fresh and precise, untroubled by specialized jargon, euphemisms, clichés, and mystifying gobbledygook. Your sentences should be clear, direct, and economical. Your tone should be natural and unstilted.

The papers that you write in school are not so different from the practical, business, or technical writing that you may do outside of school. A letter of recommendation, for example, is both informative and persuasive, just as many school papers are. It offers information about a person's past (usually narrative) and about that person's present (often descriptive) in order to make an argument for his or her future. A letter in which you apply for a job is a kind of specialized personal essay, not entirely different from some personal writing that you will do in a composition class except that in the letter of application you may pay closer attention to your audience.

Practical and vocational forms of writing are different from school writing, however, in at least one major respect. In a sense, such writing is not your own. Ordinarily, the occasion and the purpose are determined by some institutional need, not by your own choice. Even essay examinations in school may be expected to conform to a kind of established, non-personal form. They are, at any rate, not occasions for free-swinging experiments in writing. In most forms of practical and vocational writing, your writing is a medium serving a company, an institution, or something other than your own personal preferences. You can still be yourself, but you may also need to fulfill the expectations of others.

The following pages discuss some of what is expected in various forms of practical and vocational writing.

## 29.1 ESSAY EXAMINATION ANSWERS

Answering an examination question in essay form is similar to writing a short expository or argumentative paper. In studying for the course, you have become familiar with a fairly wide range of information; to answer a specific question, you must recall the relevant material, organize it, and present it in essay form.

## Reading the Questions

Because most examinations have a time limit, students often begin writing feverishly after no more than a glance at the questions. The results of such frantic haste are usually disappointing. You can use the allotted time far more profitably if you take a few minutes at the start to read all the questions and directions. If a choice is offered, decide which questions you are best prepared to answer and cross out the others. If the questions have different values, plan the amount of time to spend on each: a question worth 10 per cent, for example, should not take up 30 per cent of your time. Try to save a few minutes at the end to check your answers.

Before beginning to write, be sure to read the question thoroughly. Many answers are unsatisfactory simply because students misinterpret or forget the question in their hurry to fill the paper with words. Examine each question carefully and decide what kind of answer it requires. Don't misread or overlook key words. Notice in the following questions how a change in one word would affect the whole question:

Explain the effects [causes] of the Quebec Act of 1774.
Describe the reproduction [digestion; development] of the frog.
Discuss the structure [sources; significance] of *Moby Dick*.

Since the verb often determines the nature of the answer, take particular care to interpret it properly. Here are some of the verbs instructors commonly use in essay questions.

**analyse:** give main divisions or elements, emphasizing essentials
**classify:** arrange into main classes or divisions
**compare:** point out likenesses
**contrast:** point out differences
**criticize:** give your opinion as to good and bad features
**define:** explain the meaning, distinguish from similar terms
**describe:** name the features in chronological or spatial order
**discuss:** examine in detail
**evaluate:** give your opinion of the value or validity
**explain:** make clear, give reasons for
**illustrate:** give one or more examples of
**interpret:** give the meaning or significance
**justify:** defend, show to be right
**review:** examine on a broad scale
**summarize:** briefly go over the essentials

## Writing the Answers

Before beginning to write an answer to a question, remember that the instructor expects you to demonstrate *specific* knowledge on the subject. A succession of vague generalities will not be acceptable. Even if you are discussing a fairly broad general topic, support whatever generalizations you make with specific illustrations. Do not omit essential particulars because you assume the *instructor* is familiar with them already; the main purpose of the examination is to find out what knowledge *you* have acquired.

A scratch outline (see 20) of the main points you plan to develop in your answer may be useful as a guide in writing. But whether you make an outline or not, make a concentrated effort to set your thoughts down in some logical order: all the sentences should relate to the question asked, and each should lead to the next in an orderly fashion. Many essay answers are unsuccessful because students, although well-informed, present information in a haphazard, unrelated fashion, giving the impression that they are thoroughly confused on the subject. It is often useful to repeat the key terms of the questions and the main points you'll be making about the terms in a thesis statement at the beginning of your answer. This can serve as an organizational guide for your writing.

Remember that the *length* of the answer is not the criterion of its worth: choosing the right facts and organizing them sensibly will impress the reader far more. Avoid throwing in unrelated material just to demonstrate your knowledge or to disguise your ignorance of more pertinent information. Since the time you have to write your answer is limited, you should confine yourself strictly to what you know about the specific question asked. Your instructor is not likely to give you much credit for a short essay on the wrong subject, no matter how good it may be.

Examination answers should be written in acceptable general English. Although instructors do not expect an essay written in class to be as fully developed and as polished in style as one written at home, they do expect it to be adequate in grammar, usage, and the mechanics of writing. Even if a paper is otherwise accurate, frequent misspellings do much to lower the reader's opinion of it. Take particular care to spell and use correctly any technical terms or names that have been used in the course: *myosis, mercantile, assize, neurosis, imagery, Lamarck, Malthus, Schopenhauer.* Instructors are understandably disturbed if they think you have paid scant attention to terms you have heard in class and read in the text numerous times. Careful proofreading of the

**29.1**

*Exam*

answers will help you eliminate any careless errors you may have made and will also give you a chance to fill in gaps in information.

## Examples of Essay Answers

Printed below are essay answers in biology, history, and literature. Read each question carefully, decide what sort of answer is required, and compare the two student answers. Then read the criticisms that follow. The sentences in the answers are numbered to facilitate discussion.

QUESTION: Define *dominant* as it is used in genetics.

ANSWER A: (1) In genetics, dominant is the opposite of recessive. (2) Different characteristics are inherited by the individual by means of genes acquired from the male and female parents. (3) These genes are arranged, or carried, on chromosomes, and are paired, one from each parent. (4) A good deal is still unknown about the behavior of genes, although the science of genetics is making rapid progress. (5) Gregor Mendel, a monk, made discoveries in heredity by doing experiments with sweet peas. (6) He found that certain traits are stronger (dominant) and others are weaker (recessive). (7) Therefore, if two genes carry the same characteristic, one will be dominant over the other. (8) Examples of this are dark eyes, normal color vision, etc.

ANSWER B: (1) The term *dominant* as used in genetics refers to that situation in which one gene in a pair takes precedence over another in determining a given characteristic in the individual. (2) For example, if a child inherits a gene for blue eyes from one parent and for brown eyes from the other, he will have brown eyes. (3) This is because the brown-eyed gene is *dominant;* the blue is *recessive.* (4) He still carries both genes and may transmit either to his offspring, but one has masked the effect of the other in his physical appearance. (5) Clear dominance does not occur in all pairings, however. (6) Sometimes *mixed dominance* occurs, as in the case of sweet peas, where a cross between a red and a white parent produces pink offspring. (7) Some cases of dominance are *sex-linked;* the gene for color blindness in humans, for instance, is dominant in the male and recessive in the female.

CRITICISM: Answer A contains irrelevant general information (sentences 2–5) and does not give a clear definition of *dominant.* You cannot explain the meaning of a word simply by naming its opposite (sentence 1). "Stronger" and "weaker" (sentence 6) are poor synonyms because they have such a variety of meanings. The answer also misleads by oversimplification: sentence 7 implies that complete dominance occurs in *all* pairings of genes. It is also not clear to what species of life the two examples in the last sentence (dark eyes and normal color vision) refer.

Answer B is satisfactory. The term is clearly defined in the first sentence. Sentences 2–4 give an example of its use, distinguish it from its opposite, and add an important qualification. Sentences 5–7 note two important variants in the meaning of the term. There is no irrelevant material.

QUESTION: Compare and contrast English and Spanish colonial methods in the New World.

ANSWER A: (1) The Plymouth colony suffered many hardships in the early years of its existence. (2) This was also true of the Roanoke colony, but it eventually failed and did not survive. (3) The climate was more promising there, but it seemed as if the kind of people it included, like gentlemen unused to work, adventurers, and renegades, did not have the patience and religious fervor of the New England settlers. (4) The same was true of the Spanish colonies in Florida and elsewhere — the climate was good, but the men were selfish and had no direction. (5) The Spanish were more cruel toward the Indians than the English, and there was nothing constructive in their aims.

ANSWER B: (1) The Spanish generally thought of the New World as a reservoir of riches to be tapped. (2) The great Spanish conquerors, like Cortez and Pizarro, were explorer-adventurers whose main aim was to subjugate the native population and wrench from them whatever riches and power they possessed. (3) The Spanish method was usually to impose a military dictatorship upon a restive populace; the domination depended on military force. (4) The English, on the other hand, thought of the New World colonies as a *permanent* extension of English civilization. (5) Their methods were not to immediately extract native riches, but to plant the seeds of English life in the new continent. (6) Unlike the Spaniards, the English generally emigrated in family units, placated rather than subdued the native inhabitants, invested labor and capital in the New World soil, and awaited long-term fruits. (7) Settlement was their aim rather than exploitation.

CRITICISM: More than half of answer A (sentences 1–3) contrasts *two English colonies* rather than *English and Spanish colonial methods*. Mention of climate in sentences 3 and 4 is also irrelevant to a question dealing with methods. "Selfish" and "had no direction" need further explanation, as do "cruel toward the Indians" and "nothing constructive."

Answer B is much more satisfactory than A. The basic differences in aim and the consequent differences in method are fairly well stated. The first section of the answer (sentences 1–3) describes Spanish methods; the second (sentences 4–7) presents the significant differences in English aim and method.

**29.1**

*Exam*

QUESTION: Explain the significance of E. J. Pratt's *Brébeuf and His Brethren* in the development of Canadian poetry.

ANSWER A: (1) *Brébeuf and His Brethren* by E. J. Pratt was published in 1940 in the midst of WW II. (2) It is a long poem about the Jesuits. (3) It won the Governor-General's Award for poetry and has been widely praised. (4) Among Pratt's contemporaries were F. R. Scott, A. J. M. Smith, and Dorothy Livesay. (5) It is an important poem because it is concerned with

1) Canadian history
2) myth-making
3) realism
4) narrative

(6) Other writers in this tradition are Oliver Goldsmith, Dorothy Livesay, Isabella Valancy Crawford, Archibald Lampman, and Don Gutteridge. (7) *Brébeuf and His Brethren* combines in a single narrative all the themes of the earlier narratives. (8) Therefore, it is truly significant.

ANSWER B: (1) E. J. Pratt's *Brébeuf and His Brethren,* the winner of the Governor-General's award for poetry in 1940, is an important landmark in Canadian poetry. (2) A narrative poem describing the martyrdom of the Jesuit missionaries of seventeenth-century Canada, Pratt's poem represents the high point of a tradition of Canadian narrative poetry begun in the late eighteenth century. (3) Nineteenth-century narratives such as Oliver Goldsmith's *The Rising Village* (1825) and Isabella Valancy Crawford's *Malcolm's Katie* (1884) introduce contrasted states of order versus chaos, nature versus civilization, and isolation versus community; a similar treatment may be observed in *Brébeuf and His Brethren.* Abandoning the vague imagery and sentimental diction of many of his predecessors, Pratt introduces a mosaic structure and a new level of documentary detail which focus attention on the most dramatic incidents involving the Jesuits in Canada. In his concern with re-examining and re-evaluating the past, Pratt becomes a contemporary myth-maker. Consequently, *Brébeuf and His Brethren* is the most important model for narrative poems by such later Canadian writers as Dorothy Livesay, Don Gutteridge, and John Newlove.

CRITICISM: In Answer A, sentences 1 and 4 do not specifically relate to the question. The heart of the answer seems to be sentence 5, but the unexplained list of headings conveys nothing. If these points are important, each should be developed in a separate sentence or two. Sentences 6 and 7 also seem to be relevant but are vague. *What* were the poems and *when* were they published? *What* themes from earlier narratives does Pratt use?

In answer B, the points merely listed in A are developed and made specific. The relation of the poem to both earlier and later poetic traditions is explained. All sentences are relevant and are well related to each other.

## 29.2  WRITING ABOUT LITERATURE

In most English courses students are often required to write about literature—to examine, interpret, and discuss fiction, poetry, drama. Literary analysis and interpretation are not radically different from the close reading and interpretive writing you might do in history, philosophy, and sociology courses or from your critical response to an editorial, magazine article, sermon, or letter to the editor. In much the same manner, we can examine a piece of literature critically and sort out our thoughts about it in order to understand it more fully.

Still, writing about literature is sometimes troublesome. You may sometimes find yourself thinking that "It's all a bunch of symbols and hidden meanings." You may sometimes feel that writing about literature requires a more specialized language and more advanced knowledge than you have. If an assignment calls for you to write an interpretive essay on a poem or story or play, and if you feel hopeless, or if you feel that "tearing a story or poem apart to analyse it spoils the story or poem," it may help if you remember some simple things.

First, a story or a poem or a play is created from words, and those words have been available for generations, for you, to take pleasure and instruction from them. The author wrote them to be read, though he or she may be hard to understand or may be saying something you can't respond to easily; in fact something may be said you can't accept. But you *can* understand, and the author who has offered you this creation deserves some of your time.

Second, curiosity may be a better motive for literary analysis than memorization of a page or two of literary terms. But you do have to learn to trust your curiosity when you look at a poem, for example, and be willing to ask questions: Why these words instead of others that would have served? Why doesn't the poem speak to me directly? Why do things occur in the order in which they occur? Exactly who is speaking to me? Am I meant to be the audience, or am I overhearing a speaker speak to someone in the poem? Why this? And why that? If you trust your curiosity, you can begin to find your way into a poem, for only the poem will provide answers to questions about the poem.

Third, when your assignment is to write an analytical essay about a piece of writing, unless your instructor has given a very specific assignment, it's all right to seize an interesting point— a puzzling line, a peculiar phrase, a strange incident—and use it as a focal point for your essay. Unless your instructor has spe-

**29.2**

*Lit*

cifically called for a particular kind of discussion, you should feel under no obligation to talk about everything in a poem or a play or a story. If something in it appeals to you, set yourself the task of coming to grips with its meaning.

In answering the questions that come up, or in discussing the points that interest you, use the poem or play or story that has been assigned, not your own experience. It is often tempting to treat the literary piece as a starting place for talking about similar experiences you have had, similar feelings you have enjoyed or suffered. The text of the work is the proper source of evidence and material. You should also avoid trying to paraphrase the assigned work, converting it to your own language. This may be something you need to do to aid in your own understanding, but don't paraphrase as an end in itself. When you paraphrase a poem, for example, you are writing translation, not commentary. It's helpful to remember that most human things—including stories, poems, plays, yourself, and your acquaintances—are too complex to be reduced to a simple generalization, or maxim, or to a "moral of the story." A story or a play, for example, can be read in several ways (remember that different people see you in different ways, too); there's not likely to be a single "right" way to talk about a piece of literature.

### Some Questions to Start With

Some features of literature provide good questions that may help you get started in exploring a piece of writing. Attempting to answer any one of the questions about these features may get you sufficiently involved in the writing to be able to see more questions and to understand more of what is going on.

1. **Genre.** Does the *kind* of writing that you are studying give the author a perspective that he or she wouldn't have otherwise? Does it create limitations for the author, or does it offer special advantages? What can a writer do in a poem that can't be done in a short story? What can be done in a play that can't be done in a poem?
2. **Speaker.** Who controls what we learn from the literary work? Who is telling the story? Who is speaking in the poem? Is the author speaking, or is it someone else? What difference does it make? Why does the author choose to tell the story, present the poem, or show the drama in that particular way? What distance is there between the author and us, or between the author and the speaker? Whose version of events are we reading?

3. **Setting.** What is the setting? Is it localized and shown in specific detail? If it isn't, why isn't it? What kind of environment do the characters live in? What effect does it have on them?

4. **Character.** How do we learn about the characters? If a poem is at issue and no characters appear except the speaker, how do we learn about him or her? Are the characters revealed by their words, by their actions, by both? What difference does it make? Are they identifiable as individuals, or do they seem to be representative types?

5. **Style and tone.** How does the author speak to us? What does the author reveal about himself by the way he speaks? If characters speak, do they have distinguishable styles? What do they reveal about themselves? What will the vocabulary tell us about the speaker or speakers? Does the style of the sentences tell anything about the speaker or about the work? What images and figures of speech occur? How do they determine the tone of the work?

6. **Structure and rhythm.** Why is the work arranged as it is? What part of the structure gets primary attention? What part seems to get the least attention? How is the tempo of the work controlled? When does the author slow down the pace of the work? When is the pace speeded up?

## Some Suggestions for Writing and Literary Study

If you have plenty of time for your writing, and if your instructor permits you to support and amplify in some detail your own critical commentary with material gathered in research, the following classification of types of literary study may help you to focus on a subject when you are planning a paper about a work of literature. (This classification is based largely on a list of areas for literary research compiled by B. Bernard Cohen in his *Writing About Literature*.)

1. **Textual analysis.** One kind of literary criticism is devoted to a close examination of the text itself—preparation and publication, revisions, errors or misprintings, various editions, and so forth. Part of the meaning of Book III of *Gulliver's Travels* was clarified, for example, with the discovery—some 175 years after initial publication—of a short passage that had been printed in the first edition but had been deleted thereafter. It is unlikely that you will do highly specialized textual research for the papers you are assigned in undergraduate courses, but you can often find a subject in existing textual problems (such as the effect on the meaning of Keats' "Ode·on a Grecian Urn" of the punctuation of the last two lines).

**29.2**

2. **Relationships among the author's works.** It is sometimes useful to examine the work in hand by considering it in the light of the author's other works. For example, it may be possible to understand the manner of *Gulliver's Travels* better by considering it along with "A Modest Proposal" and some of Swift's other satires.

3. **Relevance to biography.** Some papers on literary subjects can profitably examine the particular circumstances in the author's life that helped give shape to the work.

4. **Study of the creative process.** If primary sources such as letters and diaries are available, it is possible sometimes to study a given work for what it reveals about the creative process. Why did Swift write the four books of *Gulliver's Travels* in an order other than that in which they are printed?

5. **Relation of the work to literary theory.** It is also possible to develop fruitful explorations of a work by examining it in the light of theories about art and literature current when the work was written.

6. **Impact of the times on the work.** Sometimes it is interesting to approach a work as an artifact, to determine how it records and reflects the ideas, events and perhaps language of its time.

7. **Relationship of the work to literary tradition.** A work of literature can be studied in terms of the literary habits, assumptions, and techniques the author has inherited from other writers. You might examine *Gulliver's Travels,* for example, to see how Swift adopted, rejected, or refined the techniques of satire that were already in use.

8. **Relationship of the work to a particular subject area.** Sometimes you can find a worthwhile subject for a paper by looking at a literary work for what it reveals about a particular field of interest or idea. You could, for example, increase your understanding of *Gulliver's Travels* and write something of interest about it by focusing on what it says about English politics.

9. **Reception of the work.** You can often learn a great deal about a work by discovering how it was received in its own day or at any later time.

## 29.3 BUSINESS LETTERS

Although letter-writing is not always taught in composition courses, it is one of the most important forms of written expression. In many situations, letters are the only means you have to make yourself heard. They deserve your best effort.

What you say in a letter and the way you say it will depend upon your purpose, the person you are writing to, and, above all, upon the way you customarily express yourself. Courtesy and reasonableness, even in a letter of complaint, are always best in business correspondence. Beyond that, you should be familiar with the conventions of correspondence, so that the form and appearance of your letters will make the intended impression. The form established for business letters is standard for most kinds of formal correspondence.

Neatness, clarity, and directness are the chief virtues of a business letter. It should include all relevant information (such as dates, prices, description of merchandise) and should be as brief as possible and still be clear. The tone should be courteous, even if you are complaining about an error or poor service.

The sample letter of application on page 404 illustrates the form and tone of a typical business letter. Notice the position and punctuation of the heading, inside address, greeting (salutation), and close.

## General Appearance

Select stationery of appropriate size and good quality, with envelopes to match. Good stationery costs little more than an inferior grade, and it will make a much better impression on the person who receives your letter. For business letters the standard sheet is 21.5cm x 28cm, the same size as ordinary typing paper.

Typed letters are expected in business correspondence, and they are increasingly popular for personal correspondence. In typing your letter, leave generous margins and centre the body of the letter so that the page will look well balanced. Space paragraphs distinctly, using either block or indented form. Block paragraphs are set flush with the left margin of the letter; they are separated by a line of space, as shown in the sample on page 404. For indented paragraphs, begin five spaces from the left-hand margin. Be consistent in form. If a letter runs to more than one page, use a separate sheet of paper for each page and number the pages at the top.

**29.3**

**The heading.**  A heading should be typed in the upper right-hand corner, giving the writer's complete address and the date. The standard form is the block pattern, with end punctuation omitted.

The name of the city, the province, and the date are written out as illustrated below:

902 21 St. S.W.
Calgary, AB [or Alta.]
T2M 0L5
1978 01 05 [or January 5, 1978]

If you use a letterhead which includes the address, type the date below it, flush with the right-hand margin or centred, depending on the design of the letterhead.

**Inside address and greeting.** The inside address of a business letter gives the full name and address of the person or firm to whom it is directed. It appears flush with the left-hand margin, at least one line below the last line of the heading. No punctuation is used at the ends of the lines. If you wish to mention the person's title or position in the firm, put the designation immediately below the name in the inside address:

Ms. Linda Peterson
Personnel Director
Allen, Swift and Company
4863 Portage Avenue
Winnipeg, MB [or Man.]
R3L 1B1

The greeting, or *salutation,* appears below the inside address, separated from it by a line of space. In business letters, it is followed by a colon. If the letter is addressed to a particular individual in a firm, you may use either the name or an impersonal greeting:

Dear Mr. Keiser: [or Dear Sir:]    Dear Miss Jenkins: [or Dear Madam:]

Until recently it was customary to use the masculine form of address (*Gentlemen: Dear Sir:*) if the letter was addressed to the firm as a whole or to an individual whose name was unknown. Since the recipient is just as likely to be a woman as a man, however, alternative salutations are becoming more widely used. One acceptable salutation is simply the name of the company or, if appropriate, the title of the individual or department:

Dear Sir or Madam:    Dear Editor:    Dear Matthews Camera Company:

**Close and signature.** A conventional expression called the *complimentary close* is used at the end of the letter. Only the first word of the close is capitalized and a comma customarily follows.

The general tone of the letter will suggest how formal the close should be:

| Formal | Less formal |
|--------|-------------|
| Yours truly, | Sincerely yours, |
| Yours very truly, | Sincerely, |
| Respectfully yours, | Yours sincerely, |

The close can be either flush with the left-hand margin or in the middle of the page.

The signature is always written in longhand below the close. For clarity, however, you should type your name below your signature. A woman may indicate her marital status in parentheses if she wishes, but this practice is dying out among businesswomen.

**Addressing the envelope.** Both the address of the person to whom you are writing and your own address should be clear and complete on the front of the envelope. A block style — with the left-hand margin even — is the standard form for both addresses.

No punctuation is used at the end of the lines in this form. A comma is used between the names of a city and the province, which are put on the same line; the Postal Code is placed directly below; a space separates the second letter from the second number.

Grande Prairie, AB
T8V 3X7

When you abbreviate street designations, use the standard forms (*St.* for *Street, Ave.* for *Avenue, Blvd.* for *Boulevard*). For names of provinces, use those abbreviations given in your dictionary (*Alta., Ont.*) or the new two-letter abbreviations being introduced by Canada Post (AB, ON).

Use an envelope that matches your stationery and fold the letter to fit. With long business envelopes, a standard sheet (21.5 cm x 28 cm) is folded horizontally into three sections. With short business envelopes, it is folded once across the middle and then twice in the other direction.

## Letters of Application

Most prospective employers now prefer to receive a short letter of application accompanied by a résumé. Although the letter should be brief, it is often helpful to make reference to why you want to work for a particular company or what you feel you can offer the

**29.3**

*Let*

**Heading**

856 East Hillside Drive
Burnaby, BC
V5B 1K4
1978 06 15

**Inside address**

Dr. Robert Gruen
Director of Research
Bloch-Peterson Foundation
780 West Augusta Boulevard
Vancouver, BC
VON 1B3

**Salutation**

Dear Dr. Gruen:

Your classified notice in the current Journal of Pathology indicates
that there is an opening for a bacteriologist on your staff.  I would
like to apply for the position.

**Body**

I feel that my experience in bacteriological research would suit me
very well for the type of research Bloch-Peterson specializes in.  My
résumé, which is enclosed, gives the details of my academic and professional background.

If I can provide any other information, I shall be glad to do so.
I can be available for an interview at your convenience.

Sincerely yours,

**Close**

*Joanne Trestrail*

Joanne Trestrail

Résumé

Joanne Trestrail
856 East Hillside Drive
Burnaby, BC
V5B 1K4

(213) 267-1927

Objective         Applied research, especially in some area of disease
                  control and prevention.

Experience        June 1976-present
                  Vancouver Board of Health
                  Assist Dr. Lucille Lesiak in epidemological studies,
                  concentrating on communicable diseases among Vancouver
                  elementary-school children.  Do analytical laboratory
                  when required.

                  Summer 1975

                  McGill University, Montréal, Québec
                  Helped Dr. Joseph Roth prepare the statistical tables
                  for his recently published Tropical Diseases

                  Summer 1973
                  Laboratory Assistant, Department of Bacteriology
                  University of Guelph, Guelph, Ontario

                  References available on request

Education         1975-76
                  University of British Columbia, Vancouver
                  Master of Science in Bacteriology

                  1971-1975
                  University of Guelph, Guelph, Ontario
                  Bachelor of Science in Biology

                  Summer 1974
                  McGill University
                  Seminar in microbiology and statistical techniques

Clubs and
Organizations     League of Women Voters
                  Apollo Music Club
                  Capilano Tennis Club

company. The letter should follow standard business-letter format (see page 404).

A résumé is a one-page summary of pertinent information about yourself, including personal data, educational background, and employment record. The form shown on page 405 would usually be considered acceptable, although it is not always necessary to define your objectives. It is a good idea to indicate the nature of the work you did at your places of employment, along with any specific accomplishments. You should also list any awards or honors and publications, if appropriate. If you wish to name references or people who would be willing to recommend you, a list can be inserted at the end of the resumé.

Always ask the permission of people you list as references. Give their complete addresses and correct titles (Professor, Dr., Mrs.). *Mr., Mrs., Ms.,* and *Dr.* are the only titles that are abbreviated. All others are written in full.

If you are asked to include documents (such as photographs, transcripts of academic records, or photostats), use a crush-proof envelope. If you want the enclosures returned to you, include a self-addressed, stamped envelope.

## Letters to Editors and Public Figures

People in a democratic society often wish to express their opinions to newspapers, magazines, or influential public figures. Such communications should be written in standard business-letter form and should be brief and pointed. Even if you are expressing disagreement with some opinion or policy, try to be reasonable and courteous. Your letter is much more likely to have the desired effect if it relies on facts and logic than if it presents an impassioned subjective reaction. Formal greetings and closings are usual in these letters.

Consult the appropriate section of a dictionary or an etiquette book for the proper forms of address for cabinet ministers, members of Parliament, and other government officials.

# The Research Paper

*. . . not to know what has been transacted in former times is to continue always a child. If no use is made of the labours of past ages, the world must remain always in the infancy of knowledge. — Samuel Johnson*

Anything you write *may* require some research. Whole libraries, as well as other resources, are available to you whenever you write anything. One of the decisions you make in thinking out any paper is whether or not you know enough already to handle the subject, or whether or not the subject requires more than you already know. If you don't know enough, if the subject requires information you cannot supply, then any assignment may become a research assignment.

Often the planning and writing of a research paper (also called a library paper, a reference paper, or a term paper) is a separate and special part of freshman composition and many other courses. The preparation of a research paper has much in common with other writing assignments, but in addition it provides:

1. Practice in exploring the possibilities of a subject and limiting it so that it can be treated adequately in a paper longer than those you will customarily write; research papers may often range from 1500 to 4000 words.
2. An introduction to the resources of the library and training in the most efficient ways of locating information.
3. Practice in using source material intelligently — choosing between what is useful and what is not, evaluating the ideas of others, organizing and interpreting the information.
4. Acquaintance with documentation and manuscript form typically expected in academic work and in reports and papers prepared for publication.
5. An opportunity to learn something new about a subject and to gain specialized, thorough knowledge of it.

Because the reference paper is longer and more complex than most other compositions you may be asked to write, we discuss it here in successive steps:

1. choosing a topic (30.1)
2. locating appropriate source materials (30.2)
3. preparing the working bibliography (30.3)
4. evaluating your material (30.4)

5. taking notes (30.5)
6. planning the paper (30.6)
7. writing the first draft (30.7)
8. documenting the paper (30.8)
9. assembling the completed paper (30.9)

The actual task of preparing a reference paper, however, can seldom be divided into such neat categories. The steps overlap and certain operations must be repeated as work progresses. For example, as you get into your reading, you may decide that your chosen topic needs to be modified; and as you write your paper, you may discover gaps in your information that must be filled in by further research. The best advice, perhaps, is to start on the assignment early and to take particular care in choosing and defining your topic, so that both your research and your writing will have a clear focus.

## 30.1 CHOOSING A TOPIC

One important prerequisite for writing a good reference paper is that you have a genuine interest in the subject that you are going to investigate. In some courses, the subject field may be limited by the general assignment (perhaps to various aspects of the United Nations, or to the history of a specific geographic area, or to an author or work of literature you have studied); but more often the choice of a subject will be left up to you.

In either instance, you should be reasonably certain that the specific topic you select will be one that you will like to read about, to think about, and then to write about. Since a reference paper may take as much as five or six weeks to prepare, it can easily become a chore – and be largely a waste of time – unless you feel that what you are doing is of some interest and importance. The suggestions in 18.1, Finding and Exploring What You Have to Say, are as relevant to the reference paper as they are to other kinds of writing.

### Choosing a Subject Area

Before making a definite decision on your topic, consider your various interests in and out of school. These general subjects may suggest particular topics that you might want to investigate:

1. A subject related to one of the courses that you are now taking or that you intend to take. For example, if you are going to major in business administration and you intend to take Canadian economic history next year, you might investigate the beginning of child-labor laws or early life insurance companies in Canada.
2. A subject related to your reading interests (biography, history, science fiction, detective stories) or one related to your favorite hobby or sport (music, dress design, mountain climbing, baseball).
3. A subject about which you now have an opinion but little actual information. Does capital punishment help prevent crime? Are children with high IQ's generally successful in later life? Do rapid readers retain more than slow readers?
4. A subject that has aroused your curiosity but that you have never had time or opportunity to investigate. Of what value are computers in education today? Do sunspots actually affect the weather? How has the popularity of television affected book sales?

It is easier to find a purpose and keep it before you if you select a topic that ties in with one of your current interests.

## Limiting the Topic

As soon as you know what general subject area you would like to concentrate on, find a specific topic within that area that can be treated adequately and profitably in a paper of the assigned length. Keep these considerations in mind when you are narrowing your topic:

1. **Length of the reference paper.** An undergraduate reference paper is not expected to be the last word on a topic; neither is it intended to be a disconnected listing of commonplace facts or a superficial summary of a complex topic. Limit your topic enough so that your treatment of it can be reasonably thorough. The danger of selecting a topic that is too narrow is far less than the danger of choosing one that is too broad and lacks focus. (See 18.1, Examining a Situation for Possible Subjects.)
2. **Availability of source material.** Before you begin to read and take notes, find out whether or not the more important books and periodicals that you will need are available in the library. Since half a dozen or more sources are usually required for a

**30.1**

*Topic*

reference paper, you should be certain that enough material is available before you begin your research.

3. **Complexity of the source material.** For some subjects (chemical structures of synthetic rubber, for example), the available material may be too technical for a general reader to understand — and perhaps too complicated for you to interpret without a good deal of study. You will probably be better off, even in a technical area, with a topic of current general interest.

Here are some steps to take to help you determine your approach to your topic:

1. **Do some preliminary reading.** Spend a few hours reading background material in one or more general or special encyclopedias, in some magazine articles, and perhaps in newspaper articles, if your subject is of current interest and likely to be covered by the daily press.

2. **Check reference sources.** Look through the library card catalogue and the guides to periodical literature to see how the general subject you have chosen may be broken down into smaller units. A broad subject like *aviation* might first be limited to *commercial aviation,* then to the *functions of the Canadian Transport Commission (CTC),* and then still further to *recent safety measures enforced by the CTC.*

3. **Define your idea as precisely as possible.** Even though you probably still will not be able to make a final statement of the central or controlling idea of your paper, your preliminary reading should have given you a reasonably accurate idea of the focus of your paper. This will help give direction to your research, so that you won't later have to discard much material as useless.

## 30.2 LOCATING APPROPRIATE SOURCE MATERIALS

One purpose of the research paper is to acquaint you with the resources of your library so that you can locate the information you need quickly and efficiently. On most subjects, the material in the library is so extensive and so varied in form (books, periodicals, encyclopedias, newspapers, pamphlets, microfilm) that to keep from being hopelessly lost you need to know something about the essential works in your subject, the methods used to index and catalogue material, and the quickest way to obtain this information.

This section deals with library facilities and the various aids that will help you find the material for a reference paper. Librarians are always willing to help students with their research problems, but every student should also be willing to help the librarians, too, by showing some knowledge of the standard sources of reference.

## The Library Card Catalogue

The card catalogue is an alphabetical card index of the items in the library. The cards, filed in drawers or trays, are located in the main reading room or other central spot. Most card catalogues, in addition to listing all books in the library, give the titles of periodicals (and indicate what copies the library has), encyclopedias, government publications, and other works.

Almost all books are listed alphabetically in three places in the card catalogue of most libraries: by author, by subject, and by title. The cards issued by the Library of Congress, like those reproduced on page 412 for *Canada's Energy Crisis* by James Laxer, are almost universally used for cataloguing.

You can save yourself many hours of thumbing through books that are not relevant to your subject by learning to interpret and evaluate the information given in the card catalogue. The subject card includes the following information (keyed to the circled numbers on the card):

1. **Subject.** The subject heading on the catalogue card tells in general what the book is about. In this instance, the general subject is energy policy. Also listed on the card (in item 7) are the other subject headings under which the book is catalogued.
2. **Call number.** The call number in the upper left-hand corner tells where the book is located in the library. In most libraries, borrowers obtain books by filling out a slip with the call number, author, title, and the borrower's name and address. If you have access to the stacks, the call number will enable you to locate the book you are looking for.
3. **Author's name.** If you are already familiar with the subject you are investigating, the author's name may tell you whether the book is likely to be authoritative.
4. **Title and facts of publication.** The date of publication is sometimes an important clue to the usefulness of a book. For ex-

**30.2**

*Lib*

**Subject card**

ENERGY POLICY—CANADA. (1)

(2)
HD
9574    Laxer, James. (3)
C22      (4)    Canada's energy crisis / James Laxer. — Toronto : J. Lewis
L38             & Samuel, 1974.
         (5)    136 p. ; 21 cm.                                   C74-4379-X
         (6)    Includes bibliographical references.
                ISBN 0-88862-065-9 : $10.00.   ISBN 0-88862-064-0 pbk.

         (7)    1. Petroleum industry and trade—Canada.   2. Petroleum industry and trade
                —United States.   3. Energy policy—Canada.   I. Title.
         (8)  HD9574.C22L38              333.8'2'0971            75-309222
                                                                      MARC
                Library of Congress                  75

**Author card**

HD
9574    Laxer, James.
C22       Canada's energy crisis / James Laxer. — Toronto : J. Lewis
L38     & Samuel, 1974.
          136 p. ; 21 cm.                                   C74-4379-X
          Includes bibliographical references.
          ISBN 0-88862-065-9 : $10.00.   ISBN 0-88862-064-0 pbk.

          1. Petroleum industry and trade—Canada.   2. Petroleum industry and trade
          —United States.   3. Energy policy—Canada.   I. Title.
        HD9574.C22L38              333.8'2'0971            75-309222
                                                                MARC
          Library of Congress                  75

**Title card**

                    Canada's energy crisis.

HD
9574    Laxer, James.
C22       Canada's energy crisis / James Laxer. — Toronto : J. Lewis
L38     & Samuel, 1974.
          136 p. ; 21 cm.                                   C74-4379-X
          Includes bibliographical references.
          ISBN 0-88862-065-9 : $10.00.   ISBN 0-88862-064-0 pbk.

          1. Petroleum industry and trade—Canada.   2. Petroleum industry and trade
          —United States.   3. Energy policy—Canada.   I. Title.
        HD9574.C22L38              333.8'2'0971            75-309222
                                                                MARC
          Library of Congress                  75

ample, if you are looking only for information on developments in 1978, this book will not be helpful.

5. **Number of pages, illustrations, height.** The number of pages in the book suggests how extensive its coverage. This book is of medium length—136 pages of text. The indication of height—21 cm—is for librarians.

6. **Special information.** The catalogue card indicates that the book contains a bibliography that might prove helpful in directing you to other sources. None of the books listed, however, would be later than 1974, the year in which this particular book was published.

7. **Other subject headings.** The list of other subject headings under which the book is catalogued may provide ideas of other subject areas to look under for more material; it may also provide a further clue to the contents of the book.

8. **Facts for librarians.** The information at the bottom of the catalogue card—such as the Library of Congress classification (HD9574.C22L38)—is generally for the use of librarians.

See 30.3 page 417, Preparing the Working Bibliography, to see what information from the library catalogue card should be included on your own bibliography card.

## Trade Bibliographies

The bibliographies published for booksellers and librarians should be consulted to locate a library book not listed in the catalogue or to learn if a book is still in print. The most important include

> ***Books in Print.*** A listing by author and by title of books included in *Publishers' Trade List Annual,* which lists—by publisher—all books currently in print.
>
> ***Canadian Books in Print.*** A listing by author and title of books bearing the imprint of Canadian publishers or Canadian subsidiaries of international publishing firms and currently in print.
>
> ***Cumulative Book Index.*** The complete publication data on all books published in English, each listed by author and by title.
>
> ***Guide to Basic Reference Materials for Canadian Libraries*** (1974).
>
> ***Paperbound Books in Print.*** An especially useful source since some important books are available *only* in paperback.
>
> ***Subject Guide to Books in Print.*** An invaluable index to *Books in Print.*

**30.2**

*Lib*

## Periodical Indexes

A great deal of essential material, particularly on current topics, is available only in periodicals, which may range from popular magazines and newspapers to technical journals and learned publications. This material is catalogued in various guides and indexes, some of them published monthly, others annually. Knowing how to use periodical indexes will not only simplify the task of research but will also enable you to make your reference paper more authoritative and up to date. Most libraries also have lists of the periodicals they hold which tell also where the periodicals are indexed.

***Readers' Guide.*** The most generally useful of all periodical guides is the *Readers' Guide to Periodical Literature,* which indexes the articles in more than 120 magazines of general interest. It is published monthly in paperbound volumes which are afterwards gathered in large cumulative volumes covering a year or more.

The entries in the *Readers' Guide* are listed alphabetically both by subject and by author. The abbreviations used in the listings— for the titles of periodicals, the month of publication, and various facts about the article itself—are explained on the first page of each volume. On page 415 is a reproduction and explanation of three consecutive main entries from a monthly issue.

**Other periodical indexes.** In locating sources for a reference paper you may find it useful to refer to one of the specialized periodical indexes listed below. Most of them appear annually; the year after the title shows when publication began. The indexes are listed alphabetically.

> ***Applied Science and Technology Index*** (1913). Subject index to periodicals on science, technology, and related subjects.
>
> ***Art Index*** (1929). Author and subject index for fine-arts periodicals and museum bulletins.
>
> ***Bibliographic Index: A Cumulative Bibliography of Bibliographies*** (1938).
>
> ***Biography Index: A Cumulative Index to Biographical Material in Books and Magazines*** (1946/47).
>
> ***A Bibliography of Canadian Bibliographies*** (2nd ed., 1972).
>
> ***Book Review Digest*** (1905). Author, subject, and title index to published book reviews; gives extracts and exact references to sources.
>
> ***Business Periodicals Index*** (1958). Subject index to periodicals on all phases of business, including particular industries and trades.

## Sample entries from the *Readers' Guide*

(1) **POWELL, Joseph L. Jr**
Not-so-cool Jody Powell. C. Mohr. il pors N Y
Times Mag p20-1+ My 15 '77 •

(2) **POWER resources**
Energy (cont) Sci N 111:249 Ap 16 '77
Nightmare life without fuel; Time essay. I.
Asimov. Time 109:33 Ap 25 '77
Permanent energy shortage. Progressive 41:5-6
Ap '77
*See also*
Coal supply
Energy policy

### Conferences

Opening the debate; Time Inc's energy con-
ference. il Time 109:27-8+ Ap 25 '77

### Conservation

Adventures in alternate energy;
Michael Hackleman: electric truck is wind-
powered, too. E. Moran. il Pop Sci 210:
78-9 Ap '77
At the grass roots, a rush to save fuel. il
U.S. News 82:17 My 2 '77
Close to home. A. J. Mayer. il Newsweek 89:
25-6 My 2 '77
Energy management: a crisis in industry. H. L.
Breckenridge. bibl f Intellect 105:352-4 Ap '77
Job for energy misers. M. E. Marty. Chr Cent
94:463 My 11 '77
Moral equivalents and other bugle calls; Time
essay. S. Kanfer. Time 109:25 My 2 '77
Plugging the leaks. Sci Am 236:57-8 Ap '77
Tale of two suburbs: near Chicago and outside
Cologne. P. Delaney; B. Seaman. il Time 109:
23-4 My 2 '77
*See also*
Energy policy

### Economic aspects

Economic impact; energy policy. M. Ruby and
others. il Newsweek 89:20-2+ My 2 '77
For some firms, there's a bonanza ahead. il
U.S. News 82:30 My 9 '77
Getting more energy. D. Pauly and others. il
Newsweek 89:27-8 My 2 '77
$1 trillion—the cost of meeting U.S. energy
needs. il U.S. News 82:19-20 My 2 '77
Will energy conservation throttle economic
growth? with interview with J. R. Schlesinger.
il Bus W p66-72+ Ap 25 '77

(3) **POWERS, Stefanie**
Problems and pleasures of living together; interview, ed by I. Silden. pors Harp Baz 110:
114-15+ My '77

From Readers' Guide to Periodical Literature. Vol. 77, No. 7 (June 10, 1977).
New York: H. W. Wilson Co., 1977, p. 97.

### Explanation

Entry **1** is a *subject entry*. An article about Joseph L. (Jody)
Powell, titled "Not-so-cool Jody Powell," written by C. Mohr
and illustrated with portraits, appears on pages 20–21 and is
continued elsewhere in *The New York Times Magazine*, May 15,
1977.

Entry **2** is also a *subject entry*, followed by a list of titles on power
resources. This entry is subdivided into more specific topics, and
cross references to related subjects are also listed.

**30.2**

*Lib.*

Entry **3** is an *author entry*, but because the article is an interview
with the "author," an editor's name is also listed.

*The Canadian Book Review Annual* (1975-).

*Canadian Periodical Index* (1938-), a continuing serial, which includes the index to *The Financial Post,* a valuable source for Canadian subject matter.

*Catholic Periodical Index: A Guide to Catholic Magazines* (1930).

*A Checklist of Canadian Literature and Background Materials,* 1628-1960.

*The Education Index* (1929-1964). Author and subject index for educational periodicals, books, and pamphlets.

*The Canadian Essay and Literature Index* (1973-).

*Essay and General Literature Index.* Author, subject, and title index to essays, articles, and miscellaneous works published in collections since 1900.

*Humanities Index* (1974). Author and subject index to periodicals from various countries; devoted to articles in the humanities; valuable supplement to the *Readers' Guide.*

*Poole's Index to Periodical Literature* (1802-1881). Subject index to American and English periodicals, many of which are no longer published but still important; precedes coverage of *Readers' Guide.*

*Canadian Government Publications;* a monthly catalogue (1953-).

*Social Sciences and Humanities Index* (1907-1974). Author and subject index to periodicals from various countries; devoted chiefly to the humanities and social sciences; formerly titled *International Index to Periodicals;* now superseded by two separate indexes.

*Social Sciences Index* (1974). Author and subject index to periodicals focussing on the social sciences; supplements *Readers' Guide.*

*Ulrich's International Periodical Directory.* Classifies international periodicals by subject area and indicates which periodical index covers them.

*Vertical File Index: A Subject and Title Index to Selected Pamphlet Material.*

## Encyclopedias

The following general encyclopedias are authoritative and include many bibliographies and cross references; all are regularly revised and several are supplemented annually with yearbooks:

| | |
|---|---|
| *Catholic Encyclopedia* | *Encyclopedia Americana* |
| *Chamber's Encyclopaedia* | *Encyclopedia Canadiana* |
| *Encyclopaedia Britannica* | *Encyclopedia of the Social Sciences* |

Many subject areas, from art to science, are covered by more specialized reference works that go into more detail than general encyclopedias, for example, Norah Story's *The Oxford Companion to Canadian History and Literature* (1967), a supplement to which appeared in 1973, edited by William Toye. You should be able to find most of these by browsing in the reference room of your library. The librarian will also be able to tell you what reference works exist for your area of interest.

## Yearbooks and Annuals

The following annuals provide up-to-date facts and figures on a wide variety of subjects, particularly those of current interest.

*Canada Year Book.* Annually updated facts, figures, and other valuable information about Canada.

*Canadian Almanac and Directory* (1847-).

*Canadian Annual Review of Politics and Public Affairs* (1960).

*Information Please Almanac, Atlas and Yearbook* (1947-).

*The World Almanac and Book of Facts* (1868-). This is one general reference that any student can afford to own.

*Yearbook of the United Nations.* Activities of the United Nations.

## Guides to Reference Materials

Many other specialized reference works can be found by consulting the following guides:

Barton, Mary N., comp. *Reference Books: A Brief Guide for Students and Other Users of the Library.*

*The Reader's Adviser: A Layman's Guide to Literature.*

Shores, Louis. *Basic Reference Sources: An Introduction to Materials and Methods.*

Walford, Arthur, J., ed. *Guide to Reference Material.*

Winchell, Constance M. *Guide to Reference Books,* updated 9th ed. by Eugene P. Sheehy (-1975).

# 30.3 PREPARING THE WORKING BIBLIOGRAPHY

**30.3**

*Res*

A working bibliography is a list—on note cards—of the books, magazine articles, and other published works that you intend to consult when gathering material for your reference paper. The number of references you should collect will depend on the nature of the assignment, but it is always best to begin with more than you will probably need. If your working bibliography includes only a bare minimum of sources, you will probably have to take time later to find more: a book you want from the library may already be out on loan; one article on your list may prove to be too technical; another may merely repeat material you have already collected.

Whether your initial bibliography contains many sources or relatively few, you will probably want to add others as you get into your research and find new avenues you want to explore.

Each entry in your working bibliography should be written on a separate card, either a 12.7cm x 7.6cm or 10cm x 15cm. With only one reference on each, cards can be rearranged quickly for alphabetizing; new ones can be inserted in the proper places and useless ones discarded. You may want to use 12.7 x 7.6 cards for the working bibliography and 10 x 15 cards for taking notes, since the larger cards will obviously hold more data and will also be readily distinguishable from your bibliography cards.

Bibliography cards for different types of references are illustrated on page 419. Each card should include all the facts you will need to identify the reference and obtain it from the library. It should also have all the information you will need in preparing the final bibliography. The punctuation suggested here is a standard form for bibliographies (see page 439):

1. **Author's name,** with the last name first, followed by a period. If the book is edited, use the editor's name, followed by a comma, followed by *ed.* If the article or pamphlet is unsigned, write the title first on the card.
2. **Title of the book,** underlined and followed by a period, or title of the article, in quotation marks and followed by a period.
3. **Facts of publication:**
   a) **For a book:** the city of publication, followed by a colon; the name of the publisher, followed by a comma; and the date, followed by a period. Former practice often left out the publisher's name, and usage is still divided. However, unless you are told otherwise, it is always best to include it.
   b) **For a magazine article:** the name of the magazine, underlined and followed by a comma; the date of the issue, followed by a comma; and the pages covered by the article, preceded by *pp.* and followed by a period.
   c) **For a journal article:** the name of the journal, underlined and

## Sample bibliography cards

**For a book by one author**

> 785.09
> E 94    Even, David. *Orchestral Music:*    ①
> *Its Story Told Through the Lives*
> *and Works of Its Foremost Composers.*
> New York: Franklin Watts, Inc.
> 1973.

**For a book, edited**

> 301.451
> L 616    Lerner, Gerda, ed. *Black*    ②
> *Women in White America: A*
> *Documentary History.*
> New York: Random House,
> Pantheon Books, 1972.

**For a signed article in an encyclopedia**

> Reference    ③
> Room
> Shelf 12
>         Myers], R[aymond] R.
>         "Paints, Varnishes, and
>         Allied Products."
>         *Encyclopaedia Britannica.*
>         *Macropaedia* 13, 1974.

**For a magazine article**

> Periodical    ④
> desk
>         Pearsall, Robert Brainard.
>         "The Presiding Tropes of
>         Emily Brontë." *College*
>         *English*, 27 (January 1966),
>         266–273.

**For a journal article**

> 051
> For    McQuade, Walter. "Management    ⑤
> V.90    Problems Enter the Picture at
>         Art Museums." *Fortune*,
>         July 1974, pp 100–103, 169, 173.

**For an unsigned newspaper article**

> Periodical    ⑥
> desk
>         "Unlucky Striker." *The Globe*
>         *and Mail*, September 27,
>         1978, p. 6, col. 1–2.

**30.3**

Res

followed by a comma; the volume number in Arabic numbers; the date, in parentheses, followed by a comma; the page numbers, without *p.* or *pp.*, followed by a period.

   **d) For a newspaper article:** the title of the item (other than mere headlines); the name of the newspaper, underlined and followed by a comma; the date, followed by a comma; the section number, followed by a comma; the page number, preceded by *p.* and followed by a period. The column number may be added after the page number, separated from it by a comma, preceded by *col.,* and followed by a period.

4. **Library call number,** or the location of a reference work in the library. This information, placed in the upper left-hand corner, should be written just as it appears in the card catalogue, so that you can easily relocate the reference if the need arises. See also 30.9, page 439, The Final Bibliography.

5. **Index number,** a number or code that you assign to the work, should be placed in the upper right-hand corner of the card. This same number should be used on any note cards you make that refer to this source.

   The difference between a magazine and a journal will usually be apparent from content and format. Magazines generally have a wide public appeal and are published weekly or monthly, with dates corresponding to the issue. Each issue begins with page 1. Journals are of more limited appeal (e.g., *The Canadian Journal of Economics*) and are published less frequently than magazines (many are published quarterly); the date does not always correspond to the actual date of issue ("Autumn" could be issued between September and November). Therefore the volume and issue number are more important, especially since pagination is usually continuous throughout an entire volume (e.g., Volume 1, number 2, might begin on page 233).

## 30.4 EVALUATING YOUR MATERIAL

Since writing a reference paper is in part an exercise in critical judgment, it is important that you learn to evaluate the sources you use. Try to find and use the most informative books and the most authoritative material available.

### Facts to Consider in Evaluating

Writers engaged in writing their first reference papers on unfamiliar subjects are not expected to know offhand that a work by author A is wholly worthless or that author B is considered the foremost authority on the subject. They can, however, arrive at a fairly accurate estimate of their sources by considering these facts:

1. **Date of publication.** If your subject is one for which recent facts are important, see that the sources are up to date. The most recent edition of a book or an encyclopedia will generally be more useful and authoritative than an earlier one.
2. **Completeness.** With magazine articles, it is better to read the original article as it was printed in full instead of a condensation or reprint of it. Similarly, books are usually more comprehensive than articles, though you should determine that the book's author is reputable. Check the bibliographies in the books you look at for sources often referred to. Encyclopedias should usually be used only as a place to start your search for information, and never relied on heavily.
3. **Facts and opinions.** Distinguish carefully between an author's facts and opinions. Label the opinions "So-and-so thinks that. . . ." In general, pay more attention to *facts* (unless your paper is about various opinions), since you will need facts to support your own opinions.
4. **Objectivity of the source.** A book or an article based in large part upon an author's opinions or biases—particularly when the subject is controversial—should not be used as your sole authority on the matter. Read material on the other side of the question before reaching a conclusion.

When you are in doubt about the reliability of a source, a librarian or your instructor may be able to give you advice. Reviews in the more specialized journals evaluate books in their own fields. *Book Review Digest* may also prove helpful. Taking the time to read reviews of books may help you judge their reliability. And, of course, after you have worked a while on your subject, you will be in a better position to evaluate the material yourself.

## 30.5 TAKING NOTES

Accurate and full notes are essential for writing a good reference paper. You can save time when taking notes if you approach the problem efficiently. Don't try to take down everything you read; instead, spend a little time looking over the book, the article, or the pamphlet to see if it contains the information you want. If you have given enough thought to formulating and narrowing your

**30.5**

*Notes*

topic, you will have a pretty clear idea of what you are looking for.

When examining a book, look first at the index and the table of contents to see in what sections your subject is treated. See also if there are any tables, graphs, bibliographies, or further references that might be useful. Skim each chapter or article to find out what it covers. Then go over it again carefully, taking down the notes you will need.

Notes should be taken on either 12.7cm x 7.6cm or 10cm x 15cm cards so that you can later arrange the material according to the plan of your paper. It is usually a waste of effort to try to take notes in numbered outline form since you probably won't know the final plan of your paper until you have finished your research. What is important is to have each note card accurate, clearly written, and clearly labelled. Each note card should contain these essential parts, as illustrated by the sample cards shown on page 423:

1. The **heading** at the top of the card, showing what material it contains.
2. The **index number** to identify the source and **page number,** accurately noted.
3. The **content,** facts or opinions (summarized in your own words or directly quoted) accurately recorded.

Notes that cannot be readily interpreted a week or a month after they have been written are obviously of little use; so too are incomplete or carelessly written notes. You can avoid a good deal of tedious, unnecessary work, including rereading and rechecking, by following these simple rules:

1. Use *one side* of each card only. Your material will then be easier to classify and arrange, and you won't run the risk of overlooking a statement on the back of a card.
2. Include only *one major point* or a few closely related facts from the same source on a single card. If the information is too extensive to write on one side of a card, use two or three cards and number them in sequence.
3. Get all the information accurately the first time you consult a source so that you won't have to make extra trips to the library.
4. Put all *direct quotations* in quotation marks, including all statements, single sentences, and phrases that you copy word for word from any source. If you omit a word or words in a direct quotation use ellipsis periods (...) to indicate the omission (14.2). If you are paraphrasing the source, state the idea in your own language. (See 30.8, page 431, Plagiarism.)

## Sample note cards

**Direct quote**

> Origins of Parliament                     Maurois
>                        Hist. of Eng., 146
>
> "The convoking of the different 'Estates'
> of a Kingdom (military, priestly and
> plebian), in order to obtain their
> consent to taxation, was not peculiar
> to England in the fourteenth Century."                    ①

**Summarized material**

> Incidence of neurosis                     ②
> among the poor
>                        Harrington
>                        Other Amer., 119
>
> Though there is a myth that the
> richer you are the more neurotic
> you are likely to be, the truth is
> just the opposite: poor people
> suffer from mental illness more often
> than people in any other social class.

**Statistical data**

> Enrolment in institutions        Stat. Abstract        ③
> of higher education (1000's)      (1976)  112
>
> |         | 1940 | 1950 | 1960 | 1970 | 1975 |
> |---------|------|------|------|------|------|
> | Total   | 1708 | 1851 | 2008 | 2525 | 2747 |
> | Public  | 603  | 641  | 701  | 1060 | 1214 |
> | Private | 1105 | 1210 | 1307 | 1465 | 1533 |

5. Write your notes in ink (pencilled notes may become blurred with frequent handling) so that you won't have to recopy them. When you use abbreviations, be sure that you will know later on what they mean.

It isn't necessary to write out all your notes in complete sentences; practical shortcuts such as the omission of *a, the, was,* and other such words are good for summarizing material. If the method you use for taking notes in lectures or on your own textbooks has proved successful, use it also for your reference paper.

Accurate notes are one of the chief tools of scholarship. Early and careful practice in taking them is excellent training that may be useful in later work.

## 30.6 PLANNING THE PAPER

The central or controlling purpose of a reference paper should be clearly in mind long before you have finished investigating all your resources. You should know, for instance, whether you are trying to reach a conclusion about two opposing viewpoints or whether you are trying to explain an event or situation. When you have gathered a sufficient amount of material to put your topic in focus, it is time to formulate a thesis sentence (18.1, page 228) that will state your controlling purpose and to outline the order in which you will develop your material.

### Examining and Arranging Your Notes

First read through all your notes to refresh your memory and determine the general order in which you will arrange your material. Then arrange the notes in piles, grouping together all the notes on a particular aspect of your subject. The headings at the top of each card will be useful in helping you sort and arrange your material. At this stage, you should note any gaps in your material that will have to be filled in with further reading before you start your first draft.

If any of the notes you have taken no longer seem relevant to your purpose in writing, put them aside in a tentative discard pile. Almost anyone engaged in research finds that a good deal of carefully recorded material has to be discarded. Don't succumb to the temptation to include material that has no bearing on your thesis simply because it is interesting or because you worked hard to find it.

## Making a Preliminary Outline

When you have arranged your note cards to your satisfaction, state the central idea of your paper in a thesis sentence (not in two or more sentences nor in the form of a question). Then make a rough outline showing the order in which you intend to present your material. Each point in the outline should contribute in some way to the development of your central idea or thesis. Often your instructor will want to see your working outline before you go much further with the work. To crystallize your plan and to make it possible for your instructor to examine it and make suggestions, you should follow standard outline form. At this stage, a topic outline is generally sufficient; if necessary, you can later expand the entries into complete sentences. (See 20, Organizing Your Material, for a discussion of outlining and outline form.)

Neither your preliminary outline nor your thesis sentence needs to be considered as final. It is better, in fact, to make a reasonably flexible outline so that you can make whatever changes seem desirable as you write and revise your first draft.

## 30.7 WRITING THE FIRST DRAFT

A reference paper should represent your writing at its best—in terms of organization, sentence structure, wording, and emphasis. The most convincing proof that you have actually learned something new from your research is the way you have evaluated, organized, and expressed your material. Instructions concerning the proper form of footnotes (30.8) and bibliography (30.9) should be followed to the letter. The paper should be as neat as you can possibly make it, with each part in its proper order and all errors in spelling and punctuation carefully corrected.

Make certain that you are thoroughly familiar with your material before you begin to write. You should have the information on your note cards so well in mind that you can write rapidly and with confidence once you start. For this reason, it is a good idea to review your notes once more just before you begin writing.

This draft should be written in the same way you would write the first draft of any other important assignment (as discussed in

**30.7**

Draft

21, Writing the First Draft), but with ample room left for documentation. You can leave spaces between the lines or at the bottom of the page to insert the necessary footnotes. Some writers insert the documentation in the text of the first draft to help determine final placement and space requirements:

> The theory reserved the most desirable characteristics for northern people. Those of the south were pictured as jealous, superstitious, cowardly, lascivious, cruel, and inhuman.[3] Because of this belief,

---

[3]Philip Butcher. "Othello's Racial Identity," Shakespeare Quarterly, 3 (July 1952), 246.

---

> Shakespeare's choice of Othello as the victim of Iago's plot makes it especially convincing to the audience.

Or the footnotes may be put all together on a separate page or handled in any other way that will be convenient when you make the final copy.

If a passage seems to need more facts or further documentation, don't interrupt your writing to do the necessary additional research. Put a question mark or some other notation in the margin, continue with your writing, and look up the material after you have finished the first draft.

Most reference papers are written in a rather formal, impersonal style. Usually there's no need to refer to yourself at all, but if you do, the reference should be brief. (It's also better to say "I" rather than use "the writer" or other third person references.) Remember, however, that impersonal writing does not have to be flat or lifeless. The information itself will provide the interest if you express it clearly and directly.

## 30.8 DOCUMENTING THE PAPER

Any paper based on the writing of others should acknowledge each and every source from which an idea or statement is taken. In a reference paper the acknowledgments are made by footnotes—notes at the bottom of the page or at the end of the paper (numbered to correspond to numbers in the text) that show exactly where the information was obtained. The method of documentation recommended by most instructors in English and the humanities is described on pages 433-437 and illustrated in the student paper beginning on page 442. (Your instructor will tell you where to put your footnotes, but if you are in doubt, the bottom of the page is always correct.)

## Where Footnotes Are Needed

When drawing on the work of another writer or researcher, you owe him or her the courtesy of giving credit where credit is due. You also owe your *readers* the courtesy of providing the sources of your information so that they can judge them for themselves and find additional information, if desired. Failure to document borrowed information is at best carelessness; at worst, it is plagiarism, which means offering material written by someone else as your own work (see page 431). Footnotes are essential in two situations:

1. **After direct quotations.** Each statement taken word for word from a printed source should have a reference number at the end of the quotation and be properly identified in a footnote. The only exceptions to this rule are well-known expressions, such as familiar Biblical quotations ("Blessed are the poor"), famous lines from literature ("Something is rotten in the state of Denmark"), and proverbs ("A bird in the hand is worth two in the bush").

2. **After all important statements of fact or opinion taken from written sources and expressed in your own words.** Facts include figures, dates, scientific data, and descriptions of events and situations about which you have no firsthand knowledge, such as what happened at a session of the United Nations, how coffee is cultivated in Brazil, or the role of Madagascar in World War II. Opinions and interpretations that are not actually your own would include statements such as one writer's reasons for the growing popularity of soccer in Canada, or an opinion on seal hunting from a newspaper editorial.

In some publications, footnotes are also used for comments or additional information that the writer does not wish to include in the text. In freshman reference papers, however, this practice should be kept to a minimum; if a statement is worth making, it usually belongs in the text.

**30.8**

*Doc*

Footnotes are *not* needed for statements that would pass without question. These include obvious facts ("Certain chemicals cannot be used in the preservation of foods in Canada"), matters of common knowledge ("The British North America Act was passed in 1867"), general statements and expressions of the writer's own opinion ("The medical and biological sciences have made unbelievable progress in the last twenty years").

If you have a full page in your draft without any references, you should probably check it again to see if any documentation is needed. A great many footnotes on a single page may indicate that some of the material could better be combined or rephrased to eliminate unnecessary references.

The following sections discuss some things to consider in integrating footnoted material into the text of your paper.

## Using Direct Quotations

In incorporating material from sources into your research paper, you will often have to decide whether to quote directly or to restate the material in your own words. In general, direct quotations are preferable only in these situations:

1. **Important statements of information, opinion, or policy.** Whenever the *exact* wording of a statement is crucial in its interpretation, it should be quoted in full:

   Faced by much opposition, Mackenzie King, in 1942, described his government's policy on conscription as: "Not necessarily conscription but conscription if necessary."[2]

2. **Interpretations of literary works.** When a statement or opinion in your paper is based on a passage in a poem, essay, short story, novel, or play, quote from the passage so that the reader can see the basis for your interpretation:

   The closing passages of *Moby Dick* also suggest that the whale represents some omnipotent force hostile to man. Ishmael says that Moby Dick rushed at the ship with a "predistinating head," and that "retribution, swift vengeance, external malice were in his aspect . . . in spite of all mortal man could do."[1]

When you are writing a paper that requires frequent references to a literary work, however, you need to footnote the edition of the text you are using only once, the first time you use a quotation.

Thereafter, you may identify quotations by giving (immediately after the quotation, in parentheses) the page numbers for fiction; the line numbers for poetry; the act and scene for drama (followed by the line numbers if in verse):

> Man, who once stood at the centre of the universe, confident that he was the end of Creation and could claim kinship with the angels, is now shrouded in a "mist" that isolates him from God and shuts off all his questioning about the problems of ultimate order. As Webster says of the Cardinal in *The Duchess of Malfi*, Man,
>
> > which stood'st like a huge pyramid
> > Begun upon a large and ample base,
> > Shalt end in a little point, a kind of nothing. (V.v.96–98)

3. **Distinctive phrasing.** If your source states some idea or opinion in a particularly forceful or original way that would be weakened by paraphrasing, quote the exact words:

> Russell does not believe that our age lacks great ideas because religion has declined: "We are suffering not from the decay of theological beliefs but from the loss of solitude."[13]

A quotation should be smoothly integrated into the text of your paper. Even though its source is given in a footnote, it should be preceded by some brief introductory remark such as "one leading educator recently said that ...": "as Desmond Morton points out...": "an editorial in *The Canadian Forum* argued that...." The best way to learn about integrating quotations is to observe how professional writers handle them—for example.

> Another English critic described Canada as "a sort of half-way house in letters between U.K. and U.S.A.," and therefore found no surprise in Leacock's having discovered "the hilarious mean between American and English humour":
>
> > His fantastical ideas are often in the nature of American hyperbole—but they are developed in English fashion as a rule, in a quiet and close-knit narrative which has none of the exuberance of the typical American humorist.[8]
>
> The notable exception is J.B. Priestly, who finds specific and positive qualities in Leacock's "outlook, manner, and style," which, he says, not only "belong to the man but ... to the nation"....[9]—R.E. Watters, "Stephen Leacock's Canadian Humor"
>
> In two essays included in his much-acclaimed recent book, *Language and Silence,* George Steiner describes several ways in which, in his view, "A language shows that it has in it the germ of dissolution ":

**30.8**

*Doc*

> Actions of the mind that were once spontaneous become mechanical, frozen habits (dead metaphors, stock similes, slogans). Words grow longer and more ambiguous. . . . —Ronald Gross, "On Language Pollution"

See 14.1, Quotation Marks Around Quoted Material, for a discussion of ways to set up long and short quotations from both prose and poetry.

## Paraphrasing

Although a reference paper relies heavily on the writings of others, it should not consist simply of a long string of word-for-word quotations from sources. As always, it should reflect your own style. Except in the situations described in the preceding section, information from secondary sources will be *paraphrased*—restated or summarized in your own words. Otherwise the paper will have a jumbled, patchwork effect that may distract or confuse the reader. Compare the two following passages for effectiveness:

> TOO MANY DIRECT QUOTATIONS: Authorities disagree about the dating of these pyramids. Professor Sheldon Muncie says, "The preponderance of evidence collected by investigators in recent years points to a date no earlier than 1300 A.D. for the construction of the lowest level."[1] Professor William Price basically agrees with him: "Bricks of this type were not used in the surrounding areas until the late fourteenth century."[2] But Robert McCall found that "The radiocarbon readings are completely out of line with the standard textbook dates; the original substructure is at least 700 years older than Muncie's earliest estimate."[3]

> PARAPHRASE: Authorities disagree about the dating of the pyramids. Professors Sheldon Muncie and William Price concluded, on the basis of the type of brick used and other evidence, that they were begun no earlier than the fourteenth century.[1] But Robert McCall's radiocarbon readings indicate a date earlier than 600 A.D.[2]

The best way to paraphrase a passage is to absorb the content and then to write it down from memory in your own words. When you have finished, you should check it for accuracy and any unconscious borrowing of phrases and sentences. Remember that even though the words are your own, the information or ideas are not; you will still have to use a footnote to identify the source.

## Plagiarism

Most writers know that copying another's work word for word without giving the author credit is considered plagiarism. But they often assume that this practice is frowned on only when long passages are involved — whole pages or paragraphs. Consequently, they feel free to copy phrases and sentences without using quotation marks and footnotes. Actually, any uncredited use of another's information, ideas, or wording is plagiarism. Under the mistaken notion that they are paraphrasing, students often reproduce sources almost exactly, changing only a word here and there. An honest paraphrase, however, is one in which the *ideas* of the source are stated in the writer's *own words*. The following examples show the difference between genuine paraphrase and plagiarism of source material:

ORIGINAL SOURCE: (from J.A. Corry, "Free Trade in Ideas," *Our Sense of Identity,* Malcolm Ross, ed., p. 277): It will be urged here that most of the arguments of [John Stuart] Mill's *Essay on Liberty* still apply. . . . Freedom of expression is a necessity of life for the free flexible society which admits that it is not sure of final answers and wants to feel its way by experiment, by trial and error. It is meaningless to talk about proceeding experimentally unless we have the fullest possible observation and report on the result of the experiments. Every individual is now deeply affected by the social and political experiments we undertake daily. Our society is so complex and it is so difficult to know exactly what the results of these experiments really are that we need the widest possible ventilation of grievances.

STUDENT VERSION A: Nineteenth-century arguments for liberty still apply. For the free society that confesses to not knowing all the answers must grope its way by trial and error. Therefore, full observation and report on the result of such experiments must be available. This is so because every individual is daily influenced by social and political experiments. Thus, in our complex society the widest possible airing of grievances is a must.

**Plagiarism.** By omitting any reference to Corry and Mill, the writer implies that the ideas are his or her own. In organization the paragraph follows the source very closely — a similar order of ideas and the same number and structure of sentences. Many of the words and phrases are taken directly without the use of quotation marks to indicate this fact. In other cases, word order has been simply rearranged and synonyms substituted (*confesses* for *admits, grope* for *feel, influenced* for *affected, airing* for *ventilation*).

**30.8**

*Doc*

VERSION B: J.E. Corry, citing Mill's *Essay on Liberty,* stresses the continuing need for freedom of speech in a society which admits to not knowing all the answers and which must therefore proceed experimentally. He concludes that because these experiments—both political and social—affect everyone in our complex society, great latitude must be allowed for dissent.[1]

**Paraphrase.** The writer admits, both in the text and in a footnote, that the ideas used are Corry's. He states them in his or her own words and does not slavishly follow the source. Quotation marks are unnecessary, since none of the phrases are Corry's.

ORIGINAL SOURCE (from Lionel Trilling, "F. Scott Fitzgerald," *The Liberal Imagination,* p. 42): Thus, *The Great Gatsby* has its interest as a record of contemporary manners, but this might only have served to date it, did not Fitzgerald take the given moment of history as something more than a mere circumstance, did he not, in the manner of the great French novelists of nineteenth century, seize the given moment as a moral fact. . . . For Gatsby, divided between power and dream, comes inevitably to stand for America itself.

VERSION A: Of course the one thing that makes *The Great Gatsby* interesting is its picture of the life of the twenties, but if it were only this it would by now be out of date. Instead, like the great French novelists, Fitzgerald made the particular moment a moral symbol. Gatsby, the main character, divided between power and dream, represents the American dilemma.

**Plagiarism.** This version does not reproduce the source as closely as Version A of the passage from Corry; it more subtly plagiarizes the original. Again, the writer gives no indication that the ideas expressed are not his or her own. The wording, except for "divided between power and dream," is largely original. The comparison between Fitzgerald and the great French novelists is not original, and implies a critical breadth suspiciously beyond the range of most undergraduate writers.

VERSION B: As Lionel Trilling points out, *The Great Gatsby* is much more than a record of the manners of the twenties. In miniature, Gatsby represents America, "divided between power and dream."[1]

**Paraphrase.** The writer credits Trilling as the originator of the ideas he presents. He also puts quotation marks around the one phrase he uses verbatim.

## Numbering and Spacing of Footnotes

In the text of the paper, the footnote number is placed *at the end of the quotation or statement* for which the source is being given; it is never placed before the borrowed material. The number is raised slightly above the line and is placed outside the end punctuation of the statement to which it refers: "... nearly 400 000 in 1978."[13]

Footnotes are generally numbered consecutively throughout the paper in Arabic numerals beginning with 1. If the last footnote on the first page is numbered 3, the first footnote on the second page will be numbered 4, and so on. It is impossible to say how many footnotes should appear in a paper of a given length because the number varies with the type of subject and the kind of sources used; however, the typical student reference-paper contains from two to four footnotes on a page. Studying some footnoted articles or books will help you see how the system works.

In typed manuscript, footnotes are single spaced (but separated from each other by an extra line of space) and the first line of each is indented as for a paragraph. Set footnotes apart from the text with a short line extending about 2.5 cm from the left margin, as shown in the sample paper on pages 442-463.

## Footnote Form

Generally, each footnote should contain at least four essential facts (the information a reader would need to locate the source): the author's name, the title of the work, the facts of publication (publisher, place, and date), and the specific page or pages of the source used.

Practices in footnote form vary, chiefly in punctuation and kinds of abbreviations. This section follows the form recommended by the second edition of the *Style Sheet* of the Modern Language Association (MLA), the form most often used in academic writing in the humanities. Alternative systems are frequently used in scientific papers (see p. 438). Follow carefully any changes your instructor may want made in the form described here.

## Footnotes for Books

**First reference.**   Study the sample footnotes below, noting the order of the information and the punctuation used between each element. The first time you refer to a book in a footnote, include as much of the information as is relevant in each case. However,

**30.8**

*ftnt*

if the author's full name has been given in the text, it need not be repeated in the footnote. This is sometimes called a *split note.*

### A book with one author:

¹ Pierre Elliott Trudeau, <u>Federalism and the French Canadians</u> (Toronto: Macmillan, 1968), p. 10.

### Two or three authors:

² Walter S. Avis and A.M. Kinloch, <u>An Annotated Bibliography of Writings on Canadian English</u> (Toronto: Fitzhenry & Whiteside, 1978), p. 58.

### More than three authors:

³ Carl F. Klinck and others, <u>Literary History of Canada</u> (Toronto: University of Toronto Press, 1965), p. 187.

[The Latin abbreviation *et al.* may be used instead of *and others.*]

### An edited book:

⁴ <u>Letters of Noah Webster</u>, ed. Harry R. Warfel (New York: Library Publishers, 1954), p. 352.

[If the editor's name is more relevant to the citation than the author's, put that name at the beginning of the footnote: Harry R. Warfel, ed., *Letters of Noah Webster.*]

### An article in an edited book of selections written by various authors:

⁵ George Whalley, "Where Are English Studies Going?" <u>In the Name of Language</u>, ed. Joseph Gold (Toronto: Macmillan, 1975), pp. 131-160.

### A translated book:

⁶ M.H. Scargill, "Le développement de la langue anglaise au Canada," <u>Histoire littéraire du Canada</u>, ed. Carl F. Klinck <u>et al.</u>, trans. Maurice Lebel (Québec: Université Laval, 1970), pp. 308-317.

### A book for which no author is given:

⁷ <u>A Manual of Style</u>, 12th ed. (Chicago: Univ. of Chicago Press, 1969), p. 27.

### A revised edition:

⁸ James C. Coleman, <u>Abnormal Psychology and Modern Life</u>, 5th ed. (Glenview, Ill.: Scott, Foresman, 1976), pp. 254-55.

### A multivolume work, all volumes published in the same year:

⁹ John E. Robbins, ed., <u>Encyclopedia Canadiana</u>, revised ed. (Ottawa: Canadiana Co., 1972).

[Note that if the footnote includes a volume number, the abbreviation *p.* or *pp.* is omitted.]

A multivolume work, the volumes published in different years:

¹⁰ Harold Child, "Jane Austen," in The Cambridge History of
English Literature, ed. A. W. Ward and A. T. Waller, XII (London:
Cambridge Univ. Press, 1914), 231-33.

[The volume number in this instance precedes the facts of publication.]

A book that is part of a series:

¹¹ Thomas Chandler Haliburton, The Sam Slick Anthology, Canadian
Paperback series, ed. R.E. Watters and W.S. Avis (Toronto: Clarke,
Irwin, 1969), p. xxi.

**Subsequent references.**   For subsequent references to the same
work that do not immediately follow the original reference, a
short form should be used: the author's last name only, if not more
than one work by the same author is being cited, and the page
number:

¹² Trudeau, p. 150.

If two sources by the same author have been previously cited,
the short form must also include the title, to make clear which
work the note re-refers to. A shortened form of the title may be
used:

¹³ Trudeau, Federalism, p. 150.

If the book has no author, the title should be used:

¹⁴ A Manual of Style, p. 92.

See page 437 for the use of *ibid.* in footnotes.

## Footnotes for Magazine, Journal, and Newspaper Articles

Footnotes for magazine and newspaper articles are handled in
much the same way; the volume number is used in footnoting an
article from a scholarly journal and may also be included for a
magazine if thought necessary.

Signed article in a magazine:

¹⁵ Gary Geddes, "The Writer That CanLit Forgot," Saturday Night,
November 1977, p. 84.

Unsigned article in a magazine:

¹⁶ "Canada's Heritage Sites," The Financial Post, November 1977,
p. 36.

**30.8**

*Ftnt*

Article in a scholarly journal:

> [17] Arthur R.M. Lower, "History as Pageant," <u>Dalhousie Review</u>, 54 (Spring 1974), 5.

[The abbreviation *p.* or *pp.* is omitted if the volume number is given.]

Signed article in a newspaper:

> [18] Eugene Forsey, "Dangers in the Bill to Amend Canada's Constitution," <u>The Globe and Mail</u> (Toronto), July 7, 1978, p. 7.

[Locate newspaper articles by section or column, if possible.]

Unsigned articles and subsequent footnotes to the same article are handled in the same way as unsigned articles in magazines. Subsequent references to articles in periodicals may be shortened in the same way as those for books (see p. 435).

## Footnotes for Other Sources

These sample entries will help you arrive at a form for various source materials you may use.

Encyclopedia articles:

> [19] Dorothy MacPherson, "Indians of Canada," <u>Encyclopedia Canadiana</u>, rev. ed. (Ottawa: Canadiana Co., 1975), V, 249.

[If the article is unsigned, begin with the title. Notice that the volume number is given in Roman numerals, and that the abbreviation *p.* or *pp.* is omitted.]

Biblical citations:

> [20] Matthew 6:26-30.

[Often the identification is given in parentheses immediately following the quotation, rather than in a footnote, and very familiar quotations, such as "Thou shalt not steal," are not footnoted.]

Material at second hand:

> [21] Robert M. Stamp, "Canadian Education and the National Identity," <u>Journal of Educational Thought</u>, December 1971, p. 17, in <u>Canadian Schools and Canadian Identity</u>, ed. Alf Chaiton and Neil McDonald (Toronto: Gage, 1977), p. 29.

[Both the original source and the source from which the material was taken are given.]

Bulletins and pamphlets:

²² The Labour Force, December, 1976, Statistics Canada, Labour
Force Survey Division, Cat. No. 71-001 (Ottawa: Statistics Canada,
1977), p. 24.

Unpublished dissertations and theses:

²³ H. Rex Wilson, "The Dialect of Lunenburg County, Nova Scotia,"
Diss. Univ. of Michigan, 1958, p. 48.

[Titles of unpublished works are usually enclosed in quotation marks.]

**Use of *ibid.* in footnotes.**   As used in a footnote, the abbreviation
*ibid.* (for the Latin *ibidem,* "in the same place") means that the
reference is to the same book or article as the preceding footnote. It can be used only to refer to the work listed in the footnote *immediately* preceding and *only* if the two footnotes appear
on the same page:

²⁴ Margaret Mead, Blackberry Winter (New York: Wm. Morrow, 1972),
pp. 86-87.

²⁵ Ibid., p. 93.

Because it stands first in a footnote, ibid. is capitalized; because
it is an abbreviation, it is followed by a period. Ibid. is not usually italicized, but usage varies; follow the recommendation of
your instructor.

The use of ibid., and of Latin abbreviations in general, is
decreasing in academic writing. Usually it is just as simple to use a
shortened reference to author and title (as illustrated on page 435)
as it is to use ibid.

**Other abbreviations in footnotes.**   Standard abbreviations such as
those for provinces (*Oshawa, Ont.; Brandon, Man.*) are commonly used in footnotes. The following abbreviations may also be
used to save space. (Follow the recommendation of your
instructor about whether to underline those from Latin.):

| | |
|---|---|
| anon. | anonymous |
| ca. or c. (*circa*) | about a given date (*ca.* 1490) |
| ch., chs. | chapter, chapters |
| col., cols. | column, columns |
| ed. | edited by or edition (2nd ed.) |
| et al. (*et alii*) | and others (used with four or more authors); you may also simply write "and others" |
| e.g. (*exempli gratia*) | for example (preceded and followed by a comma; note the periods) |

**30.8**

*Ftnt*

| | |
|---|---|
| ibid. (*ibidem*) | in the same place (explained above) |
| i.e. (*id est*) | that is (preceded and followed by a comma) |
| l., ll. | line, lines (in typewritten copy it is better to write these out, to avoid confusion with the figures 1 and 11) |
| MS., MSS. | manuscript, manuscripts |
| n.d. | no date of publication given |
| n.p. | no place of publication given |
| p., pp. | page, pages (the word *page* is never written out in footnotes) |
| rev. | revised edition or revised by |
| sic | thus (placed in brackets after an error in quoted material to show that you are aware of the error; seldom used by contemporary writers) |
| trans. or tr. | translated by |
| vol., vols. | volume, volumes |

## Alternative Forms for Footnotes

Research papers in the sciences and social sciences often use systems of reference to sources quite different from the system just described, which is one generally used in the humanities. The references have the same purpose — to give the author, title, and facts of publication of articles and books used, to acknowledge the source of materials, and to make it possible for a reader to go directly to a source for further information. The details of form vary considerably among the different scientific and technical fields and often among the books and journals within a field. If you are writing a paper for a course in the sciences, you will need to follow your instructor's specification of which system to use or study the form of a particular journal or style manual and follow its practice. Whatever system you follow, do not shift from one system to another in your paper: consistency in form is essential in the use of footnotes.

Any description of footnotes makes their use seem much harder than it really is. If you have good notes with the exact sources of the facts clearly recorded, it is relatively simple to keep track of the necessary sources in the first draft and to place them in the final paper in the proper form.

## 30.9 ASSEMBLING THE COMPLETED PAPER

In preparing the final copy of your research paper, refer to the suggestions given in 28.2, Manuscript Form. You will also find it useful to study the sample student paper on pages 442-463. Proofread your final copy carefully before turning it in. A well-researched paper can be seriously marred by careless errors and inconsistencies.

## The Final Bibliography

The finished research paper concludes with a bibliography of the sources used in the paper. If the list includes only those books, articles, and other sources that have been documented in the footnotes, the bibliography is titled "List of Works Cited." If the list also includes references that you have explored in depth but have not cited directly, the bibliography should be labelled "List of Works Consulted." Your instructor will tell you which form you should use.

Your bibliography cards (30.3) should contain all the information you need to compile the final bibliography. The form for a bibliography differs somewhat from footnote form:

Footnote entry:

[1] Edgar McInnis, <u>Canada: A Political and Social History</u> (Toronto: Clarke, Irwin, 1959), p. 379.

Bibliography entry:

McInnis, Edgar. <u>Canada: A Political and Social History</u>. Toronto: Clarke, Irwin, 1959.

Follow these general guidelines and the examples that follow for an acceptable bibliography form:

1. List all entries in alphabetical order, by the author's *last name,* or, if the author is unknown, by the first significant word of the title (disregard *A* or *The*). When two or more works by the same author are listed, use a line of twelve dashes, followed by a period, for all but the first work.
2. Do not give the page numbers for books, but do list the inclusive pages for articles in periodicals and newspapers.
3. Do not separate the list according to kinds of publications. Since the bibliography for most student papers is short, all sources should appear in the same list.
4. Do not number the entries.

Punctuation varies in different bibliographic styles, mainly in the use of commas, colons, and parentheses. The form shown in the examples illustrates one widely used style, but be sure to note carefully any different practices your instructor may want to follow.

**30.9**

*Biblio*

## Bibliography Form for Books

### One author:

Atwood, Margaret, The Edible Woman. Toronto: McClelland & Stewart,
     1969.

### Two or three authors:

Daymond, Douglas, and Leslie Monkman, eds. Literature in Canada.
     Toronto: Gage, 1978.

[Notice that only the first author's name is listed last name first—
for purposes of alphabetizing.]

### More than three authors:

Blair, Walter, and others. The Literature of the United States. 3rd
     ed. 3 vols. Glenview, Ill.: Scott, Foresman, 1969.

### Two books by the same author:

Garner, Hugh. The Silence on the Shore. Toronto: McClelland &
     Stewart, 1962.

------------. The Sin Sniper. Toronto: Pocket Books, 1970.

[Notice that these books are arranged alphabetically by title.
Remember to disregard *A* and *The* when alphabetizing.]

### An edited book, especially one of another writer's work:

Shakespeare, William. The Complete Works of Shakespeare. Rev. ed.
     Hardin Craig and David Bevington, eds. Glenview, Ill.: Scott,
     Foresman, 1973.

### An edited collection; date of publication unknown:

Reed, William L. and Eric Smith, eds. Treasury of Vocal Music. 6 vols.
     Boston: Branden Press, n.d.

### A translation:

Pasternak, Boris. My Sister, Life. Trans. Olga A. Carlisle. New York:
     Harcourt Brace Jovanovich, 1976.

### An encyclopedia article:

McG[uire], W[illiam] J. "Persuasion." Encyclopaedia Britannica.
     Macropedia 14, 1974.

### Reprint:

Dexter, Walter. The London of Dickens. 1923; rpt. Philadelphia:
     Richard West, 1973.

## Bibliography Form for Periodicals

### Signed article in a magazine:

Wanzel, Grant. "Architecture as Cultural Action." Canadian Forum,
     September 1978, pp. 20-23.

### Unsigned article in a magazine:

"Canada's Last Growth Industry." Saturday Night, December 1977, p. 3.

Article in a scholarly journal:

Hill, Archibald A.  "The Green Knight's Castle and the Translators."
     The Canadian Journal of Linguistics, 17 (1972), 140-158.

Newspaper article:

Morris, Jan.  "Legacy of Good from Empire."  The Globe and Mail
     (Toronto), August 25, 1978, p. 7.

Unpublished dissertation:

Smith, Wallace Joseph.  "The Fur Trade in Colonial Pennsylvania."
     Diss. Univ. of Washington, 1950.

## Final Order of Contents

The research paper, usually submitted in a manila folder or binder, should contain all the parts in the order assigned. Typically, the completed paper has the following units. Make sure that you include any other material (such as your first outline or first draft) that your instructor asks for.

1. **Title page.** The title of the paper should be centred; your name, the date, the course number, and any other information your instructor requests should be put in the lower right-hand corner—unless you are told otherwise.
2. **Outline.** Some instructors will expect you to turn in your final outline (topic or sentence outline) and the thesis sentence. The revised outline should correspond to the organization of the final paper.
3. **Text of the paper.** The final copy of the paper must be complete with footnotes, charts, and diagrams wherever needed. The numbering of the text normally begins on the second page, with Arabic numerals centred at the top or at the top right-hand corner.
4. **Bibliography.** The bibliography follows the text but begins on a new page, each page being numbered as a part of the text.

This extended explanation may suggest to you that writing a research paper is an impossible task to accomplish in a mere five or six weeks of work. It isn't. Done carefully, with due attention to each of the stages outlined in this section, it may be accomplished with no more effort than you would use for your other course work. And if your research paper represents your best effort, you will find the assignment a satisfying one and good training for later work.

**30.9**

*Biblio*

The following pages present a sample student paper, complete with outline, text, and bibliography. It may be helpful for you to study its style and content and the way quotations and footnotes are handled.

GLOSSOLALIA:   ITS PLACE IN

TODAY'S CHURCH

John Robertson
Religion 448 [Course]
March 31, 1978 [Date submitted]

GLOSSOLALIA:  ITS PLACE IN TODAY'S CHURCH

Thesis statement:  A resurgence of interest in and reported instances of glossolalia has led to a renewed controversy about its place in modern Christian society.

Introduction:  "Glossolalia," which means speaking in tongues, is usually thought of as a phenomenon of fundamentalist Christian churches, but an objective survey will show that it has a long history in Christianity and that both glossolaliasts and non-glossolaliasts should be able to come to a mutual understanding of its place in today's religion.

   I.  Background and history of glossolalia

      A.  Outside the Judeo-Christian tradition

      B.  New Testament roots

         1.  Occurrence at Pentecost

         2.  Paul's reaction and opinions

      C.  Later reception of glossolalia

      D.  Contemporary interest

         1.  Modern instances of glossolalia

         2.  Reactions from various fields

II.   The contemporary controversy

    A.   Negative views of glossolalia

        1.   Threatens the unity of the church

        2.   Gives unrealistic picture of Christianity

    B.   Positive views of glossolalia

        1.   Brings self-authenticating knowledge

        2.   Brings life filled with Christian spirit

III.  Negative features of glossolalia

    A.   Features based on Paul's equivocal position and its effect

    B.   Features that distort its position in the church

IV.   Positive features of glossolalia

    A.   Features that promote individual religious faith

    B.   Features that benefit the church as a whole


Conclusion:  Since there is no one answer to the question of the place of glossolalia in today's religions, both glossolaliasts and non-glossolaliasts should remember some key points about each other's position and exercise mutual tolerance and understanding.

GLOSSOLALIA:  ITS PLACE IN TODAY'S CHURCH

Glossolalia is an English word made up of two words--<u>glossa</u> and <u>lalien</u>. Literally, the term means "to speak in tongues." In its more common usage, the term denotes the spontaneous and seemingly random and sometimes meaningless vocal sounds uttered by a person while in prayer or in some other uncommon psychological state that may resemble a trance. More precisely, the speech of a glossolaliast has been defined as an effortless flow of usually complex structure with the repetition and inflection characteristic of language.[1]

At present, many Christians find confusing this strange phenomenon which seems to go along with a fundamentalist understanding of literal faith. Some critics refer to it as "fluent nonsense, esoteric self-indulgence, and infantile babble."[2] But there are glossolaliasts who often question the spirituality of Christians who do not speak in tongues.

The purpose of this paper is to examine the history of ecstatic speech, to present the views of both glossolaliasts and non-glossolaliasts, to look at each side objectively, and finally to arrive at an understanding that is workable and acceptable with respect to both.

The phenomenon of speaking in tongues does not belong solely to the Judaeo-Christian tradition. Numerous examples of similar phenomena are

---

[1] Morton T. Kelsey, <u>Tongue Speaking</u>: <u>An Experiment in Spiritual Experience</u> (New York: Doubleday, 1964), p. 1.

[2] Watson E. Mills, "Reassessing Glossolalia," <u>Christian Century</u>, 87 (Oct. 14, 1970), 1217.

2

found in the ancient religions of the Near East as well as in the ecstaticism of the Hebrew prophets. Tongue-speaking of the contemporary church is clearly seen by its adherents to be rooted in the New Testament itself. The practice appears to have evolved out of a desire on the part of religious converts and devotees to have some visible proof of their being possessed by the Spirit of God. Evidently, glossolalia was an accepted proof in the first century.[3]

At Pentecost a soul-stirring experience dramatically affected the lives of those converts who were expecting some significant revelation from God. Consequently, the account in Acts 2 indicates that a number of those present broke forth spontaneously in ecstatic speech. To many in the crowds the converts appeared merely to be drunk. But, for the converts, the experience was a manifestation of the inflowing of the divine spirit. Paul maintained that the Spirit revealed its presence in the believer's life through special gifts (1 Cor. 12:10, 12:28-31) and among these he listed the gift of speaking in tongues.[4]

Paul discusses tongues in the context of his exhortation "concerning spiritual gifts" and their importance to the body of Christ. He suggests that tongue-speaking is a gift of the Holy Spirit, but is subordinate to the gift of prophecy or speaking with understanding (1 Cor. 14:1, 5:6-9). The factionalism caused by tongue-speaking in the Corinthian church apparently prompted Paul to implement strict disciplinary measures

---

[3] Watson E. Mills, Speaking in Tongues: Let's Talk About It (Waco, Texas: Word Books, 1973), p. 18.

[4] Mills, Speaking in Tongues, p. 19.

3

(1 Cor. 14:26-33). In 1 Corinthians 13, Paul indicated to the Corinthians

a more excellent way--the way of love. He urged them to "put away childish

things" (1 Cor. 13:11).[5]

In no way did Paul present a thorough, descriptive analysis of the

nature and value of glossolalia.[6] On the contrary, he was content to deal

pastorally with the problem in Corinth since the "spiritual ones" had over-

emphasized glossolalia to the neglect of prophecy in the vernacular.[7]

Hence, the controversy.

St. John Chrysostom, patriarch of Constantinople from 397 to 407, said

that "glossolalia was something that used to occur but now no longer takes

place."[8] Little did he know that some three million twentieth-century North

Americans would have the experience of speaking in tongues.

Glossolalia was generally overlooked and dismissed as something in-

dulged in only by the "lower" strata of Protestantism--"lower educationally,

socially, and economically." "Higher" class church members thought of it

as meaningless babble of a few Pentecostals and other spiritually immature

individuals.[9]

Such was the generally held view up until April 3, 1960; something of

a theological bombshell exploded when the Rev. Dennis J. Bennett, then of

---

[5] Mills, Speaking in Tongues, p. 19.

[6] Clark H. Pinnock, "A Truce Proposal for the Tongues Controversy,"
Christianity Today, Oct. 8, 1971, p. 6.

[7] Mills, Speaking in Tongues, p. 20.

[8] Watson E. Mills, "Glossolalia, Christianity's 'Counterculture'
Amidst a Silent Majority," Christian Century, 89 (Sept. 27, 1972), 949.

[9] Mills, "Glossolalia," p. 950.

4

Van Nuys, California, announced from the pulpit of his highly "respectable"
Episcopal church that, "the Holy Spirit did take my lips and tongue and
form a new and powerful language of praise and power that I myself could
not understand."[10]  This was the first instance of glossolalia among the
so-called non-Pentecostal denominations.

In the decade of the sixties, interest in glossolalia increased,
mainly due to an upsurge in the behavior outside of the Pentecostal movement in various main-line denominations.  The largest groups are found in
the Episcopal, Baptist, and Presbyterian Church, although there are over
forty denominations involved in the practice of ecstatic speech.[11]  As a
result of this increased activity, writers in a number of fields have dealt
with the issue:

Journalism:  From this view there was no theoretical framework; jour-
nalists leaned more toward sensationalism.  Many experiences began characteristically with hallucinatory experiences such as seeing a light and
ending with an emotional experience such as speaking in tongues.[12]

Theology:  This view often dealt with whether glossolalia and the
behavior associated with it should be encouraged, condoned, or forbidden in
the Christian worship service.  The opinion of many authors was that while,
through history, glossolalia had done no harm to the church, neither had it

---

[10] Donovan Bess, "'Speaking in Tongues':  The High Church Heresy," The
Nation, 197 (Sept. 28, 1963), 173.

[11] Mills, "Reassessing Glossolalia," p. 1217.

[12] Felicitas D. Goodman, Speaking in Tongues:  A Cross-Cultural Study
of Glossolalia (Chicago and London:  The University of Chicago Press,
1972), p. xviii.

5

been of any particular value.  Usually articles in this field dealt with
what should be done.[13]

Psychiatry:  Since glossolalia was not ordinary behavior and was
associated with various states of consciousness, psychiatrists often have
classified it as psychotic.  Some writers have felt it was a pathological
reaction and linked it with schizophrenia and hysteria, but others argued
that it was not pathological.[14]

Anthropology:  This view took a cross-cultural approach to the study,
giving a much more comprehensive view.  By using a functional approach to
analysing the data, some anthropologists demonstrated that glossolalia
might be a component in the process of commitment to a movement with impli-
cations for both personal and social change.[15]

In order to view glossolalia objectively, it is necessary to examine
the positive and negative views of glossolalia and then  examine some of
its positive and negative consequences.  A non-glossolaliast might argue
that glossolalia is a serious threat to orderly worship and episcopal authority.  There have been instances where the practice has led to factionalism and divisiveness.  Tongues are a smoke screen put forward by
Christians who are otherwise afraid to really get involved in the ethical
demands of a new life in Christ.  Tongue-speech means nothing, linguistically, and is therefore gibberish--a kind of esoteric nonsense.  There is
no room in Christendom for the spiritual snobbery that inevitably results

---

[13] Goodman, p. xix.
[14] Goodman, p. xxi.
[15] Goodman, p. xx.

6

from glossolalia. God simply does not deal in such trivialities and obscurities.[16]

The occurrence of tongue-speech throughout history in the church reveals that the whole phenomenon is a fad that can be explained in sociological terms. In the mid-twentieth century, tongue-speech is just another of the happenings within the church. It is quite at home with kindred phenomena such as spiritualism, mysticism, mental telepathy, and demon possession. Acts such as glossolalia are a serious threat to the unity of the church.[17]

There can no longer be indifference within the church about glossolalia. "To speak or not to speak" is not the central point any longer. More important is the implication of the notion that God approves of such gibberish. Non-glossolaliasts argue that Christians should not tolerate such nonsense in the name of religion. Christians are not on a spiritual high, and God is not concerned with any latent ecstatic feelings some might have. Christianity should be projected realistically and responsively in this century. There is no place for the language of angels here. Christians should stop bickering over issues that at best are peripheral and get on with the matter of Christian unity.[18]

On the other hand, a Christian glossolaliast might contend that non-glossolaliasts cannot be expected to know of its many blessings--of the self-authenticating knowledge the gift itself brings--for most have not

---

[16] Mills, Speaking in Tongues, p. 15.

[17] Mills, Speaking in Tongues, p. 16.

[18] Mills, Speaking in Tongues, p. 16.

7

experienced the gift of tongues. That is why it is difficult for glossolaliasts to accept criticism. There is a tendency to stereotype something
the critics know very little about. It can be compared to writing a
critique on apple pie à la mode without ever having tasted it.[19]

One must accept the fact that tongue-speaking is an extraordinary
gift. In fact, many glossolaliasts believe it is the only manifestation
of the Spirit. Many people from virtually every walk of life have given
testimony to the power of the Spirit known as glossolalia--lawyers, doc-
tors, ministers, politicians, professors, businessmen; glossolalia knows
no boundaries.[20]

Granted, personal testimony is not the best kind of evidence, but many
encounters follow the same lines, which tends to add validity. Often there
was severe reservation about the value of glossolalia. Many were raised
in a religious tradition where the practice was taboo. Yet, to the glossolaliasts, before the gift was received, their lives were empty and lacked
the spiritual integration they now enjoy. After much prayer and earnest
seeking there came a point where God's Spirit was no longer resisted, and
their lives became filled. They were then able to speak in tongues to the
glory of God. This second blessing, they say, is what Christianity is all
about. All are invited to join in an unending search for the unlimited
power that can come only through absolute surrender to the Holy Spirit.[21]

---

[19] Mills, Speaking in Tongues, p. 17.

[20] Mills, Speaking in Tongues, p. 17.

[21] Mills, Speaking in Tongues, p. 17.

8

When the controversy began back in the early sixties, most of Christendom was polarized into two camps with no middle ground. The intervening years have seen much maturing on both sides, but there is still a long way to go. Today, many would not be so absolute in their rejection of the validity of tongues because as the phenomenon has grown, the stiff resistance has waned. Also, those who favor glossolalia have become less insistent in their definitive claims about the necessity of the gift for all Christians because their number includes well over three million persons from every walk of life. Glossolalia has increased to such proportions that its adherents are not necessarily compelled to justify their spiritual behavior. And those who do not speak simply find it increasingly difficult to assign such a large segment of faith to hell. A stand off? Watson E. Mills says probably not.[22] There is still today as in the beginning a basic lack of understanding of the primary issues being raised by the tongue movement. This information gap touches the majority who do not speak in tongues and even a considerable number who do. Mills believes that circumstances have caused the two camps to be a little more friendly, but there still exists a huge gap between the two viewpoints. Further, it seems that the subject is so emotional and complicated that there can be little hope for a significant change in attitude until everyone is willing to be open and share what insight they possess.[23]

In order to understand the controversy more clearly, we have to understand both the good and the bad features of glossolalia.

---

[22] Mills, Speaking in Tongues, p. 18.

[23] Mills, Speaking in Tongues, p. 18.

9

As discussed earlier, there are many negative features of speaking in tongues such as the disunity which results. The most damaging evidence can be taken from 1 Corinthians 14. The Apostle Paul found himself in a delicate position. He could not discriminate against one of the charismatic gifts in which he himself abundantly shared; neither could he approve of the way it was used in the church at Corinth nor of the importance placed upon it. Therefore, he proceeded carefully, tactfully, and diplomatically in a balanced appraisal of the gift. He did this in a masterful way by comparing "tongues" with "prophecy" which resulted in a downgrading of speaking in tongues.[24] The following is a brief list of points of comparison and contrast between tongues and the greater gift of prophecy.

The manifestations are incomprehensible. If spoken sound has no precise meaning it is spoken out into the air (1 Cor. 14:6-9). Since tongues cannot be understood without interpretation, the Apostle indicated this gift is inferior to that of prophecy.[25]

Speaking in tongues benefits only the individual, and is of no use to the congregation. The man who speaks with tongues speaks the language of ecstasy (1 Cor. 14:2-4); he does not speak to men; nobody understands him; he speaks in the Spirit, consoling only himself. On the other hand, the man who prophesies preaches the word of God; he speaks to men; he builds up others; he encourages and consoles others (1 Cor. 14:35).[26]

---

[24] Carl D. Tuland, "The Confusion About Tongues," Christianity Today, Dec. 6, 1968, p. 7.

[25] Tuland, p. 8.

[26] Mills, Speaking in Tongues, p. 145.

10

Tongues do not supply any of the spiritual needs of the congregation,
nor the world. But prophesying brings some revelation of truth, some
knowledge in spiritual things, some message from God, or some teaching
about the Christian life.[27]

Tongues do not advance spiritual fellowship. Paul stated: "But if
the sounds of the speaker's voice mean nothing to me, I am a foreigner to
him and he is a foreigner to me" (1 Cor. 14:11). The simple conclusion
that tongues do not produce communication with others even in the church
is of serious consequence for the believers.[28]

Tongues are of no benefit to the world. Having shown that praying in
tongues was not even understandable to the believers, Paul showed that
likewise it did no good to those outside the church. Paul drew a conclusion that, though figurative, indicated the value he placed on tongues
involving prayer in public: "rather five intelligible words than 10,000
in the language of ecstasy." It illustrated the Apostle's conviction that
purely emotional worship had little value when compared with conscious,
well-balanced, fruitful worship.[29]

Tongues do not promote a conscious religious life. With this point,
Paul began his most damaging argument against the use of tongues. Even
praying in tongues becomes a subconscious act, to the exclusion of the
conscious moral participation of our mental facilities. "If I use such
language in my prayer, the Spirit in me prays, but my intellect lies

_____

[27] Tuland, p. 9.

[28] Tuland, p. 8.

[29] Tuland, p. 9.

11

fallow" (1 Cor. 14:14). This means that humans make their emotions the
basis of their belief and religious experience. This relationship is inferior to the conscious relationship of the Spirit-filled mind with God,
truth, and humanity.[30]

Tongues can remove Christ from the centre. Some tongue-speakers truly
exalt and magnify Christ; however, some do not. Those who have studied
tongues and behavior associated with it are alarmed at the preoccupation of
many tongue-speakers with themselves, their own feelings, their own enjoy-
ment. Christ taught that all must die to ourselves. We must forget about
our feelings and our moods and give ourselves completely in His service.
Everyone should be more concerned about serving Christ in the world than
edifying themselves.[31]

Paul's presentation in 1 Corinthians 14 left hardly anything in favor
of glossolalia. Speaking in tongues was lowered to the level of almost
complete uselessness. Laudable as any sincere effort may be to promote
true Christian belief in a decadent world, speaking in tongues seems to be
highly overrated as a means of making known salvation as a transforming
experience, involving the whole person, including the mind. Paul's
message was that any doctrine, any teaching of the church, though rich in
itself, can be wrongly elevated to a position it does not deserve. Points
of secondary importance can become so prominent in the opinion of certain
groups that they are presented as if they were the most essential parts of

---

[30] Tuland, p. 9.

[31] Mills, Speaking in Tongues, p. 145.

12

the Gospel, and the divine credentials of those particular groups. Over-accentuation of any doctrine is a distortion of the Gospel. This is what Paul tried to counteract when he discussed speaking in tongues.[32]

The majority of people view glossolalia in terms such as those which have already been presented. But some of the more positive aspects and effects of glossolalia and the views of some who see great benefits in tongue-speaking must be considered. Some of the more positive effects are suggested below.

Spiritual excitement. The whole charismatic movement, and tongue-speaking in particular, has certainly caused some spiritual excitement in the churches. Even more remarkable is the fact that many of the formal, liturgical churches have been in the forefront of the movement. Many observers see this as a significant factor. Churches that are more formal and structured in their worship patterns, in which spontaneity and overt emotions are stifled, are ripe for ecstatic eruption. This has been evident in the lives of individual Christians and in the services of worship. Not all excitement is good, but nothing is more deadening than the indifference and lethargy which pervades so much of Christendom. The stimulation of interest in a spiritual phenomenon, the lively debate about it, and the wide distribution of information about this charismatic experience have all brought new life into many churches and into many individual Christian lives.[33]

The reality of God. In a day when the "God is Dead" theology was

--------

[32] Tuland, p. 9.

[33] Mills, Speaking in Tongues, p. 145.

13

raising serious doubts in some minds about the reality of God and all
spiritual experience, glossolalia came as a confirming sign to many people
that God was there, working an amazing miracle in their lives. Overwhelming Christian assurance usually accompanies the tongue experience. Most
Christians live in a day of hearsay religion. They have heard about Paul,
and they know that Martin Luther took his religion seriously. Yet, for
many church members, there is simply no direct evidence of the presence and
power of God in their own lives. Tongue-speaking is a visible sign of the
Spirit's work in the life of the Christian.[34]

Group Bible study. The debate about tongues has provoked some of the
most serious Bible study ever seen in our churches. In living rooms, club
rooms, Sunday School classes, conferences, college campuses, and a dozen
other places, there have been groups of Christians earnestly pouring over
the scriptures. No other subject had involved them in such intense study
of the Bible; yet, there they are from all walks of life, of varying ages,
eagerly searching the scriptures for understanding of this amazing spiritual phenomenon. This Bible study will bear rich fruit in individual lives
and in renewed vitality in the churches.[35]

A sense of joy. Anyone who has participated in or witnessed the
fellowship of a group of Christians, praying and witnessing in tongues, is
certain to be impressed by the overwhelming sense of joy in their lives.
Joy was one of the dominant characteristics of the New Testament church,
but it is hardly characteristic of our institutional churches today. Many

---

[34] Mills, Speaking in Tongues, p. 146.

[35] Mills, Speaking in Tongues, p. 145.

14

pastors, staff members, and church members are generally concerned with how
to keep attendance from falling, how to meet the budget, how to settle conflicts, and whether or not to move to the suburbs. In other words, many
of the problems which overwhelm institutional churches just do not matter
very much to glossolaliasts. They are happy in a barn, a storefront, or
somebody's basement. They are irrepressibly joyous in the Spirit, in being
together, and in sharing their experiences with Christ. Any Christian is
bound to see a note of authentic New Testament witness in such a spirit as
this. It rebukes and chastens the institutional church for its hang-ups
on worldly concerns. The most important result of the outbreak of tongues
may be this devastating exposure of the sinful preoccupation of our institutional churches and of individual Christians with material values.[36]

The shattering of human self-sufficiency. Many critics have charged
tongue-speakers with overweening pride and self-righteousness. They accuse
them of saying, in effect, "Look at us, we are more spiritual than you; we
have the baptism of the Holy Spirit." Wayne E. Ward states that in his
experience with glossolaliasts he has discovered very little individual
or group snobbery. In fact, their absolute humiliation before God and
their willingness to become fools for Christ's sake seem to him to be basic
to the tongue experience. Many tongue-speakers have told him this was the
heart of their tongue experience: willingness to become utterly foolish,
self-abasing, helpless instruments of the Spirit's power. This is a
shattering dethronement of human pride and self-sufficiency.[37]

---

[36] Mills, Speaking in Tongues, p. 146.

[37] In Mills, Speaking in Tongues, p. 146.

15

James L. Slay goes on to declare that a human being is a very proud
and self-centred individual. All of this disappears when one is utterly
and completely dominated by the Holy Ghost. Speaking in tongues may seem
foolish to many, but it is strong and valid evidence of complete self-
abnegation. When all is yielded to the Lord He will come and dwell within
us. Slay states:

> We know we are possessed by the Spirit when He speaks through
> our prayer and praises to our heavenly Father. In this way,
> too, He reveals to a wasted world that He lives within us.[38]

Pervasive love. It would be hard to find a group of Christians today
who have suffered more rebuke and ridicule than the tongue-speakers. They
have been soundly condemned, in high places and low, from the pulpit and the
pew, in print and in words unprintable. Yet, there has seldom been a word
in retaliation against their critics. At the same time, their critics have
gone into tirades of vituperation and character assassination. Their
motives have been impugned, and they have been dismissed as psychotics.
Even those outside their number can not help but have a sense of awe at the
unfailing love which so many tongue-speakers have shown their critics.[39]

To the glossolaliasts there seems to be an intensification of the work
of the Holy Spirit, meaning that God is preparing them for the return of
His Son.[40]

Ray H. Hughes states, "In the shadow of the return of Christ, believers

[38] In Wade H. Horton, The Glossolalia Phenomenon (Cleveland, Tenn.:
Pathway Press, 1966), p. 243.

[39] Mills, Speaking in Tongues, p. 147.

[40] Horton, p. 177.

throughout all Christendom should arise and appropriate the power which is provided through the Baptism of the Holy Spirit."[41]  This has led to an even more vigorous sharing of the Christian witness among glossolaliasts, another aspect in which most Christians fall short.[42]  Also, this inten- sification has led many tongue-speakers to even more victorious Christian living.  The test of any faith is the way in which it strengthens the believers to cope with the struggles of life.  Many tongue-speakers show a renewed power to face temptation, to overcome despair and depression, to forgive those who have hurt them, and to live in the joy of Christ.  Surely there are exceptions, but this is a prevailing attitude which has been observed among glossolaliasts.[43]  Therefore, glossolaliasts feel that speaking in tongues is undiminished in its value to the church today.  It brings edification to the speaker at all times and to the congregation whenever it is interpreted.  It is still a sign of the Spirit's presence in the church as He declares to our generation the wonderful works of God.[44]

In any event, many will still ask, "But why tongues? Why not our own language?"  To ask the question is to answer it.  When our native tongue is spoken, the words are those in our minds, words that are in choice, inflec- tion, nuance, and color, manifestations of our personalities.  When tongues are spoken, as the Spirit gives utterance, the words spoken are those in the mind of the Spirit, words that manifest His personality unfettered by

---

[41] In Horton, p. 177.

[42] Mills, Speaking in Tongues, p. 147.

[43] Mills, Speaking in Tongues, p. 148.

[44] Horton, p. 65.

17

the censorship of the human ego.  These words are, therefore, an exquisitely

personal self-manifestation of the Holy Spirit.[45]

In this controversy it is clearly evident that there are some conflicts

in beliefs and some points which can never really be cleared up.  Therefore,

since there is no true answer to the conflict, both sides might do well to

remember some of the following guidelines.

Non-glossolaliasts, in order to further Christian unity, may do well

to remember:

1.  Accept glossolalia as a legitimate though non-normative
    phenomenon which may attest to God's spirit.

2.  Accept the glossolaliasts as brothers and sisters even
    though they are unwilling to forego what the non-
    glossolaliast believes to be an outdated and irrelevant
    sign of the Spirit's power and presence.

3.  Admit that important insights can be gained from those
    who speak in tongues.

On the other hand, glossolaliasts who are concerned with developing

meaningful dialogue with non-glossolaliasts should consider the following:

1.  Recognize that while glossolalia is a legitimate sign,
    it is not the sole sign of the presence of God's spirit
    and, consequently, it can not be normative.

2.  Avoid the kind of statement which implicitly or explicitly
    declares that the gift of tongues is clearly superior to
    all other gifts.

3.  Admit that rejection of glossolalia is not rejection of
    the Holy Spirit.[46]

---

[45] Howard Erwin, "As the Spirit Gives Utterance," <u>Christianity Today</u>,
Apr. 11, 1967, p. 10.

[46] Watson E. Mills, "Reassessing Glossolalia," p. 1218.

18

Perhaps the wisest course of action for all concerned is neither to forbid nor require speaking in tongues, to remember that glossolalia is a gift of the Holy Spirit but not the sole gift, and to exercise mutual tolerance in the context of Christian love.

19

List of Works Consulted

Bess, Donovan. "'Speaking in Tongues': The High Church Heresy." The
     Nation, Sept. 28, 1963, pp. 173-177.

Erwin, Howard. "As the Spirit Gives Utterance." Christianity Today,
     Apr. 11, 1967, pp. 7-10.

Goodman, Felicitas D. Speaking in Tongues: A Cross-Cultural Study of
     Glossolalia. Chicago and London: The University of Chicago Press,
     1972.

Horton, Wade H. The Glossolalia Phenomenon. Cleveland, Tenn.: Pathway
     Press, 1966.

Kelsey, Morton T. Tongue Speaking: An Experiment in Spiritual
     Experience. New York: Doubleday, 1964.

Lindell, Harold. "Test for the Tongues Movement." Christianity Today,
     Dec. 8, 1972, pp. 8-10.

Mills, Watson E. "Glossolalia, Christianity's 'Counterculture' Amidst a
     Silent Majority." Christian Century, 89 (Sept. 27, 1972), 949-955.

_____. "Reassessing Glossolalia." Christian Century, 87 (Oct. 14,
     1970), 1217-1219.

_____. Speaking in Tongues: Let's Talk About It. Waco, Texas:
     Word Books, 1973.

Pinnock, Clark H. "A Truce Proposal for the Tongues Controversy."
     Christianity Today, Oct. 8, 1971, pp. 6-8.

Stark, Thomas. "What About Speaking in Tongues?" Christian Herald,
     Jan. 7, 1972, p. 12.

Tuland, Carl D. "The Confusion About Tongues." Christianity Today,
     Dec. 6, 1968, pp. 7-10.

This glossary lists the words and constructions that most often cause confusion in writing; it is not, however, a replacement for a good dictionary. Many of these items are discussed in more detail in the relevant chapter of the *Handbook,* for example, *lay, lie* in chapter 8, Verbs, and *who, whom* in chapter 7, Pronouns. The index lists the usage entries that appear within the *Handbook.*

**a, an.** The choice of *a* or *an* depends on the initial sound of the following word rather than the initial letter. Use *a* before words beginning with a consonant sound, *an* before words beginning with a vowel sound: **a** boat, **a** used boat, **a** European country, **an** alligator, **an** F, **an** hour.

**accept, except.** *Accept* means "receive" or "approve of"; *except* means "exclude" or "with the exclusion of":

> Everyone has **accepted** the invitation **except** Sam.

**advice, advise.** *Advice* is a noun meaning "counsel" or "recommendation"; *advise* is a verb meaning "give advice" or "make a recommendation":

> I **advise** you to follow your instructor's **advice.**

**affect, effect.** *Affect* is a verb meaning "influence" or "assume the appearance.of"; *effect* is a noun meaning "result":

> The weather **affected** our tempers.
> The frightened child **affected** a defiant look.
> The **effects** of radiation are not yet completely known.

*Affect* is also a noun, a technical term used in psychology meaning "emotion," and *effect* is a formal verb meaning "to bring about."

**aggravate, irritate.** In formal English, *aggravate* means "make worse" and *irritate* means "annoy": *aggravate* the condition; an *irritating* habit. In general and informal usage, *aggravate* and *irritate* both mean "to annoy": his voice *aggravated* me; the mosquitoes were *irritating.* But since the use of *aggravate* to mean "annoy" might irritate some readers, it is better to maintain the formal distinction.

**ain't.** A non-standard contraction meaning "aren't" or "isn't." *Ain't* is not considered appropriate in writing (or in speech) in Canada.

**all ready, already.**   *All ready* is an adjective phrase meaning that everything or everyone is prepared; *already* is an adverb meaning "previously":

> Finally the car was loaded and we were **all ready** to leave.
> The train had **already** left when we got to the station.

**all right.**   The only acceptable spelling. Avoid *alright* or *alrite*.

**all together, altogether.**   *All together* is an adjective phrase meaning "in a group"; *altogether* is an adverb meaning "wholly":

> The sale items were **all together** on one table.
> That's **altogether** another matter.

**allude, refer.**   To *allude* is to make indirect mention of something; to *refer* is to state directly:

> I knew that his remark about trees **alluded** to the unfortunate incident at the picnic.
> He **referred** to the second chapter in order to make his point.

**allusion, illusion.**   An *allusion* is a brief, indirect reference to a person, event, literary work, or the like. An *illusion* is a misleading appearance:

> She made an **allusion** to Yeats' "Second Coming."
> The little boy's smile created an **illusion** of innocence.

**almost, most.**   *Almost* is an adverb meaning "very nearly"; *most* is an adjective meaning "the greater part of":

> He **almost** wrecked the car.
> **Most** drivers try to be careful.

Although in speech *most* is sometimes used to mean *almost*, the two words are not interchangeable.

**a lot.**   Always two words. Do not use *alot*.

**a.m., p.m.** (or A.M., P.M.)   The abbreviations should always be used with numbers to refer to a specific time:

> The train leaves at 5:56 **p.m.**

Do not use the word "o'clock" with *a.m.* or *p.m.* [not *eight o'clock p.m.*]; do not use *a.m.* or *p.m.* without a specific time [not We're going to a party this *p.m.*].

**among, between.**   *Among* usually refers to more than two; *between* refers to two only. However, *between* is sometimes used in informal English for more than two. *Between* is always used when the reference is to individual items, even though an "item" might consist of more than one unit:

> We had to choose **between coffee and cake** [as one item] **and punch and cookies.**

Do not use *or* between the items: *between him and her* [not *between him or her*].

**amount, number.** In general and formal usage, *amount* is used to refer to something as a mass: a large *amount* of black dirt; a certain *amount* of money. *Number* is used to refer to individual items which are countable: a large *number* of plants, a *number* of people.

**and etc.** The use of *and* with *etc.* is redundant because *etc.* (*et cetera*) means "and so forth."

**and which, but which.** The use of *and* or *but* with a relative pronoun (*who, which, that*) in an adjective clause is superfluous and defeats the subordination; only the pronoun should be used:

> The sea anemone is a fascinating creature **which** [not *and which*] looks more like a plant than an animal.

**anymore.** Except in negative constructions (He doesn't go to school *anymore*), this adverb is not in general use in the sense "these days": The team is losing a lot of games *anymore*.

**anyone, any one.** These words are not interchangeable. *Any one* refers to one of a certain number of items or people; *anyone* is a singular, indefinite pronoun and refers only to a person:

> You may choose **any one** of those books to read.
> **Anyone** who pays the entrance fee may enter the race.

*Everyone, every one,* and *someone, some one* are similar.

**as.** When used as a conjunction to introduce adverb clauses, *as* is often less exact than other adverbs such as *while, when,* or *because:*

> While [not *as*] we were eating, we talked about the election.
> We stopped to rest under a tree because [not *as*] the sun was so hot.

**awhile, a while.** *Awhile* is an adverb meaning "for a certain period of time." *A while* is a noun:

> Can you stay **awhile?** [adverb modifying *stay*]
> Can you stay for **a while?** [noun, object of the preposition *for*]

**bad, badly.** *Bad* is the adjective, *badly* the adverb. Although *bad* is the preferred form following a linking verb (I feel *bad;* the situation looks *bad*), *badly* is sometimes used, especially after *feel* (she feels *badly* about hurting you). Many people object to such uses of *badly,* however, and it's just as well to avoid them in writing. Similarly, avoid using *bad* when *badly* is called for: The day started off *badly* [not *bad*] and got worse.

**because.**   See *reason is because.*

**behind.**   Most Canadians use *behind* rather than *in back of:* The bike is *behind* the garage

**being that.**   To introduce a dependent clause of reason or cause, *being that* is an unacceptable substitute for *because, since,* or *for:*

> **Because** [not *being that*] I was so tired, I decided not to go to the party.

**but that, but what.**   Even though *but that* and *but what* are used informally in dependent clauses, *that* is preferable in most writing: I don't doubt *that* [not *but that*] he'll be there.

**but which.**   See *and which.*

**can be, able to be.**   *Able to be* is an awkward expression when used with a passive infinitive: Canoes are *able to be* carried easily by two people. *Can be* is preferable: Canoes *can be* carried easily by two people.

**can, may.**   In written edited English, *can* is used to express ability, *may* to express permission:

> **Can** you dance? **May** I have this dance?

*Can* is frequently used informally in the sense of permission (*Can I go too?*), but it is best to avoid this use in writing.

**can't hardly.**   Such common expressions as *can't hardly* and *couldn't scarcely* are double negatives, because *hardly* and *scarcely* mean "almost not." Use *can hardly* instead: I *can hardly* hear you.

**can't help but.**   This is an established idiom, but many writers avoid it, using instead *cannot but* (formal) or *can't help:*

> I **cannot but** feel sorry for him.
> I **can't help** feeling sorry for him.

**capital, capitol.**   The *capitol* is the building which houses the state or national legislative bodies in the United States. For all other meanings, use *capital.*

**case.**   Often deadwood that should be removed.

> AS DEADWOOD: **It was often the case that** we stayed in town for dinner.
> BETTER: We often stayed in town for dinner.

**censor, censure.**    *Censor* means "repress" or "remove objectionable parts of"; *censure* means "condemn" or "disapprove," often in an official sense:

> Some restricted movies have been **censored.**
> The M.P. who used foul language in the Commons was **censured** by the Speaker.

**centre around.**    Although this is a commonly used expression, it is considered illogical by many. Use *centre on* or *revolve around* instead.

**cite, site.**    *Cite* is a verb, most often used in the sense of "quote" or "refer to"; *site* is a noun meaning "location," or a verb meaning "place in a certain location":

> Dictionaries often **cite** the way a word has been used by different writers.
> We've found the perfect **site** for a picnic.

**complement, compliment.**    *Complement* is a noun or verb referring to completion or fitting together; *compliment* is a noun or verb suggesting praise:

> She saw a hat that would be the perfect **complement** for her suit.
> Nancy **complimented** Theodore for having the sense to come out of the rain.

**conscientious, conscious.**    *Conscientious* is an adjective meaning "scrupulous" or "upright"; *conscious* is an adjective meaning "awake" or "aware":

> Pamela was **conscientious** about every responsibility she took on.
> Stephen was **conscious** of the noise in the background.

**considerable, considerably.**    *Considerable* is the adjective, *considerably* the adverb. Using *considerable* as an adverb is nonstandard:

> It was a **considerable** amount of money.
> The weather was **considerably** [not *considerable*] colder last year than this.

**contact.**    Although in wide use, *contact* in the sense of "get in touch with" (I'll *contact* you soon) is disapproved by some; in formal edited English a more precise word is preferable: *see, call,* or *write.*

**continual, continuous.**    Although the distinction has largely disappeared, *continual* refers to an action that occurs repeatedly over a period of time, *continuous* to an action that is in uninterrupted flow:

> The **continual** ringing of the phone began to annoy Joe.
> Many old people live with a **continuous** fear of being robbed.

**could of, would of.**   These are mistaken expressions derived from the spoken contractions *could've* and *would've*. Use *could have* and *would have* in writing.

**credible, creditable, credulous.**   *Credible* means "capable of being believed" (a lie can be credible); *creditable* means "worthy of being believed" (a lie should not be creditable); but *credulous* means "willing to believe on the slimmest evidence."

**data.**   Although *data* is widely used in informal usage for both the singular and plural, *datum* is used as the singular in formal writing.

**detract, distract.**   *Detract* means "take away from"; *distract* means "to turn aside" or "divert the attention."

> The amount of litter on the ground **detracted** from the pleasantness of the park.

> The wailing sirens **distracted** us from our conversation.

**different from.**   This is the general idiom, but *different than* may be used to avoid an awkward sentence:

> Life in a small town is **different from** life in a large city.

> Living on a farm involves a **different** life-style **than** living in a city does.

OR:  Living on a farm involves a life-style **different from** that in a city.

**disinterested, uninterested.**   Even though both words are commonly used to mean *uninterested,* a distinction should be maintained. Use *disinterested* to mean "impartial": *Disinterested* judges are better than *uninterested* ones.

**done, don't.**   All varieties of standard English call for *did* in the past tense in all persons: I, you, he, she, it *did* [not *done*]. The past participle in all persons is *have* or *had done. Don't* is the contraction for *do not; doesn't* is the contraction for *does not:* I, you *don't;* he, she, it *doesn't* [not *he don't*].

**due to.**   Although widely used to mean "because of" (Due to the rain, he stayed home.) many insist on using this phrase only with forms of *to be:* His absence was *due* to the rain, where *due* is an adjective modifying *absence.* Nevertheless, *due to,* like *owing to,* is now widely used by many established writers.

**due to the fact that.**   In most situations, this phrase is deadwood: His failure was **due to the fact that** he didn't study. Better: He failed because he didn't study.

**either . . . or.**   Singular subjects joined by *either . . . or* or *neither . . . nor* are generally considered singular, and take a singular verb:

> Either the bicycle or the moped **is** the transportation of the future.

If both subjects are plural, the verb is plural:

> Either bicycles or mopeds **are** the transportation of the future.

**eminent, imminent.** *Eminent* is an adjective meaning "note-worthy" or "famous": an *eminent* ambassador. *Imminent* is an adjective meaning "about to happen": The storm is *imminent.*

**enthuse.** This verb is a back formation from *be enthusiastic about* or *show enthusiasm.* While *enthuse* is fairly common in speech, it is generally better to use another form in writing.

**etc.** The abbreviation for *et cetera,* "and so forth." Do not use *and etc.* and avoid *etc.* in essays.

**every one, everyone.** See *any one, anyone.*

**exist.** Often deadwood: The traffic jams that *exist* at rush hour cause a lot of hot tempers to flare. Better: Rush-hour traffic jams cause a lot of hot tempers to flare.

**expect.** Colloquial in the sense of "suppose," "presume," or "think": I *expect* it's about time for dinner. Use a more precise word in most writing.

**farther, further.** In formal English *farther* is used to refer to measurable physical distance: How much *farther* do we have to walk? *Further* refers to abstract degree: We will study these suggestions *further.* The distinction is not always adhered to in informal writing. If in doubt, it is better to maintain the distinction.

**fewer, less.** *Fewer* is used to refer to countable items, *less* to something considered as a mass:

> **Fewer** people are here today than yesterday.
> If there are **fewer** people, it means **less** work for the clean-up crew.

**flaunt, flout.** Although frequently confused, these words are not synonyms: *flaunt* is to make a show of, or display something ostentatiously; *flout* is to disregard, or treat with scorn:

> Everyone was tired of the way he *flaunted* his wealth.
> Some people always *flout* the traffic laws.

**former, latter.** Used to refer to the first or last of two items only. If there are more than two items, use *first, last.*

**get, got, gotten.** In North America, both *got* and *gotten* are acceptable forms of the past participle of *get:*

> He could have **gotten** [or **got**] more for his money.

Many idioms with *get* are standard in all levels of writing: *get up, get away from, get ahead.* But some expressions are considered informal and should be avoided in student writing: *get on one's nerves, get away with murder, gets me* (for "annoy"), *get* in the sense of "hit" or "struck."

**good, well.** *Good* is an adjective: a *good* time; this cake tastes good. *Well* is either an adjective, in the sense of one's health, or, more usually, an adverb: The team plays *well* together. Since *good* is an adjective, it shouldn't be used in place of the adverb *well:* The car is running *well* [not *good*] since it was tuned up.

**half.** Both *a half* and *half a* are standard; the choice usually depends on sound and idiom: He ate *half a* pie; He ate *a half* serving. *A half a* is redundant.

The number of the verb is determined by the noun accompanying *half:* Half the children **are.** . . . Half the pie **is.** . . .

**hang.** People are *hanged,* pictures and other objects are *hung.* This distinction is not always made for people, but it is for objects.

**hardly.** Since *hardly* is a negative that means "almost not," don't use another negative with it. See *can't hardly.*

**he or she.** Although *he* has traditionally been used as the pronoun when both sexes are meant, more writers are using *he or she* (*him or her, his or hers*). If constant repetition of *he or she* sounds awkward, try rewriting the passage so as to use the plural (*they*).

**hisself.** Non-standard for *himself.*

**imply, infer.** *Imply* means "suggest"; *infer* means "assume" or "draw a conclusion" from a suggestion or implication:

> Even though she didn't say anything, her expression **implied** that she thought her friend was acting foolishly.
> We **inferred** from the manager's remarks that we would not be getting raises this year.

Because *infer* is sometimes used to mean *imply,* your context should also make your meaning clear. In any case, maintain the distinction between the two words.

**in, into.** *In* generally refers to a location within, *into* to the action of going toward the location:

> She decided to sit **in** the chair that she had bumped **into** in the dark.

**in back of.** See *behind.*

**incredible, incredulous.** *Incredible* means "very hard to believe"; *incredulous* means "not believing, skeptical":

> The Olympic gold-medal winner showed **incredible** precision and control on the balance beam.
> John was **incredulous** at the story the old soldier was telling.

**irregardless.** Non-standard for *regardless.* Since both *ir-* and *-less* are negative affixes, *ir-* is redundant.

**is when, is where.**   Often incorrectly used to introduce an adverb clause as a definition:

> INCORRECT: Theatre-in-the-round **is when** the audience surrounds the stage.
> BETTER: A theatre-in-the-round is one in which the audience surrounds the stage.

**its, it's.**   These two words are often carelessly confused. *Its* is the possessive form of the pronoun *it:* everything in *its* place. *It's* is the contraction for *it is* or *it has: it's* raining; *it's* begun.

**kind, sort.**   *Kind* and *sort* are singular when used with *this* or *that* and should be used with a singular noun and verb: *this kind* of book is my favorite, *that sort* of person annoys me. If the idea is plural, use *these* and *those: these kinds* of books are . . . , *those sorts* of people. . . .

**kind of a, sort of a.**   Although frequently occurring in speech, *kind of a* is considered informal in writing: We'll never see that *kind of a* day again. The *a* is unnecessary. Use *that kind of day.*

**last, latest.**   *Last* refers to the final item in a series of something that is completed: the *last* chapter, *last* inning. *Latest* refers to the most recent in an ongoing series: the *latest* book I read (I'll read others), the team's *latest* defeat (we hope it's the last).

**later, latter.**   *Later,* a comparative adjective, refers to time: the *later* the hour, the longer the shadows. *Latter,* an adjective or a noun, refers to the second of two items named. See also *former, latter.*

**lay, lie.**   *Lay* is a verb meaning "to put or place"; it takes an object: *lay* the books on the desk. *Lie* is a verb meaning "to recline"; it does not take an object: **lie** down for a nap. The principal parts of *lay* are *lay, laid, laid:* He *laid* the books on the desk. The principal parts of *lie* are *lie, lay, lain:* She *lay* down for a nap.

**learn, teach.**   The student *learns,* the instructor *teaches* the student. The use of *learn* for *teach* is considered non-standard [not I'll *learn* you some manners].

**leave, let.**   *Leave* means "depart or abandon"; *let* means "permit": *Let* us *leave* this place. Using *leave* for *let* is considered nonstandard.

**let's us.**   Since *let's* is a contraction for "let us," *let's us* includes a redundancy.

**lie, lay.**   See *lay, lie.*

**like, as.**   To introduce a prepositional phrase of comparison, use *like:*

> He looks **like** [not *as*] his father.
> Some people **like** the Joneses try to keep up with their neighbors.

To introduce a clause of comparison (with a subject and verb), use *as, as if,* or *as though:*

> It looks **as if** [not *like*] his father is not coming.
> She wanted to be a lawyer **as** her mother had been.

The use of *like* as a conjunction has become more widespread recently, but it is ordinarily better to use the preferred forms *as, as if,* and *as though.*

**likely, liable, apt.**   Both *likely* and *liable* suggest that something will occur, but in formal usage *liable* is restricted to an unpleasant or disastrous occurrence:

> The tornado is **liable** to damage a large part of town.
> BUT: The tornado is **likely** to veer away from town.

The use of *apt* to suggest an occurrence is colloquial: She's *apt* to appear soon. In formal usage, *likely* is preferred in this instance; *apt* is used only in the sense of aptitude: She is very *apt* at needlepoint.

**line.**   Often overused, *line* in the following sense can be considered deadwood: He was in the legal *line* of work. Better: He was in law.

**loose, lose.**   The spelling of these words is sometimes confused. *Loose* is an adjective meaning "not tight" (*loose* sleeves), or a verb meaning "release" (*loosen* the rope). *Lose* is a verb meaning "misplace" (don't *lose* it).

**may, can.**   See *can, may.*

**may be, maybe.**   *May be* is a verb phrase suggesting possibility; *maybe* is an adverb meaning "perhaps":

> He **may be** the next mayor.
> **Maybe** it will rain this afternoon.

**moral, morale.**   The adjective *moral* means "ethical" (a *moral* code of conduct); the noun *moral* refers to the ethical significance or practical lesson (the *moral* of a story). The noun *morale* means "state of mind": If all the workers do their share, the *morale* of the group will be good.

**myself.**   A reflexive or intensive pronoun, used to refer back to *I* in the same sentence:

> I hurt **myself.** I, **myself,** am the only one to blame.

It is not more elegant to substitute *myself* for *I,* as in this sentence: My friend and *myself* were invited. Avoid this usage.

**nohow, nowheres.**   *Nohow* is non-standard for "not at all"; *nowheres* is non-standard for "nowhere."

**not ... no.**   Constructions such as "I don't have no money," or "The tickets will not cost you nothing" are called double negatives, because the second negative needlessly repeats the meaning of the first one. They are common in some dialects, but are not appropriate to written or spoken standard English.

**number, amount.**   See *amount, number.*

**of, have.**   Do not use *of* for *have* in expressions such as *could have* and *would have*. See *could of.*

**of which, whose.**   *Whose,* the possessive form of the pronoun *who,* is generally used to refer to persons; *of which* is the possessive form most often used for inanimate objects:

> One of the most interesting colonial Canadians was Joseph Howe, **whose** ideas still sound very modern.
> It was a huge house, the rooms **of which** were dank and mildewed.

Often, however, *of which* is awkward; *whose* is generally used in such cases: ". . . the room *whose* walls were painted orange."

**off of.**   A colloquial expression that means no more than *off:* He jumped *off* [not *off of*] the cliff.

**party.**   Colloquial in the sense of "person": Are you the *party* who wanted to see me? Use *person* in your written work.

**piece, peace.**   Do not confuse the spelling of these homonyms: *piece* means "portion"; *peace* means "absence of hostility."

**phenomena.**   The plural of *phenomenon,* a fact or event. If you use *phenomena,* be sure to use a plural verb.

**plenty.**   As an adverb, *plenty* is colloquial: This coffee is *plenty* hot. Use *very, quite,* or a more precise word in your writing. In the sense of "more than sufficient," the general phrase is *plenty of:* We have *plenty of* time.

**plus.**   *Plus* is a preposition meaning "with the addition of"; its use as a conjunction (John *plus* Mary went to the dance) is best avoided; use *and*. A phrase using *plus* should not affect the number of the verb; but *together with* is preferable:

> The old apartment complex, **plus** the new townhouse section, cr tains a total of 225 units.

*Plus* is also used as a noun (The new lights are a *plus* for the city), but many consider this usage journalese or jargon.

**practicable, practical.** The two words are not interchangeable. *Practicable* means "feasible or usable, but not necessarily proved successful." *Practical,* on the other hand, implies success in its application to living. An electric car may be part of a *practicable* solution to urban pollution problems; putting on the spare tire is the *practical* method of dealing with a flat tire.

**precede, proceed.** *Precede* means "to go before"; *proceed* means "to continue," "to move along":

> The mayor's car **preceded** the lieutenant-governor's in the parade.
> Let's **proceed** with the meeting.

**principal, principle.** *Principal,* both as an adjective and a noun, means "chief" or "foremost": the *principal* of a school, the *principal* reason for success. *Principle* is a noun meaning "rule of conduct or action": the *principle* governing the operation of a windmill, *principles* for living.

**raise, rise.** *Raise* is a transitive verb, taking an object, meaning to cause (something) to move up; *rise* is an intransitive verb meaning to go up:

> Every morning when I get up I **raise** the window shade.
> Yeast causes bread dough to **rise.**

As a noun, *raise* "an increase in pay" is typically Canadian; *rise* is British.

**real, really.** *Real* is an adjective, *really* an adverb, although in speech *real* is often used as an adverb: We had a *real* good time. In writing, distinguish between the two:

> Their disagreement was **real.**
> You did a **really** fine job.

**reason is because.** A phrase containing a redundancy since *because* means "the reason that." The preferred phrase is "the reason is that":

> The **reason** we are late **is that** [not *because*] an accident tied up traffic for hours.

**reckon.** Informal or colloquial for "think": Who do you *reckon* will win the Grey Cup? In writing, use "think" or "feel."

**respectful, respective.**  *Respectful* is an adjective meaning "considerate of" or "honoring"; *respective* is an adjective meaning "particular" or "in a certain order":

> He is very **respectful** of his instructors.
> Each application was placed in its **respective** file.

**set, sit.**  See *sit, set.*

**shall, will.**  In current Canadian usage, *will* is generally used with all persons in the verb for the future tense. In formal usage, however, *shall* is used in the first person for the simple future (I *shall ask*), *will* in the second and third persons (she *will ask*). For the emphatic future, the use is reversed: *will* is used in the first person (I *will win*), *shall* in the second and third (they *shall leave*). *Shall* is not a more elegant term than *will*.

**sic.**  *Sic,* a Latin word meaning "thus" or "so," is used only in quoted material, within brackets, to indicate an error in the source. It is used less often today than formerly.

**sit, set.**  The verb *sit* (as in a chair) is intransitive, not taking an object: *Sit* down. The verb *set,* meaning "put (something) down," is transitive, taking an object: *Set* the plants on the balcony.

**some.**  *Some* used as an adverb (I was *some* tired) is regional; edited English would use *somewhat* or a more precise descriptive word. *Some* used as an adjective (That was *some* concert) is informal; it is best avoided in writing.

**someone, some one.**  See *anyone, any one.*

**sort.**  See *kind.*

**somewheres.**  Non-standard for *somewhere.*

**stationary, stationery.**  *Stationary* is an adjective meaning "fixed in position," "immobile." *Stationery* is a noun referring to writing materials. One way to remember the difference is to recall that both *stationery* and *letter* contain *er*.

**supposed to, used to.**  Because in speech the *-d* ending of *supposed* is assimilated to the *t-* of *to,* the *-d* is sometimes left off when phrases such as *supposed to* and *used to* are written. Remember that they are regular verbs in the past tense, and thus require the final *-ed*.

**sure, surely.**  In conversation, the adjective *sure* is often used in place of the adverb *surely:* We *sure* enjoyed the new exhibit at the museum. Avoid this "bob-tailed" adverb in writing, *surely* being the adverb:

> We **surely** enjoyed the new exhibit at the museum.
> *Better:* We **certainly** enjoyed the new exhibit at the museum.

**suspect, suspicion.**   *Suspect* is a verb meaning "distrust" or "imagine": The police *suspected* foul play. *Suspicion* is a noun; used for *suspect*, it is inappropriate in writing.

**their, there.**   Confusion of these two words is usually a careless error in spelling: *their* is the possessive form of *they: their* house, *their* problem. *There* is most often used as an adverb or an anticipating subject: she is over *there. There* are five horses in the corral.

**themselves, theirselves.**   *Themselves* is a plural reflexive or intensive pronoun: they hurt *themselves. Theirselves* is not a standard English form.

**that kind.**   See *kind, sort.*

**till, until.**   Interchangeable as prepositions or conjunctions: Wait *till* [or *until*] I get there. Notice that *till* is not a shortened form of *until*, and should not be spelled with an apostrophe. The form *'til* is occasionally seen, especially in "poetic" writing, but is an unnecessary contraction and does not appear in most dictionaries. The spelling *untill* is obsolete.

**to, too.**   Confusion of these two words is usually a careless error in spelling. The preposition *to* is far more common than the adverb *too*, which means "also," "besides," or "very."

**try and, try to.**   Both are accepted idioms: *try and* is the more common in colloquial English: *Try and* get your work done on time. *Try to* is the preferred form in formal English: *Try to* get your work done on time.

**type of.**   The shortening of this phrase to *type*, as in *this type car* should be avoided. The preferred form is seen in *this type of car.*

**unique.**   Although a common enough practice, avoid using *more unique* and *the most unique* in writing. Many people find these usages distasteful because *unique* applies to things in a class by themselves: a *unique* design.

**used to.**   See *supposed to.*

**wait on.** A localism in the sense "Wait for." In writing, this phrase should be used only in the sense "serving a customer."

**want, want to, want that.** In the sense "ought" or "should," *want* is informal: You *should* [rather than *want to*] review your notes before the test. In statements of desire or intention, *want to* is the standard idiom: *I want you to get* [not *for you to get* or *that you get*] all you can from this year's work. In such constructions, *want that* and *want for* are non-standard.

**was, were.** *Was* is the past tense of *be* (*is*) in the first and third person singular: I, he, she, it *was*. *Were* is the past tense for second person singular (you *were*) and first, second, and third person plural: we, you, they *were*. "We was" or "you was" are non-standard.

**we, I.** *We* (the "editorial we") should not be used when I is meant: I [not *we*] base my [not *our*] conclusions on information I received from several hotel managers.

**who, whom.** Although the distinction between *who* and *whom* is disappearing in many contexts, follow this general guideline: use *who* when it is the subject of a verb, even in subordinate clauses; use *whom* in all object positions (object of the preposition, direct object):

> **Who** is going to the play?
> **Whom** are you taking to the play? (You are taking whom?)
> He is a man **who** never compromises his principles.
> He is a man of **whom** it has been said, "He never compromises his principles."

**whose.** See *of which, whose.*

**wise.** This suffix is well established in many words (*likewise, otherwise*); but it is bad form to use this suffix indiscriminately by making your own combinations, as *business-wise, politics-wise.*

**would of.** An error for *would have.* See *could of, would of.*

# Index

Page references in **boldface** type refer to the most important discussion of a topic.